20 CENTURIES OF
GREAT PREACHING

VOLUME ELEVEN

MAIER

to

SANGSTER

1893–

20 CENTURIES OF GREAT PREACHING

An Encyclopedia of Preaching

VOLUME ELEVEN

MAIER
to
SANGSTER

1893–

CLYDE E. FANT, JR.
WILLIAM M. PINSON, JR.

Donald E. Hammer
Research Associate

WORD BOOKS, Publisher
Waco, Texas

20 CENTURIES OF GREAT PREACHING. Volume Eleven:
MAIER TO SANGSTER

Copyright © 1971 by Word, Incorporated, Waco, Texas.
All rights reserved. No part of this work may be reproduced in any form, except for quotations in reviews, without permission from the copyright holders. For permission to reprint previously copyrighted material, write to the original owners.

Library of Congress Catalog Card Number: 78-156697
Printed in the United States of America.

Scripture quotations marked RSV are from the Revised Standard Version of the Bible, copyright 1946 and 1952 by the Division of Christian Education of the National Council of the Churches of Christ in the United States of America, and are used by permission.

Quotations from *The New English Bible, New Testament,* © The Delegates of the Oxford University Press and The Syndics of the Cambridge University Press 1961, are reprinted by permission.

Scripture quotations credited to Moffatt are from James Moffatt, *The Bible, A New Translation,* copyright 1922, 1924, 1926, 1935 by Harper & Brothers.

Special Thanks:

We are grateful to Helen Smith Shoemaker for her gracious assistance by supplying material for the article on her husband and for furnishing the included sermons, and to Word Books for the use of the picture of Samuel Shoemaker; to Leslie Weatherhead for supplying previously unpublished sermon manuscripts; to James Stewart for his helpful correspondence in locating sermon materials; to Myron L. Boardman, executive director, Foundation for Christian Living, for providing us with sermons by Norman Vincent Peale, and to Mrs. Norman Vincent Peale for reviewing and revising those sermons as printed, as well as providing a helpful description of her husband's methods of sermon preparation; to Martyn Lloyd-Jones for his assistance in obtaining unpublished sermons, and to T. Omri Jenkins, Westminster Chapel, London, for his help in completing the study of Lloyd-Jones. A special word of thanks is due to James I. Packer, warden, Latimer House, Oxford, England, for his excellent evaluation of the pulpit ministry of Martyn Lloyd-Jones, as well as his encouragement and assistance in other phases of the work; to Paul E. Sangster, principal, Balls Park College, Hertford, England, for supplying us with the portrait of his father, W. E. Sangster, and for his help in locating sermon materials; and to Leslie Davison, general secretary, the Methodist Church Home Mission Department, London, England, for graciously presenting us with a photograph of Sangster.

Contents

WALTER MAIER	1
Biography	3
Sermons	11
Unfailing Light for the Lengthening Shadows	11
Christ First—For the Home!	18
Keep America Christian!	27
What Is God's Purpose in War?	36
Full Freedom from Fear	45
SAMUEL SHOEMAKER	55
Biography	57
Sermons	77
Another Approach to Conversion	77
The Christ of the Resurrection	82
Our Emotions	87
Maundy Thursday Night	92
How Can We Surrender a Situation to God?	96
Lord, Teach Us to Pray	101
LESLIE WEATHERHEAD	107
Biography	109
Sermons	120
The Sunday After Easter	120
Believing	124
Follow the Directions	127
Supposing You Met Jesus	131
Where Is This Risen Christ?	136
FULTON J. SHEEN	143
Biography	145
Sermons	155
Pain	155
The Woman at the Well	159
To Caesar and to God	165
Temptations	171

CONTENTS

JAMES STEWART 179
  Biography 181
  Sermons.. 191
    Sacrifice and Song... 191
    The Power of His Resurrection........................ 198
    The Desire of All Nations 203
    Generosity Without Limit 209
    The Divine Strategy 213

NORMAN VINCENT PEALE 219
  Biography 221
  Sermons.. 233
    Be Glad You're Alive 233
    Try Prayer—Amazing Things Will Happen..... 238
    Believe You Can and You Can 244
    Problems Are Good for You 250
    New Strength over Old Weaknesses 256

MARTYN LLOYD-JONES 263
  Biography 265
  Sermons.. 275
    The Importance of Spiritual Thinking 275
    Facing All the Facts 286
    Beginning to Understand 298
    Self Examination 308
    Spiritual Allergy.. 318

W. E. SANGSTER 331
  Biography 333
  Sermons.. 340
    Drunk and Mad 340
    Good Without God... 345
    The Pledge of Those Glorious Scars 351
    And After Death—What?................................. 356
    When Hope Is Dead—Hope On!..................... 363

Illustrations

Walter Maier 2
Samuel Shoemaker 56
Leslie Weatherhead 108
Fulton J. Sheen 144
James Stewart 180
Norman Vincent Peale 220
Martyn Lloyd-Jones 264
W. E. Sangster 332

Abbreviations of the Books of the Bible

Old Testament	Authorized	Douay
Genesis	Gen.	Gen.
Exodus	Exod.	Exod.
Leviticus	Lev.	Lev.
Numbers	Num.	Num.
Deuteronomy	Deut.	Deut.
Joshua	Josh.	Josue
Judges	Judg.	Judges
Ruth	Ruth	Ruth
1 Samuel	1 Sam.	1 Kings
2 Samuel	2 Sam.	2 Kings
1 Kings	1 Kings	3 Kings
2 Kings	2 Kings	4 Kings
1 Chronicles	1 Chron.	1 Par.
2 Chronicles	2 Chron.	2 Par.
Ezra	Ezra	1 Esdras
Nehemiah	Neh.	2 Esdras
Esther	Esther	Esther
Job	Job	Job
Psalms	Ps.	Ps.
Proverbs	Prov.	Prov.
Ecclesiastes	Eccles.	Eccles.
Song of Solomon	Song of Sol.	Cant.
Isaiah	Isa.	Isa.
Jeremiah	Jer.	Jer.
Lamentations	Lam.	Lam.
Ezekiel	Ezek.	Ezech.
Daniel	Dan.	Dan.
Hosea	Hos.	Osee
Joel	Joel	Joel
Amos	Amos	Amos
Obadiah	Obad.	Abdias
Jonah	Jon.	Jon.
Micah	Mic.	Mich.

Old Testament	Authorized	Douay
Nahum	Nah.	Nah.
Habakkuk	Hab.	Hab.
Zephaniah	Zeph.	Soph.
Haggai	Hag.	Aggeus
Zechariah	Zech.	Zach.
Malachi	Mal.	Mal.

New Testament	Authorized and Douay	New Testament	Authorized and Douay
Matthew	Matt.	1 Timothy	1 Tim.
Mark	Mark	2 Timothy	2 Tim.
Luke	Luke	Titus	Titus
John	John	Philemon	Philem.
Acts of the Apostles	Acts	Hebrews	Heb.
Romans	Rom.	James	James
1 Corinthians	1 Cor.	1 Peter	1 Pet.
2 Corinthians	2 Cor.	2 Peter	2 Pet.
Galatians	Gal.	1 John	1 John
Ephesians	Eph.	2 John	2 John
Philippians	Phil.	3 John	3 John
Colossians	Col.	Jude	Jude
1 Thessalonians	1 Thess.	Revelation	Rev. (Apoc.)
2 Thessalonians	2 Thess.		

20 CENTURIES OF
GREAT PREACHING

VOLUME ELEVEN

MAIER

to

SANGSTER

1893–

WALTER MAIER

1893–1950

WALTER MAIER, photograph from Paul L. Maier, *A Man Spoke, A World Listened*. Used by permission of McGraw-Hill Book Co.

WALTER ARTHUR MAIER

1893	Born in Boston, Massachusetts, October 4
1912	Graduated from Concordia Collegiate Institute, Bronxville, New York
1917	Ordained and installed as assistant pastor of Zion Lutheran Church in Boston
1920	Served as executive secretary of the International Walther League
1922	Became professor of Semitic languages and Old Testament interpretation in Concordia Seminary, St. Louis, Missouri
1930	Began to serve as radio speaker for the International Lutheran Hour
1950	Died January 11

WHEN WALTER A. MAIER was only a few weeks old he became seriously ill and suffered a violent convulsion. His mother described the crisis:

> We thought he would die of convulsions. The doctor gave him only a short time to live if the spasms didn't stop. Papa and I knelt at our bedside and prayed in agony. That night the fever broke and the convulsions stopped. We watched to see if they would return, but he slept on peacefully. Later we found that both of us were thinking the same thing at the time: perhaps God had some special purpose in sparing the child.[1]

After this experience both parents assumed that their son would enter Christian service. He did—and he served so effec-

---

1. Paul L. Maier, *A Man Spoke, A World Listened* (New York: McGraw-Hill Book Co., 1963), p. 8.

tively that he became one of the best-known churchmen in America.

LIFE AND TIMES

Walter A. Maier was born in Boston, Massachusetts, on October 4, 1893. He graduated from Concordia Collegiate Institute in Bronxville, New York, in 1912. Already his abilities were evident. In the school yearbook his name carries the following notation: "President of the class of 1912, valedictorian, vice-president of the student body, chairman of the press committee, Alma Mater correspondent, baseball player, and business manager of the yearbook." His classmates remember him as a popular, personable, outgoing young man. But they also remember that he had a deep interest in serious study.

Theological training and further graduate work took him to Boston University, Concordia Seminary in St. Louis, Missouri, and Hartford University. He was especially proficient in Old Testament studies and Semitic languages; he earned a doctor's degree in Semitics in 1929.

Maier was ordained as a Missouri Synod Lutheran minister in 1917 and was installed as assistant pastor of the Zion Lutheran Church in Boston. He was only twenty-four years old, but his sermons attracted wide notice.

World War I soon consumed Maier's attention. He volunteered for the chaplaincy. He also secured permission to minister to the spiritual needs of prisoners of war in the Boston area. He wanted to serve these men as a minister of the gospel, but he also wanted to explain to them the principles of American democratic government. Because of his German ancestry, Maier was able to preach to the German prisoners in their native language.

Not all of his time was spent with prisoners of war. Maier served at army camps as a Protestant chaplain. After the armistice, he returned to Boston. There, in addition to his student and pastoral responsibilities, he continued his ministry to prisoners of war. He served effectively as a chaplain to German prisoners. At first, the prisoners suspected that he was a tool of the American government, and they met him with jeers. In order to win their confidence, Maier organized a special Christmas celebration in 1918. He led a group in the singing of carols and distributing of gifts to the prisoners. Then he invited the dumbfounded Germans into the mess hall where they were treated to a feast. After the festivities, he led the entire group into the chapel for a worship service. He concluded the service by leading the group in singing "Stille Nacht" ("Silent Night"); and when the evening was over, Maier had earned the trust of all the prisoners.

The twenty-five-year-old minister won the respect both of the Germans and of the Americans in the area. He carried on this work on his own initiative and mostly without pay. His ministry during the war was indicative of his approach to life — creative, unselfish, and zestful. Following the war years he served as executive secretary of the International Walther League; he edited the league's paper, the *Messenger*, and gained valuable experience in journalism.

Maier became professor of Semitic languages and Old Testament interpretation in Concordia Seminary, St. Louis, Missouri, in 1922. At the seminary he was not only a knowledgeable and effective teacher; he also demonstrated concern and affection for the students and an interest in the total life of his community. Not only was he concerned about his own professional field, but he also displayed intense interest in evangelism and missions. He led groups of students to survey neighborhoods to locate unchurched persons. Numerous missions and churches were established as a result of his leadership.

In 1930 Maier began his work as a radio preacher for the International Lutheran Hour. This task catapulted him to international fame. The nation's wire services and press devoted great blocks of space to his addresses. A word from him on a current issue became news. In 1935 the president of the Chevrolet division of General Motors underwrote the entire first series of the second season; the program, now put on sound financial footing, prospered. Persons all over the world heard Maier and thousands of letters indicated that their lives were changed.

In addition to his teaching and radio preaching, Maier wrote a great many books and articles. His articles totaled over eight hundred; his books numbered almost thirty. From 1935 until 1950 he wrote at least one book a year, most of them coming from his radio broadcasts.

In his preaching approach, Maier was deeply evangelistic. His sermons were Christ-centered and based on the Bible. He made it quite clear from the beginning of his radio broadcasts that he believed the Bible to be the infallible authority for the Christian life. According to Maier, man's best hope was faith in Jesus Christ, and he never softened that theme.

Yet he also linked his evangelism with ethics. He spoke forthrightly concerning problems of family life, government, and economics. Few issues escaped his attention. He dealt with personal moral issues and social sins as well. He attacked salacious literature, lewd motion pictures, alcohol, gambling, and gossip; but he also poured out volumes of material concerning racial prejudice, economic injustice, church-state separation, war and peace, and governmental corruption.

On some social issues he was a true prophet. During his era most preachers were silent on race relations—Maier was not. Again and again he dealt with the sin of racial prejudice. During the 1930s and 1940s, his was one of the few voices raised against bigotry in human relations. It is true that he was often negative in his approach and sometimes simplistic—but he did tackle the tough problems of his day.

He was only fifty-seven years old when he died January 11, 1950. His death stilled the voice of one of the most widely heard preachers in the history of the Christian faith. His life was a brilliant blending of scholarship and evangelistic concern, proclamation and application of the gospel, and conservative theology with progressive social views.

Preaching and Sermons

From 1935 to 1950 Walter Maier was the best-known radio preacher in the world. His was the voice of the Lutheran Hour that was eventually carried by twelve hundred outlets and reached an audience of five million weekly. Like Dick Sheppard in England and S. Parkes Cadman in this country, Maier's fame as a preacher was largely the result of his radio ministry.

Perhaps the most graphic description of Maier's radio preaching was given by a Mutual network executive who called his speaking technique "the soapbox delivery of a Harvard script."[2] The content of his sermons was literate, evangelical, and strongly ethical; his delivery was rapid-fire and impassioned. Many listeners were attracted to his preaching by its prophetic quality: he was referred to as "the Jeremiah of the twentieth

---

2. Ibid., p. 207.

century."[3] Intellectual listeners who were otherwise repelled by radio preaching listened to Maier because his sermons were factual and intelligible. Others were attracted by the impact of his preaching, the enthusiastic style of his delivery. Both of these elements, content and delivery, must be understood to evaluate the preaching of Walter Maier.

Maier believed that a preacher could serve a cause that was beyond reason without sacrificing intellect in the process. He was committed to the contemporary tone of his radio preaching, but he was even more deeply committed to the biblical nature of its content. At the beginning of each radio season he made a promise to his listeners concerning the Bible-centered approach of the program:

> On the threshold of the fourteenth season I give you this pledge with which each year's broadcast has begun: Every message will have a Bible text, explain a Bible truth and bring its greatest appeal in a plea for trust in the Bible's Savior. Every hymn will be sung to the glory of our Lord by those who love Him. Every prayer will be spoken in His saving name. Every sermon will be, not a political, social, or moral discussion, but a personal invitation to men of all colors and conditions in the seventy-one countries throughout the world where Bringing Christ to the Nations is heard to turn from sin to the salvation which is in God's Son, praise His holy name! Before I or other speakers in this mission of the air become ashamed of Jesus, withhold, soften, sugarcoat or deny His Gospel, may the static of divine wrath drown out every sound of this program![4]

He was true to his promise; all of his sermons were based upon scriptural texts, and the unmistakable authority of his preaching was a strict biblical authority. His theology was strongly conservative. Maier never failed to take sin seriously or to proclaim that salvation was in Christ, and in Christ alone. He had an unusually acute sense of the providence of God and saw God's hand in every event. He based his preaching on the personal relation of the individual with Jesus Christ and de-

---

3. Lester Erwin Zeitler, "An Investigation of the Factors of Persuasion in Sermons of W. A. Maier" (M.A. thesis, Concordia Theological Seminary, 1956), p. 7.
4. Walter A. Maier, *The Airwaves Proclaim Christ* (St. Louis: Concordia Publishing House, 1948), pp. 2–3.

clared that in that relationship all of life's issues should be resolved.

But the content of Maier's sermons was marked by one quality that is usually absent from the radio preaching of the theological conservative. Maier combined his solid biblical preaching with the strongest ethical emphasis imaginable. Among all of the famous radio preachers, none other ever spoke of the ethical behavior of man more directly than did Walter Maier. His sermons were inevitably contemporary in their emphasis. He urged the extension of Christian ministry into areas of social service to provide for the needs of all people. Maier was sensitive to injustice and unrighteousness. For example, he spoke prophetically of the approaching dilemma in race relations and urged a Christian solution to the problem. His approach to these problems was always practical; he spoke on the level where men live.

Occasionally he was criticized for a negative approach to certain problems. On many questions, especially the sensitive ones, his sermons devoted more time to condemning the guilty than to offering positive solutions. He repeatedly emphasized that Christ is the answer, whatever the problem; some critics said that he should have gone further by showing *how* Christ is the answer. In fairness to Maier it must be said that the positive implications of many of these sermons would have been obvious to the Christian, but perhaps to the unbeliever it might not have been so clear how Christ could and would help in the practical solution of the problems Maier discussed.

With such an articulate, ethical message, we might expect Maier's delivery to be calm and deliberate. It was anything but that. One magazine article said, "When the humble professor faces the microphone . . . he undergoes a metamorphosis. Gone are his normally soft voice and gentle approach. He shouts . . . gesticulates emphatically. . . ."[5] *Time* wrote:

> He literally shouts into the microphone at a machine-gun pace. Radio engineers have tried all sorts of tricks to modulate the tone. Once or twice they persuaded him to slow down, but it took the punch out of what he said, people wrote in to ask if he was sick and fan mail dropped off 1,000 letters a day.[6]

---

5. *Pageant,* February 1945, p. 120.
6. *Time,* 18 October 1943, p. 49.

The *Christian Herald* described his freedom from the manuscript: "The words pour out of his mouth—and soul—in a perfect torrent. A manuscript is before him, but often he forgets it as, with eyes closed, he climbs a mountain peak of inspiration and hurls wide and far his thunderbolts of warning to a lost world."[7]

Not everyone was equally impressed. Maier received the usual volume of crank mail. He kept a small file of caustic comments. One classic card from California offered this bit of pointed advice: "4 Christ's sake, change your voice. It sounds like hell!" His son wrote, "Father wanted to frame that one, but mother would have none of it."[8]

Maier was able to maintain the effect of preaching before a large audience, even though he was alone before a microphone. The *Saturday Evening Post* wrote, "The microphone becomes his audience, and to it he delivers his discourse, pointing his finger at it in stern warning, raising clenched fists toward it as he calls for penitence and spiritual rebirth, shaking his head at it intensely, as though it were the most miserable of sinners."[9] A master's thesis which investigated the factors of persuasion in Maier's sermons said, "In the broadcasting hour, the whole human race is crowded right there into that little studio with him and he is telling everyone personally the good news of salvation."[10]

At his death the *Watchman Examiner* said of Maier's style of preaching, "He was an impassioned preacher, a quality which cannot be simulated in radio preaching. The constraining love of Christ was in his voice as well as clearly enunciated in his messages. Dr. Maier was an evangelical who believed in the power of God revealed in Christ to save sinners...."[11]

The *New York Times* obituary said of him:

> Dr. Maier was one of the world's best-known Lutheran preachers.... His death stilled a most vigorous voice and energetic personality which since 1930 had built a two-station radio program into a coast to coast and finally a worldwide spiritual crusade.... Every

---

7. *Christian Herald,* March 1947, p. 43.
8. Paul L. Maier, p. 186.
9. *Saturday Evening Post,* 19 June 1948, p. 88.
10. Zeitler, p. 7.
11. "The Death of Dr. Maier," *Watchman Examiner* 38 (2 February 1950).

two months his cumulative audience was the equivalent of the population of the United States.[12]

Daniel Poling described him as "the pre-eminent voice of Protestant faith and practice."[13] Billy Graham called Maier "one of Christendom's greatest leaders," and said, "Dr. Maier must be rated among the most influential clergymen of all time."[14]

His sermons included in this selection reveal the intensely ethical, always biblical approach of Maier. "Keep America Christian!" provides a good example of the factual nature of these sermons. The outline of this sermon is simple but effective:

    I. We are losing our Christian heritage.
    II. We need God to preserve our Christian heritage.

The sermon "Full Freedom from Fear" follows the same typical two-point development:

    I. We need this freedom from fear.
    II. Christ can give us this freedom from fear.

Numerous incidents from current events as well as literature illustrate the sermon.

No doubt many people would disagree with the idea that God has any purpose in war, but Maier's development of the question "What Is God's Purpose in War?" shows his careful handling of a difficult theme. The sermon "Unfailing Light for the Lengthening Shadows," a sermon in which Maier anticipated the horrors of World War II and discussed the entire problem of human suffering, is an excellent example of the truly prophetic note in Maier's preaching. "Christ First—For the Home!" reveals Maier's approach to the problems of the family, one of his favorite ethical themes.

Each of these sermons helps us to understand the nationwide popularity of one of America's best-known Lutheran preachers.

---

12. *New York Times*, 12 January 1950.
13. *Christian Herald*, March 1950, p. 16.
14. *Fort Wayne Journal Gazette*, 13 January 1950.

Sermons

UNFAILING LIGHT FOR THE LENGTHENING SHADOWS

"In thy light shall we see light" (Psalm 36:9).

THE COMING WAR! What phantoms of terror this specter provokes! Poison gases that will penetrate any mask; air-bombers loaded with TNT that will blast away entire cities; new shells that can destroy a regiment! A world war that will bring the crashing, shrieking battle-line to our front door, that will leave civilization drained white of its life-blood, with men turned beasts, women violated, children stunted by scurvy, pestilence, starvation; a war not to end war, but to end progress — not to make the world safe for democracy, but diabolically to make it safe for international suicide.

Will these terrorizing threats be fulfilled? How eager we are to discount grim warnings and hope that somehow and somewhere our age will discover a way of escape! A widely recognized economist, no pessimistic amateur, wrote a few days ago: "The question is whether war . . . will break out tomorrow, next year, or at the turn of the forties. . . . We are all marching toward war." No yellow journalist, but "the best-informed and most completely trusted" observer in Europe voiced the same prophecy in almost identical words: "We are all marching, against our will, toward another war," and cried out: "This planet is not governed by intelligence; we are all going stark, raving mad again." With nations representing one-fourth of the world now thrown into conflict; with the toppling expenditures for armaments draining national treasuries (Great Britain built fifty-six munitions factories last year, and in our own land the military appropriations are twice as great as in 1917, the first year of the war); with diplomacy retreating from one miscarried conference after the other, while hatreds flourish, propaganda spreads, and munitions manufacturers rub their hands in anticipation of new profits; with war-torn Spain

---

Reprinted from Walter A. Maier, *The Cross from Coast to Coast* (St. Louis: Concordia Publishing House, 1938), pp. 27–38.

and China witnessing the depth of degeneracy to which the brutalized race can descend, as an automobile races through Barcelona with a human head for a radiator cap or as an aviator scores a direct hit upon a schoolhouse and kills fifty children, the question is not, "Will there be another war?" but, "When war comes, how and where can we find light and guidance for our hearts and souls?"

The same searching plea for light arises when we measure the long shadows of other fears that fall far over the land. Public-minded men and women behold the growing indebtedness, the menace of inflation, the civil war called labor trouble, widespread poverty in a land of plenty, the persistent problems of unemployment, and they repeat, "Where can we discover the sustaining light of comfort when the evil day breaks upon us?"

Even more personal and inescapable than the menace of future calamities are the tragedies that even now are upon many, the darkness of affliction, blow upon blow, loss upon loss, sorrow upon sorrow, under which some of you stagger as your eyes try to pierce the night for a single ray of light. These heart-breaking adversities besides the anguish of souls that have not made peace with God, that have lost their way in sin and, groping for human help, have felt themselves plunged into deeper blackness—these menaces to our happiness, multiplied, it seems, as never before in many lives, combine to make millions repeat, "Where is the light for the gloom that encircles our age—light for our souls, our hearts, our minds?"

How I thank God that it is now given to me to show you

UNFAILING LIGHT FOR THE LENGTHENING SHADOWS

as that promise of heavenly illumination is pledged to us in the words of Psalm 36, verse 9: "In thy light shall we see light."

I. HUMAN LIGHT OFTEN FAILS!

When the psalmist wrote these words, he deliberately rejected one of the popular delusions of our day, the fallacy that human reason alone can always radiate enough light to guide men through the gathering shadows of adversity and give them peace and joy in the midst of sorrows. It is true, of course, that God has endowed the race with marvelous mental powers for overcoming earthly evil, so that often we can meet our difficulties intelligently and develop far-sighted plans to avert national catastrophe and individual calamity. Yet even in this sphere some of our problems prove too complicated for logic, and then our proposals are no better than a flickering candle, blown out forever by the first gust of a fitful wind. Moreover, as soon as reason ruthlessly rides over the precepts of the Word of God and the laws of morality and fair dealing, as soon as men believe that they can light the lamps on the path of their own destiny without God's Law and against His Word, just so soon they place the sign of failure on their projects, no matter how enthusiastic the support of technical experts and world-renowned scientists.

Painfully have the past years proved, with world-wide demonstration, that reason, rebelling against God and setting aside His laws, brings nothing more than a *mirage* on the desert of life or treacherous pirate lights that lure men to destruction. How repeatedly, since these messages were first broadcast, have not the masses acclaimed men who are going to lift the nation out of its trouble and bring happiness and prosperity to our people! Where are they today? How often have not heralded plans submitted to end our financial stagnation proved nothing more than pretty sky-rockets, that illumined our night with a momentary flash, only to die out and leave the firmament blacker than before! We were told that the scarcity program, the planned destruction of vast quantities of God-given food supplies, would maintain price levels. What if throughout the world the protest was raised that this was a sinful waste of divine blessings and would never succeed? The hard-headed, we-know-it-better-than-God policy persisted, and mountains of foodstuffs were burned or thrown into the ocean. Now comes the inevitable admission that this folly, for which our world may yet pay in scarcity and famine, was a total failure. That confession came from Brazil, where annually for seven years the government systematically destroyed immense portions of the coffee crop. Although 52 million bags of coffee, or more than 10 billion pounds, were wantonly thrown into the flames, we are told that the whole program had collapsed and would be entirely abandoned. Any similar device that runs counter to the Word of God, no matter how attractive it appears on paper, is doomed to collapse. The light in the lamps of godlessness will always fail.

This truth finds its application in a dozen other major difficulties, when even in purely secular, civic, and social affairs human reason has proved insufficient. We hear university presidents declare that American education has failed, that our high schools and colleges frequently do not build character, in spite of the fact that we have more schools, larger schools, better schools, costlier schools, than any other nation in history. How can there be any unfailing light in lecture halls and classrooms where the existence of God is sarcastically questioned, its truths made the brunt of malicious hatred?

We are troubled by the clouds of crime hanging heavily over this Christian country, which, with the exception of Russia, leads all civilized nations in lawlessness. True, we have more laws than any other people and more law-enforcement officers; but what good are the best legal codes and the greatest corps of criminal experts in the face of easy bribery and corruption that dim the torch of justice?

We want light for the multiplied problems of the home, and we spend hundreds of millions of dollars for this purpose. Too often, however, we have forgotten that "except the Lord build the house, they labor in vain that build it"; and because many of our new theories of family life, our modern ideas of child-training, rule God out and compromise with sin, they can offer no lasting enlightenment for the American home.

If the mortal mind cannot solve economic problems dealing with dollars and cents that you can see and feel, how can human understanding shed any helpful light on the intangible problems of our soul? If with all our culture we are still enshrouded in darkness as, dumbfounded, we behold the unexplainable sufferings and reverses of this life, how can secular knowledge reveal the mysteries of the life to come?

Because they have learned that reason offers poor comfort for the soul, multitudes have turned to the strange cults and bizarre sects which pervert the words of our text and coax, "In our light you shall see light." It is bad enough when a politician pledges help and breaks his word; when a doctor claims to cure but kills; when a statesman guarantees peace but produces war. Yet all this is not even to be compared with the treachery by which men make theirs a religion of reason and deceitfully promise their fellow-men light, only to desert them in deeper darkness. They assert their claim to reveal the future, to bring light from the stars and planets, counsel from the palm of the hand, guidance from the cut of the cards, direction from the dead— these fortune-tellers, star-gazers, spiritist mediums, who instead bring fraud and the counsel of hell and who ought to be barred from their destructive practices forever. They pretend to banish sickness, these new religions that advertise extensively in our magazines and try to appeal to intelligence. They speak glibly of hidden power within us; they dwell on the nobility of the human race and emphasize the divine in man; but because they fail in every crisis, always shattering the *morale* of their deluded followers, we have unparalleled instances of nervous breakdowns, neurotic sicknesses, insanity, and even suicide.

What light can these we-don't-need-God, we-don't-want-Christ attitudes give those who have been hurled beneath an avalanche of human misery? Think of the lengthy dissertations on suffering by the pagan philosophers and their twentieth-century counterparts, which would leave us with the cold consolation that there is no justice on earth, no accounting for the cruel turns of destiny, no hope that we are anything more than the play-things of fate, no response to our pitiful prayers except indeed the answer of our own echo! What can the human intellect say to parents whose hearts bleed at the loss of their child? We remember Robert Ingersoll, atheist, as he stood beside the casket in the house of a friend and spoke only empty, comfortless generalities and platitudes; and I recall a mother who wrote me that after reading a modernist volume on immortality, she had less comfort over the death of her son than before she read it.

What light can reason extend to a patient mortally sick with cancer? Charlotte Perkins Gilmore, daughter of an old esteemed New England family, great-granddaughter of one of America's most distinguished clergymen, a poetess and writer of many books, was hailed as one of America's twelve greatest women, but with all this preeminence she was destitute of any illumination save the light of her own proud intellect. When that light failed, all she could do was to write a note, stating that she preferred chloroform to cancer, and then, thinking in her dull, crude, groping way that death could end it all, she committed suicide. By contrast my thoughts linger with a Christian physician at whose bedside I prayed only a few hours ago, who, during a long night of agonizing pain, resigned himself to the will of God and found joy in Christ and in the light that could never fail were life itself to stop.

II. IN GOD WE FIND THE TRUE LIGHT

You and I must have that same light and courage; and it can be ours if we believe the promise of our text, "O God, 'in Thy light shall we see light.'" When we come to our heavenly Father and meet Him in His Word, a penetrating beam is focused upon us and we see ourselves, not as we think we are, not as we want to be, not as we pretend that we are, not as others believe us to be, but in that unsparing, all-revealing, dazzling brightness without shadow or concealing we see ourselves as we are—poor, helpless, selfish, impure, self-willed. You have all heard of that mysterious light discovered forty years ago, the invisible X-ray, that penetrates flesh to help reveal, in shadow form, the dark interior of the human body; but the light of God pushes its way to the innermost recesses of the human heart, and not in shadow form, but in clear-cut picture does that flood of light lay the human soul bare and prove this ancient truth, "The heart is deceitful above all things and desperately wicked."

Have you viewed yourself in that light and discovered the sham, the dishonesty, that crowd into our lives? In that blinding light have you learned that "all have sinned and come short of the glory of God"? Not until we stand in that pitiless glare and see ourselves as God sees us, are we prepared for the highest and most blessed revelation of life. That comes when, beholding Jesus Christ and hearing Him twice declare, "I am the Light of the world," we learn our heavenly Father's grace by which we are justified, delivered from the penalty and the power of sin, saved eternally; the grace which seals redemption even for the weakest and most unworthy believer; the mercy which, as it points to the blood-bought forgiveness of our transgressions, forever puts an end to the delusion that our virtues, character, accomplishments, best deeds, are in any way, and even to the slightest degree, the cause of our salvation. You know of the helpful rays like the ultraviolet. What far greater curing of sin-sick men and their distressed souls emanates from our blessed Savior and the light of His mercies that guides us from death to life, from despair to hope, from sin to salvation!

It cost a startling price to give men this true Light. Within the last sixty years in our country seventeen scientists have laid down their lives, victims of their research for public health. They have permitted themselves to be inoculated with germ-laden serums; they deliberately contracted incurable diseases and consuming fevers; they pioneered in radium and have had their body eaten by its mysterious power; they bared their arms to be bitten by disease-carrying mosquitoes and ticks—and they paid with their lives, so that others might have a better chance to live. Nothing that we can say will do justice to their self-sacrifice, and nothing that you can do will be an adequate recognition and reward. Yet by comparison with the Savior's self-giving and the radiance sent through the world by His cross on Calvary all this human heroism recedes into an indefinable background. While these martyrs to science labored and died for the body, Jesus suffered and died for our souls. While they were heroically concerned about giving men comfort and happiness in this life, Jesus, looking beyond the swift span of our years into an eternity, lit the lamps on God's highway into heaven and the life to come.

In the light of Christ we also see the light by which we come to Him courageously, even though the pall of grim pessimism overclouds us. How faith-stimulating are these words of Jesus for those who have lost their way in life and seek restlessly for guidance, "I am the Light of the world: he that followeth Me shall not walk in darkness but shall have the light of life." Trusting faith never gropes blindly. Raymond Lull, intrepid missionary to the Mohammedans, the first Christian systematically to undertake this difficult work, chose as his motto and the expression of his confidence, during the perils that were to surround him, the cry of the psalmist, "The Lord is my Light." The church of Athanasius, uncompromising defender of our holy faith, was invaded by murderous hosts of his enemies; they penetrated into every nook and niche of the building and with dripping swords cut down many of the worshipers; yet in the midst of those shambles Athanasius, the very man whom these troops were seeking, passed through the ranks unnoticed, escaped with his life, and sang in thanksgiving, "The Lord is my Light and my Salvation; whom shall I fear?" Cling to Christ, and you, too, will be able to rejoice, "In Thy light shall we see light," cheering light for every murky day of distress; light for every sin-clouded hour; light for the perplexities of your soul, which, if unsolved, leave you in misery.

Will you not agree that the greatest issue in your life is not "how to win friends and influence people," but how to make God your Friend and be influenced by His blessing; not how to make a fortune and then spend it, but how to be rich in the grace of Christ; not how to guard the health of your body and conserve your strength, but how to keep a wholesome, happy heart and mind; not how to find the light of intellect, but how to discover "the Light of the world"?

Some of you have been resisting God. May the same illumination that struck Saul on the Damascus road, "a light from heaven, above the brightness of the sun," shine upon you and show you, penitent and prostrate before your God, the magnificence of His mercy. Some of you have been blinded by the contrast between God's holiness and your unholiness. Perhaps this message has been sent to you, as God once sent His disciple to blinded Saul, so that the scales may drop from your eyes, too, and you may behold the glorious love of Jesus. Some of you may have been searching for this very light of divine power and penetration; God grant that from today on you may be one of the people who "walked in darkness," but "have seen a great light"; for once you are Christ's, His divine radiance is imaged in your faith and life. Not only does He say: "I am the Light of the world," but in blessed promise He tells those who are His: "Ye are the light of the world." Just as Moses, who stood face to face with God on Mount Sinai for forty days and forty nights, came down from the mountain, His face dazzling with light, the refraction of God's illumined countenance, so when you are Christ's, you are marked with a spiritual halo, a light by which you can direct your fellow-men to the Savior, by which you can find brightness for dark days. When you have that light, nothing can rob you of the peace "which passeth all understanding." Should wars approach, your Savior says, "When ye shall hear of wars and rumors of wars, be ye not troubled." If you are overwhelmed by serious loss, as your money, your property, the few possessions that you have in life or the many, slip from your hands, you can ask, "Whom have I in heaven but Thee? and there is none upon earth that I desire beside Thee. My flesh and my heart faileth; but God is the Strength of my heart and my Portion forever." If the weaknesses of the body overtake you, your health is undermined or you linger on beds of pain, then that Word which brings light and life assures you, "Fear thou not; for I am with thee: be not dismayed; for I am thy God. I will strengthen thee; yea, I will uphold thee with the right hand of My righteousness." If in the closer circles of your life your hopes are crushed to earth as love turns to hatred and faithfulness to infidelity, then look to God's light, and you will find Him "that sticketh closer than a brother." When the evening of your existence approaches, as some of you begin to see the end of your pilgrimage, believe this divine guarantee of bright illumination for the close of life's day, "At eventide there shall be light." Come what may, you can direct your vision heavenward and sing:

> Sun of my soul, Thou Savior dear,
> It is not night if Thou be near;
> Oh, may no earth-born cloud arise
> To hide Thee from Thy servant's eyes!

Even when the light of this world fails and the earth begins to recede, then in that last, breaking moment you can turn to the homeland and the city which "had no need of the sun neither of the moon to shine in it: for the glory of God did lighten it and the Lamb is the Light thereof." God grant us, every one of us, not first and foremost the sharp light of a highly developed intellect, not the dazzling spotlight of human renown, not the warm, basking rays of comfort, but His own saving, comforting, strengthening, blessed Light, "the Light of the world," Jesus, our Savior! Amen.

CHRIST FIRST—FOR THE HOME!

"Learn first to show piety at home" (1 Timothy 5:4).

AMONG the most distinguished jurists ever to occupy the United States Supreme Court bench was John McLean of Ohio, remembered particularly because of his courageous antislavery ballot in the Dred Scott case. Justice McLean had been indifferent to the claims of Christ during his earlier life; but one day, after hearing a message on the blessed meaning of Jesus' death, he learned to love the Savior. Before that day of his new birth closed, he rushed home, announcing, "I have just found that Jesus died on the cross for me. Let us go to the drawing-room and pray together." Although a group of attorneys waited in that room to consult him, he declared, "I have given myself to Jesus, and now I propose to invite Him to my house." Addressing the lawyers, he continued, "You may do as you please, stay or go; but I want Christ in this home, and now I am to make my first prayer in my own house." They remained, and from that day Justice McLean lived in the positive, unshrinking faith that kept Christ first for his family. God grant that many of you who hear this appeal for repentance, trust in Christ, and the new life will be led by His Spirit to find in the ever-living, ever-loving Lord your Savior, and as the first-fruits of your faith make Christ the Head of your home!

Reprinted from Walter A. Maier, *Peace Through Christ* (St. Louis: Concordia Publishing House, 1940), pp. 65–78.

A deep reliance on Jesus' blood-bought mercies always gives the Savior the principal place in the family circle. When the jailer at Philippi, his heart pierced by penetrating sorrow over his sins, cried, as I pray God you have, "What must I do to be saved?" and then received this pledge of full, free redemption, "Believe on the Lord Jesus Christ, and thou shalt be saved," this new disciple rose from his despair and — so we like to picture the scene — in the first act of his reborn life helped bring his wife, children, relatives, servants, to Baptism, so that Christ would rule over his entire household.

Martin Luther had hardly started the titanic task of restoring the Christian faith when he sought to win the home for Jesus. Not many years after he began writing the magnificent treatises which have provoked the admiration of friend and foe alike, he prepared, especially for fathers, a short summary of the saving truth, so that they could teach their children the way to heaven. He knew that Christ had to be First in the family.

Last year when we broadcast a message of the Savior's grace, a man in Minneapolis was brought by the Spirit to accept Jesus. Immediately after the broadcast he hurried to a pastor's house, requesting help in bringing his loved ones to the Lord. Having accepted the Savior, he knew, Christ must be First in his house.

You see, then, that people in various stations of life, when they find themselves saved by grace, want the husband or the wife, their parents and their children, to have the same exalted faith that is theirs. Intensely do they long to meet their own in heaven; and to secure these blessings they know that Jesus must reign supreme in their earthly dwelling. As we declare from shore to shore — in the spirit of our message for today —

Christ First — For the Family

this is no mere personal plea. It is rather the instruction of God Himself (1 Tim. 5:4), where Saint Paul writes: "Learn first to show piety at home."

I. Christ First for the Cleansing of the Home!

This appeal is addressed by the Apostle to children bereft of their fathers. In the world of that day, much more than now, a widow could exist only under heavy handicaps; and Saint Paul reminds Christian children in such families that they must "learn first to show piety at home," love their widowed mothers, support them, and in general follow Christ's teachings. No one who understands the emphasis which both the Old and the New Testament lay on the blessedness of keeping Christ in our everyday domestic life will take it amiss when we say that today the plea, "Learn first to show piety at home!" may be regarded as addressing itself to all children and to all parents, earnestly pleading that in their family life Jesus "reign supreme and reign alone."

Many modern experts on the home, of course, often have no thought whatever of Christ. They are interested in architecture, but they do not realize that one cannot successfully build the permanently happy home without Jesus. Specialists write pretty books about furnishings and interior decorations, but they push aside the soul beauty that Jesus alone can give. Family financiers speak knowingly of expenditures, budgets, and economies, but with how little attention they sometimes regard the price Jesus paid for their soul's redemption! Domestic doctors discuss education as an aid for the better life, and though they may write many commendable prescriptions, we ought to realize that not public instruction in matters of sex but home-training in the spirit of Christ should be our watch-word. American houses need roof and wall insulation against zero weather but more than that Christ's heart- and soul-protection against the blasts of many destructive theories. Before Federal housing aid, millions in our country should have Heaven's family aid.

As long as sin rules unchecked in any home, the forces of evil that many of you know only too well seek to banish peace by promoting selfishness, lust, hatred, and a dozen other vices. Without Christ people often seem to live in a certain kind of harmony; yet be sure of this: if the Savior is not accepted and acknowledged in our earthly homes, we shall never be acknowledged and accepted in the heavenly mansions.

With the blessings Jesus offers: the complete forgiveness of purple vice and scarlet sin; the free approach to this mercy by grace through faith; the new heart and the right spirit by which temptation's lure may be restrained and fleshly lusts rejected; His constant companionship for guidance, strength, hope; His invitation, "Come unto me"; His assurance, "Thy sins are forgiven thee"; His pledge of heaven, "Because I live, ye shall live also"; with all these promises, the love of Christ should be eagerly accepted by every soul throughout the world as the most magnificent mercy that even the power and love of Heaven combined could grant sinful man. With all the additional blessings the Savior provides for our home relations: love instead of black hatred; happiness despite poverty; joy even in sorrow, the greatest wonder of our age is this, that every hovel and palace, kraal and igloo, every basement tenement and pent-house apartment, is not marked by the cross of Jesus Christ! Instead, as the Scriptures testify, "men loved darkness rather than light." I hope that you Christ-denying preachers and liberal church officials who may be listening in have finally convinced yourselves in the light of the present debacle that you must silence the twiddle and twaddle about the inborn goodness of man. If you insist on burdening your souls by denying the verdict of God's Word that "all our righteousnesses are as filthy rags," then look at American homes where, with Jesus, we approach heaven as closely as we can on earth, but where without Christ men and women may come nearer to hell, I think, than any other place in this life!

We hear much of "revival" today, and prayers are uttered from coast to coast that the Spirit would mightily restore faith in Christ to the lukewarm and indifferent; to smug, contented churches where, while the souls of men are dying, the chief concern often seems to be: "What will we have now? A turkey or a sauerkraut supper? a Christmas bazaar or a New Year's card party?" What America needs is repentance, a deep, personal, unreserved sorrow over sin and a clear knowledge of what unforgiven sin means in its misery here on earth and its endless suffering hereafter. And when the text reminds us to show godliness in the home, we realize that our repentance can well begin with the sins violating our family happiness.

Young people, for example, are systematically urged to set aside the divine code of purity and to live after their own lusts. God's command for youth, "Keep thyself pure!" and the Church's appeal that before marriage young women remain virgins and young men unsullied is laughed to scorn. Premarriage chastity is completely set aside by a growing number of young people who pride themselves that they are living full, satisfied lives, when in reality they are actually destroying their own prospects of a happy marriage, weighting their souls with sins so treacherous that the last chapter of the Bible, summarizing a hundred similar warnings, excludes from Paradise all those who continually serve the flesh.

Young people usually follow the example of their elders; and in the adult world wedding vows are often wilfully broken by the secret affairs of unfaithful husbands and wives who, imagining that they enjoy the zest of life, instead are forging fetters of death for the soul. The curse of broken marriage pledges is not only this, that it cuts off the possibility of a family's full joy, often breaks two homes, inflicts misery on the innocent, ruins reputations, frequently spreads social disease, arouses the conscience, so that many hardly know one peaceful moment, waking or sleeping; but also, a thousand times worse, the terrifying truth—mark this, you who sneer at purity!—that there is no room in heaven for impenitent adulterers.

Other family sins call for wide, yet personal repentance, when we hear the Apostle's appeal, "Show piety at home." Not once but three times in the Bible's first nine chapters Almighty God lays down the divine command for all generations, "Be fruitful and multiply!" Yet just as though there never were a Bible, as though God never existed, unnumbered husbands and wives—and, we say it with shame, many even in Christian circles—by actions that speak infinitely louder than any words say, "We will not be fruitful and multiply!" While God's Word joyfully declares, "Children are an heritage of the Lord," too many people believe that babies are a nuisance restricting ambitions and personal pleasure. So tightly does the practice of keeping the family childless clutch America today that financial journals write long articles on the astonishing profits recorded by birth-control industries, which every year help prevent hundreds of thousands of children from coming into existence. Now, not the serious physical consequences that may come from this protracted practice; not the moral collapse which follows, showing young people how the consequences of personal impurity can be avoided; not the loss which our nation sustains through families wilfully kept childless, form the most serious charge against the selfish rejection of parenthood. Sins like those of Onan still arouse the displeasure of the holy God!

Men and women nowhere sink to lower levels than in their own Christless homes. You will agree with me if you have ever seen drunken fathers or, worse, drunken mothers stagger home in an alcoholic rage. Their screaming and cursing are too terrible to describe, you will say; but the filth of drunkenness, the bruised and beaten wives, the whimpering children, the pay envelope squandered in the tavern, the loss of work, good name, and usefulness in life—even all this is only a passing annoyance in comparison with the warning of the Almighty, "They which do such things shall not inherit the kingdom of God."

And what shall I say of children who, far from showing "piety at home" by loving and obeying their parents in the Lord, have time and money for every one except the father and the mother who gave them life and supported them during their childhood years? One of the most shocking warnings in the entire Scriptures is the Biblical picture which shows us a son who despised to obey his parents, as a corpse, perhaps an executed criminal, lying unburied as the ravens eat his dead body and the eagles of the air pluck out his dead eyes. Yet that horrifying end is nothing compared with the punishment of his soul!

I speak rather plainly to you; for would you want me to use vague, uncertain language when the welfare of your home and the eternal blessedness of your soul are at stake? If we are outspoken in condemning sins against the family, we can be even more definite in showing the way to hope and happiness for this group. Where, then, you ask, can we find the power to tear out the weeds of wickedness that sometimes flourish particularly in the garden called the Christian home? Are those right who say that we must build the family with new domestic laws? Is it true that particularly the divorce statutes of the nation should be purged of their opposition to God's marriage code? But just as little as men could ever build a barricade to keep the storm-swept ocean off the length of our Pacific and Atlantic coasts, so impossible it is to stop the riptides of human passions by a protective wall of heavy law books.

Are those doctors of home troubles right whose diagnosis of our family sins reveals that we must have more enlightenment? Even worldly wisdom can help to a certain extent; but when education assumes an antichristian bias, when it deliberately degenerates into a tirade against God and His Word, it becomes an invisible TNT that can blast the home's moral and spiritual walls into irreparable ruins. So much of American culture is veering toward practical atheism that thoughtful leaders in Protestant churches are aroused. Many have come to the deliberate conclusion that their groups must follow the practice long ago adopted by my Lutheran Church, the Catholic Church, and the Christian Reformed Church. This removes the child from influences indifferent or hostile to Christ and puts education under the direct control of the churches themselves. Our entire American system for higher education demands a fundamental reshaping to the end that the most essential part of American college and university life must become not head-training but heart-training, not only brain-building but character-building.

Once more, are those right who say that the hope of the American home lies in the overthrow of the family, the program advocated by radical Socialism and atheistic Communism? We hardly need answer this question after the recent tragedies and the horror that has sickened the minds of millions throughout the world, the diabolical campaign to crush Finland and destroy its Lutheranism. It was dastardly enough when the Red bombing planes rained destruction on Finnish homes, set fire to villages, raped and killed the women; but even more repulsive is the whole communistic program for the home, that would make the wife common property, the children wards of the state—a proposal born of hell itself, as it helps to produce unparalleled numbers of unmarried mothers, a neglected childhood, a riot of divorce, and a devastation by disease unequaled in modern history. As throughout the United States the organized movement dedicated to extend this vileness to our own shores grows, we must not only oppose the encroachment of this Red terror but also with redoubled prayer invoke God's power and with increased effort seek to counteract the new support this Red scourge will receive from that doubly tragic war now fought in Europe.

Because all else fails, the cry of this hour must be: Christ first for the family! We put our appeal into this definite plea: If you live as though Jesus had never died for you on the cross, stop in this moment, which may help to decide your destiny for a blessed eternity, and pray God for guidance, so that you may have Him as your Savior and the welcome Guest in your home. Let us send some helpful Christian literature or have one of my fellow-pastors call to show you positively what Christ will do for you and yours! By His own promise the eternal Christ will bring peace into your soul, help you start a new chapter in your home life, and strengthen you by His power to love good and hate evil. If you are Christ's, let me ask that at this beginning of another church-year, when our hearts are directed toward receiving the Savior, you make pointed resolutions that Christ will be the First in your families. Young folks often think the counsel of the Church and of their parents old-fashioned and unsympathetic with youth. Believe me when I tell you that youth has no greater friend than Christ, who Himself knew the problems of young manhood and "was tempted like as we are." Plan your future home with Him! Avoid every thought of marriage with an unbeliever, for only in exceptional cases can a home divided, for Christ and against Him, have any hope of real happiness! Avoid those mixed marriages that would unite Protestants and Catholics. We have seen too much of the sorrow they produce to keep silent and refrain from warning you! Write this down as your determination, "My partner in life must be of the same true faith; we must worship the same Christ!" Plan to build your own home on the Bible, and it will be built, as the Savior Himself promised, on the immovable Rock.

Parents who know that this is the truth, keep your home a sanctuary of the Almighty! Make the family altar the symbol of the Savior's presence! Raise your voices in prayer and hymns! "Let the word of Christ dwell in you richly!" Keep all suggestive pictures from your walls, lustful volumes from your bookshelves, vile magazines from your reading-tables, programs endorsing divorce and triangle relationships off your radios! Make Christ the unseen Guest at every meal! Too many in America believe the bounties we enjoy daily as the rest of the world gazes in astonishment are automatic and can never be taken from us; but a nation even as large and wealthy as ours can be gripped by famine, and we ought to raise our hearts to God every time we are privileged to enjoy our meals. Before Michael Faraday, electrical genius, began his dinner, he prayed with such force that another scientist who visited him recalled, "I am almost ashamed to call his prayer a 'saying of grace.' In the language of Scripture it could be described as the petition of a son into whose heart God had sent the Spirit of His Son and who with absolute trust asks a blessing from his Father." How tragic by contrast is the fact that many in our country begin their meals as the animals do, without a word or thought of gratitude to Him from whom all blessings flow!

II. CHRIST FIRST FOR THE BLESSING OF THE HOME

When Jesus cleanses the home, He also blesses it with the power to meet the requirements of the text, "Learn first to show piety at home." Have you ever realized how Jesus brought comfort, strength, and help to the families that received Him, how His mercy in those ancient days carries a meaningful lesson for modern homes? Are you handicapped by want? Are you one of the Ohio relief families that tomorrow will receive apples and cornmeal as the weekly ration? The Savior whose first miracle was performed in a humble dwelling in far-off Cana as He changed water into wine for a Galilean wedding couple can direct the power of His omnipotence to "supply all your need." Instead of turning from this Savior, let Jesus prove His love in your home! Resolve: "Christ shall be First in this family!" Show your faith, and He will show you His power! Trust Him completely, and His mercy will provide for you!

Are you afraid you have closed the door on Christ because of your sins or the bad repute you or your children have brought on the family? In this very moment He stands at the entrance to your heart and home, knocking to gain welcome entrance and promising, "If any man hear my voice and open the door, I will come in to him and will sup with him." In the days of His flesh His self-righteous and scornful enemies objected, "This man receiveth sinners and eateth with them"; in Jericho He entered the house of the notorious publican with the greeting, "This day is salvation come unto this house." Believe with all your heart that the same Savior can bring peace and pardon over your threshold!

Are you clutched by religious doubts? Do you question the power of Christ to keep His word? Because some prayers have not been answered immediately and in the way specified, do you declare that Jesus has failed? Instead of protesting, "I am through with the Church!" invite Jesus to your home, as the disciples did on the Emmaus road when they pleaded, "Abide with us, for it is toward evening, and the day is far spent," and as your soul in penitent and trusting faith sings, "Abide with me, Lord Jesus," your home will be brightened by a radiant faith.

Is sickness the cross imposed on you? Many of your hearts are heavy because for long years you have not known a single day entirely free from pain. Instead of harboring dark, resentful thoughts, exalt Christ as the First in your home, and you will have the assurance that the same Savior who entered His countrymen's homes to lay His healing hands on fevered brows and to remove the pains of palsy can restore your health, if it be for the welfare of your soul, and, if not, strengthen you for greater joy!

Many young women pray that, if it be God's will, they may have a loving husband and children; yet in His wisdom God has not answered; and it may seem that the chance for this happiness dwindles each year. Rather than lapse into bitterness, protesting against what you call the unfairness of life, give Christ the first place in your heart, and as He brought joy into the family circle at Bethany with its two unmarried sisters and its unmarried brother Lazarus, so the blessed Savior can grant you overflowing happiness. He may have spared you unspeakable suffering. He may have far-reaching plans for your usefulness. If it be His will, He can still grant you the blessing of your own home.

If it seems that death has inflicted a wound that can never heal; if your eyes moisten at the sight of an empty chair; if you listen in vain for a voice forever silent and find a loneliness that can hardly be removed, don't raise your voice to accuse God! Don't charge your heavenly Father with cruelty! Ask the Lord Jesus to rule in your home, and the same ever-blessed Redeemer who proved His power by giving life back to a Galilean girl, stopping a funeral procession to restore a deceased son to his widowed mother, approaching a tomb to speak words of resurrection to the moldering remains of His friend—that glorious Christ, who Himself rose from the dead, will banish brooding darkness from your family circle by His promise, "Because I live, ye shall live also."

Hear the Apostle's appeal once more: "Learn first to show piety at home." Mothers of America, if your club duties, your social obligations, employment and business, even your church-work, interfere with the proper care of your children and prevent the necessary supervision of your home, resign from your literary and musical clubs; give up your office job; reduce the time you are spending for church suppers, ladies' aid entertainments, and stay with your children, the precious souls whom God has given you for molding! Bring them to Christ and by the Spirit's help keep them with that Savior! Live for your husband and your family!

Fathers of America, whom God has appointed the priests and guardians of the home, whom He wants to be His priests, proclaiming the love of Jesus Christ to your own beloved ones, what are you profited if you gain business success, but, without Christ, lose your own soul and see your own children similarly lost? What advantage will there be for them in eternity if you leave your sons and daughters real estate, stocks and bonds, bank accounts, but do not give them the inheritance of Christian faith? If you are too busy for Christ and His Church, too busy for prayer and the Bible, may God Almighty bring you to your knees (if necessary, by sickness, loss, reverses, collapse of hopes), so that you will realize how terrifying it is to live without Jesus, to deprive your own children of His love! Thousands of shrewd business men are sacrificing their greatest joy and blessing by keeping Christ from their family life. If you have no time for Jesus, *make* time for Him! If your bowling club, your service club, your political club, and, again, even your church club keep you away from your home and restrict your spiritual direction of your family, drop some of these activities! Remember, you must first "learn to show piety at home."

Children of America, help to keep Christ first in your family! Obey your parents gladly and willingly! Learn about Jesus! Recall how He provided for His mother during His last hours on the cross! Pray to Him morning and evening! Ask your parents to have family prayers! If you want to attend Sunday-school, send me a postal card, so that I can help you hear more of the blessed Jesus!

Let all of us, young and old, learned and simple, white and black, yellow and red, wherever we are and whatever our homes may be, resolve, our faces directed toward Christ's coming, that our Savior shall be First in our family, the Guest of our hearts and homes, until we are with Him in the unbroken eternity of His heavenly homeland! God grant it for His sake! Amen.

KEEP AMERICA CHRISTIAN!

"Turn thou us unto thee, O Lord, and we shall be turned; renew our days as of old!" (Lamentations 5:21).

Four thousand billion dollars! Who among us can really understand that staggering sum? Yet a Harvard professor of economics recently told those worried about our growing national deficit that within fifty years, provided the Federal income continues to increase as it has, the United States will be able to sustain an indebtedness of that inconceivable amount. Four thousand billion dollars! Who knows whether this figure, cruelly fantastic to many of you who would thank God if you had four dollars, represents the breaking point in American financial power? An army of experts, I suppose, will contradict this claim; moreover, we should realize that a nation's existence is not guaranteed by the amount of its money nor its destruction sealed by financial loss. A country can rebuild, sometimes better and stronger, after complete bankruptcy. The wildest inflation, when people pay hundreds of thousands in paper money for a loaf of bread or a quart of milk, need not mark the utter end of any nation.

Similarly, if we ask ourselves, What is the worst disaster that can overtake our beloved land? we ought to agree that the most devastating danger comes not from without, but from within. Just as a man can recover from ghastly surface wounds, broken or even amputated limbs, while below-the-surface diseases, like cancer or internal injury to the vital organs, prove fatal, so a nation, with its cities, towns, and villages, can regain its peace after the chaos and upheaval of war; it can be restored to health after wide epidemics of influenza or typhus; it can rise victoriously from the ashes of fire, the debris of flood, earthquake, tornado, the ruin of bombs and cannon. Yet history testifies that there is one inner loss which is final, that can remove national glory forever and permanently reduce any country, however rich and powerful. That deadliest danger is unbelief, ingratitude toward God Almighty, the blasphemous ridicule of His Word, the rejection of the Lord Jesus Christ, the denial of the cleansing blood, the contempt for the Gospel, and with this, the carnival of crime, the sweeping rule of sin, the glorification of evil. God's truth, majestic in its plain, unalterable force, warns, "The nation and kingdom that will not serve Thee shall perish," and every time an empire has collapsed—review this parade of fallen kingdoms: Egypt, Babylonia, Syria, Media, Persia, Greece, Rome, and, above all, Judah—the truth of that warning is fulfilled.

The most vital necessity for America today is, therefore, trust in the

---

From Walter A. Maier, *For Christ and Country*, Concordia Publishing House, copyright 1942, pp. 189–203. Reprinted by permission.

Lord Jesus Christ's power to forgive sins and restore us to God. That truth was recognized when the United States was founded; but because the opposition to our Lord and His Church is steadily increasing, while sinister anti-Christian forces attempt to destroy the faith which has been the heritage of millions, I appeal to you in Christ's name:

Keep America Christian!

For our text we turn to the closing words in the Book of Lamentations (chapter five, verse twenty-one), where Jeremiah, surveying his people's unbelief and their sorrow, cries out, "Turn thou us unto thee, O Lord, and we shall be turned; renew our days as of old!"

I. We Are Losing Our Christian Heritage

In this plaintive plea, "Renew our days as of old," the prophet recorded his sorrow over the tragic fact that Israel, blessed by Jehovah above all other nations; Israel, protected by divine might and heavenly love since its earliest days; Israel to whom alone God sent His prophets, His Word, and the promise of a coming Messiah, had forgotten its Creator and Redeemer. The ancient days during which the people stood close to their God had given way to a new, sin-marked era in which the Lord was ungratefully cast aside. Recalling David's golden age when Israel loyally acclaimed Jehovah; Solomon's temple, where swelling psalms joyfully sang the Almighty's praise; the reign of God-fearing kings, when Old Testament Scriptures were held in high esteem, sacrifices performed with humble repentance—and contrasting with those distant, happy days the worldliness, unbelief, rebellion against God which aroused divine wrath and summoned Nebuchadnezzar's Babylonian hordes to lay Jerusalem waste, Jeremiah breaks out into this plea: "'Renew our days as of old!' Bring back those glorious years when Israel gladly served God!"

Need I remind you that a similar, lamentable contrast exists between the America of today and of our founding fathers; that we, too, must pray with deep-souled appeal, "O God, 'renew our days as of old!'" The Book of Judges points to grave national calamities which began when "another generation" arose "which knew not the Lord, nor yet the works which He had done for Israel." Similarly a new generation has now arisen within our boundaries which does not know the God who made America great nor recognize His overbounteous mercy toward our country. Despite everything radicals may try to tell you, keep this basic truth firmly implanted in your mind: Our colonies, later the States, were settled by men and women who were Christians, who came to our shores, among other reasons, because they could here spread the Gospel, erect Christian churches, and worship the Savior according to His Word! Those early pioneers had their faults, of course, and I am not endeavoring to glorify something so far distant from us that its frailties cannot be seen; but for the most part, the people who built America were outstanding in their devotion to Christ. The Charter of Virginia assures its colonists the right to live together in "Christian peace" and instructs them to help "in propagating . . . the Christian religion to such people as yet live in ignorance of the true knowledge and worship of God." The Plymouth Charter specifies that the colony is established "to advance the enlargement of the Christian religion, to the glory of God Almighty." The Delaware Charter defines one purpose of that settlement as "the further propagation of the Holy Gospel." Maryland's Charter explains that its first settlers were moved by a "pious zeal for extending the Christian religion." The Massachusetts Bay Charter emphasizes that Boston was founded by men who wanted to bring the new world "to the knowledge and obedience of the only true God and the Savior of mankind." The early settlers of Pennsylvania came to America, according to their own declaration, for the spread of the "Christian religion." The Rhode Island Charter commits its people to the "true Christian faith and worship of God," and in the Rhode Island Compact the signers declare, "We submit our persons, lives, and estates unto our Lord Jesus Christ, the King of kings, and Lord of lords." The Connecticut Constitution in its preamble pledges the settlers to help "preserve the liberty and purity of the Gospel of the Lord Jesus Christ." The first article in the New Hampshire Charter begins: "We . . . in the name of Christ and in the sight of God." The oath that this instrument requires was to be administered in the name of "the Lord Jesus Christ, the King and Savior of His people."

Similarly, in the early days of our War for Independence, although freethinkers sometimes occupied high places, an unmistakably Christian note rang through the official proceedings. The closing words in the Declaration of Independence confessed the nation's dependence on God. The first American day of humiliation, fasting, and prayer, in 1776, was appointed by Congress so that the colonies might "through the merits and mediation of Jesus Christ, obtain His pardon and forgiveness." The first Thanksgiving Day, ordered by Congress in 1777, asked the people's prayers for God's solemn blessing and "the penitent confession of their manifold sins . . . and their humble and earnest supplication that it may please God, through the merits of Jesus Christ, mercifully to blot our sins out of remembrance." President John Adams proclaimed a country-wide fast, asking the citizens to admit their sins before the "Most High God" and with the sincerest penitence implore His pardoning mercy through the "Great Mediator and Redeemer for our past transgressions." In the midst of the Civil War, 1863, the United States Senate passed a resolution suggesting that our people seek God's help "through Jesus Christ." In a hundred different ways, it could be shown, the America of yesterday exalted Almighty God as the Supreme Ruler of our commonwealth, taught that in the Scriptures His will is revealed for the infallible guidance of men, and that Jesus Christ is the divinely appointed Mediator between God and the men who make up nations.

I am not now discussing the relation of Church and State nor pleading for intolerance or religious discrimination, both of which are condemned by true Americanism and true Christianity. I am trying to show you that the founding fathers in America were not atheists, skeptics, unbelievers, pantheists, freethinkers, Mohammedans, Buddhists, but (despite their denominational differences, which I would in no way minimize) Christians who built their hope on the Lord Jesus Christ. Here and there, in the course of years and with the freedom America offered all men, a settlement of unbelievers and atheists did spring up. For example, when the city of New Ulm, Minnesota, was planned, its founders boasted that in this community the folly of religion would be revealed by the success of irreligion. Yet New Ulm and a few other similar experiments failed dismally to function as centers of antireligious agitation. Today a Lutheran college and church steeples show Christ's victory over unbelief. On the whole, the pioneers along our Eastern seaboard, the men and women who built cities and towns in the Colonies, the first to cut down forests in the Northwest Territory, to cross the Alleghenies, to sail down the Ohio and up the Mississippi, the early farmers on our Midwestern plains, the hardy adventurers who drove covered wagons to the Rockies and then fought their way over desert or mountain passes through blister of heat or blizzard to the slopes that drop into the blue Pacific, were close to the Almighty in those days when most of our congregations were established, most of our mission groups, Bible societies, Christian charitable and educational institutions founded.

Now, however, the scene is changed. We have more churches, but not stronger churches. The clear-cut acknowledgment of the Lord Jesus Christ which marked the original American way of life is subdued. Public orators speak of God, it is true; but have you noticed how woefully infrequent is the reference to "the name which is above every name"? In some instances men of prominence deliberately refuse to mention Christ. Certain fraternal organizations, called "Christian," systematically bar His name, perhaps because they are afraid of incurring the disfavor or losing the support of anti-Biblical elements. Even some religious groups which during the hard, formative periods of this country were outspoken in their loyalty to Jesus have gone over to the left wing of Modernism. They have imposing buildings, well-paid choirs, celebrated pulpit orators, élite membership, social halls, gymnasiums; but they are without Christ, the Son of God, the one Savior. They have lost the faith of their fathers, they have compromised when God's Word demanded opposition to error and warned, "Whosoever shall deny me before men, him will I also deny before my Father which is in heaven."

At the same time, other countermovements have been set in motion against our Lord. Atheism has been systematically organized. Communism—and I mean the Bible-ridiculing, Christ-blaspheming sort—has made startling headway in the United States during the last two decades, and we may well expect that it will go forward in greater strides after the war. American Christians should realize that every atheistic Communist has sworn hostility to the Gospel of Jesus and that the higher his rank, the greater his influence, the more dangerous his hatred of the Savior.

When we thus behold the denial of the Lord Jesus in this blessed nation, generations ago dedicated to faith in His redemption; when we see the America in which, while strange, foreign sects and cults become firmly rooted, half of the entire population belongs to no church whatever and, therefore, comes under Christ's verdict "He that is not with me is against me," do you not agree that the prayer to be spoken from our innermost hearts must repeat Jeremiah's plea "O God, 'renew our days as of old' "? Bring back the America that was not ashamed to confess the Lord Jesus; the America that had days of fasting, humiliation, and penance; the America in which Sunday was a time for church attendance by the whole family; the America that wanted sermons instead of sermonettes, that listened to preachers who called sin *sin;* the America in which frontier settlers shared their homes with circuit riders or traveled for days to hear a preacher expound the Gospel; the America that had no streamlined trains, no airplanes, no radios, no electric power, no steam heat, no modern plumbing, no production lines, yet that had the Savior, and, having Him, was victorious over its enemies!

"Renew our days as of old!" we repeat as we recall the startling change which has overtaken American education. The first schools founded on this continent taught the Christian religion and were based on the Scriptural maxim, "The fear of the Lord is the beginning of wisdom." Today much of public education is pointedly antireligious, with a deep-rooted determination on the part of many teachers (whose salaries are paid from public funds) to poison young minds against the Bible. Most of you have no idea of the startling extent to which textbooks used in many public schools feature an away-from-God tendency. While recent years have witnessed a remarkable increase in school building and enrollment, on a steadily mounting scale we have been forced to erect more prisons in the battle against juvenile crime. In many cities we are training children to be mentally shrewd rather than morally good, cute and cunning instead of honest and straightforward. Because the collapse of morality and reverence constitutes a serious menace to the future of the nation, we ought constantly to ask the Almighty for a return to the early American educational ideals. They had no modern theories of training in those pioneer decades, no "progressive" systems, no theories of self-expression; but they kept first things first. For them no training was complete without the study of the Bible, the memorizing of its passages, the exalting of its truth.

True, we can never fully recapture that early American ideal since our public schools, attended by children of various, conflicting creeds, cannot give spiritual instruction or require Biblical training; but the Christians of our country can return to the colonial practice — and the conditions after the war may make this necessary — by which the churches built their own elementary schools to insure religious instruction. My own Church annually spends millions of dollars to maintain and expand a system of child training which helps the pupils keep the Lord Jesus uppermost in his mind. We gladly pay our taxes to support the public educational system; but we also believe that the nation and the churches require hearts and minds illuminated by the Holy Spirit, souls daily instructed in Biblical truth. Therefore we maintain hundreds of Christian day schools throughout the land, offering more than secular culture can legally give — a sound, Scriptural training. These schools are open to your boys and girls. Give us your children so that we can help give them to Christ! Juvenile court statistics show conclusively that youngsters thus trained have a moral and spiritual force in their lives which goes far in keeping them away from crime and closer to Christ.

Similarly, we need a return to the spirit of Christian higher education which marked our country's yesteryear, when colleges and universities were founded for the defense and spread of the true faith. Read the records of the seventeenth, eighteenth, and nineteenth centuries to remind yourself that the oldest, largest, and best universities were dedicated to the Savior in their charters, on their seals, and in their Scripture-centered instruction! Deeply we regret that many of the colleges thus called into existence by humble, Christian faith, built by Christian funds, endowed by legacies from Christian friends, have forsaken this foundation. In too many cases such schools have become hotbeds of infidelity and hatred of the Redeemer. As some of you parents know from bitter experience, young people who enter colleges as happy, trusting believers, leave as dissatisfied, sophisticated skeptics. Particularly in times like these, when the nation needs spiritual strength for its first line of defense, we must keep Christ in culture. Therefore, if you fathers and mothers want your children to attend a college in which Biblical religion, far from being assailed, will be exalted, write me for a list of spiritually accredited colleges connected with my Church!

Similarly, the plea "Renew our days as of old!" arises from a dozen different sectors of our life. Give us the early American household, with large families, mothers devoted to their home, fathers conscious of the fact that they must be God's priests among their own, children who are obedient and respectful; homes, in short, with Jesus the constant Guest and His Spirit the consecrating Power! Think of it, Christian marriage was so sacred in the Plymouth Colony that during its first seventy-one years only six divorces were granted, and these on Scripturally justified grounds! Contrast with this the reports of fifth, sixth, and seventh marriages in the United States and a divorce rate which now seems primed for a startling increase!

This "renew our days as of old!" should be spoken with redoubled sincerity now, when the burdens of war begin to press heavily. Listening to some speakers, one would imagine God plays no part in the triumph of our forces or in the just and righteous peace for which we pray. "We must win this war," it is said, "because we have the will to win." But we need more than the armies, navies, air armadas; more than hundred-billion-dollar expenditures; more than organization and strategy, bravery and sacrifice! My fellow countrymen, we need God; and since He is with those only who accept Him in humble, trusting faith, let us seek Him penitently in Christ and recognize how earnestly He speaks to us in war's visitation. Church papers do well in featuring these paragraphs spoken by a preacher in Bournemouth, England, to his congregation: "We have ignored the ringing of the church bells calling us to worship. *Now* the bells cannot ring except to warn of invasion. We have left the churches half empty when they should have been filled with worshipers. *Now* they are in ruins. The money we would not give to the Lord's work, *now* is taken from us in taxes and higher prices. The food for which we forgot to say thanks, *now* is unobtainable. The service we refused to give to God, *now* is conscripted for the country. Nights we would not spend 'watching unto prayer,' *now* are spent in anxious air-raid precautions." Similarly, of our own country it could be said: We have used our automobile tires to take us away from church on Sunday, and *now* many have no tires for the whole week. We did not send enough missionaries to convert the Japanese, *now* we must send soldiers to destroy them. We have not trained our youth for the Savior; *now* we must train them for slaughter.

II. WE NEED GOD TO PRESERVE OUR CHRISTIAN HERITAGE

We should, however, do more than cry out, "Keep America Christian!" We must act! Everyone who knows the Lord Jesus and the magnificence of His grace in reconciling a lost world to His heavenly Father must be ready to assume individual responsibility. Jeremiah does not primarily seek to start a mass movement nor ask others to act for him. He recognizes his own share, his personal duty. May the Holy Spirit awaken men with the courage of that mighty prophet who, as few others, protested ceaselessly against evil, defended the faith at all costs, resolutely championed his Lord and continually sounded the necessary note of repentance and contrition! Let American clergymen make this fearless man of God their model by clinging to the whole Word of Truth! Such loyalty may produce opposition, just as Jeremiah had to fight the chief priests and the officials in the ecclesiastical system of his day. Dare to be a Jeremiah, and you will have a Jeremiah's blessing — deliverance in danger and persecution! If necessary, the Almighty can invoke His heavenly power to sustain you in any struggle.

Laity of America, read these Old Testament prophecies to find strength and courage during disturbed days! You are not too small, insignificant, isolated, to be heard or have your objection to apostasy sustained. The man with the Almighty on his side is still a majority. Therefore, if you hear any attack on Christ, cry out in rebuke! If in church circles you meet denial of the faith, any contradiction of God's truth, raise your voice in disavowal! If in the realm of politics attempts are made to discredit the divine Word; for example, if efforts are made to introduce anti-Biblical, anti-American, evolutionary, Communist books, reading guides or courses into the public-school system of your community, start a petition to prohibit them! Take the lead in eliminating violations of Scriptural teachings and our constitutional rights! Some of you business men, blessed with a clear-cut understanding of the Savior's teaching, should enter the nation's political life and contribute the uplifting power that Christian leadership can offer. Today there is a marked need in the weighty public offices — especially those dealing with the lives of our military youth — for many more far-sighted men who know Jesus and His exalting righteousness.

Jeremiah, realizing that without God all his protests would be of no avail, turned to the Almighty in the prayer of our text. Oh, that millions from coast to coast would likewise find refuge and strength in true petition and bring down God's benediction through fervent intercession! America on bended knees, with folded hands, bowed heads, and humble hearts could win victories over foes a thousand times stronger than our enemies across both oceans. So, pray, America! Pray penitently! Beseech God in your own room, your household, your church, wherever you may be! Pray persistently, with trust which can never be defeated because you know "with God nothing shall be impossible"! By the omnipotence of heaven, if it be His will and for our individual and collective best, He can change our sorrows, stop this war, and give the world a true and righteous peace, with all oppression defeated.

Especially, however, pray as Jeremiah did when he pleaded contritely, confessing the sins of his people as well as his own transgressions! Multitudes across this nation should repeat his prayer: "Turn Thou us unto Thee, O Lord, and we shall be turned!" Come before God, you among the unconverted who have never accepted the Redeemer! Ask the Almighty, "Turn me from sin, from hell, from eternal death! Turn me from my own sinful flesh, from my own lustful thoughts, my own selfish, hateful, revengeful self! Turn me from the lure and lust of temptation! Turn me from the despair over my transgressions, from the accusation of my conscience, from the fear of death! Turn me from Thy wrath, and for Jesus' sake bring me into Thy love!" When you plead with this complete trust which takes Christ fully at His Word; when you know in the positive assurance of the Holy Spirit that the suffering which Jesus endured, the blood He shed on Calvary, the cry of anguish which there escaped His parched lips, the death He died on the cross, was all for you, so that by the humble acceptance of Him as your Savior you could be turned from sin to salvation — you are saved for earth and heaven. Then, while you cling to Christ, no power of men or devils combined can tear you from His hands. You have been born again into a new existence that has turned you to God!

Many of you (I know from your letters) could now testify that God has marvelously turned you; that the Spirit has changed men who have beaten or deserted their wives and made them repentant, loving husbands. Some of you had to be imprisoned to meet Christ and find the new life in Him; now — praise God! — drunkenness, envy, malice, unmentionable sins, have all been forgiven and conquered in your life through the Spirit who has turned you to the Father by the power of His regeneration.

Do not let anyone or anything keep you from Christ's love! Ask God to turn your mind so that instead of doubting, you gladly accept the glorious truth which even mighty intellects have acclaimed! Beseech the Spirit to direct your heart from the treacherous clinging to worldly treasures! Last week a sailor on the doomed tanker *Allen Jackson*, instead of fleeing to a lifeboat when the torpedo struck the ship's side, remembered eighty dollars left in the locker and ran to salvage his wallet. But he sold his life for money he could never enjoy. While his shipmates escaped, he was drowned. To avoid spiritual death, beseech your heavenly Father for the strength required to cut loose from all destructive entanglements! Ask God to turn your life from the slavery of sin to the service of your neighbors and your country in this hour of its need, so that perishing souls may be restored by a word of Christ's grace and truth you may be privileged to speak!

Plead with God in the faith of Jeremiah to turn you wholly to the Savior in body, soul, heart, mind, and spirit! My fellow redeemed, may the joy of a saved, sanctified life be yours! By the power of rebirth and reconciliation to the heavenly Father, you, as believers in Christ, can be a mighty force in restoring the "days as of old," in keeping America Christian. God bless you in your love for the Savior, and God bless a Christian America, for Jesus' sake! Amen.

WHAT IS GOD'S PURPOSE IN WAR?

"They chose new gods; then was war in the gates" (Judges 5:8).
"As many as I love, I rebuke and chasten" (Revelation 3:19).

WHEN the Civil War dragged on into its fourth year and the struggle seemed indecisive, despite the fact that the North had more money and more men, President Abraham Lincoln, weary of bloodshed, wrote these amazing lines: "God wills this contest and wills that it shall not end yet. By His mere great power over the minds of the contestants, He could have saved or destroyed the Union without a human contest. Yet the contest began. And having begun, He could give the final victory to either side any day. Yet the contest proceeds."

Next week America begins its fourth year of fighting in World War II. How foolish and fantastic the predictions now seem which in 1941 foretold the end of this struggle in six months, a year, two years! If our experts cannot foretell the time and manner of earthly peace, they of themselves certainly cannot explain the facts of spiritual peace. As the struggle continues, our thoughts should be like Lincoln's. We, too, should know that by the Lord's "great power over the minds of the contestants" He could have averted this war or given final victory a year, a month, a week, after it started.

Therefore we ask, "What are our heavenly Father's intentions as the shocking agonies of conflict multiply?" This war will be recorded as history's most frightful slaughter. It will kill more civilians than any other struggle up to this time. It will destroy more by hunger and epidemic, and the years after the armistice will bring terror to many parts of the earth. To this add the misery in the souls of hundreds of millions, the black, destructive forces created and enlarged by this strife, the trillion dollars and more spent for purposes of slaughter, the hundreds of billions of dollars lost in bombed cities, all the woe and wickedness of war combined, and we realize that if Lincoln had reason to seek for the divine design in the four years of Civil War, which financially cost less than eleven days of this World War, then certainly we have reason to ask—and this is our question for today:

WHAT IS GOD'S PURPOSE IN WAR?

Under the Holy Spirit's enlightening guidance we find His two chief purposes: the punishment of unbelievers and the purifying of the believers, indicated in these passages: "They chose new gods; then was war in the gates" (Judg. 5:8), and "As many as I love, I rebuke and chasten" (Rev. 3:19).

From Walter A. Maier, *Jesus Christ Our Hope*, Concordia Publishing House, copyright 1946, pp. 117–33. Reprinted by permission.

I. HE USES THIS CONFLICT TO PUNISH SINNERS

Right at the outset let us be clear on the basic fact that there is a supreme, all-powerful Ruler of the universe who is directly connected with all war. The Bible calls everyone who says, "There is no God," a "fool"; and this folly was never more gross and glaring than now, with the world smoking from the ruins left by fury and hatred. How desperate would be our distress, how hopeless our future, how misplaced our prayers, how misshapen our entire existence, how devilish the whole earth, if boasting unbelievers were right in claiming that our Lord does not exist! If there is no Sovereign of the universe, if man dies like a dog, if no Judgment follows in the hereafter to punish the wicked, then away with purity and patriotism! Down with law and order! Destroy Christian churches and schools! Blast all truth, love, virtue, honesty out of existence! Every man for himself! Let each one get what he can, though he crushes his fellow men as he gets it! — these are the cries of blind avarice raised by far too many Americans.

How puny men can deny the Almighty's existence when they hear the message of grace in Christ's Cross; when they see the startling evidence of His power in the world, as in the marvels of their own body; when they trace His hand throughout history in the rise and fall of empires, in the doom and defeat of wicked leaders; how some of you can write me that you are atheists when your own reason testifies that you have a God, and even the lowest savages know that there is a Supreme Being — all this is one of the most convincing proofs for the utter sinfulness and degeneracy of the race. Since not one but ten thousand passages of Scripture prove the Lord's blessing; since a million miracles in nature, the system of billions of stars above, the mystery of a trillion marvels in the submarine world below, unite in testifying to an eternal Creator, a heavenly Sustainer, a divine Designer, accept Heaven's truth and bow humbly before your God! To deny that He lives and rules is to commit mental, moral, spiritual suicide.

Neither make the related mistake of concluding with many modern, Scripture-ridiculing preachers that the Lord is only a vague, weak, shadowy force, a spirit so far removed from this world and so little concerned about its affairs that He permits events to take any course they will, while He remains untouched by our weal and woe. The Bible sharply contradicts this. "He" is "not far from every one of us," the Apostle declares. "In Him we live and move and have our being." The true God, the one and only God — Father, Savior, and Spirit — is so close to us that our globe, far from being a section of the sun accidentally torn loose by a huge wandering star (many of your boys and girls are taught this today in tax-supported high schools) is His creation, under His constant guidance and direction. He is so near to us that in every need we can come to Him for help and hope.

Again, we must not think of God as a cruel war lord, who delights in agony, exults in massacre, revels in blood. That is the hideous, blasphemous caricature of the Almighty drawn by many militarists and those who pile up war profits. They like to ease their conscience and promote their cause by picturing the shedding of blood as a holy, sacred privilege, by promising that those who fall in battle will because of these sacrifices be lavishly welcomed into eternity. But listen to Scripture when it protests, "Scatter Thou the people that delight in war"! Hear the Lord say that David cannot build the Temple because he fought too many battles! Note that the Scriptures clearly declare, God "doth not afflict willingly"! It was not easy, humanly speaking, for Him to permit the second world conflict and its casualties. He wants all men to be saved. He who sent His Son for their redemption is grieved every time the horrors of this struggle destroy an unbelieving soul, an unrepentant life. If Christ, our heavenly King, wept hot tears of loving sorrow when He looked over the haughty, sinful capital of His people; if He cried, "O Jerusalem, Jerusalem," when He thought of the enemies who would soon level the city with the ground, will you not agree that if He were with us today, His tears would flow for the millions in America, Great Britain, France, Holland, Belgium, and the South Sea islands, yes, even for those in Italy, Germany, and Japan who have been killed in the cruelty of this conflict? To Jesus, the soul even of the most treacherous enemy is worth more than the earth's accumulated treasures. Therefore let us today, in the New Testament grace, refuse to speak of any international strife as a holy war, Christ's war, God's war. As we see the Savior, who never fought in battle, although merely His glance could send His enemies prostrate; as we behold the Lord of mercy, who never killed a single person, even though His enemies crucified Him, let us recognize that this struggle has come upon us with His permission, but not with His pleasure; that He hates war; that He denounces those who love it, promote it, protract it, profit by it; that He in all truth is the God who pleads for peace, offers peace, blesses peace, exalts peace!

Why, then, did He permit this war to come? We find the first answer in the repeated statements of Scripture which show that all bloodshed, even the most justified, even wars for defense, wars against oppression and tyranny, wars for righteousness, are a punishment for those who rise up in rebellion against Heaven. When Jehovah announces the conflict with Babylon, He declares, "I will punish the world for their evil, and the wicked for their iniquity." From the beginning of history until this moment international strife has come as the penalty of unbelief. Our text emphasizes this truth in a short but startling way by the words of Deborah, the Old Testament heroine, who knew war, not on the home front but on the battle front. To her there were no delightful aspects of bloodshed, no teas and theatricals, no increased income and double salary. War to her was a shrieking, horrifying, death-dealing penalty; and she recognized that the children of Israel were overrun with enemies, because they forsook the

Almighty, who had made them His own people, and deliberately "chose new gods," the false gods of their heathen neighbors, manmade idols. The struggle in Deborah's day, which brutally oppressed the people for twenty years, came, so the Old Testament clearly declares, as a punishment to help Israel learn the folly of its sins, recognize the Lord's power, and penitently return to Him who was its only Help.

Today we should realize clearly and personally that it must likewise be said of masses in America, "they chose new gods." Time was when our country, which has received larger, more numerous, and more sustained blessings than any other nation, mightily acclaimed the true God and recognized Him as the Source of all hope and strength. The founders of the colonies from which the United States grew; the brave souls who crossed the Atlantic when it took months, not hours, to span the ocean; the pioneers who left the sea coast and against overwhelming odds forged ahead through the wilderness over untracked mountains and unbridged rivers to establish the first cities and towns in the valleys of the Ohio, the Mississippi, the Missouri Rivers; the men and women whose prairie schooners inched their way over the Rockies and then down toward the Pacific shores—these pioneers knew God. Read the charters of the original thirteen colonies; see how early America built churches as well as schools and colleges dedicated to Christ; recall how from their meager funds they sent missionaries to win the red men for Jesus, how they printed the Bible, and how Congress officially gave its endorsement! They had their sins and weaknesses, these founding fathers, but they had the Lord, and therefore they had victory.

Today, however, the God who gave us this land as the fullest answer to human needs is not good enough for millions of our countrymen. They abuse His name in profanity; they pass His churches unconcernedly; they leave His Word unread, His Gospel unheard, His invitations unaccepted; they flout His laws, question His existence, attack His truth. As Israel of old, they worship "new gods," the gods of money —blood-money sometimes, gained from the conflict which costs others their lives. Again, multitudes bow down before the "new gods" of evil desire. New York police officials declare that at Times Square alone more than 400 teen-age girls, who roam the streets as pickups, could be taken into custody every night if the authorities had a place to put them. Masses are worshiping the "new gods" of pleasure, with theaters featuring risqué performances that take in more money than ever before and taverns overcrowded until the early morning hours; the "new gods" of pride, which make many look for power and victory to themselves, their generals, scientists, financiers, production leaders, but not to the Almighty. At a time when America should "ask for the old paths, where is the good way, and walk therein" and, returning to the blessed Trinity, find rest for its souls, peace for its land, "new gods" are found in many homes, with a conservative State like Oregon now showing more than twice the number of divorces of ten years ago, with lust taking the place of love and marriage made a mockery. There are "new gods" in many schools, which, instead of promoting an education beginning with "the fear of the Lord," work for a disregard of the All-merciful and His Word; they produce clever, sophisticated, oversmart children, but not devoted, obedient, disciplined, respectful boys and girls. There are "new gods" in American industry, where employer and employee, seeking not what they can give, but what they can get, forsake the faith and prostrate themselves before the idol of their own power. Even in some churches the God of our fathers has been dethroned in favor of the new, man-made god of modern, anti-Bible, anti-Christ creeds. Just when this rejection of the Redeemer was at its highest and this choosing of "new gods" at its widest, World War I began; and because the masses did not learn the lesson of repentance and reliance on the Lord, twenty-five years later came World War II, far more shocking than the first—both divine punishments for widespread wickedness. Unless we now repent and return to Christ, World War III can start with annihilation bombs, destruction from the sky, and mass murder almost indescribably worse even than we now know.

Our Father's first purpose in the present conflict is to fulfill the repeated threat of His punishment on unbelief, blasphemy, rebellion against His grace. By permitting this struggle to go on, He is hurling many of His enemies to the ground, destroying those who would assail His name. Witness the appalling price Germany is paying for its battalions of Bible critics and Scripture scoffers! See the arm of divine vengeance reach out for Japan, long guilty of opposing the Church! But consider especially that the Lord of Hosts is speaking to America with lengthening casualty lists! In a single day we now spend for this war almost three times the cost of the entire Revolution. Our total national debt at the end of World War I is consumed in one hundred days of World War II. All this should serve to emphasize God's call to repentance by which He would beg: "O America, 'return unto Me, and I will return unto you!' Reject these 'new gods' that can bring more brutal bloodshed, and turn to Me, the Lord who made you, loves you, redeemed you, and wants you to be His!"

The Almighty is also speaking to many of you individually through this war in which, as your hopes crashed, you have sustained heavy loss. When things went well, some of you declared that Jesus, if He ever existed, might be good enough for the weak, the suffering, the ignorant, but *you* certainly did not need Him. The poor and the simple could keep the Lord of the Bible if they wished, but *you* were making "news gods," the idols of achievement and power, the idol of yourself, your supposed strength and brilliant ability. Now that sickness or sorrow, loss of health or wealth, brutality or bereavement, shake you out of your stupor, you ought to recognize that your suffering comes as the penalty of rejecting your Redeemer. You are paying the heavy price for your transgressions, while your heavenly Father is trying to arouse you to the realization that you are lost without the Savior, that it is time — high time, over time — for you to confess Him your Redeemer.

Therefore on this Sunday, the last in the church year, which by ancient, praiseworthy custom is set aside as a day of repentance and humiliation, may all of us in this vast radio mission, we in the studio, you at home or away from home, in autos or trains, in camps or ship quarters, in your boarding rooms or college dormitories, in hospitals or sanatoria, in public institutions or prisons, join in a nation-wide plea of repentance and pray sincerely and fervently: "O God, our gracious Father, we have sinned repeatedly against Thee. We have often neglected the preaching of the Gospel, forsaken the assembly of Thy believers, denied Thy Son, our only Hope; we have often broken Thy commandments, every one of them, by wicked thoughts and desires, by selfish, hate-filled words, by evil, destructive deeds. Oh, for the sake of Thy Son, our Savior, who Himself took our sins away, assuming their guilt, their sentence, their punishment, their curse, as on the cross He suffered, bled, and died for us, grant us the assurance that all our iniquities have been canceled and the handwriting against us blotted out by His blood! Receive us, as Thou hast promised; restore us; renew us through Thy Spirit, so that, born again through faith in Christ, we can live to please Thee! O God the Father, have mercy upon us; O God the Son, have mercy upon us; O God the Holy Comforter, have mercy upon us; for Jesus' sake!"

Now, if this appeal is made in truth and trust, it can help shorten war, reduce the shocking terrors of bloodshed, restrict the occurrence of further conflicts. But if we, unto whom *"much is given"* and of whom *"shall be much required,"* refuse to repent and return to the God of our fathers, then bitter, heartbreaking days may lie before us. Even peace may not bring the answer to our problems. The skyrocketing incomes of these war years have so pampered many in our country that they may not be able to endure any postwar letdown. Without a deep Christian foundation, masses in the United States will face difficulty in meeting the stern demands of the years ahead. Politicians may promise halcyon days, golden prosperity, Utopia, a warless, wantless world; scientists may claim, as some recently have, that within the next century man will live 125 years on the average and will never grow gray or fat, that our increased knowledge will bring us increased peace; but with all the advances in skills and sciences the future may bring, the deepening of human knowledge alone cannot pave the way to prosperity, individual or national. The I.Q. of some notorious criminals is higher than the average of university faculties. No; these bleeding years remind us America needs God more desperately today than ever before; for if we refuse to smash the new, false gods to pieces, we may yet suffer more than the worst we have endured.

II. HE USES THIS CONFLICT TO PURIFY BELIEVERS

The same war which punishes sinners comes to believers, with its myriad sorrows, not as a penalty, but as a means God uses to purify and strengthen their trust. We have the glorious assurance, even though we cannot understand it, that for the faithful all the cruelty of conflict, the drowning of thousands on the high seas, the crashing of ten thousand planes, the bombing and blasting of hundreds of thousands in air raids, the agonizing death of millions on the battlefields, the total destruction of ten millions of civilians, were permitted by the Father's higher wisdom because they were to bring His children to unseen but marvelous blessings.

Once more this takes us back to the immeasurable height and depth, the endless width and breadth, of the Savior's love. We think we know what love is; yet how overawed, humble, powerless, we are when we meditate on Christ's love. He gave His own sinless life for those who hated Him, constantly opposed Him, daily blasphemed Him, viciously persecuted Him, diabolically slandered Him, brutally lashed Him, and criminally crucified Him, pure and innocent as He was. That love, which endured the shame and agony of the cross, included you. Whenever sad, downhearted, lonely, you wonder whether anyone in the whole world cares for you; whenever you have trouble in your family as your nearest and dearest turn against you; when, during these long years of war, your sins have added to your woe and tried to separate you from the guarantee of grace, what joy can be yours to know that Jesus has promised, "I will never leave Thee nor forsake thee"; that He has sealed with His own blood the heavenly pledge for the forgiveness of all your sins, including those which make you shudder when you recall them!

Now, if Christ loved you so that He went to the cross to remove the burden of your sins, to suffer their penalty for you; if—and may the Holy Spirit lead you to believe this with your whole heart, soul, and mind—your Savior has defeated hell and gained heaven for you; if He would make you, a child of wrath now, a child of God; and if, as the climax of His compassion, you need only believe and come contritely to Christ to be assured of salvation, then His mercy will never strike you with cruel, cutting punishment. Since Jesus, your Lord and Redeemer, paid the whole price demanded by divine righteousness for wiping out your transgressions; since He went the whole way in bringing you back to God; since He broke down every barrier separating you from the Father's love; since "the blood of Jesus Christ, His Son, cleanseth us from *all* sin," as a believer, you have no more guilt for which you can be punished. God loves you.

Therefore even the sorrows which the redeemed are called upon to bear are evidence of His grace, not proof of grim anger, according to Christ's own words "As many as I love I rebuke and chasten." How wonderful beyond all words! We could not believe this mercy if it were not pledged us by our Savior Himself; but it is His own assurance that every affliction which befalls us, every burden and loss we endure, every opposition and enmity we must suffer, comes to us, as Christ's followers, from His compassion. If you are sick in bed as you hear this Gospel grace yet know Jesus as your Savior, you can cry out, "All this pain is proof of my Father's love." If war has made some of you young folks postpone your marriage for four or five years, do not become hard, bitter, grim; rather seek the Holy Spirit's help for patience and, trusting Him, believe that somehow this delay is for your best! If in the moral letdown of war your husband or wife has left you, this unfaithfulness may seek to crush you to despair; but looking to the Cross, you can declare, "It was Heaven's love that permitted this anguish to overtake me." Even if the saddest, the hardest, and, humanly speaking, the cruelest of all blows strikes, and your son, perhaps your only child, is killed in action, then, as you weep in almost uncontrolled sorrow, believe, although you cannot explain this, that since your boy was Christ's, the Lord called him because He loved him, and "the sufferings of this present time," even death on the battlefield, "are not worthy to be compared with the glory which shall be revealed in us."

How, you are clamoring to ask, can misery, pain, even death, be evidence of love? Here we must take our frail and faulty reason captive, ask the Spirit's help in learning to think God's thoughts and trust His promise that "all things," including the worst wickedness of war, "work together for good to them that love God." The reverses and the restrictions which our all-knowing Father's grace permits us to suffer teach us sympathy and open our hearts to the needs of others. The Lord wants us to forget ourselves and help others. Therefore we often meet the same afflictions which overtake our fellow men, in order that we, personally knowing their pain, can extend the helping hand of compassionate encouragement.

Again, the sorrows which divine love sends us should help us realize how weak and insignificant we are of ourselves, how sorely we need heavenly strength. Ours, of course, is the age of power pacts and supermen, when in swollen pride we are all tempted to disregard divine guidance. To rebuke this haughtiness, to keep us from further sin, to make us more reliant on our Redeemer, come the chastenings of the Lord. In many instances, as your letters show, blasphemers have been brought low on their sickbed to give them time to think of God and return repentantly to Him. If the Almighty has taken away your bodily health to make you spiritually strong; if the war has left you men and women in the service lonely, separated from your loved ones, so that the Holy Spirit could impress you with His constant companionship and thus deepen your faith; if the Father wants to enrich your soul through material loss, draw you closer to Him by leading you away from the world; if He removes the earthly props on which you mistakenly rest your courage, to help you build your hope on Jesus' blood and righteousness, then how marvelous, merciful, magnificent this divine love which chastens and rebukes you to insure your salvation, fortify your faith, and strengthen your devotion to the Savior! If we were left to ourselves, we should destroy our own souls in selfishness; but Christ, our precious Redeemer, loves us too much to permit that, and so we meet restraints and reverses which would keep us humble, obedient, trustful of His mercy.

Therefore sincere believers have always recognized in these marvelous words of Jesus, "As many as I love I rebuke and chasten," the mercy which through Christ makes each blow a blessing and every adversity an advantage! When Dr. Arnold, the devout headmaster at Rugby, lay on his deathbed, suffering intensely, he told his son, "Thank God, Tom, for giving me this pain. . . . I feel it is very good for me . . . and I do so thank Him for it." In the same trusting reliance Saint Paul praised the Lord for his afflictions and said, "I . . . glory in my infirmities." Job could exult, "Though He slay me, yet will I trust in Him." You too can have this assurance if you are blessed by a real, personal, saving faith in Jesus.

The wartime sorrows which the churches have sustained can likewise help, again through the Holy Spirit, to refine and purify. Outwardly the Savior's cause has suffered shocking losses. Thousands of church buildings have been bombed or roboted out of existence. Never before, even under the most fiendish Roman persecutors, has so much Christian property been destroyed as in the hundred-million-dollar devastation of European churches. Never before have so many ministers of God been killed by persecution and warfare as in our generation. Never before have so many missionaries been interned as at present, when in the South Pacific alone the Japanese have removed 700 Kingdom messengers from their fields. But if the churches come out of this conflict closer to Jesus and repentant of the pride, the formalism, the denial of the Savior's atonement, which marked and marred many of them; if they learn to testify unflinchingly to the truth, then, as the congregations of the catacombs were spiritually more powerful than those of the cathedrals, so the woe of war can bring tremendous benedictions to Christ's Church.

Much, therefore, depends on the attitude of the teachers and preachers. If they submit themselves wholly, unselfishly to Jesus and His Word, they can show us the way out of our difficulties. We read a few days ago that an attempt is now being made to organize pastors into a clerical union. How shocking the very thought that men whose lives should be consecrated to the Savior can think of restricting their activities to a forty-hour week, of demanding double pay for overtime, of insisting that they work with only certain classes! The American clergy does not need to be unionized; much of it needs to be revitalized by returning to its Redeemer.

We have passed Thanksgiving, and our thoughts are directed to

Christmas. Oh, that every American would heed the appeal issued by Bible organizations and repeated from the White House itself, asking that we read our Scripture daily between these two vital holidays! However, let us not read the sacred pages to find what was recently called "our own righteousness," but to discover anew the royal Redeemer's mercy for our sinfulness! Then, even as sorrows increase, each one of us can find joy, peace, rest, greater than we have known before. With the cry "On your knees, America! Repent, America! Return to Christ, America! Back to the Bible, America!" our embattled nation can go on to God-pleasing victory. Almighty Lord, precious Savior, strengthening Spirit, teach us all the vital lessons of this war for Jesus' sake! Amen!

FULL FREEDOM FROM FEAR

"Fear not: for I have redeemed thee" (Isaiah 43:1).

OUR reasons for fighting this global conflict, our hopes for the postwar world have been summarized in "the Four Freedoms": freedom of speech, freedom of religion, freedom from want, freedom from fear. The first of these is not new in our country, thank God! It was written into the Constitution and has flourished throughout the United States as in no other nation. The fact that we are able to use our most widespread radio facilities and address you in behalf of our Lord Jesus Christ is a tribute to our free government and the eminently American attitude of the Mutual Broadcasting System. With all the power and resources we have, let us battle against every attempt to regiment public opinion or restrict free expression!

The second liberty, the freedom of religion, is likewise an old privilege for us. Thank God again that we have no state church, no gestapos or commissars who control our worship or censor our preachers! Church and State are constitutionally separated. Help keep them separate, so that no denomination ever assumes control of our political

---

From Walter A. Maier, *Victory Through Christ*, Concordia Publishing House, copyright 1943, pp. 192–205. Reprinted by permission.

affairs and no administration shows favoritism to one religious group or persecutes another!

The third liberty, however, the freedom from want, is new, as it seeks to give everyone in all the world "the right to adequate food, clothing, shelter, medical care; the right to security." No nation in history has ever been able to preserve people from poverty, unemployment, famine; and we doubt whether even a country with our resources can banish every want from the lives of its own citizens. It takes more than human ingenuity and machines to furnish food, clothing, shelter. We still need God to bless our seedtime and harvest, give increase to our flocks, and prosper our labor. If, with reliance on the Almighty, man's best thought is devoted to helping the poor, feeding the hungry, healing the sick, we should indeed invoke God's blessing on such efforts to relieve the undersupplied, the undernourished, the underprivileged.

It is the fourth liberty, however, the freedom from fear, which particularly concerns us today. The Government generously promises us security against the haunting terror that new wars will continually arise. "The use of force," we are told, "must be made less and less feasible on earth, until it finally becomes impossible," and a warless era dawns with a world-wide reduction of armaments. What a glorious picture of peace, blessed peace, always in all the earth! Yet that freedom from fear and bloodshed — often predicted in the past, but never more frequently than in these last decades of the most widespread, devastating wars — will never be fully realized. Our blessed Savior Himself, foreseeing the very days in which we live, has warned us that, as the world hastens to its end, there shall be "wars and rumors of wars, . . . for nation shall rise against nation, and kingdom against kingdom." Besides, some fears are even greater than war's terrors, and these cannot be removed even by a government as considerate as ours. To dispel the shadows which daily darken your soul, you must have heavenly strength. You need — and this is my message to you —

FULL FREEDOM FROM FEAR,

found only through faith in the Lord Jesus Christ and such promises of God's Word as that offered by these seven simple words of our text (Isaiah, chapter forty-three, verse one), "Fear not, for I have redeemed thee!"

I. WE NEED THIS FREEDOM FROM FEAR

This "Fear not!" of Isaiah is only one of more than a hundred Scripture passages which cry out in effect, "Be not afraid!" Bible critics have sought to remove some of these "Fear nots" as though they had crept in by mistake. But a hundred, or even a thousand, pledges of triumph over terror would not be too many in our fright-filled years.

Think of the legions of phobias which relentlessly make men and women cringe before the thought that they will lose their most precious possessions. People fear the loss of health; and not thousands, but millions, in the United States are gripped by actual pain or the torture of imaginary disease. Again, many fear that they will lose their money, their investments, their home, their food, their work. And while in overprosperous periods like these such forebodings recede into the background, they are never completely banished from the mind. Multitudes fear the loss of their mental powers and shrink from the specter of insanity. Still others fear the loss of their good name and reputation. They cower before the thought that some evil which they thought safely hidden in the buried past will be uncovered. Unnumbered men and women are tormented because they dread the loss of love, the breakup of the family, the banishment of home happiness. Far worse, however, is the insistent voice of a guilty conscience that emphasizes God's wrath, the fear of unforgiven sins, the torture of hell. And in the most crushing combination of fear men know they are affrighted by the prospect of their own death and of facing the just, holy God. If you have never seen an unbeliever die, you have been spared one of life's worst terrors.

Some of you, of course, are completely satisfied with yourselves. You smile confidently and say: "Fear? Why should I be afraid? I have everything I need. I am not afraid of God or man. If hardship comes, I can take it. And when it is time for me to die, I will not whine or whimper. I will go with a smile on my face." But will you? Many who similarly rejected the Almighty actually became cringing cowards in their last breath. David Hume, philosopher and infidel, ranted against the Cross, ridiculed Christ, and at the same time confidently claimed that when his time for leaving life came, he would face death cheerfully. His housekeeper, who was with him to the end, asserted that when his agnostic friends visited him, he put on a brave front; but she added: "When he was alone, the scene was different. His mental agitation was so great as often to alarm me greatly. He struggled to appear composed even before me; but to one who had attended his bedside for many days and nights, who witnessed his disturbed sleep and more disturbed wakings, who frequently heard his breathings of remorse and frightful startings, it was no difficult matter to determine that all was not right within. This continued and increased until he became insensible. I hope that I may never be called upon to witness a similar scene."

Convicted murderers have sneered that they would walk to the electric chair or up the gallows stairs without assistance, since death meant nothing to them. But read Warden Lawes's account of his years at Sing Sing, in which he tells how often hardened killers had to be dragged to their execution! If you shout back into your radio that the day before yesterday in South Carolina the first woman to be executed in that State walked to the electric chair calmly, declaring, "I am ready to die," then read the full newspaper account, which tells you that she carried a Bible with her! — despite your defiance of God and His goodness, there is a judgment which you cannot escape, a death you must die. The prouder, more over-confident, more contemptuous, your blasphemy now may be, the more appalling your despair when all the window dressing of your supposed courage disappears.

Picture to yourselves the crushing burden unrelieved fright imposes! Ask any physician to describe its consequences, and he will tell you plainly it weakens the energy of your body, lessens its resistance, interrupts its normal processes, and, if the fear habit becomes fixed, finally produces illness. Many of you have worried yourselves sick. Some of you will go to a premature grave unless you gain new confidence.

Again, worry affects the mind. It not only prevents its victims from thinking and doing their best but also banishes calm and quiet. It undermines courage, builds imaginary barriers, makes people suspicious of their neighbors, leads them to seek sinister motives behind innocent actions, to find only gloom and pessimism in life. One of the reasons for the startling number of nervous breakdowns and cases of mental disorder is this, that too many people, refusing to trust God fully, become the victims of continued, unmitigated worry. This is tragic enough, but the spiritual burdens fear imposes are even more serious. It makes people put a question mark behind God's promises, doubt their salvation in Christ, wonder whether they have committed the unpardonable sin, and feel themselves lost forever, when in truth no one can ever be lost who trusts this plain promise of Scripture, "Believe on the Lord Jesus Christ, and thou shalt be saved!"

What, then, do men need? What must you have to escape these destructive forces? Money? You cannot buy peace of mind and a calm heart, even with heaped millions. When one of the financial leaders of America fell fatally sick, a Christian friend comforted him at his bedside and started to sing, "Come, ye sinners, poor and needy!" That multimillionaire, whose whispers controlled stock-exchange movements in this country and abroad, the financial leader whose wish was law for a hundred boards of directors, responded brokenly: "Yes, sing that for me! I feel poor and needy."

Can position and power grant freedom from fear, a quiet, rested mind? Before President Andrew Jackson's second term expired, the man who had risen from a log-cabin poverty to the highest position in the United States stormed out to meet a delegation, which three times had asked to see him, and cried: "Gentlemen, people envy me in this White House, and they long to get here; but I tell you that at the end of the second term I am glad to get out of it, for it is a perfect hell." The last sultan of Turkey spent $900 each night to have his bedroom guarded. In Germany Adolf Hitler rules with a sweep that even dictators rarely wield. But few people are permitted to see him privately. When high officers come for an audience, they are first searched for concealed weapons. Dictators fear death.

Can success and achievement provide a serene confidence? William Makepeace Thackeray, genial British writer, found recognition throughout the civilized world. But one day, while he sat in a Paris restaurant, he glanced to the other end of the room and wondered who the miserable wretch was whom he beheld there. He arose to investigate and found that he was looking at himself in a mirror.

Can science, culture, education free men from their sins? If learning could liberate, why are there so many suicides among the intelligentsia, such crude superstition among cultured leaders? Why the large number of nervous breakdowns and mental disorders, despite all our schools and colleges?

Can you sidestep fear by having fortunetellers reveal the future? Not one of these servants of superstition—the astrologers, the numerologists, tea-leaf readers, crystal-ball gazers, dream interpreters, palmists, graphologists, their forecasts, the dream books, the fraudulent sixth and seventh books of Moses, the rabbit's feet, the good-luck rings—can ever relieve you of your solicitude for the future. African natives converted to Christ give up their amulets and charms. A missionary to that continent states that in front of a lay preacher's hut he found rows and rows of necklaces and charms and, upon inquiring, learned that these had been placed there by the natives who had turned to Jesus and put their trust in Him. But in our enlightened country people are paying an estimated $125,000,000 a year to fortunetellers of various kinds, who ought to be banned because of the evil and sorrow they provoke.

Can you free yourself from fears by following the new creeds and mail-order religions which promise to produce supermen? They are just as dishonest as the vicious deception recently revealed, when beautifully decorated packages for the soldiers, after the contents on the top had been removed, were found to contain nothing but paper and colored straw. It is bad enough if people are thus robbed of their money, but it is far worse if men and women are defrauded spiritually by cults which offer deliverance only to substitute delusion.

Can federal laws or social programs grant release from fear? Thank God, we have a Government that says: "Don't worry about your job; we will give you employment insurance! Don't be afraid of losing your bank deposit; we will give you savings insurance! Don't be afraid of drought or blight; we will give you crop insurance!"—there are limits, however, even for the wealthiest nation. When things go wrong in your family and you fear that your home will be broken, no Congressional action can help you. If you feel some terrible hidden disease gnawing at your vitals, not even a special Presidential act can remove this terror. If you are lashed by the relentless fury of your conscience, no program by men or angels can free you from such fear. When you come face to face with death and think of the eternity in which you must stand before your God to answer for your transgressions, you need divine forgiveness and assurance.

II. CHRIST CAN GIVE US THIS FREEDOM FROM FEAR

While all human hopes of freedom from the tyranny of our fears fail, we have God's radiant assurance in our text, "Fear not, for I have redeemed thee!" This is likewise but one of many Scriptural promises pledging our salvation. Now fewer than three dozen Old and New Testament passages proclaim in clear, clarion tones: God has redeemed us! Because this can become a glorious day of inner rebirth, if only you will stop resisting the Spirit and listen closely to God's pledge, "I have redeemed thee," I ask: Postpone your after-dinner nap for a few moments! Come out of the kitchen! Lay your magazine or newspaper aside! Give these next minutes to God! To *redeem* sinners means to secure their release from punishment, to pay the ransom required for their freedom; and that, nothing less, God did for you. You were hopelessly enslaved in sin, and He made you free by His grace. You were lost in your iniquities, but His love found you. You were sentenced to everlasting death, but He secured your acquittal for life. You were condemned to hell, but He pardoned you for heaven.

How marvelous the way in which God redeemed you! No ordinary ransom could secure your release. Hear this and humble yourselves before the Almighty: He sent His only Son to save you. You parents know how hard it is to give your sons even for the nation's defense. Will you not bow thankfully before the Father's surpassing love that sent His Son Jesus not for His friends but for His enemies? No payment in money could buy you back to God, for the errorless Word explains, "Ye were not redeemed with corruptible things, as silver and gold, . . . but with the precious blood of Christ." Your rescue was no exchange by which you gave something to the Lord in return for your deliverance, as when captives of war are mutually released by belligerent nations. God did everything from start to finish.

While the Holy Spirit pleads with you to accept Jesus, harden not your heart! "Behold, now is the accepted time; behold, now is the day of salvation!" Get right with God today! Do not wait for tomorrow's uncertainties! When you receive and trust this marvelous promise of redemption, fear is defeated, then you are Christ's, He will constantly guide, guard, and protect you as His own precious redeemed. If Jesus shed His blood on the cross, took your place in suffering the punishment of your sins; if He loved you so much that He bore the burden, the curse, the guilt, the punishment of all your transgressions, can you not see that He whose mercy never changes will be close to you on every pathway of duty? The moment you accept the Lord Jesus "even the very hairs of your head are all numbered." Your life is not ruled by blind, cruel "fate." You are not the victim of "bad luck." "The cards are not stacked against you." Rather does everything that comes to you day after day flow from the Savior's magnificent mercy to strengthen your faith, increase your courage, and help you overcome fear. I read recently of a four-year-old child, alone, happy and undisturbed in the coach of an express train roaring at high speed through storm and night. When a passenger asked him, "Well, little man, aren't you afraid here all alone at night on this noisy train?" the youngster smiled and said, "No, my daddy is the engineer up ahead." Once in childlike faith you have been reconciled with your heavenly Father through Christ, no matter how uncertain the road of life before you may be, how black the world about you may seem, your Father is always up ahead to guide your course and guarantee your soul's safety.

Believe that through Jesus you are God-controlled; that, if necessary, your heavenly Father will draft His miracles and might to bless you! A cottage near Warsaw, Poland, is marked with an iron tablet praising the Lord's power. The villagers, explaining why it was placed there, will tell you of a God-fearing peasant named Dobry. Things had not gone well with him. His rent was long in arrears, and finally the time came when the landlord would evict him. On the evening before, as church bells called to prayer, Dobry and his family knelt to sing Paul Gerhardt's "Commit Thou All Thy Griefs and Ways into His Hands!" In the midst of the song a queer noise was heard at the window. Dobry arose, raised the glass, and saw the raven which his grandfather had once tamed and then set free. Can you imagine his surprise to find that the bird had brought him a costly ring, studded with precious stones? It proved to be the king's ring; and when Dobry returned the costly jewel to the palace, he was rewarded so generously that he could build a house of his own. To commemorate his deliverance from the fear of midwinter homelessness, the grateful man placed on his door the iron tablet, featuring the ring, the raven, and the hymn. If every American Christian family which has experienced God's glorious intervention could similarly call attention to Heaven's help, millions of homes would be marked with a tablet commemorating His divine power.

How often and how miraculously in the present war has our gracious Father not given His children the courage to declare, "Though an host should encamp against me, my heart shall not fear: though war should rise against me, in this will I be confident"! How vital, too, that the men and women in our nation's armed forces know the Lord Jesus and the fear-destroying faith in His mercy! Give our fighting men the best equipment money can provide, but first supply them with spiritual weapons, Baptism and the power of faith! Some of the happiest letters we receive come from soldiers, sailors, marines, airmen, who find courage in Christ's Gospel. Up on the bleak Aleutians, after one of our broadcasts, the soldiers raised $125 in a free-will offering to help expand our work. An aviator, ferrying a bomber to Africa, heard our message 20,000 feet above South American jungles and was strengthened for his dangerous task. Men on the Pacific battle front have gratefully received these broadcasts. From ships in the Atlantic, from submarines, from scores of camps, from privates and high officers, come thanks for God's Word, and at the same time repeated pleas to maintain and enlarge this radio mission, particularly for the men and women in our fighting forces.

Even when Christians meet reverses, they still have David's confidence, "I will not be afraid of ten thousands of people that have set themselves against me." This is not exaggeration nor mere wishful thinking. How, do you suppose, can a God-fearing wife bear a godless husband's ridicule and refuse to take recourse to divorce? How can Christians meet sudden calamity, permanent injury to their body, loss of members or senses, and, instead of groveling in fear, courageously face the future? How can believers endure wasting, destructive diseases, excruciating pain, while unbelievers often take the coward's way out in suicide? God's children have faith, and defeating fear, they can exult with Saint Paul, "Whether we live ... or die, we are the Lord's."

Regrettably, many of you who know the Lord Jesus are still ruled by fear. Some of the Negroes in the Civil War days were brought north by the underground railroad, the secret journeys by which they hid in friendly homes during the daytime and under the cover of night traveled from one hospitable town to another. As soon as they reached Canada, of course, they were free. On one of the trains which drew into the Toronto station, a woman who had helped hundreds of slaves cross the border, saw a colored man still hiding in the corner, afraid that he was being pursued. She cried out in reassurance: "Joe, why are you crouching there? You are a free man on free soil! Praise the Lord, Joe!" Similarly, with Christ you have crossed the boundary from sin to grace. You are free! Praise the Lord by refusing to cringe in fear! "Stand fast ... in the liberty wherewith Christ hath made us free!"

What can still put fright into your heart? The memory of your past sins? Jesus took them all away. They exist no longer. They have been forgiven and forgotten. Are you afraid because you do not feel that you have been redeemed? Martin Luther was once asked whether he felt that his sins were forgiven, and the great man of God replied, "No, I don't *feel* that they are forgiven; I *know* they are, because God says so in His Word." Your heavenly Redeemer does not say, " 'God so loved the world, that He gave His only begotten Son, that whosoever' feeleth that he is saved 'should not perish, but have everlasting life.' " But He does declare, "By grace are ye saved." That must be true!

Are you worried because the consequences of your sins may be revealed and bring you disgrace? Take it all to Christ! He will not only forgive you. He will also grant you strength to bear the results of your own folly!

Does your conscience assail you on the charge that your sins are too ruinous and repeated to be forgiven? Does the devil whisper into your heart: "There is no hope for you. You have committed the unforgivable sin"? Find courage in this sure pledge of Scripture, "The blood of Jesus Christ, His Son, cleanseth us from all sin"!

Do you fear that you may not be included in the Savior's grace, that the artificial restrictions men have set up may bar you? Build immovable hope in this all-embracing promise, "Fear not, for I have redeemed *thee*!" — That includes everyone. No racial or social bar can keep you away from the Lord Jesus.

How sorely millions in our country need this courageous victory over fear! We are in the midst of trying times. Who can assuredly see the end of our difficulties? One of the cruelest of all delusions is the too frequent promise that after the war a golden age will come, the most splendid period in history, when right and truth, democracy and prosperity, will reign as never before. But the Bible warns us that in the latter times and before Christ comes to judge the quick and the dead, "men's hearts" shall fail "them for fear." Unless God is over-merciful, we must look for international upheaval and the wide spread of atheism. You cannot kill myriads of human beings, destroy hundreds of millions of dollars' worth of property, spend hundreds of billions for purposes of war, and then expect that somehow human ingenuity, statecraft and diplomacy will find a way for national and individual affairs to roll on more smoothly than ever before. Only God can avert greater suffering than this generation has already endured; yet in this world of sin and sorrow His Son, our Redeemer, looks down upon those who come to Him in humble, contrite, self-denying faith; and the heavier their burden, the louder the roar of powerful enemies, the more bitter the battle — the surer will be His comfort, the nearer His presence, the clearer His sustaining assurance. Come peace or war, health or sickness, gain or loss, prosperity or adversity, life or death itself — may the Savior's triumph over all terror constantly re-echo this victory promise in your heart, "Fear not, for I have redeemed thee!" Amen!

FOR ADDITIONAL INFORMATION ABOUT WALTER MAIER:

Arndt, William. "Walter Arthur Maier." *Concordia Theological Monthly* 21 (March 1950), 163 ff.

Clinard, H. Gordon. "Walter Arthur Maier—Suffering Is Judgment and Mercy" in "An Evangelical Critique of the Use of the Classic Biblical Solutions to the Problem of Suffering by Representative Contemporary Preachers." Th.D. dissertation, Southwestern Baptist Theological Seminary, 1958.

Glass, Grayson. "The Ethical Content in the Preaching of Walter A. Maier." Th.M. thesis, Southwestern Baptist Theological Seminary, 1959.

Maier, Paul L. *A Man Spoke, A World Listened.* New York: McGraw-Hill Book Co., 1963.

Sulston, Kenneth Hartley. "A Rhetorical Criticism of the Radio Preaching of Walter A. Maier." Ph.D. dissertation, Northwestern University, 1958.

For other sermons by Walter Maier:

The Airwaves Proclaim Christ. St. Louis: Concordia Publishing House, 1948.

Peace Through Christ. St. Louis: Concordia Publishing House, 1940.

Also: *The Cross from Coast to Coast* (1938), *America, Turn to Christ* (1944), *Courage in Christ* (1941), *Let Us Return unto the Lord* (1947).

SAMUEL SHOEMAKER

1893–1963

SAMUEL SHOEMAKER, photograph, courtesy of Word Inc.

SAMUEL MOOR SHOEMAKER

1893	Born in Baltimore, Maryland, on December 27
1908	Enrolled in St. George's, an Episcopal school for boys, Newport, Rhode Island
1912	Entered Princeton University
1917	Arrived in Peking, China, on October 29 to teach
1919	Became executive secretary of the Philadelphian Society at Princeton
1920	Enrolled in General Theological Seminary, New York
1921	Joined the staff of Grace Episcopal Church, New York
1922	Returned to Princeton as executive secretary of the Philadelphian Society
1924	Received call to become rector of Calvary Episcopal Church, New York
1925	Began work at Calvary Episcopal Church
1928	Led in construction of Calvary House
1930	Married Helen Smith
1948	Received D.D. degree from Virginia Theological Seminary and S.T.D. from Berkeley Divinity School
1952	Accepted rectorship of Calvary Episcopal Church, Pittsburgh
1955	Helped found the Pittsburgh Experiment
1961	Announced his retirement
1963	Died October 31

IN A LETTER to his wife to be opened after his death, Samuel Shoemaker wrote the following credo:

> As I sit in the study on a beautiful, cool August afternoon, I look back with many thanks. It has been a great run. I wouldn't have missed it for anything. Much could

and should have been better, and I have, by no means, done what I should have done with all that I have been given. But the over-all experience of being alive has been a thrilling experience. I believe that death is a doorway to more of it: clearer, cleaner, better, with more of the secret opened than locked. I do not feel much confidence in myself as regards all this, for very few have ever "deserved" eternal life. But with Christ's atonement and Him gone on before, I have neither doubt nor fear whether I am left here a brief time or a long one. I believe that I shall see Him and know Him, and that eternity will be an endless opportunity to consort with the great souls and the lesser ones who have entered into the freedom of the heavenly city. It is His forgiveness and grace that give confidence and not merits of our own. But again I say, it's been a great run. I'm thankful for it and for all the people who have helped to make it so, and especially those closest and dearest to me.[1]

Two months after writing this letter, Shoemaker died. His description of life as "a great run" was appropriate. He dashed through life at breakneck speed involving himself in a bewildering number of ministries. Thousands of persons whom he had helped were thankful for his "great run."

Life and Times

Samuel Moor Shoemaker was born into a wealthy Maryland family in Baltimore on December 27, 1893. His first years were spent largely in the family's summer home known as Burnside. When Shoemaker was fourteen, his family enrolled him in St. George's, an Episcopal school for boys in Newport, Rhode Island. He excelled in student activities, but he was not especially outstanding in his studies. During his senior year he served as one of the six prefects, business manager of the school's monthly magazine, secretary of the drama club, president of the musical club, vice-president of the St. George's Society, president of the Missionary Society, and editor-in-chief of the school yearbook.

In 1912 he entered Princeton University. During his four

---

1. Samuel M. Shoemaker, "Credo," *Faith at Work*, January–February 1964, p. 14.

years there he maintained the same rapid pace he had set at St. George's. Although active in many organizations, he did not neglect the academic demands of college, as evidenced by his winning an award for excellence in English. He also displayed a sensitive social conscience. In an editorial in the *Daily Princetonian*, March 1, 1916, Shoemaker and four others openly protested military drill and war propaganda at the university. The editorial stated that "colleges are not the place for drilling or for instruction in military matters; patriotism which shoulders a rifle is not the only kind of patriotism."[2]

After receiving his degree from Princeton, Shoemaker went to China to work for the Princeton-in-Peking project. His responsibility was to teach insurance and to instruct two groups of adults who were interested in the Christian faith. To his dismay his groups dwindled rapidly, and he struggled to find the reason for the diminishing attendance. Shoemaker felt that this struggle was the turning point of his life and ministry. He concluded that his ineffectiveness was due to his lack of commitment to God's will. He thereupon committed himself without reservation to God's direction. Concerning this experience he said, "I felt no emotion about this and saw no stars nor bright lights; but afterwards I felt light and at ease, as if life had slipped into its right groove at last."[3] He began to share his experience with others and found that they were receptive.

Shoemaker returned to the United States in the summer of 1919 to attend General Theological Seminary in New York, but he was persuaded to become executive secretary of the Philadelphian Society at Princeton for one academic year. He delayed enrolling in the seminary until 1920. After a year of seminary study, he joined the staff of Grace Episcopal Church in New York and gained valuable experience in pastoral duties. He also engaged in additional study in psychiatry, psychology, and preaching. In 1922, with the approval of his bishop, he returned to Princeton to serve another term as executive secretary of the Philadelphian Society. His interest in students remained strong throughout his life. Many of his speaking engagements were on college and university campuses. He spent long hours counseling students.

---

2. Helen Smith Shoemaker, *I Stand by the Door* (New York: Harper & Row, 1967), p. 19. Reprinted by permission of Harper & Row, Publishers.
3. Samuel M. Shoemaker, "The Turning Point," *Faith at Work,* March 1963, p. 41.

In 1924, while traveling in the Near East, Shoemaker received a call to become rector of Calvary Episcopal Church, situated in a downtown transition neighborhood of New York City. Shoemaker accepted this challenging opportunity and arrived in New York on May 15, 1925. During his first year at Calvary, Shoemaker began to assemble an effective staff of workers. He also developed a creative plan to involve the church in ministry to the entire community. Shoemaker wrote in his diary, "It has always seemed to me that a vital church should be reaching, not only the settled working people with homes and families, but also those without any place in society, the homeless, friendless, faithless derelicts who have lost everything. While we work with people of sufficient privilege to find their way into the rectory and church, what is happening to men in the Gas House district to the east of us?"[4] The Calvary Mission, an operation geared to the needs of alcoholics, resulted from Shoemaker's concern. The birth of Alcoholics Anonymous was directly related to this ministry.

The number of persons involved in the activities of Calvary Church increased rapidly. Two years after Shoemaker had arrived, the attendance in the morning worship had increased by more than two hundred. Shoemaker began reaching beyond the walls of the church by holding outdoor services. In addition, he revitalized the church school. One of the most significant achievements was the building of Calvary House in 1928. Calvary House had three main functions: it was the center for meetings of the parish, it was a home for most of the members of the church staff and their families, and it was a training center for ecumenical leadership in the church at large.

In 1930 Shoemaker married Helen Dominick Smith, daughter of Alexander Smith, U.S. senator from New Jersey. She was a member of the Calvary staff when he proposed to her—on a frozen golf course in Briarcliff, New York. After their wedding in the Princeton chapel she continued to be deeply involved in the life of the church and in her husband's ecumenical ministry. She ministered through her hospitality. A staff member of Calvary recalls:

> Sam's sense of humor now seemed to be matched by that of his wife as his hospitality was heightened by her graciousness.... Guests always found delicious

---

4. Helen Shoemaker, p. 188.

fruit juice and well-chosen, well-prepared dishes awaiting them.[5]

Her Christian ministry extended beyond the local parish. She has served as executive director of the Anglican Fellowship of Prayer, written numerous books and articles, and addressed the Congressional Wives' Breakfast. She has also served as a member of the board of directors of Faith at Work and has been active in other denominational, ecumenical, and charitable organizations. In addition she ministered as a homemaker and a mother to two daughters, Sally and Helen.

In 1952, after a long and successful ministry in New York, Shoemaker accepted the rectorship of Calvary Episcopal Church in Pittsburgh, Pennsylvania. There he applied the principles learned in his New York experiences. He was particularly eager to relate the Christian faith in a personal and dynamic way to the lives of laymen. He wanted to see laymen develop the ability to express their faith in a positive and forthright way. At first his efforts were viewed with some skepticism. Most of the parishioners preferred to express their faith by contributions or weekly attendance at the church, and some by participation in church and city organizations already established. An article in *Fortune* magazine stressed the change which began to come upon the church under Shoemaker's leadership: "If these inclinations gradually changed it was because of what the conservative parishioners saw happening to their sons and daughters. For the fact was among the younger people Dr. Shoemaker scored his biggest success."[6] In 1955 Shoemaker was instrumental in founding the Pittsburgh Experiment, an effort to involve laymen in small groups to help them apply Christianity to their daily lives in vocation and business. He formed a series of couples' groups in which young couples carried on dialogue and explored what is involved in "becoming a Christian." He and his wife established some twenty prayer-study groups which met weekly. All of these activities were designed to train laymen in prayer, witness, and action.

After ten years of distinguished service at the Calvary Epis-

---

5. Irving Harris, "S. M. S. – Man of God for Our Time," *Faith at Work*, January–February 1964, pp. 20–21.
6. Duncan Norton-Taylor, "Businessmen on Their Knees," *Fortune*, October 1953, p. 248.

copal Church in Pittsburgh, Shoemaker retired January 1, 1962, having announced his retirement the previous March. Plagued with ill health, he died on October 31, 1963. Thousands sensed the loss of a helpful friend who had touched their lives through his ministry of writing, counseling, guiding small groups, radio preaching, and pastoring.

Shoemaker's many and varied interests consumed his vast energy and led to great accomplishments. He produced a book almost every year, preached in several radio series, and spoke on scores of college and university campuses. He concentrated, however, on the work of his own parish. He sensed the desperate need for a revolution in the life of local congregations. He was unwilling to admit that the church had no future and that the Christian movement would have to sidestep the institutional church in order to make progress. In an article in *Christianity Today* he wrote, "I have wanted the Church, the old, organized Church, to be part of any awakening in which I was involved."[7] He was by no means blind to the faults of the institutional church. In fact much of his energy was spent in exposing the failures of institutional Christianity and proposing cures for these failures.

As a means of church renewal, he emphasized the role of the laity, especially in small groups. Norman Vincent Peale declared, "Without question, the rise of the small group movement . . . came about largely through Sam Shoemaker's leadership."[8] The new magazine of the small group movement, *Faith at Work* was established partly to give expression to this interest. Shoemaker believed that every church needed small groups of Christians meeting for spiritual refreshment. The small group movement emphasized personal piety but did not neglect the larger dimensions of the Christian faith. Shoemaker's own interest in social concern indicated his desire that these groups share more than personal pietism. Bardwell Smith in the foreword to Shoemaker's biography writes, "He has sometimes been criticized for not having a social ethic at all, for being concerned for individuals alone. This is not accurate, however much one might challenge his conviction that creative social change occurs primarily through the changing of individuals."[9]

---

7. Samuel M. Shoemaker, "The Church and Awakening Groups," *Christianity Today*, 10 October 1960, p. 6.
8. Norman Vincent Peale, "The Unforgettable Sam Shoemaker," *Faith at Work*, January-February 1964, p. 16.
9. Helen Shoemaker, p. xvi.

It is true that Shoemaker's basic emphasis was upon the individual. His deep commitment to evangelism is one indication of his individualistic approach. In her biography of her husband, Helen Shoemaker wrote, "Sam's great interest was in enlisting people for Christ—and he never saw fewer than three people a day from the time he began his personal counseling when he was a very young man until the time he retired from Calvary Church, Pittsburgh, in 1961."[10] Many came to a new life in Christ as a result of their encounters with Shoemaker. He felt that a person who had experienced Christ would not be able to keep silent about that experience. He wrote, "The real truth is that the depth of an experience of Christ may be measured by our inability to keep still about it. The real thing overflows."[11] Shoemaker believed in a conversion experience. He wrote, "What I should like to see, for people in my own church, is as definite spiritual conversion as the Methodists and Baptists talk about, and then these people helped and trained and brought into the Church by the ancient apostolic rite of Confirmation."[12]

In his last major message to his church, "Can Our Kind of Church Change Our Kind of World?" Sam Shoemaker set forth his basic convictions. The following excerpts are, in a sense, a summary of the beliefs he championed:

> The church exists to convey to all men the message of Christ and to build the Kingdom of God in the earth. It has no life, no reason for being, apart from the fulfilment of this supreme and destined task.
> The church is therefore not an end but a means. It was not the church which "God so loved that he gave his only begotten Son," but the world which he so loved. The church is the company of those who, having heard the message of Christ, have responded, and discovered the meaning of life in him; and henceforth can have but one aim, to reach all men for him, in obedience to his last command....
> The church's success or failure, therefore, is not to be determined by the fine state of its buildings, or the length of its rolls of members, but solely by what it is doing to reach the untouched, at home and abroad.

---

10. Ibid., p. 84.
11. Samuel M. Shoemaker, *Conversion of the Church* (New York: Fleming H. Revell Co., 1932), p. 85.
12. Samuel M. Shoemaker, *How to Become a Christian* (New York: Harper & Bros., 1953), p. 75.

To read many of the church's pronouncements, to listen to many clergy "talk a good fight," you would think the church's task were clear to all members of it, and they were all hot after it. But when you take an honest look at the church, you know perfectly well that, in most places, it is so bogged down in its means that it has forgotten its ends. . . .

Christianity has truly been called a religion of ecstasy. You cannot live in the presence of a Risen Lord, and of his fiery Holy Spirit, without a continuous, grateful excitement burning in your soul. . . .

It must be perfectly obvious to anyone that what the whole church needs, from top to bottom, is a deeper conversion, a profounder experience of the power of the Holy Spirit. We have often recognized this, then gone about expecting it to happen through sterile and ineffectual means. Awakening has never in history come from regular ecclesiastics getting together to "do something." It has come from inspired nobodies, whom first the church ignored, then condemned, then (if they got powerful) took over, and finally domesticated. It is of no use to look for hope in time-consuming, money-spending commissions that wind up in a long report nobody reads. Let us look to see where the Holy Spirit is at work now. Maybe we can learn something.

Whatever the old-new phenomenon of "tongues" means, it is amazing that it should break out, not only in Pentecostal groups, but among Episcopalians, and moreover in places among Anglo-Catholic Episcopalians. I have not had this experience myself. I have seen people who have, and it has blessed them and given them power they did not have before. I do not profess to understand this phenomenon. But I am fairly sure it indicates the Holy Spirit's presence in life, as smoke from a chimney indicates a fire below. . . .

What I am saying is, instances of just what the church needs are already at hand. . . .

For a moment take a look at our world. It is living fast. Everywhere is the great scientific dynamic and achievement. There is fear in every sensitive heart. There is drivenness, want of satisfying emotion, increase of unreason, rebellion, loss of regard for personality, easy dismissal of the spiritual as irrelevant or even nonexistent. There is gnawing loneliness, and vague, intense bitterness. Besides the eternal fact that "most men live lives of quiet desperation." . . .

What, then, shall we do?

First, let us admit our almost wholesale failure, while giving thanks for what God has been able to do in spite of us. If we remain convinced that we are basically "all right," and just need a little polishing up, we shall not seek a remedy that goes deep enough to heal, nor find an answer sufficient to empower. . . .

Second, let us go on our knees in a deep and penitent surrender to God for our sins—yours and mine, not just other people's. . . .

Third, let us pray. We all know something of private prayer, and prayer in church. We must learn another kind: prayer with others, "where two or three are gathered together," as he said. . . .

Fourth, we need the strengthening fellowship of such groups. We shall come to know and love these people, so that we can share together in honesty our victories and our defeats. . . .

Fifth, we shall then be able to witness to others, by life and by word. When the "shine" and "sparkle" are there, it will not be hard to open the conversation. It is not a matter of personality, it is a matter of Grace. . . .

Am I asking the church to change completely its philosophy of its work? Yes, I am. I have no doubt about the faith. I have the gravest doubt about what the church is doing to make the faith live in and for the world. I believe the church must push aside the lumbering mass of organizations with which it is now encumbered, and take a fresh look at its work in the world.[13]

The best explanation of Shoemaker's approach to life and ministry is found in the poem "I Stand by the Door: An Apologia for My Life." Although it sounds paradoxical, Shoemaker felt that to run "the great race" one must "stand by the door."

I stand by the door,
I neither go too far in, nor stay too far out,
The door is the most important door in the world—
It is the door through which men walk when they find God.
There's no use my going way inside, and staying there,
When so many are still outside and they, as much as I,
Crave to know where the door is.

---

13. Samuel M. Shoemaker, "Can Our Kind of Church Change Our Kind of World?" mimeographed address supplied by Helen Smith Shoemaker.

And all that so many ever find
Is only the wall where a door ought to be.
They creep along the wall like blind men,
With outstretched, groping hands.
Feeling for a door, knowing there must be a door,
Yet they never find it . . .
So I stand by the door.

The most tremendous thing in the world
Is for men to find that door — the door to God.
The most important thing any man can do
Is to take hold of one of those blind, groping hands,
And put it on the latch — the latch that only clicks
And opens to the man's own touch.
Men die outside that door, as starving beggars die
On cold nights in cruel cities in the dead of winter —
Die for want of what is within their grasp.
They live, on the other side of it — live because they have not
    found it.
Nothing else matters compared to helping them find it,
And open it, and walk in, and find Him . . .
So I stand by the door.
Go in, great saints, go all the way in —
Go way down into the cavernous cellars,
And way up into the spacious attics —
It is a vast, roomy house, this house where God is.
Go into the deepest of hidden casements,
Of withdrawal, of silence, of sainthood.
Some must inhabit those inner rooms,
And know the depths and heights of God,
And call outside to the rest of us how wonderful it is.
Sometimes I take a deeper look in,
Sometimes venture in a little farther;
But my place seems closer to the opening . . .
So I stand by the door.

There is another reason why I stand there.
Some people get part way in and become afraid
Lest God and the zeal of His house devour them;
For God is so very great, and asks all of us.
And these people feel a cosmic claustrophobia,
And want to get out. "Let me out!" they cry.
And the people way inside only terrify them more.
Somebody must be by the door to tell them that they are spoiled
For the old life, they have seen too much:
Once taste God, and nothing but God will do any more.

Somebody must be watching for the frightened
Who seek to sneak out just where they came in,
To tell them how much better it is inside.

The people too far in do not see how near these are
To leaving — preoccupied with the wonder of it all.
Somebody must watch for those who have entered the door,
But would like to run away. So for them, too,
I stand by the door.
I admire the people who go way in.
But I wish they would not forget how it was
Before they got in. Then they would be able to help
The people who have not yet even found the door,
Or the people who want to run away again from God.
You can go in too deeply, and stay in too long,
And forget the people outside the door.
As for me, I shall take my old accustomed place,
Near enough to God to hear Him, and know He is there,
But not so far from men as not to hear them,
And remember they are there, too.
Where? Outside the door —
Thousands of them, millions of them.
But — more important for me —
One of them, two of them, ten of them,
Whose hands I am intended to put on the latch.
So I shall stand by the door and wait
For those who seek it.
"I had rather be a door-keeper . . ."
So I stand by the door.[14]

Preaching and Sermons

During his year of service at Grace Episcopal Church in New York, Shoemaker studied homiletics at Union Theological Seminary. There he took courses two days a week from Harry Emerson Fosdick and G. S. Johnston Ross, "the delightful and witty Scotsman, brilliant as only Scotch Presbyterian preachers can be."[15] This study proved to be rich experience for Shoemaker. He said:

> I do not pretend to be in the class of those men as a preacher, of course, but I do know that I owe much of

---
14. Helen Shoemaker, pp. ix–x.
15. Ibid., p. 38.

what little homiletical gift I have to their inspiration. No man can preach who is not excited about preaching, and these men made it exciting.[16]

Those who later heard Sam Shoemaker preach agreed that he also made preaching an exciting experience for others. Cuthbert Bardsley, bishop of Coventry Cathedral in England, recorded his impression of Shoemaker's preaching in 1929, the first time Bardsley heard him preach:

> Doctor Shoemaker spoke like a machine gun! The words poured forth in a torrent. He gave one the feeling that he had much to say and very little time in which to say it. He was ablaze with a passionate conviction, filled with a deep concern—unlike some preachers he was convinced about the reality and the love of God and overflowing with a deep concern. . . . Since that moment, over 30 years ago, I have heard him preach on many occasions. Always, and increasingly, I have realized that I was in the presence of one of the great prophetic voices of the world.[17]

Bardsley later called the experience "inspiring but terrifying," one that made upon him "the impact which all true prophecy should have." Bardsley recalled, "It made me glad and sad. It made me cry out 'Thanks be to God,' and it made me exclaim 'Woe is me.' "[18]

It was no accident that Shoemaker was enthusiastic on that occasion. He held a deep conviction that preaching must be practiced with enthusiasm. He regarded it as a matter of life and death, and he was scornful of those preachers who preached dull, lifeless sermons:

> Some men preach with about as much enthusiasm as a railway official walking through the train and calling, "Tickets please": he will help you if you ask him, but it is not a matter of life and death to him. Well, preaching *is* a matter of life and death. You ought to be prepared and

---
16. Ibid.
17. Cuthbert Bardsley, "Foreword," . . . *And Thy Neighbor: Sam Shoemaker Talks about Creative Living* (Waco, Tex.: Word Books, 1967), p. vii.
18. Ibid.

know just what you want to say, aim at it, hit it hard, and then stop.[19]

Shoemaker's conviction was not a matter of mere emotion. The sermon held a high place in his philosophy of ministry, and although he was deeply impressed with the significance of the liturgical service, he believed that the sermon was superior in reaching "untouched people" for the church:

> Like it or not, more new people, more untouched people, are reached through the preached word than through any liturgical service however beautiful; and the spoken word has always been one of God's means of grace to the souls of men. Do it the very best you can. Put into it every power you have. God will honour and use it, if you offer it to Him from the time the sermon is conceived till you walk down from the pulpit.[20]

Shoemaker also believed that too much can be made of preaching, especially when the personality of the preacher is emphasized more than the truth of the gospel. But he was impressed that the sermon had more effect upon people than is generally realized.[21] He was not unaware, however, of the skepticism of many people who doubted the value of preaching, particularly in the light of the small degree of change evidenced by many people who are regular sermon-listeners:

> It is easy to grow skeptical about sermons when you realize how many people there are who have been listening to them for ten, twenty, forty years yet seem little changed by what they have heard. But do not belittle the indirect and unconscious influence of preaching, nor the possible effect upon someone seeking or in need who happened to come to church that day.[22]

For Shoemaker, preaching was primarily *witnessing*, not arguing. He said, "This is not all there is to preaching, but it is a

---
19. Samuel M. Shoemaker, *The Church Alive* (London: Arthur James, 1952), p. 21.
20. Ibid.
21. Helen Shoemaker, p. 117.
22. Samuel M. Shoemaker, *Beginning Your Ministry* (New York: Harper & Row, 1963), p. 105. Reprinted by permission of Harper & Row, Publishers.

very essential ingredient, and people almost never hear it."[23] If people heard about the recent spiritual experiences in the lives of other Christians and in the life of their minister, then Shoemaker believed that the truths of the gospel would come alive in the congregation, "eventuating in experience with its own uniquely convincing confirmation of 'the Word.' "[24] This philosophy of preaching was a necessary corollary to Shoemaker's intense belief in the worth of small groups of believers, sharing together their contemporary experiences in the faith.

Furthermore, this concept of preaching as witnessing suited his involvement with Christian evangelism. But Shoemaker was careful to point out that his concept of evangelism could not be equated with some forms of "the old Evangelism":

> Does some of this sound too much to you like some forms of the old Evangelism? I hope not, because I think that awakening in our time must supersede old-fashioned Evangelism, with its probable emotionalism, intellectual obscurantism, Puritanical rules, and frequent self-righteousness. I think also it must go much deeper than the merely sacerdotal kind of Catholicism, with so much stress on outward forms and often so little on a changed heart. I think it must understand, but not be too much bowled over by, the insights of the intellectuals and the academics who talk mostly to the few of their own kind. One has the feeling that God must have for us an awakening which includes the warm enthusiasm of the Evangelicals, the genuine Sacramentalism of a true Catholicism with its steady emphasis on forgiveness and grace, and the intellectual honesty and social passion without which many moderns (rightly, I think) will not listen to us, and which would give to the Holy Spirit a wider as well as a deeper channel through which to work via the Church of this time.[25]

If evangelism was a preeminent emphasis in his preaching, then it was a very broad and balanced evangelism, one with both "intellectual honesty" and "social passion." Nevertheless, in common with the "older evangelism," Shoemaker emphasized the importance of the minister's own devotional life:

---

23. Ibid., p. 116.
24. Ibid.
25. Ibid., p. 124.

> Possibly one can do no better than share the ways that he has found helpful himself. I begin with a chapter from the Old Testament, and one from the New—just read right through. Others find an arranged lectionary, or the Bible Reading Fellowship, more helpful. It is impossible to strike gold every time, but at times you will. You will mix scholarship, devotion, homiletical search: I defy you to keep them separate as you read.[26]

Other parts of his devotional experience which were significant for both his own personal life and his homiletical preparation included the practice of intercessory prayer, the use of the Book of Common Prayer, and the use of a "quiet time," described as a time "when we shall be still before God, with a pad and pencil to note down anything that seems specially worthy of remembering.... Ask God in."[27] All of these daily experiences with God, however, must be based upon a larger, more inclusive experience, one more determinative of the direction of ministry. Shoemaker was convinced that no minister could lead others into the new life in Christ who himself had not experienced "at least some change of heart, some awareness of the Hand of God at work in one's life, something—mystical or practical—like a feeling of 'call' to the ministry...."[28] He was fond of quoting Dr. G. S. Johnston Ross, his professor of homiletics at Union Theological Seminary, who said, "A preacher must have an arresting personal religious experience."[29] For Shoemaker, this arresting personal experience must also be a continuing experience, an intimate knowledge of the workings of God in one's own life. He asked, "How can you speak out of experience when you have not had, and are not now having, the experience itself?"[30]

Yet this experience was not to be a dead end within the preacher himself, a self-serving satisfaction of spiritual success. It must be communicated to others. In fact, Shoemaker felt that a Christian could test the validity of his faith by his ability to communicate that faith to others:

> Test yourself by this: Can I get across to other people

---

26. Samuel M. Shoemaker, "Christ, the Parson, and Prayer," *Pastoral Psychology* 8 (October 1957): 27.
27. Ibid., p. 32.
28. Samuel Shoemaker, *Beginning Your Ministry*, p. 114.
29. Ibid.
30. Ibid., p. 115.

what I believe about Jesus Christ? If not, what real good am I to them, and what real good am I to Him?[31]

People, not theories or ecclesiastical structures, were central in the preaching of Sam Shoemaker. He stressed the priority of human needs and the necessity of the preacher's sensitivity to such needs. He maintained that the church was occupied with the wrong things, that she was concerned with maintaining the institution rather than with ministering to people. He charged that the church had become a system of "committee-ized Christianity," desperately in need of "the human touch."[32] He felt that some ministers were afraid of people, afraid to have real contacts with them in a personal way. He noted that "most ministers lend books because they will not share themselves,"[33] and that the average clergyman's best intention was "to get a job thoroughly done, not to get a person thoroughly changed."[34] Likewise he deplored the tendency of educated people to become frightened of emotion, therefore failing to come to grips with their deepest needs.[35]

To meet these needs, Shoemaker recommended preaching to the individual: "Most sermons will be sermons to individuals—not public hammerings, but talking aloud with a congregation about something that is on the mind of one we know, and therefore probably on the minds of many."[36] In order to promote this kind of preaching, he recommended that the minister engage in frequent conversations with individuals regarding their needs. Shoemaker regarded the words which the preacher heard day by day from the people in his parish as the best source of material for the sermon, because these conversations do not present abstract ideas, but concrete, living problems. He quoted with approval the words of F. B. Meyer: "Tell people on Sunday what they have been telling you through the week, and they will listen to you."[37]

According to Shoemaker, too many sermons were merely

---

31. Samuel Shoemaker, *How to Become a Christian*, p. 74.
32. Samuel M. Shoemaker, *With the Holy Spirit and with Fire* (New York: Harper & Bros., 1960), p. 89.
33. Samuel Shoemaker, *The Conversion of the Church*, p. 99.
34. Samuel M. Shoemaker, "Where Goes the Glow," *Christian Century*, 29 April 1953, p. 517.
35. Helen Shoemaker, p. 117.
36. Samuel Shoemaker, *The Conversion of the Church*, p. 114.
37. Samuel Shoemaker, *Beginning Your Ministry*, p. 107.

academically conceived or sociologically oriented, rather than being directed toward the ordinary man who needed conviction and conversion.[38] In *A Young Man's View of the Ministry*, he spoke of some preaching that was misdirected:

> When a minister of the church begins to put off the Lord Jesus Christ for a lot of thin, man-made philosophies, when he begins to base his message on poet and sage and sociologist, rather than on the word of God, and when he preaches ethical programs from his pulpit as the whole solution of the world's need, it is simply time he went on the lecture platform instead.[39]

In keeping with this emphasis on the practical, personal nature of religious experience, Shoemaker emphasized the need for understandable language in the pulpit. In *The Conversion of the Church* he wrote:

> Terminology kills a great deal of religious work: the terms are stilted, technical, pious, and drive off the people who most need touching. Let us develop a natural vocabulary that puts religious ideas into ordinary language.[40]

In *Beginning Your Ministry* he listed "Three Good Rules" for preaching, one of which was, "Say it simply." He urged preachers to "speak conversationally in simple, homely, pictorial, vernacular language," and warned that "we shall reach few with big words and polished sentences."[41] He was also fond of quoting Sam Jones's statement on practical preaching: "Don't put the hay so high that the mules can't get at it! Spread it on the ground, then the jackasses and the giraffes can both get it!"[42]

But with all of his insistence upon simplicity, Shoemaker did not discount the need for imagination in preaching. He regarded pictorial preaching as strong preaching, and said that "if you see it clearly, you can say it effectively."[43] He urged beginning

---

38. Helen Shoemaker, p. 118.
39. Samuel M. Shoemaker, *A Young Man's View of the Ministry* (New York: Association Press, 1923), p. 22.
40. Samuel Shoemaker, *The Conversion of the Church*, p. 84.
41. Samuel Shoemaker, *Beginning Your Ministry*, p. 109.
42. Ibid.
43. Ibid.

preachers to allow their imaginations to play upon a subject until they could see it vividly with the inner eye, and then they would be able to picture it adequately for other people.

He also urged them to develop true originality in proclamation:

> And, as one must not fear to make his "own" emphases so long as he does not neglect other great truths, so he must seek to develop his own style and way of preaching. We can learn much from others, but we shall do well not to imitate them, either in style of composition or in delivery. Write as much as you can, so as to learn how to write. Say it simply and as colorfully as you can. Let it be your own, both in conviction and expression.[44]

Nevertheless, the pulpit should not be used as a personal platform for the preacher, but rather as a point of involvement with his people: "There is a use of 'I' which is egotistical and out of place, but there is a use of 'I' which includes the preacher with the people. A lot depends on your tone and inflection."[45]

Originality, in turn, will lead to variety; and variety, according to Shoemaker, is not only the spice of life, but also of the sermon. He believed that the sermon should include different moods, emphases, levels, and hues. He recognized that in every congregation there was the usual mixture of saints and worldlings, the simple and the mature, and "the sinners open or hidden." Therefore, the preacher should use "imagination, pathos, humor, bromidic simplicity, a little advanced theology (not too much), earthiness, comfort, challenge, raising your voice sometimes in anger, softening it in sympathy, not fearing true sentiment but avoiding sentimentality like the plague."[46] In short, Shoemaker believed that the pulpit should be a place of genuine conversation with the community of faith.

Nor did Shoemaker feel that humor was out of place in the sermon. He himself had an excellent sense of humor, and others delighted in his fellowship. He was particularly gifted at telling stories. While he warned against "professional pulpit jokers," he also said that "a Christian without humor is a blight."[47] Indeed, it is almost impossible to keep humor out of

---

44. Ibid., p. 111.
45. Ibid., p. 112.
46. Ibid., p. 113.
47. Ibid.

religion, especially because of "our absurd sense of self-sufficiency in the light of our real weakness and His strength, and our prideful self-importance over against His majesty."[48]

What method did he use to prepare his sermons? Shoemaker himself described his sermon preparation:

> A couple of mornings a week took up the sermon. I kept my typewriter conveniently near, so that I could wheel round in my desk chair and put down whatever was "coming" at that time—sermon, aphorism, idea. I kept at the left side of my desk four little three-by-five boxes, one for sermon ideas, one for quotes, one for "the next book," and one for people—names and addresses and phone numbers of those I wanted to keep in touch with currently. Then would come lunch, at home or with someone outside.[49]

Irving Harris said of his method, "His sermons were invariably pounded out swiftly, despite interruptions, in three hours or so—on double-spaced sheets, some of which could be sent to the newspapers 'hot off' his old portable."[50] Shoemaker then took these four or five typewritten pages with him into the pulpit Sunday by Sunday, and few new listeners ever guessed that he was using a manuscript. When he was once asked why he used a manuscript, he answered, "I know my own limitations."[51]

Although Shoemaker used a manuscript in delivering his own sermons, he recommended another method to young ministers. In *Beginning Your Ministry* he said, "If possible, learn to speak without a manuscript; I did not do this but I wish I had."[52] He realized that good content could be wholly wasted through poor delivery; and so to those who did use a manuscript, he said:

> Don't look down into your manuscript: look out to your people, making contact with them through your eye. . . .
> If you must have a manuscript, you must not seem to read it. Read it over beforehand to yourself two or three

---

48. Ibid.
49. Helen Shoemaker, p. 68.
50. Harris, p. 22.
51. Ibid., p. 23.
52. Samuel Shoemaker, *Beginning Your Ministry*, p. 107.

times, and once say it aloud. It should be possible for you to look down three or four times to a page when preaching, but yet to leave an impression that you are hardly even speaking from notes. A man with his eyes glued to a manuscript can be no preacher. Adopt a conversational tone with them from the first; almost in the mood, "As I was saying. . . ."[53]

In evaluating the preaching ministry of Samuel Shoemaker, Bardwell Smith wrote:

The power of his preaching lay in its being truly existential and at the same time faithful to the full biblical context. Without question, he stressed certain themes to the partial neglect of others. Sam was not what one would call a "balanced thinker"; he was hardly a scholar. But what he dealt with in his sermons was the heart and core of the Christian message: the centrality of a God who in creation, governance, and redemption calls men into obedience, into loving service to the world.[54]

But perhaps Shoemaker himself said it best in the conclusion of *Beginning Your Ministry,* in "A Personal Word with You":

I hope that as you come near the close of your ministry you will be able to say what I often say, that if I had had a thousand lives, I should have spent them all just where I have spent the one life I did have.[55]

---

53. Ibid., pp. 118–19.
54. Helen Shoemaker, p. xv.
55. Samuel Shoemaker, *Beginning Your Ministry,* p. 127.

Sermons

ANOTHER APPROACH TO CONVERSION

1 John 4:20

I THINK it is unquestionably true that the reason why Christianity has made even the progress it has made in this wayward world is that it has brought God closer to man than any other religion. In this faith, we do not lift ourselves by our boot-straps up to Him, He comes down to us in the Person of His Son.

But this is not all done through the historic fact of the coming of Christ. It must be made actual and real as this great general fact becomes real to each one of us through experience. In a way, the Incarnation takes place all over again each time He comes into the life of any one of us. And unless this happens on a personal scale, the great historic revelation is made of no effect. There are quantities of people who have been within the range of the church and the influence of its faith, many who are now within that range, for whom the whole thing remains unreal. The gap has never been closed. God is far away from them, and they look wistfully at the whole experience of faith as a starving man looks through the windows of a lavish restaurant.

Why is this? Why is it that many people who would like to have faith cannot find it? What will close the gap for them, and make the whole experience of God and faith real to them?

We say, often very truly, that sin is what keeps people from God. They do not want to let go of something that is holding them back, something they do not want to surrender. There is an old secret, a present wrong, a habit or an attitude they do not want to give up. There is someone they won't forgive, or something they won't do that they know God wants them to do, little as they know Him. We can become so discouraged about ourselves, so faithless towards life, that we cut ourselves off from any fresh sources of encouragement and hope; so that this becomes also a sin. These two things—a specific

---

Previously published by Calvary Episcopal Church, Pittsburgh, and reprinted by kind permission of Mrs. Samuel Moor Shoemaker.

wrong we will not let go of, and a confirmed attitude of hopelessness — can remain with us so long that they become frozen and virtually irremovable, like some old radiator valves in our house that have not been turned off for so long it would break the threads if you turned them off now. Thundering against sin does not help such people. Another approach must be made.

Again, often the first thing an unbelieving person says to an enthusiastic believer is that he is troubled theologically. He doesn't understand what is meant by the Trinity, or why do we believe in the divinity of Christ? It is true that such a person may never have listened closely to any reasoned presentation of our grounds for such faith, and it may help him if, without contentiousness or scorn, we give him a few good reasons for "the faith that is in us." But many a time I have set forth the reasons, and the person sees the reasonableness and validity of them, but still the faith does not come. It is usually a help to find us ready to discuss the matter, and not to withdraw from spoken unbelief as if it were by nature blasphemous; and the arguments themselves may be new to him. Yet the whole thing may not carry conviction. Some other approach to faith is needed, some other way of dealing with this particular person. We often forget that people who consider themselves primarily intellectuals, and think that they are won and moved only by reasonable considerations, are also human beings whose values and approaches to life have in them great quantities of emotion, just like all the rest of us. One has seen intellectual people switch their intellectual convictions from unbelief to belief, without faith ever penetrating into the deeper areas of their lives or seemingly doing them very much good.

There is another approach ready to hand which is often forgotten or not realized. You find it in a verse in 1 John 4:20, ". . . he that loveth not his brother whom he hath seen, cannot love God whom he hath not seen." It would be easy to look at this from the strictly moral viewpoint, and make it only mean that unless you give up any prejudice or anger or hatred felt towards another person, you cannot love God. And we would be back in the first approach which we said does not always work. What this verse may mean, taken in a larger sense, is that unless or until we find some other human being that we can trust, we may be unable to trust God. Until we feel from some human being a concerned and disinterested caring, we may not feel it possible that there is a greater caring that proceeds finally from the very Heart of the universe. The first genuine, feelingful experience we ever have of the love of God may be that which comes through the prism of a human relationship in which we first feel genuine and disinterested love. Theoretically this psychological approach may not seem to be the only one: people sometimes experience an awareness of God when they are entirely alone. But practically we shall find that the one thing that may begin letting through the love of God is someone's understanding that gets through to us and gives us hope and a new release.

This is tremendously important for children, both little and more mature. The word "father" as applied to God must contain principally one association, i.e. one's human father. If the main content in that relationship is fear, it will carry over to God: if the main content is love, that will carry over to God. A remarkable man, Harry Hadley, was superintendent of a rescue mission which my old parish in New York ran. His father was Samuel Hadley, himself a wonderfully converted man (he is mentioned in William James's *Varieties of Religious Experience*) and superintendent of the Water Street Mission. His son was a wastrel all his father's life, and was not converted until his death; but the son often said to me, "When I call God 'Father,' I don't have to make much change in its content." Whatever else you give or fail to give to children, give them affection, lots of it. It is not inconsistent with discipline, but it greatly modifies how discipline is administered. They charge our unlovingness to God, or they are helped to believe in His perfect love by our imperfect love. This is not spoiling and doing everything they want; but it is a deep assurance of love that a child knows he can count on. "If he cannot love, and feel love from, his human father and family whom he has seen, how can he feel it from God whom he has never seen?"

This is often the only thing that gets through to mentally and emotionally disturbed people. One can hold all the right attitudes, and say nothing but the correct words; but these may not make the slightest impression on someone in a deep depression. It must have some human caring in it, and personalness, if it is to heal and redeem. A clergyman friend of mine with a genius for compassion was chaplain of a state hospital. In one of the wards there was a woman who had long been impossible to reach. She could not be coaxed to speak. The chaplain went on doing all he could for her, and would sometimes speak to her of the love and forgiveness of God. Months went by. Then one day, as he started out the door, he looked back and saw her looking after him. He went back and said, "Is there anything you wanted to say to me?" "Yes," she said, "I murdered my babies." The chaplain said, "God can forgive this, too, if we are penitent; let us ask Him for forgiveness." From that moment she began to get well, and has been back with her family for years. This chaplain knows how to deal with sick people, but he also cares. "If a depressed woman does not find some helper who cares for her in her lonely despair and whom she can know as a compassionate human being, how shall she come to have trust in an invisible God Who has always seemed far away?"

All Christians ought to be seeking to win others to Christ and His way of life and His fellowship, the Church. This is one of the two primary jobs of a minister, the other being the care of people already convinced and won. It is equally the job of every Christian layman.

Once I thought that the main equipment for this work was a knowledge of what the Christian faith is, and that is important. I did not know then how important it is to know and understand people and to care for them — how possible it is to win your argument but lose your person, how people are not just naked brains but a complex of many factors, all of which must enter into a Christian decision. It will not be our rectitude so much as our understanding that will draw them — not so much our ability to answer abstract questions as our ability to meet concrete human situations — not so much our clarity in statement as our ability to mesh with the feelings and conditions of the other person. For the moment, God and the Christian faith are distant: we are present. We cannot in ourselves "be" the whole of the Gospel, but we can be natural and human and warm and concerned. Many times we fail with people spiritually, not because they are obdurate and unapproachable, but because we ourselves go about it the wrong way — and, let us confess it honestly, all of us go about it the wrong way sometimes.

A young Christian woman met a man a few years her senior socially. They got into a conversation which turned to religion and she gave him a pretty good witness and "fight talk," all in good spirit. Then she asked for help with him from me, and he said he would like to talk. He began by saying what he thought about the conventional concept of a God Who would damn infants and heathen who were not baptized, when it was not their faults, and I told him I believed in no such God and thought that if anybody was going to be pitchforked into hell for the failure of these people to believe and be baptized, it was the Christians who did not trouble to get faith across to them. I felt he was fighting God, not just intellectually, but emotionally; and asked him if he had ever been badly hurt emotionally, what kind of relationship he had with his family, and did he agree with me that loneliness was our great personal problem? "Couldn't agree with you more," he said. The barriers began to come down. As I gained his confidence I asked him what was the worst thing he'd ever done, and he broke down and told me of something that had once happened that had ever since dogged his conscience. In the cleansing honesty of those few minutes, when he began to feel that God might forgive and restore him, he began to be a new kind of person. When I suggested we ask God for forgiveness, he was ready for me to pray for him. He said to me, "I have not found God yet through this, but I have found understanding. If someone had met me in this way years ago my whole life would have been different." I think that through this encounter he found that spiritual faith was both more reasonable and more available than he had thought; and now as he seeks to pray and to study the Scriptures and go to Church, he will find other people to help him, other ways to give him encouragement. We gave him some things to read that might help him in his thinking, but the personal encounter was what began to melt down the hard resistance. "If a man does not find someone to trust whom he can see, how can he come to trust the God whom he has not seen?"

This means that while we are outside the Christian faith we may best be brought within the range of its influence through people who have this faith and try to live by it. We may need, in a sense, to be a little bit converted to them, at least for a time, so that later on we may be completely converted to Christ, for good and all. We must get through the representative to the Lord Himself, but in point of time the representative may come first. When the late Rev. Robert Norwood was leaving Canada to come to the United States, he was talking one day with his archbishop, who complimented him on his great ministry in Canada. Norwood said, "Your Grace, I don't know whether I've made Christians or Norwood-ites out of these people." And the wise archbishop said, "Probably both — that is the way God often works."

And it means that after we come within the Christian faith and fellowship, our immediate next responsibility is to seek to become the kind of people God can use to repeat the process with other people on the outside. The Church does not exist just to minister to the needs of the people within it, but to make out of them the kind of servants who can serve Him and others in just this same intermediary way. We need to become the kind of people of whom it may truthfully be said by others, that if it hadn't been for our love and concern, wisely and prayerfully surrounding them, they would not have found Christ. So that, as the outsider needs to be just a little converted to someone already Christian in order to be greatly converted to Christ afterwards, so we who are "already Christian" need to be a little converted to those outside — not just to the good ones, but to the bad ones; not the ones we like and love easily, but the ones we do not like or love at all — not converted to the sinfulness in them, but to them as human beings, reconciled, concerned, doing everything that we can to identify ourselves with them, and to become to them such people as may be their first step towards Christ.

Do you see how organically important this makes the Church? Christianity can never be purely individualistic discovery of Christ. We are all interdependent in this world anyway, and still more interdependent when it comes to the things of the Spirit. We are intended to be helped by others in our initial discovery of faith. We are intended to help each other in the fellowship of the Church. And we are intended to become the kind of person that enables other people to believe in God.

"He that loveth not his brother whom he hath seen, cannot love God whom he hath not seen."

THE CHRIST OF THE RESURRECTION

"I am the resurrection, and the life" (John 11:25).

WE GATHER HERE TODAY to celebrate the most astounding event in history, the Resurrection of Jesus Christ from the dead. The Church and the Bible do not explain the Resurrection: they are explained by it, and they start with it. There would have been no Church and no Bible unless there had first been the fact of the Resurrection. On Good Friday Jesus died an apparent failure, His friends scattered and His movement stopped. But on Easter He rose again from the dead, His friends reassembled, and His movement started up again, never to stop. The Resurrection explains these things. It is an event of the same order as the Creation itself. It inaugurates a new creation.

Today let us think about the Christ of the Resurrection. For if there is one explanation of the Resurrection, it lies in Him Who arose that first Easter Day. To Him alone this happened, for to Him alone could it happen. He walked this earth in the simplest of human form, a man like ourselves, feeling, suffering, hoping like all the rest of us; yet when they came to make some estimate of Him, to summarize what had taken place in those three luminous years, the human category alone would not hold Him. In some unique, miraculous way "God was in Christ," and he "that had seen Him had seen the Father." His miracles, even His Resurrection, do not explain Him: rather He explains them, and they flow from Him, being what He is. This does not take away, thank God, from His humanity, His understanding of us mortal men. I would not stand here heaping eulogy upon Him — He needs none of it — but I would simply add the voice of my own witness to the witness of the historic Church in all Christian ages, that He is the divine Son of God; and that on this day which we keep, He rose from the dead. He Himself is the Center of this divine drama and its climax on Easter, as He Himself is the Center of history and its clue.

Of Himself He said, as simply as one can state a fact, "I am the resurrection and the life." This is one of the gigantic statements He sometimes made about Himself. No other man ever made such claims for Himself, unless he were beside himself. Who but God can call Himself "the resurrection and the life"? Those who would call Jesus merely a good man must reflect that, if He be no more than a good man, then He is not good at all: for these statements about Himself are either unanswerably true, or they are inexcusably false. It appears that we must take Him on His own terms, or not at all. To the best of our thinking, He is not merely man at his highest reaching up to God: He is God at His most merciful reaching down to man.

Previously unpublished sermon, by kind permission of Mrs. Samuel Moor Shoemaker.

Now there are, I think, four places where we discover Jesus to be "the resurrection and the life."

I. He is the *resurrection of the human soul.* There is nothing distinctively Christian about belief in immortality: nearly all kinds of religion and some people with little religion believe in the survival of the soul. This is almost a natural instinct, and normal human beings want to survive death. But Christian immortality is a different thing from the natural wish for survival. Our faith in personal immortality is anchored in the Resurrection of Jesus. We rely on His strengthening words, "Because I live, ye shall live also." He pioneered the way for us. His Resurrection made clear to us what Christian immortality is — not the vague wandering on of lonely and orphaned spirits, floating somewhere between earth and heaven — but the continuation of ourselves, in communion with Him and with one another. We are not a drop that falls into the sea of being and is lost in it; we are individual and responsible souls that return to their Creator. Christ's Resurrection has immeasurably strengthened our faith in the resurrection of the human soul.

II. But in Christ, also, we find the *resurrection of the body.* In one article in the Apostles' Creed is the statement, "I believe . . . in the resurrection of the body." What do we mean by this? Do we mean that the particles of matter which make up our present bodies, and which will one day be dissolved into "dust and ashes," will come together again and form this same body over again? It cannot be. St. Paul says, "flesh and blood cannot inherit the kingdom of God." But he also declares that there is a "spiritual body," not a spirit only, but a "spiritual body." It is not exactly like the natural body, but it is more like it than pure spirit can be. He seems to be saying something that we moderns can best understand if we call it the survival of full personality — not just individuality, not just soul, but the whole self, with something that corresponds to the body of the present time.

Now the foundation of this belief is in the Resurrection-body of our Lord. As you read the various accounts of the Resurrection in the four Gospels, you will find that after the Resurrection Jesus was sufficiently unlike Himself for them to take time, in some instances, to recognize Him, yet sufficiently like Himself to let them know Him. His Presence would suddenly materialize, and suddenly vanish. He would come through a closed door, and yet eat a piece of broiled fish. The indication is of something which is both material and physical, in a combination we cannot now understand altogether; but perhaps this is less difficult now than ever before, since we have now discovered that the smallest particle of matter is a little universe of whirling energy.

The resurrection of the soul and the resurrection of the body, both guaranteed by Jesus who is "the resurrection and the life," lie on the other side of the experience of death. Death came as a result of sin. They are linked together in the Bible. St. Paul says that the last enemy to be destroyed is death; and that is the enemy which Jesus destroyed by His own rising again from the dead. We might say that the first enemy to be destroyed, here and now in our present life, is sin. Sin in men and sin in nations, this is what our troubles root in. We shall get no solution for our lives nor for our world until we find out what to do with human sin. Our greatest practical need today is for a resurrection from those things which drag life down, break up homes, destroy fellowship in communities, and make war in the world.

III. This begins with *resurrection in human character and personality* through Christian conversion. Think of the eleven men who gathered together to behold the Risen Lord. They had been simple villagers, many of them fishermen. They had been drawn to Him by what He said and did; and they began sloughing off the smallness and sinfulness of their lives in response to this amazing Person, this life and truth which was making existence a new thing for them. Conversion was a zigzag slow process for Simon Peter, a sudden cataclysm later for Saul of Tarsus; but the same Lord overcame and transformed them both.

The wonder of Christian conversion has never ceased. A good and well-adjusted church-woman became aware that she did not have a dynamic and multiplying faith, and was seeking for something vital. She asked someone whether life would always be a struggle between two selves fighting within her; and she was told that one of those selves was sin. She thought it over. She surrendered that lower self to God in repentance, and she accepted a new life from Christ. Since that day she has been living in the tremendous power of a living faith. A very serious operation was found necessary while she was away from home: she took a plane home and slept quietly. She went through the operation without fear and had a marvelous convalescence. Her own radiant faith touched many other lives, and in some it was decisive for it has brought them to faith and victory. That is resurrection in human life, and Christ is "the resurrection and the life."

A young businessman who had systematically expelled all faith from his life discovered that he could not make a go of his marriage. Somewhere he read of both a philosopher and a scientist who said there was a Power in the universe that men could tap for their own help. He asked for simple instruction on how to pray, and says, "For the first time in my life I felt this outside Power." It improved his health, it gave him a new kind of happiness. It began mending his home. The Bible is taking on meaning for him. Life is a new thing. He says he wishes we "could get these things across to the Ph.D. fellows. I am supposedly well educated, with four degrees from leading universities in this country. Can you explain how I went through all those years of education and still learned nothing of ultimate values, nothing of good and bad conduct? How can the universities turn out such a lopsided product?" Are some of us just such lop-sided products of modern secular education, not knowing the rock whence we were hewn? There is beginning to be resurrection in his life, and Christ is "the resurrection and the life."

IV. But what we need most of all is resurrection throughout those nations which have kept a connection with their Christian backgrounds through freedom and democracy. We need *resurrection in Christendom itself.* Our nation has been thrust into a position of leadership for which we are not prepared. As Hermann Hagedorn says, "We are one hundred and thirty-five million people, and we must grow up, overnight, or make the world one final Hiroshima." Nothing can prepare us for that but a revival of Christian faith and the assumption of Christian discipleship and responsibility by millions of our people. A while ago I had a letter from someone who had listened to a broadcast: it contains the philosophy and faith that our people everywhere need. Listen to it: "The sun is streaming through my window. There is cheer and good-will pervading the atmosphere of my home, my church, my town, even my country. In spite of the political heat and confusion, there is in our land a spirit of cooperation and a desire to help those in need here and abroad. What bothers me is that the majority of our people are not aware that the blessings we enjoy are the by-products of Christianity. We are living so far from our forefathers that their devotion to God, dependence on His guidance, and submission to His will, are simply a part of history. The fact is that without their devotion to God, their dependence on Him, this great, wide, wonderful land would quite possibly be many small, independent, suspicious countries, each with a law to themselves. Because of their trust in God they were able to see the value of complete cooperation for the common good of all. Our money is inscribed with that trust. Let us start trusting. . . . We need a conscience to guide our land. The Church must be that conscience, a living, vital organ to set the standard for other activities. We need to get the approval of the Almighty and the stamp of His discerning Presence back on our own people. Then and only then will commodity traders, political deceivers, laborers who want increased wages without giving a full measure of work, businessmen who hide extreme profits away in complicated financial reports—only then will this brand of people feel the weight of their wrongdoing; for it is wrong to put selfish interest first. To me Communism is not just the Russian form of government, it is Anti-Christ. Christ stands for the dignity and integrity of the individual: Communism stands for obliterating the individual as such. Unless we who have the Light are willing to put aside selfish, temporary interests—and get interested in global Christian warfare, taking the Light to dispel the gloom that increasingly threatens oppressed people everywhere—that darkness will cover our own delightful land. The time is now. If we do not want war, then we must be positive in our action, gird on the armor God has given us, and conquer in His

Name.... We must stop screaming 'Down with Communism' and shout victoriously 'Up with Christ!' We must move on, or we shall most certainly lose the ground we now claim. We must pray without ceasing and live accordingly. We must not be surprised at opposition but rather expect it, for it is darkness and it is afraid of Light. I am a housewife, twenty-six years old. Often I have been prone to say 'just a housewife,' but this morning I am thanking God that I am free to keep my home, rear my children and welcome my handsome young husband home in the evening. Both of us in our teen-age years knew what it was to be cold and hungry, but despair had no claim on us. Did we not live in America? The Eternal God planted hope in our hearts. We were sure that all things would work together for our good, because we loved Him, and were pledged to live according to His purpose. We now have two little daughters, one six, one nearly three. We are not wealthy, but we are young, and we can work, and do we not live in America? Personally we are living as near to God as we know how to. We believe this way shall win. We will work for it. Will you of the clergy encourage others who may be lax or visionless to reach out and renew their experience in God? I feel that our nation needs a rebirth of holy living and holy loving, and I know of no other way for it to come than through the already organized Church. Let us work, Sir, or the night will be upon us."

I wish that letter might find its way into millions of American homes. For there is in it the clear lift of spiritual resurrection. That woman knows her Lord, and she knows her Christian philosophy as related to the world's affairs. Do we? Do we need to "get the approval of the Almighty and the stamp of His discerning Presence" back on us? Are we "willing to put aside selfish, temporary interests"? Do we love our country under God as she does? And are we working for the Christian "way" as she says she and her husband are doing? "Our nation needs a rebirth of holy living and holy loving, and I know of no other way for it to come than through the already organized Church." Can the Church count on you? Are we willing that that rebirth begin in us, now in this crucial instant in our lives and the life of the world? Or shall we go on as we are, hoping that others will shoulder the responsibility? If we do, what she says will come true, "the night will be upon us." The darkness of deepening night—or the Light of Christ's Resurrection, in life, in home, in church, in nation, in the world. "I am the resurrection, and the life." Shall we pray to Him today that His Resurrection may make us rise to newness of life in Him?

OUR EMOTIONS

Mark 12:33

THIS MORNING I am not going to ask you to "do" anything, nor to produce anything, nor to believe anything. If in any small way I should achieve what I believe God would like me to achieve through this talk, I believe a lot of you would go out of here doing and producing and believing as you never did before, not in response to anything that is said to you from without, but in response to a release from within. I want to talk with you about our emotions.

Today if it were possible, I wish the Spirit of God might use what I say to touch some of the hidden springs that lie deep and unseen within you, heaped over with second thoughts, like sticks and leaves upon a spring in a woodland. These places lie way down below the facades with which we surround ourselves, even from our dearest — perhaps most of all from our dearest. If we could only help to clear away just a few of those sticks and leaves, so that the pure water of genuine and untrammeled emotion might flow out from the real center which is you and myself, perhaps we should have done what we were meant to do.

Most of us know that the greatest satisfaction we ever feel within ourselves is a feeling of wholeheartedness. We may feel this when we are able to throw ourselves into a golf game, or when we work in our gardens, or when we tackle a desk full of papers, or when we have a good heart-to-heart talk with someone. We feel that, for a moment, or a few hours, we are "in one piece," we are doing one thing with no remainders of ourselves left over to be preoccupied with something else. We have "found" ourselves by "losing" ourselves. Our emotions are free.

But this is one of the rarest experiences that people can have, and some people hardly ever have it. We think we must trust and love other people sparingly, prudentially, watching our step at every pace. We begin treating ourselves in this calculating way. And we do the same thing with God. If Thoreau was right, and "most men live lives of quiet desperation," is it not due to the fact that only about a quarter of ourselves is really involved in most of our human relations? We do not feel free to let ourselves feel freely. Therefore we are dry and unsatisfied within.

The feeling of wholeheartedness is such a good one that of course it has many counterfeits. People think they are experiencing this feeling when they come into a room or group of people, and "take over."

Previously published by Calvary Episcopal Church, Pittsburgh, and reprinted by kind permission of Mrs. Samuel Moor Shoemaker.

They think they find it by unleashing the drives of ego in the family, or amassing power for themselves at the job. They think they find it in the satisfactions of human love sought on a selfish basis; or in drink or narcotics; or in the pursuit of an artistic outlet. Each of these things may contain a real element of wholeheartedness. But we discover soon or late that real and lasting wholeheartedness must have within it a good deal of reciprocity, and unselfishness. Unless our feelings mesh with the feelings of others, so that a kind of current is set up, and others are experiencing wholeheartedness also, we may be chasing a shadow.

We sometimes hear people speak of the importance of "being yourself." That would be excellent if we knew who we are. Many of us do not. Our ideas of ourselves are too mistaken, too grandiose, too mean, too self-deceived, too self-critical, to leave us any room to be simple and free and ourselves. The Greeks created this word, "Know thyself." But we cannot know ourselves apart from some touchstone and norm outside ourselves. I can't even tell what I look like, or whether I've got a decent shave, without a mirror. And just so I cannot tell whether I am terribly self-deceived, or offensively solemn, or annoyingly cheerful, or overweeningly proud, or foolishly self-distrustful, unless I see myself in, and in relation to, others outside myself.

More than this, I can only know myself or be myself in relation to something which is in the nature of the Absolute—not that I shall ever achieve intimacy with this, or even likeness to this; but I must keep looking at Something supremely good, if I am to achieve even a fraction of the goodness I feel myself drawn to reach for. Freedom is to be drawn irresistibly by this Ideal Good, as well as driven from within by some compulsion to be like it. No one helps me to do this by telling me to "Be yourself." I am sick of myself—I want to get away from myself long enough to form a clearer estimate of myself. They help me when they discover a little piece of the real "me" and give me some confidence about it. To be told to "be yourself," when you are tied up with a hundred tensions, is just to add one more tension. I only am "myself" in free relation to God and to other people.

How often in our daily contact with the family, or with the others at the office, or in the important situation of talking with someone who asks help of us in trouble—how often do we feel truly free with these people, so that we do and say the spontaneous things which are always in some sense a risk, but which by their own spontaneity release us and the people with us? Rational thought must always have some place in our human communications, and may sometimes act as guard on too free an expression of our feelings; but it often destroys the spontaneity and wholeheartedness of what we do. A reaction may soon become shopworn and stilted when we have thought about it too much, "fitted" it (like trying on a glove) to see if it is appropriate here or here. You can kill all the spontaneous life out of a remark or a course of action with someone by turning it over too much in your mind, asking whether it measures up to business success, to the Dale Carnegie kind of suggestions about getting on with people (many of them excellent, if we can put them into practice naturally), and even — heaven help us! — by asking whether it is "Christian"! The ideal thing, and the thing you find at times in very real people, or at real times in less real ones, is these expressions of thought and emotion that fulfill all the best of the rules and precepts, but do not occur because we have consulted the books, but because we were feeling as we should in this situation with this person. There is a phrase in Psalm 42:7, "Deep calleth unto deep," which I have always interpreted psychologically as meaning that we communicate with others more fully through our subconscious than through our conscious minds; and if we can dip down into the feelings which lie deeper than thought, we shall probably come up with much more of truth and of reality than in any effort we may make to deal with the person or situation before us.

Where does "tact" come into this? What I am saying to you would constitute the very essence of tact. For tact, I would remind you, means "touch." It means some kind of contact. We cannot just say everything that occurs to us raw in the mind; but much of what we call tact is superficial and artificial. True tact reaches through to the other person, and means not alone politeness on our part, but an understanding of their situation and their feelings at a given moment. Tact always concerns the immediate moment, as well as the total situation, and requires a lightning calculator because situations change so fast.

We are not encouraging the human "gusher" who says all that he feels, without regard to its length, or whether it hurts others unwittingly. Some people pour their emotions over you, and they are about as welcome as a waiter pouring hot soup down your shirt-front. The world is full of terrible talkers, who do not communicate at all. Some other people say little, yet give much.

And we shall beware of the prodders and priers who, in the attempt to establish rapport with you, try to make you talk so as to reveal yourself. This is a sure way to cut off self-giving. One may have to wait for the moment to come, and it may never come; for we may not be the person to unlock this particular individual. We must not dig nor push. Real release of emotion in self-giving is one of the greatest experiences that can ever come to anyone; but it cannot be whipped up at will.

What we are talking about is really healthy emotion. We must rescue this good word from its detractors. They have got us to thinking that nearly all emotion is excessive and uncontrolled emotion. We need to feel, and to express, and to receive from others, genuine emotion. That emotion always needs some control; but it is not the false control of dryness — it is the real control of coming from an inwardly released person. We often become over-emotional because we have been under-emotional for so much of the time. We have been "sitting on" our emotions; and when they get free, they explode. The answer is not to sit on them harder, but to seek the kind of release which has in it also the right kind of control.

What has the Christian faith to do with this? Haven't we all seen people whose religion seemed to take an already very dried up personality and dry it up altogether? And haven't we seen people for whom religion was not sound emotional release, but fanaticism? Yes: we must admit we have seen both of these. But Jesus did not put His final emphasis on belief, nor on conduct: He put it on feeling. The sum of the whole matter was to love God with all our hearts and souls and minds; and our neighbors as ourselves. Love means emotion. We can at least care and serve, and this too is a kind of love. But back of this there must be a will-to-love.

Everything stems from God's love for us. He poured this out for us in the life and death and resurrection of Jesus Christ. Forget most of your old moral and theological associations with Jesus Christ. Think of Him now as Someone with Whom you can be yourself. Seek to be very simple and very honest, not because He knows all about you anyway, but because He loves you and you are safe with Him. Half our theological acceptance and half our moral rectitude are bolsters of our ego, keeping up with the religious and moral Joneses. Forget the Joneses, and think about Jesus. It is our pretense that damns us. We put up a front, even with God. Let His love melt it right down to the ground. We are all very needy, and all very sinful, and all very ashamed, and all very much in need of a strengthening kind of comfort. There is a lot of fear in us, and you can say the very worst of us and much of it will actually be true. You can also say that we would not be coming to church at all unless there were some spark of response to God which is the best thing in us. We are a mixed bag—every one of us. The person who makes the most effort to be relaxed is probably the most tense and self-conscious. And many who are surrounded by friends and family are the most lonely. We need some human approval—much more do we need Divine approval. We shall certainly not get the latter by being "good," and complete approval from God is only the steady possession of the wholly self-deceived. What we can have from God, and what we need much more than approval, is love—the knowledge that He knows all about us, disapproves of a lot of it, and goes on loving us just the same.

If we will stop assuming we have this because we belong to a church, or because we are nice and good people, or because we believe all the things we ought to believe theologically, and just realize that we have it for no other reason in the world than that God is like that, we may be able to let a little of the love we need seep into our souls and our subconscious. Wells have always fascinated me. You dig a hole at a right spot, build yourself a dry wall to hold back the earth from collapsing into the hole; and lo! from nobody knows quite where the water starts seeping in and filling the well. You can draw it out, and more will seep in. It just seems to "come." It takes a certain amount of faith and a certain amount of judgment to dig a well; but there is a lot of water under the earth that seems to have been put there for man's use.

Some of us fear to sink the shaft and dig a well of faith. What if there were no water? Or we dug in the wrong place? Yes, all these mistakes may occur. But there is one bigger mistake yet, and that is to go dry for want of any water at all. And that is what people are doing who refuse to dig a well of faith, and let the water which is the Grace of God seep in from the sides. Grace is as definite an entity as water or electricity. We can be in touch with it. It can come to us. We must dig the well, and we must not seal up the walls so nothing can get through to us, way down deep there where it is dark and we do not know everything that is going on, nor understand till later that it was Grace that was pouring in there all the time. The "Everlasting Mercy" gets through to us in His own uncharted ways when we open ourselves to Him. The task that looks too big for you, the burden that looks too heavy for you, the pain that looks too sharp for you, can all be met with the addition of the help from God that comes largely in the form of an awareness that we are being loved by Him, and perhaps also by His people. It is not weakness but strength to realize these things about ourselves. We live in a day that worships the reason of intellect, and the action of will. We have forgotten something. We have forgotten the needs and the powers of the heart. We need more healthy emotion.

The great Spanish writer and philosopher Unamuno, thinking of Goethe's dying words, "Light, light, more light," declared passionately, "No, warmth, warmth, more warmth; for we die of cold not of darkness. It is not the night that kills but the frost."

Our great Christian religion exists, I believe, not so much to make our thinking about God right, and not so much to order our conduct aright; but rather to help us to believe that "God is love." The greatest mistake we can make is not theological error, nor even wrongdoing: it is to refuse to let ourselves be loved by God. As a child is a healthy child, not when it has no faults, but when it knows the security of great love from father and mother, so we are healthy children when we know ourselves to be surrounded by the love of our Heavenly Father. We shall err and we shall sin and we shall doubt: but if we come back again and again to Jesus Christ as the sure sign of the Father's love we shall live from an inward center that is like a well that is ever being drawn on, but keeps ever filling up. I believe God's Love is the final groundwork of this amazing universe in which you and I were given the unspeakable privilege of life.

MAUNDY THURSDAY NIGHT

Luke 22:15

WE are all thinking about the Upper Room tonight. Our Lord is seated at the head of the table. The apostles are there—all twelve of them together for the last time. As our eye runs over that little company, it stretches out and becomes a very large company—the company of the people who love Jesus personally. All of them, all down the centuries —they are all there. And we are there with them. For He does not change, and the holy meal of fellowship does not change, and the fellowship itself does not change.

Fellowship is one of His greatest gifts to us. There is the fellowship of human congeniality and love, and it is very rewarding. But it belongs to a few. Not many can enjoy it with more than a very few. Then there is the fellowship that Jesus Himself creates, where He is always Third Party. That is an endless fellowship. It brings together everybody and anybody. Not in an indiscriminate mass, but with the kind of individuation which is only possible where there is recognition and respect, such as are born of knowing that we both love the same wonderful Person. There is no tie in the world like that. All may share in it. The fellowship never grows so large but that there is room for one more—not only in the fellowship, but in our own hearts—those hearts that Jesus Himself has widened with His own love.

Spiritual fellowship is one of the deepest impulses of our nature. Our Lord said to them that night, "With desire have I desired to eat this passover *with you* before I suffer." He longed to be with them. There would come to Him a strength from that which would make the next dark twenty-four hours different. He would give something to them that would help carry them through the black days till Easter came. With all that faced Him, with all the suffering that Judas and others caused Him, I believe He enjoyed that last evening with them. If joy was not possible for Him, then I think He underwent the suffering of the fellowship that night in order that we might enjoy the fellowship now. "There is joy for all the members,/In the sorrows of the Head," as the old hymn has it. I am sure that He wants us to enjoy one another in Him tonight. I am sure He wants us to feel about each other, "With desire have I desired to take this Communion *with you*." There is something organic, lifelong, unbreakable in the Christian fellowship. Something through which He intends to come, and through which he always *does* come.

"One of you shall betray me," He said. "And they began to be sorrow-

---

Previously unpublished sermon, by kind permission of Mrs. Samuel Moor Shoemaker.

ful, and to say unto him one by one, Is it I?" *Self-questioning, self-doubt,* is one of the essentials of fellowship. So often in the world we are outwardly humble, but inwardly we feel proudly sure that we are right. In the Christian fellowship just the reverse is true. Outwardly we feel free to be ourselves, to let out our hearts, to make our mistakes, because we know that the fellowship will understand. Our humility is inward: it lies in constant self-questioning, self-doubt. "Lord, is it I?" Peter blusters away about his loyalty, and protests that he will go to prison and death for Jesus—he feels the confidence to say all this in the fellowship. But he has missed the deeper note of fellowship somewhere. If he had questioned himself more, he would have failed less terribly. There is no fellowship in Jesus unless, with our fellows, we give the best we have, share what we think, pool our thoughts—but always with the remembrance, "I may be wrong." Great and terrible failures come in the fellowship of Jesus. In that fellowship, all must say, because all must keep a certain self-questioning, self-doubt, "Lord, is it I?"

Then He instituted the fellowship-feast. He wanted something outward to remind them forever of the inwardness of this wonderful, sad, tremendous evening. He took the Bread and Wine which were usual at this Jewish meal, and suddenly identified them with Himself. Had He thought it over—or was it a flash of genius that came to Him while He sat there? We do not know. But forever after the Bread was His Body, and the Wine was His Blood. The symbol lay, and lies, not in the physical similarity of bread to the body, or wine to blood, but in the *brokenness* of the Bread, in the *outpoured-ness* of the Wine. They and we should forever come into fellowship with Him, and with one another in Him, through the repetition of this Holy Communion. In a sense, it is never a repetition, though we use the same wonderful words time after time. For each time, when there are people there longing for Him, longing for fellowship with each other in Him—longing for victory and peace and faith, and longing for the caring of others and the chance to serve others which put behind us our solitariness, the loneliness of our souls—each time, He comes afresh and anew. It is never the same twice. He is giving us something tonight that He never gave to us before.

There arose a dispute among them. Which should be considered the greatest? Don't let us condemn them for intruding such a contention at such a time: they were at least honest enough to come out with what they were feeling. And Jesus very gently brings them back to the right spirit. "The kings of the Gentiles lord it over them . . . but it shall not be so among you. He that is the greater among you, let him become as the younger. Whosoever shall be first among you shall be your servant." John tells us how He acted all this out in an incident. He poured water into a basin and began to wash the disciples' feet, and to wipe them with the towel wherewith He was girded. I think He washed their feet because they were dusty and tired and needed washing—for no other nor ulterior reason. He always made parables of what He did, but He did not act in order to create parables. He saw a need, and He met it. This was what He had to say about greatness. This *was* greatness: lowly, ministrant service where there was need. That was greatness. There was no chance for effusive thanks, or any of the usual "psychic income" that means so much to us when we have served others and are praised for it. Just service, as the sign of fellowship. But He added, "If I then, your Lord and Master, have washed your feet, ye ought also to wash one another's feet. For I have given you an example, that ye should do as I have done unto you."

Then Jesus said a wonderful word to them: "Ye are they that have continued with me in my temptations." It simply means, "It is you who have stood by me through my trials" (Luke 22:28, Moffatt). How should you have felt if He looked into your eyes, and said those words to you? He might have. He may be saying them to you tonight. He is far beyond trials like that now, beyond death and pain and defeat, glorious in His majesty and heavenly glory—but He is not beyond concern with His cause on earth. If "God so loved the world"—if He loved this wayward planet rather especially, as we love a wayward child—then He is as concerned about it as ever. His cause here is still perhaps the dearest thing in the universe to Him. He lives in that cause, lives in us who try to maintain and extend it. His cause has trials and difficulties in plenty, and they are His. Where we stand up for the right, and are responsible, and care, and pray, and give of ourselves, we stand by Him. When some of our beloved who have slipped within the veil from us come up before His throne, do you not think there are some of them to whom He says words very much like this, "It is you who have stood by Me in My trials"? And for our encouragement tonight, He may be saying those words to us. Let us ask Him to make us worthier to hear Him saying them to us. Let us pray for this faithfulness in fellowship, to Him and to one another.

Then came the failures in fellowship. Jesus must have seen a look of weakness pass over the face of Peter, and He said, "Simon, Simon, Satan hath desired to have you that he may sift you as wheat: but I have prayed for thee that thy faith fail not; and when thou art converted, strengthen thy brethren." What a mixture of warning and encouragement! Dear blustery old Simon, sure he would not fail, protesting it with the utmost confidence—and within a short time going down like corn in a windstorm, and saying, "I don't know the man!" But he had the grace to weep himself into genuine repentance; and I suppose that, during all the black hours of that night, and Good Friday, and the Sabbath, the words rank in his ears, "When—not if, but when—thou art converted, strengthen thy brethren." It was a repetition of His first confidence in him, when He called that weak reed a Rock, and said He would build His Church upon the insight of his faith. And Judas. Peter's denial was the result of a sudden, gusty temptation: Judas's betrayal, of a settled plan. Some think he was sincere, and believed that if the situation were precipitated, Jesus would be saved. It may be so. We do not know. All we know is that Judas had somehow put himself beyond hearing words such as Peter heard—words with deep warning in them, but also profound hope. All of us have at some time denied our Lord, and most of us have at some time betrayed Him. He lets people like us come into His fellowship, and when we have un-fellowshiped ourselves by our sins, He lets us come back into it again, by the miracle of His forgiveness. Whether we go out "into the night" as both Peter and Judas did, depends on our weakness—any of us may do it at any time. Whether we *stay* there with Judas, or whether we come back into the light again, depends upon whether we remember what Christ has said to us. Judas forgot. Peter remembered.

They went out. And there was Gethsemane, and the trial, and the Crucifixion. For a time it looked as if the power that had been generated in that Upper Room was lost forever. But it was recaptured after the Resurrection, at the time of Pentecost. That seems to have been the time when the corporate power and awareness of the Church began to flame up. They knew that the Lord was not on this side of tragic death, as He was on this night; but on the other side of glorious Resurrection. In Him that old fellowship was renewed, in far greater power than they knew on this night. Their faithfulness to Him and to each other is the only reason why we can meet here tonight. All down the centuries have come both kinds of church—the outward, historic, institutional church; and the inward, personal, spiritual church. Both are needed, as we need bodies and souls. But it is a tragic thing to miss the soul of the church, which is fellowship, in being so much concerned with the outward church.

Let me say three things about the fellowship.

First: *it is the Body of our Lord.* His extended life in the world is wrapped in the fellowship of His believers. The flame of faith feeds on the fuel of discipleship and fellowship. People do come into authentic and unmistakable fellowship with Him through fellowship with us who know and love Him. We are not worthy that this should be so—but it stands, not in any worthiness of ours, but in His own commission, which has never been withdrawn.

Second: *the fellowship is our chief concern.* The fellowship is the bridge between Christ and the world. No wonder bridges are guarded in days like these: they are the means of communication, and the enemy would cut them off. We must guard our bridges between God and man; and the chief of them is the fellowship. Let us love it and cherish it. Let us care for it and provide for it. Let us love the people within it, and seek every day to enrich their lives and help them to greater and greater power.

Third: *the fellowship is the hope of the world.* Even in these days the fellowship is unbroken. We know that in the smothered countries from which we seldom hear, and even the enemy countries from which we are cut off entirely, there are people like ourselves tonight, praying, believing, hoping, working. The fellowship is out to build the Kingdom. Our Lord lived and prayed and died and rose again for the Kingdom. The fellowship is His leaven on earth, His way of building the Kingdom. Let us pray that there may be born a very great hope in our hearts tonight, and a very great determination, that the faith and the freedom and the fellowship which we know in Christ shall be made known to all men.

God bless us all, and all mankind, and lead us deeper and deeper into fellowship with Him and with each other in Him!

HOW CAN WE SURRENDER A SITUATION TO GOD?

2 Kings 18–19

WE have often spoken about the surrender of our wills and our selves to God, and we shall often do so again; for the secret of finding a living faith and a living God lies in a sufficiently thorough giving of ourselves to Him through Christ in faith, and nothing else really brings any lasting peace of mind or heart. It is not the difficulty of finding God which keeps us from knowing Him, it is the wilfulness of our own hearts, wanting our own way. There is likely to be an occasion when we make this general, overall surrender of ourselves, if we ever make it; for we do not ooze into it by osmosis or general exposure—we come into it by an act of faith, made by our own free wills.

But our path to this general and comprehensive surrender (by which I do not mean a perfect surrender, which probably none of us makes in this world, but rather one which affects all the areas of our life) is likely to lie in the surrender to God of a particular situation which is

---

Previously published by Calvary Episcopal Church, Pittsburgh, and reprinted by kind permission of Mrs. Samuel Moor Shoemaker.

on our minds and in our hearts. It may be a troubling and unwelcome situation about which we fret and stew and worry; or it may be a situation in which we desperately want something we know we are meant not to have. The problem is: how can I surrender this situation which I dislike, or this other situation which I like all too well, to God, and find His mind on it?

Let me give you some examples of what I mean.

Here is a man near forty whose wife has left him after some fifteen years of married life. He is desperately lonely, and after the first relief of having her out of the way, he finds that he misses her dreadfully and wishes they could patch it up again, as they had to do once before. He hears a Christian message, and goes to the man who delivered it, asking for help. He begins by saying, "I suppose a person has to have a need before he can find the kind of religion you are talking about." Yes, the answer was, and would you like to say whether you have this kind of a need? Then the story came out. Quite a happy life together, but as time went on, the man was expecting his wife more and more to do as he wished. She became an accessory to his own life. He knew he had been demanding and inconsiderate. "Ever tell her you recognized this?" he was asked. No, he had not: the stubborness of his will extended to a refusal to admit he was wrong. He began to see that most of the situation was of his own making. But he had neither the wisdom nor the grace to unmake it. What should he do?

There followed some talk about Grace—about the living power of God coming down on people and their situations, when they ask Him to do so. He had been staying away from church for years, not saying his prayers except now and then to ask God to get him out of his jam without waiting long enough to give Him a chance to do it. His loneliness and rebellion and frustration came out in a flood of cleansing tears. Sometimes tears are like a pelting rain on a street, which cleans it completely of leaves and dirt and rubbish, and carries them down the drain. Self-pity may be melting into penitence: it was with him. It was suggested he stop the car in which the two men were riding, and that they put the whole situation in God's hands. Was he ready for this? Yes, he saw no other way. Some surrenders come from desperation, not yet from the drawing of God's love except indirectly. He had never prayed with anyone else, but this was no time to consider shyness or formalities.

"Dear God," he stammered out through the shaking of his tears, "help me. Show me what I ought to do. Forgive my selfishness. Bring us together again if that's your will." Here, you see, was no formal prayer of selfish desire; here was an honest effort to find God and His plan. There followed a talk about loneliness, and he began to see that what he really wanted was not to be loved, but to learn how to love. There simply is not enough love in the world ever to satisfy a love-hungry, selfish person. The problem is to get him over living in and for himself. He begins to see himself as he has never done before. After a while the tears stop, and the sign of relief comes into his whole expression. A new kind of person emerges from the old shell of selfishness with which he has encased himself for so long. Some elementary helps are offered, about his own prayers, about the church, and he is introduced to a man in his company who has just made a similar decision, so that they may meet in a new way and on a new level, and perhaps be the start of a Christian group in that company. Now the letter he writes to his wife will not be a self-pitying plea to come back to a man who, in time, will do just what he did before — it will be an honest confession of what he sees now about himself, with the hope that she too may find the same dynamic faith he has begun to find, and that they will work out their situation as God wills and guides them to do it. That man has learned to surrender his situation to God, and himself with and through the situation.

Here is a different one. A man falls desperately in love with his friend's wife and she with him. The four go on being good friends, see a lot of each other, and this love affair goes on right in the midst of what seems like the friendship of two couples. The man is a Christian, and wants to find the Christian solution to the jam he has gotten into, involving three other people and their children. But how does one surrender such a complicated situation to God?

There is a Puritan and legalistic approach to this which some would call Christian, but many of us would not. It comes shaking a moralistic finger, saying, "This must stop. This is full of danger and sin. It must be broken off at once." But, as the man himself said, this is going to hurt several people almost beyond repair. Must he reject the woman, hurt her, refuse to see her again? This might be a safe and selfish course for his own soul; but the situation he has created has involved him in some responsibility. He may have a much more difficult thing to do than just break it off. He may have to redeem it.

But how? This man is burning up with infatuation for a woman not his wife, and she for him. The heavy hand of law can cause him to break it off as wrong; but it will take the deft hand of grace to change his emotions. He is told that probably he simply does not have the willpower to do it of himself, and only as God melts down some of the animal heat in the situation, and changes something deep in his emotions, can there be any real solution. There is a good long talk, and here again some cleansing tears. There is no "pat" answer, no infallible moral rules. But it begins to appear that two things are indicated: (1) that he offers his situation to God in as full surrender as he can, taking his hands off it as completely as possible, letting it go into the hands of God. Not easy, this, and maybe not even possible except as God gives the present grace and strength to do it, almost as if God lifts it off us rather than we let go of it. God has been at work already, in disturbance and guilt-feelings about it all, in the remembrance of marriage vows, in the realization that here is cause for a break that will hurt many people or else a new course must be found. But human passions are strong, and the human will is weak. It is no time for anyone to shake a finger or moralize: only understanding of the situation can help the man to face it as it must be faced.

Then comes prayer. He says, "I feel we have been sort of praying as we have been talking, with Him near us all the time," and that is true. But then comes the really asking God in on it, opening the doors and windows of the mind and heart to Him. And when the prayer is ended, even through blurred eyes, there shines again the first look of hope and he says, "This is the first time I have seen any daylight in the situation."

And (2) there comes another indication, and it is that he talk this over with the woman involved, telling her of what has happened and seeking to draw her into the Divine Encounter also. It is just possible that the whole thing has been allowed that some great good come of it: God is constantly redeeming our sins and their results and turning them to some good the moment we turn them over to Him. God does not cause man's sin, and could have done something better without it; but God always has another move to make, beginning where we are. This man has found God. The woman may find God through him. The whole situation may be redeemed because God has been allowed to come in at one corner of it. So does Grace work, and law has no counterpart to it. Remember, the Pharisee condemners wanted to stone the woman taken in adultery, but Jesus said, "Neither do I condemn you; go, and do not sin again." They were so self-righteous in their moral zeal, and Jesus was so merciful while making the moral point clear. Which attitude redeems the person that has done the wrong?

Here is another situation, apparently at the present insoluble. A young man lives with a mother and stepfather. There is not a great deal of money so that he might go and live in college, he must live at home. And there is constant bickering and strife, to the point that it takes from his ambition and the dynamic of creative living. He has to work hard even to keep going. Some would leave home under the conditions, and I have known situations where it was a choice of a family's domination or God's will in a young person's life, and separation was the only thing, at whatever cost. This situation does not seem of this kind, however, and he feels he ought to stay there and see it through. How can he? Really only as he surrenders his situation to God. It is pretty hard to surrender that situation to God. It concerns the atmosphere in which he is forced to live all the hours when he is not at school. And he is still young. Yes, but the old truth is still in force: there are two matters, what happens, and how I take what happens and what I let it do to me. I cannot perhaps change the situation, but I can change my attitude towards the situation. There is such a thing as a calm at the center of a whirlwind, and there is such a thing as living in the midst of a thorny and unhappy situation with quietness and peace of heart. There will be, I suspect, times when one will lose one or both of these; but they will return when we bring the situation once more into God's hands.

And so this young man is not battered and bruised by his situation — he is challenged by it, but he sees some values in it that would escape anyone who was not trying to see it from God's angle. For instance: he sees that his present suffering (and it is real suffering) may be his foundation for understanding other people's suffering, and he longs to help them in vital, spiritual ways. If he longs to do it, the chances are he will do it in the end. He does not enjoy his situation, but he certainly is not overcome by it, and he sees spiritual possibility in it. So he goes on getting his education and living his life in the strength of a Power not his own. Young as he is, he has learned the secret of surrendering his situation to God.

There is an ancient and moving story in the Old Testament, at 2 Kings 18 and 19. The armies of Sennacherib of Assyria "came down like the wolf on the fold," as Byron's verse has it, and took Samaria, and then the fortified cities of Judah, and were pressing hard for Jerusalem. The good King Hezekiah bought Sennacherib off by stripping silver from the temple and the palace. But there was no real appeasing him. The Assyrians came near the city and demanded the king. He sent out three emissaries, who were told to report to the king that he was trusting a weak reed in Egypt, and they had God's word for it to go up and destroy the land. Sennacherib's messengers spoke their reviling and demeaning words in the people's language, so that as many of the people as could overhear might listen to the taunts, not to trust King Hezekiah in his reliance on the Lord, but to trust the king of Assyria, and he would take them away and give them a safe and comfortable slavery. The king had told the people not to answer him, and they did not. But the emissaries brought the threatening and overbearing message to Hezekiah. And King Hezekiah did a wise thing: he sent some of his men to Isaiah the prophet to ask his wisdom; and Isaiah's counsel was to go on trusting God, and the Assyrians would hear a frightening rumor and return to their own land. But then a second time Sennacherib's threatening messengers bore down on Hezekiah with historic evidence that their armies were greater than tribal gods. Fear can be so contagious! Evil can strut and stalk so that it is terrifying! Shall we trust in God and in faith, in the great intangibles and invisibles of Faith and Grace — or shall we trust in the overmastering power of passion and evil and naked force?

What did Hezekiah do? This time he did not go to Isaiah, he went to God Himself. "Hezekiah received the letter from the hand of the messengers, and read it; and Hezekiah went up to the house of the Lord, and spread it before the Lord." And when Hezekiah prayed, he did not go into a dream-world of wish and fancy, he told God that Sennacherib was mocking Him, but he also told Him these kings of Assyria had "laid waste the nations and their lands, and have cast their gods into the fire." But these were no gods really, only wood and stone and the works of men's hands, and that was why they were destroyed: there was no ground for trusting them in the first place. But now God, the true God, was involved and insulted. And would He save from the Assyrians' hand—why? Nothing said of this adding to the glory of Hezekiah or even of Jerusalem, but "that all the kingdoms of the earth may know that thou, O Lord, art God alone." And then Isaiah sent another encouraging message, that God had told him He was going to answer Hezekiah's prayer about Sennacherib. And that night, sure enough, some plague or scourge struck the Assyrians' camp and slew a hundred and eighty-five thousand of them. And that's a lot of Assyrians—and it's a lot of victory.

So when the Assyrians come down on us, and come they will, let's consult a good Isaiah if one is handy, but let's consult the Lord in any case, for He is always handy. Let us "spread it before the Lord," wide open as Hezekiah did. And as we put our situation in His hands, He gives a victory we could never have expected!

LORD, TEACH US TO PRAY

Luke 11:1

WE all know in our own experience, I think, that whatever the outward form or association of our religion, it is really alive and at work when we pray. It is a question whether merely following some ethical standard is in any true sense what Jesus Christ came to teach us. We must feel the reality of the Power behind all things—God—and be in touch with Him, and include Him on all our activities. We must know something to His direct influence over us, controlling, guiding, forgiving, caring for us. Religion is relationship with God; and, as much

---

Previously published by Calvary Episcopal Church, Pittsburgh, and reprinted by kind permission of Mrs. Samuel Moor Shoemaker.

of relationship is talk and communication, prayer is the communion between God and ourselves.

Whether anything happens in prayer depends on what kind of god God is. If He created the universe, and gave everything a primeval push, and then retired beyond where we can get in contact with Him, prayer is a vain effort. But if He be "the God and Father of our Lord Jesus Christ," He is not like that. He is concerned for the creation He made, and concerned with the people in it who are meant to be His children. Most people in our day believe in some kind of God. There are very few atheists. Someone said an atheist is just a theologian with the jitters. But there are many who think God so great and so impersonal that He cannot possibly mean anything personal to us, and we cannot even say that He is a "personal" God.

Let me try to answer that, not from my own wisdom, but from that of the man who graduated at Princeton with the highest honors in all its history—*signe cum laude*—the late Dr. Henry Norris Russell, of the department of astronomy. One evening he had been giving us some head-splitting figures on the size of the universe. Talking with him afterwards, I said, "Dr. Russell, how is it possible that an infinite God can have time for us?" He replied (and I recall his exact words), "The trouble is that your infinite God is not infinite enough. If He is really infinite, He can dispatch the affairs of this universe in the twinkling of an eye, and then have all the time in the world for you." I have never forgotten it. He was a great scientist, and a great Christian. His word gave great lift to a young man seeking foundations for his faith!

Prayer not only depends on what kind of a god God is; it depends upon the pray-er, and the kind of prayer that is offered. Awhile ago I was called to talk with a late teenager in the hospital. She said to me, "I've been kind of sore with God lately." I said, "Why?" She said, "I have asked Him to do a lot of things, and He hasn't answered my prayers." Well, I suggested we think about this a little. A person who has been ignoring God for a long time gets in some kind of a jam; and then all of a sudden rushes to Him with some telegraphic orders about what He should do. What kind of chaos would result if God tried to answer all the little selfish prayers of all the little selfish people in the world? The deep question is: Is God our celestial office-boy, or are we His earthly servants? Is prayer a means of getting God to change His mind in our behalf, or is prayer seeking to find His mind and will? Our small children ask us for unreasonable and selfish things, and sometimes we give them to them because there seems no other way to express our love for them. God seems to me to do the same thing. But, as there comes a day when you can reason with a child about what to do about a request, so God looks for the day when He can reason with us. The childish "gimme-gimme" prayer begins to give way to the more mature prayer of, "Lord, what do You want me to do? What is Your will in this situation?"

This means we cannot separate prayer from the rest of life. Many of us do what that girl did: we live our lives as we please, and then when things get into a snarl, we ask God to get us out of it. Soon or late we must face the implications of prayer. And they are principally that we become more and more the kind of people who pray because we love God and His will. Prayer is not calling in the fire department; prayer is seeking to live so that the house does not get on fire. Prayer is not the "last resort," it is the first thought in every situation—or at least the second. Either we shall bring the rest of life more in line with God's whole will and plan, or else prayer will be like nothing so much as the crying of a spoiled child. In the last analysis, prayer implies conversion. For conversion is the decision to turn our wills over to the will of God; and unless this has been done once in a decisive way, we shall not repeat it again and again in prayer, which is just wherein prayer should primarily consist. Prayer is communion between two people that increasingly know each other. And one of these "people" is very decidedly a Senior Partner in the relationship. Do any of you check in at the office in the morning to see what the boss wants you to do that day? I think that is very nearly what our morning prayer ought to be.

Some weeks ago Bishop Pardue was having a Quiet Day for his clergy; and he quoted at secondhand from Emerson a threefold idea about prayer. The first is that we are praying at all times, we are never not praying; "prayer is the soul's sincere desire," and what we keep desiring with all our hearts is what we really pray for. Second, prayers are being answered all the time. What we long for without cessation increasingly becomes a fact. Strong desire draws out of life what it wants and thinks it needs. Third, we must therefore be careful what our true prayer is, the real desire of the soul. Our deepest motivation is our prayer. This is why the service of Holy Communion begins with a prayer to a God "unto whom all hearts are open, all desires known." This is why merely saying words is not praying, but deep desiring— maybe as we walk along the street intensifying our determination about something we want to do or to get—is our real prayer. Right in the midst of the most selfish prayer in the world, we may catch ourselves and ask God to forgive the wrong of it and lift it to something better. We can pray to pray in the right way.

Speaking of that, people are often in a quandary about how to pray in certain complex situations. A child is born that appears to be defective. Shall one pray for healing? Certainly—that seems best of all if it be in God's greater plan. If there should not be healing, should the child be taken home when one considers the effect upon other little children there; or should the child be placed where it can receive expert care? The most pressing thing is the anguish of the parents, asking how to pray aright. Surely one is meant to pray for the healing; and for guidance in the right care of the child, should the full healing not be granted; and for grace to accept all this in such a way that real good comes out of real tragedy. Inevitably the question arises whether this was "God's will." One recoils from this. How can God will a defective child? It looks more as if something had slipped in nature. But we must not say that God has nothing to do with such a situation. He can give comfort and strength to anguished people, a peace deeper than pain, a strength greater than shock. He will guide as to right decisions. He will help to bear what must be, intellectually considered, a mystery. One does not bring to such a situation a dumb and enforced resignation, but a desire to surrender the situation in all its mystery and tragedy to God, asking what His will is now, in and for the situation. The capacity to bear something that cannot be understood is one of the gifts God alone can give to us. Let us not so much look for the perfect attitude in such a situation, or even to say the perfect words. Let us pour out the anguish we feel, ask for strength and guidance, and leave it to God how He will minister to us.

Some people have a strange idea that it is right to pray about "spiritual" matters, and wrong to pray about "natural" or "secular" matters. They think its right to pray for more faith, or even more health, but never for more income even when they need it. Do you think all God is interested in is the Sunday "you," but not the Monday-to-Friday "you"? Do you think He is only interested in the money you put in the plate, but not the money you put in your pocket or your bank-account? I cannot find any real dividing line between the spiritual and the natural, the sacred and the secular. It seems to me that all of life is sacred in which God is included, and all life is secular from which He is excluded. Your job is as sacred as mine, if we both try to do them for God and with His help. Pray about whatever interests you. Pray about those things that threaten God as His rivals in your life — things like success and power. It isn't religion that interests God, I think, but life — all of it. He may change our present attitudes towards these natural interests, but I think whatever interests us interests Him. Dr. John W. Suter says, "What we ought to be praying about on Sundays are things that keep us awake nights between Sundays."

Nothing that concerns prayer is more important than getting straight on the matter of prayer and prospering events. I still hear many people who ought by now to know better say things like this: "Why did this terrible thing happen to her? She is such a wonderful Christian." Have you never considered the Cross of Christ? That happened to the Best this world ever saw when He was thirty-three and at the height of His usefulness and power. Christ on a Cross — and you asking why something dreadful should come to you or someone else that is trying to live a good life? There is no guarantee in Christianity against trouble: there is guarantee against defeat. But we must consider all this in connection with something St. Paul said, "All things work together for good to them that love God" (Rom. 8:28). When you have begun to put your trust in God, and turned you life and situation over to Him as fully as you can, and prayed about everything, and stopped trying to manage it yourself, you will discover just that—"all things work together for good." God takes some things out of our hands, and handles them better than we can. This concerns the ultimate best, not the immediate wish always. It will take faith to see and feel it sometimes. Everything depends on the depth of our commitment to God. It would not be true to say that when you pray you get everything you ask for; but it would be true to say that the more you pray, the better things go. God keeps you from self-centered worry, from licking the wounds of disappointment, from seeing life only as it converges on yourself.

This means that prayer is effective, not when we can point to this or that answer, but when the whole of life is more and more caught up on the fullness of God's will for us. Effective prayer is not measured by how much we manage to get out of God, but by how much of God we manage to let into daily living. Heightened energy, deepened faith, greater health of body and spirit, the conquest of moods, power to forgive people and accept their forgiveness of us—these are the things that result from prayer—not just getting what we think we need.

I do not believe that prayer ever changes God or His will of love; it cannot make Him more concerned than He was already without our prayers. It is not giving Him a new idea. Prayer links us up to God and may link others. Prayer may affect events, I believe it does; but it adds nothing whatever to God's wisdom and benevolence. It only makes us more receptive to the things He wants to give us. And the great shift-over from immature to mature prayer concerns the increasing desire to want what He wants, rather than to demand what we want.

This brings us to what should be the pattern prayer of all our praying—not as touching the words we use—the Lord's Prayer must forever be this—but as touching the deep attitudes out of which we pray. And this recalls Jesus' prayer in Gethsemane, as found in Mark 14 verse 36: "Father, all things are possible to thee; remove this cup from me; yet not what I will but what thou wilt." There may, I believe, have been considerable spaces between those three brief words. The first is an affirmation: "Father, all things are possible to thee." We affirm God's full power over all life, all events. We say, there is nothing that might not happen—we are in the hands of a good and powerful God! That puts prayer in its setting. Then comes the heart of the natural desire: "Remove this cup from me." He must have hated death, it was so inappropriate for Him. Life was His word. He recoiled from it. And He prayed honestly for what He desired, even if He knew it was not the final stage of His prayer. We must do the same: it is a form of honesty with God. And then comes the purified prayer, "Yet not what I will but what thou wilt." Death was not so bad as missing God's full purpose for Him which might only be fulfilled through the Cross. That was what He really wanted and really prayed for. It must be so with us. With whatever struggle (and we cannot but think it was a superhuman struggle for Him to turn from "remove this cup" to "yet not what I will but what thou wilt") it is this which brings us to the place of power in prayer. This does not mean sad resignation: this means willing and glad cooperation. This means prayer that may carry us to our own Calvary, but it means prayer with Resurrection wrapped in the dark folds of its struggle and mystery.

Lord, teach us to pray as You prayed in Gethsemane!

For additional information about Samuel Shoemaker:

Shoemaker, Helen Smith. *I Stand By the Door: The Life of Sam Shoemaker.* New York: Harper & Row, 1967.
Shoemaker, Samuel Moor. *Beginning Your Ministry.* New York: Harper & Row, 1963.
———. *Extraordinary Living for Ordinary Men.* Excerpts selected by his daughter, Helen Shoemaker Rea, and the staff of *Faith at Work.* Grand Rapids: Zondervan Publishing House, 1965.
———. *How You Can Help Other People.* New York: E. P. Dutton & Co., 1946.
———. *Twice-born Ministers.* New York: Fleming H. Revell Co., 1929.
———. *Young Man's View of the Ministry.* New York: Association Press, 1923.

For other sermons by Samuel Shoemaker:

. . . And Thy Neighbor: Sam Shoemaker Talks About Creative Living. Arranged by Cecile Cox Offill. Waco, Tex.: Word Books, 1967.
The Gospel According to You, and Other Sermons. New York: Fleming H. Revell Co., 1934.
Also: *Christ and This Crisis* (1943), *Confident Faith* (1932), *National Awakening* (1936).

LESLIE WEATHERHEAD

1893–

LESLIE WEATHERHEAD, photograph, courtesy of Leslie Weatherhead.

LESLIE DIXON WEATHERHEAD

1893	Born October 14 in London
1919	Served the English Methodist Church, Madras, India
1922	Served as a minister in Manchester
1925	Became pastor at Brunswick Methodist Church, Leeds
1936	Became pastor at the City Temple, London
1949	Delivered Lyman Beecher Lectures on Preaching, Yale University
1955	Elected president of the Methodist Conference
1960	Retired from active pastorate

"GOD'S PSYCHIATRIST" might be considered by many as an appropriate tag for Leslie D. Weatherhead. It is not entirely an accurate description of him; he is not a psychiatrist at all, but a Christian minister. Yet he gained world renown through his skillful relating of psychology and religion in his preaching, counseling, and pastoral responsibility.

LIFE AND TIMES

Leslie D. Weatherhead was born in London in 1893. His parents, of Scottish descent, were staunchly grounded in Reformed and Free Church tradition. His father served actively as a Presbyterian layman. He administered strict though not unkind discipline to his children.

Perhaps Weatherhead's mother influenced his life even more than his father did. She gave to her son the practical affection and individual attention which was later to characterize his own ministry to other persons. In his book *Jesus and Ourselves*, Weatherhead pays a tribute to his mother: "I am not in any doubt as to how my own Christian experience began. The altar before which I knelt first was my mother's knee. . . . Jesus to me then was all gentle, kind, loving, tender, sympathetic."[1] Weatherhead's home combined love, laughter, fun, religious experience; such an environment made him want to serve God and man in some special way. He determined to be a medical missionary. The cost of medical training, however, prevented him from entering medical school. But his concern for healing never left him. He bridged the gap between religion and medicine by uniting healing with the pastoral ministry.

During World War I he served as a second lieutenant. After the armistice was signed, he became a chaplain in Mesopotamia and Persia, the countries now called Iraq and Iran. In 1919 he became minister of the English Methodist Church in Madras, India. During Weatherhead's travels a Christian doctor in Mesopotamia aroused his interest in psychology as an aid to the Christian ministry; the doctor emphasized the good that chaplains were doing in practical psychotherapy.

Weatherhead married the daughter of a missionary and returned home to England. He worked intensely on his new interest, psychology. He gained valuable clinical experience and enrolled for studies in theology and in psychology. He associated himself with doctors and psychiatrists, as well as with theologians, in his classroom studies and various professional and practical organizations. He earned an M.A. degree from the University of Manchester and a Ph.D. degree from the University of London.

His early years in the ministry were stormy. Some in the Methodist church considered him unorthodox; they feared his efforts to unite psychology and religion. At that time the teachings of Freud were looked upon as threats to the Christian faith and to the Christian church. Psychiatrists were considered by some as representatives of the devil. It is no wonder that Weatherhead's revolutionary approach created concern among fellow ministers.

The first pastorate in which he put his beliefs into practice on a wide scale was at the New Brunswick Methodist Church in Leeds. The church prospered under his leadership. He established counseling centers and various liaisons with the medical and psychiatric community. In addition, he wrote books which gained wide readership; some of the most famous

---

1. Leslie D. Weatherhead, *Jesus and Ourselves* (New York: Abingdon Press, 1931), p. 262.

of his writings during this time at Leeds were *Psychology and Life, Psychology in Service of the Soul,* and *The Mastery of Sex through Psychology and Religion.*

In 1936 he became pastor at the City Temple in London, the church pastored by such famous preachers as Joseph Parker and Joseph Fort Newton. He served the church for more than two decades, retiring in 1960. His ministry was balanced. He stressed evangelism, education, altruism, and worship; but the aspect of his ministry for which he became famous was his stress on the relation of religion and psychology. This theme is by no means sounded in all of his sermons, yet in a sense the concept undergirds everything he has done.

He believes that man suffers from guilt, that he needs to recognize and confess his guilt, and that he longs for forgiveness, acceptance, love, and fellowship. Furthermore, Weatherhead stresses that healthy persons do not constantly turn in upon themselves, but turn out in caring for others.

If one ingredient of wholesome living has been stressed by Weatherhead more than any other, it is love. In his 1949 Lyman Beecher Lectures on Preaching at Yale he said:

> Neurosis or nervous breakdown is in ninety per cent or more cases caused by a sense of deprivation of love at some point in the emotional development of the patient. I said in "a sense" of deprivation of love, because often a person imagines that love is withheld when it is not intentionally withheld and may not be actually withheld, but if the patient thinks it is, it has the same effect on the personality.
>
> By love in these sentences I don't mean *philos* and I don't mean *eros;* I mean *agape.* I hope that sounds as impressive to you as it does to me! And I would define that as endless good will and appreciation. Now a little child coming into this world should ideally be surrounded by love in that sense; appreciation and good will, the attitude that makes his own self-respect blossom, the attitude that is said to spoil him, though when in doubt – this to all parents – when in doubt, spoil. The world is so hard to people – don't add to the hardness of the world, so when in doubt, spoil.[2]

---

2. Edgar DeWitt Jones, *The Royalty of the Pulpit* (New York: Harper & Bros., 1951), p. 297. Used by permission.

Weatherhead believes that of all the institutions in the world, the church can best offer persons what they need for wholeness. He insists that the Christian faith holds out to people those very things which modern psychology has proved to be essential for human well-being; in a sense, psychology has verified the Christian faith. But more important, for Weatherhead Christian psychology isolates those elements of Christian practice and doctrine most important for the welfare of human beings. Thus in his preaching, counseling, and general ministry he stresses guilt and confession, forgiveness and acceptance, love and fellowship, and the need for persons to serve others.

Another feature of Weatherhead's ministry and of the services at City Temple was intercessory prayer for the sick. He insisted that many persons experienced healing through intercessory prayer. He never indicated that intercessory prayer was a substitute for medicine, but rather saw it as an aid to medicine.

His approach to intercessory prayer was very specific. Never did he lead his people to pray in general for the sick. In fact, he refused to lead them in the type of bland prayers which merely requested that God might help a person to get better. In his Lyman Beecher Lectures he set forth his viewpoint on intercessory prayer:

> We had at the City Temple a young nurse of twenty who was lying in St. Bartholomew's Hospital very dangerously ill, unconscious, unable to take nourishment. We say to the congregation, if we have the permission of the relatives, "Now here is Nurse X. She is in such-and-such a ward. She is lying there ill. Will you pray for her in this way: Imagine that our Lord is moving up the ward. Now imagine that He is standing by her bedside. Now imagine that He is laying His hands upon her. Don't let your mind wander. Our Lord is now laying His hands upon her.
>
> Believe that at this moment her mind, her deep unconscious mind, is responding to Him; believe that your love and caring are making an atmosphere, a psychic atmosphere around Nurse X which gives the healing power of God a better chance. Now believe that at this moment she is beginning to recover. Don't let your mind wander. (You have to say that to people or else in a

few minutes their mind is off on something else.) Believe that you are doing imaginatively and by faith what you would do if our Lord were here in the flesh. You would take her into His presence. Now hold her there for a moment. Christ is there, she is there. We are providing the atmosphere in which He can work. Without that faith He could do no mighty work.[3]

Weatherhead rendered great service by pioneering in a dramatic way the relating of religion and psychology. But obviously there were those who for varying reasons vigorously opposed such tactics in prayer. Because of his emphasis on the positive aspects of life, to the seeming neglect of the negative, there were those who felt that his ministry was England's counterpart to that of Norman Vincent Peale in America.

Throughout his ministry Weatherhead had critics. He overcame much of the early criticism directed at him on the basis of supposed unorthodoxy. In 1955 he was elected president of the Methodist Conference. Yet some still considered him soft on the question of sin, overly sentimental, and neglectful of social issues. It is true that he emphasizes the personal more than the social. He stresses that men should turn out to others in ministry, but he has seldom stressed the need for men to grapple with the social evils which so malform human life.

As pastor, preacher, and psychologist Weatherhead blazed significant trails for the ministry. Perhaps one of his greatest services was pointing out often, forcefully, and simply, that love must be given a high priority in Christian ministry. He once said:

> Be relevant, be simple, and then I would say be loving. I think the most beautiful thing I ever heard said about a preacher was this. Somebody said: "Why is it that he has such power over people, and why do they come so far to hear him?" and the answer was this: "He puts his arms around the whole congregation and no one feels left out." . . . The great preachers have been great lovers. The great preachers have been the people who made simple, homely folk, such as you and me, feel that they were loved.[4]

---

3. Ibid., pp. 294–95.
4. Ibid., p. 290.

Preaching and Sermons

Leslie Weatherhead has been regarded primarily as a psychological preacher, but his distinction should be far wider. In a preface to a collection of sermons, *That Immortal Sea,* Weatherhead indicated his range of interest: "I have tried to choose, from the many sermons I am called upon to prepare, those which illustrate a wide variety: theological, expository, evangelistic, philosophical, psychological, and so on."[5] He added that he did preach topical sermons on occasion but that he never published them because they rapidly become dated.

Horton Davies referred to Weatherhead as "a preacher of the full-orbed Gospel who is both an apologist of great ability and a superb literary craftsman. Even if all his psychological sermons were to be eliminated, he would still command attention since his other sermons (which are the vast majority) are among the best examples of modern preaching."[6]

Many of Weatherhead's sermons show his indebtedness to the contributions of the psychology of religion, and among his most familiar themes are the effects of guilt, the restoring powers of love, the worthiness of human personality, the efficacy of the Christian community, and the values of intercessory prayer—although his sermons on prayer and the miracles sometimes seem more influenced by studies in extrasensory perception, or even spiritualism, than the Christian faith.

But he is also interested in the role of preaching in conversion; Weatherhead believes that "preaching aims at securing those conditions in which it [conversion] can happen." Even though conversion is the gift of God, the context for conversion must be the community of God gathered together in worship. Nevertheless, "it cannot be engineered by man in cold blood."[7] But the preacher is enabled by the power of the Holy Spirit to make real the transforming presence of Christ. Many of Weatherhead's sermons reveal his interest in the conversion of the individual to the Christian faith: sometimes as he describes the problems that could only be solved in Christ; sometimes as he preaches on theological subjects, such as the power of the risen

---

5. Leslie D. Weatherhead, *That Immortal Sea* (New York: Abingdon Press, 1953), p. 7.
6. Horton Davies, *Varieties of English Preaching* (London: SCM Press, 1963), p. 140. Used by permission.
7. Leslie D. Weatherhead, *Psychology, Religion and Healing* (New York: Abingdon Press, 1951), p. 465.

Christ or his love for humanity; sometimes as he examines critically the claims of a secular world, in apologetic sermons like "The Advantages of Atheism" and "Whose Voice Shall I Trust?"

Weatherhead's sermons are distinguished by their personal illustrations: an analysis of one group of sermons, *That Immortal Sea,* revealed thirty-one references to personal experience or the experiences of those known personally to the preacher.[8] Literary citations are frequent: *That Immortal Sea* contains thirty-seven separate references made to material from twenty-seven different authors. Tennyson, Browning, and Shakespeare are cited most frequently, but many other authors from the contemporary period are included. Macleod described his sermons as "masterpieces of the art of literary expression."[9]

Weatherhead is fond of anecdotes from history: one volume of sermons contains nineteen of them. The same volume reveals seventeen illustrations taken from foreign lands — primarily Palestine and India, because Weatherhead lived in both of those countries for a brief time. Occasionally he quoted from theologians, philosophers, and preachers.

Rather unexpectedly, Weatherhead's sermons are marked by a careful interest in New Testament exegesis. Many of his sermons reveal a consistent effort to interpret the New Testament from the Greek text. In his book on the parables, *In Quest of the Kingdom,* there are twenty-eight references to sixteen different biblical commentators. Weatherhead cannot be regarded preeminently as a great expositor of Scripture, but his sermons do reveal an honest study of the scriptural setting for his texts.

The language of his sermons is particularly fine. Weatherhead believes in being mentally honest and realistic, and he is impatient with theological clichés and glib affirmations. In the preface to *Over His Own Signature* he says that he spent two periods in a hospital confinement in 1956 testing "poetic imagery, beautiful language, traditional theology, religious words made familiar by centuries of repetition" by the standards of "sincerity and truth in realistic usefulness to the hearer." As a result of that study, Weatherhead's sermons began to reveal a new freshness, and occasionally even a radical departure from traditional ideas. Nevertheless, he never contented himself

---
8. Davies, p. 148.
9. Donald Macleod, "Review of *Key Next Door,*" *Princeton Seminary Bulletin,* September 1961, pp. 82–83.

with destructive criticism but set the direction of every sermon toward a positive reconstruction of Christian values.

Part of Weatherhead's success must be attributed to his own personality. He projected a friendly, pleasant look in the pulpit. He was skillful in his use of humor, and his speech was marked by homely analogies and colloquial English—even slang. Macleod described him as "a master of English conversational style, in a class by himself," and said that his flawless delivery made his sermons exciting.[10] His voice was finely modulated and appealing.

One young preacher who heard him deliver his Yale lectures described six qualities which distinguished Weatherhead's presentation at Yale, and which were responsible for the sensational reception he received:

(1) The obvious humility and sincerity of the man; (2) the delicious sense of humor with which he spoke, and the refreshing freedom he displayed . . . he was not afraid to display genuine emotion, nor to depart from the manuscript; (3) the fact perhaps that he did not actually use a manuscript, but spoke freely and vigorously from an outline only; (4) his liberal and effective use of vivid, apt and telling illustrative material; (5) his ability not merely to talk about great and effective preaching in an interesting and compelling fashion, but more importantly his ability to *demonstrate* it . . . ; (6) his ability to cut across the stereotyped method of developing ideas. . . . One of the transitional phrases that he often used . . . "I wonder if you will agree with me in this?" or "Is this, do you think, an overstatement of the matter?" or "Will you follow me now in this further consideration of the matter?"[11]

Weatherhead's sermons are clearly developed and give evidence of a solid outline. His patterns of development are greatly varied. Occasionally they take the form of a simple contrast, as in "Babel or Jerusalem?" or "This Haunted World." Three-point sermons are common, as in "Whose Voice Shall I Trust?"; the sermon "Master and Lord" uses four points to establish Christ's claim to divinity. In "The Advantages of Atheism" he lists twelve different flaws in the atheist's reasoning ("dents

---

10. Ibid., p. 82.
11. Jones, p. 302.

in the atheist's armour"); these flaws in turn form links in the chain of the Christian's defense. Frequently, as in this sermon, his development is not textual; but in every case he follows a coherent development for his thoughts.

Weatherhead uses strong and colorful imagery in his sermons. His description of nature occasionally approaches the grandeur of Wordsworth, one of his favorite poets:

> Above him the stars flashed like gems in the splendor of the velvet night, at its darkest just before the dawn. It was early on the Lord's day and he longed to worship with those he had been compelled to leave. He turned toward Jerusalem, far in the east, and behold the darkness was breaking. He had had his back to it, gazing mournfully at the black, hostile sea as yet unillumined by the dawn. But now the great splendor had begun. The color spread across the sky. Daffodil first with gleams of pale green and primrose light, then the faintest pastel pink rapidly deepening to crimson and gold.[12]

As beautiful as it is, this particular passage might have been better suited for the Victorian era of opulent description; Weatherhead is really at his best in smaller cameo descriptions.

His sermons are usually based upon central Christian themes which he sharply relates to the needs of his congregation. Occasionally he deals with Christian social relationships, as in his book *In Quest of the Kingdom;* but Weatherhead's printed sermons do not reveal much discussion of contemporary social problems.

Macleod criticized Weatherhead's message as often "more soothing than challenging," lacking in a rugged Christology, and said that his picture of Christ sometimes is nothing more than "a sweet companion of the road who is vital and knows all the answers."[13] Macleod also noted his "absence of timeliness":

> One is confronted with the customary moral problems of the individual and their possible solution . . . [but we] would never suspect that this preacher lived in a world where such great ideas and movements as existential-

---

12. Leslie D. Weatherhead, *Over His Own Signature* (New York: Abingdon Press, 1955), pp. 141-42.
13. Macleod, p. 82.

ism, the new orthodoxy, the liturgical revival, and so forth, were afoot.[14]

Davies reports that some regard Weatherhead's preaching as "mawkish and sentimental," an opinion which Davies definitely does not share, although he admits that "occasionally the pathos degenerates into bathos."[15] It is fair to say that Weatherhead emphasizes comfort more than challenge; perhaps he does not project enough sober strength for rugged times.[16] On the other hand Weatherhead might point to his sermons in *The Key Next Door* on the "harsh words of Jesus," with their insistence that Christ's friendship must eventually be transforming, no matter how loving and accepting it is in the beginning.

Davies's summation of Weatherhead's preaching is fair, and it gives an accurate evaluation of his work as a preacher:

> He has harnessed the theoretical and practical insights of modern psychology to the integrating imperatives and dynamics of the Christian Gospel.... Yet he has never limited himself to psychological preaching. He has been equally concerned with the culture and discipline of the spiritual life in public and private worship, with the doctrinal sermons that expound the nature of God in Christ and the Divine purpose for mankind, and, increasingly in recent years, with bringing the doubting or daunted intellect into the captivity of Christ.
>
> His preaching is marked by profound compassion, a comradely interest in all types and conditions of humanity, a sustained encouragement of all who are trying to live as disciples of Christ, and a variety of interest that have carried him triumphantly through a ministry in the "goldfish bowl" of London's City Temple for twenty-four difficult years in history.[17]

Those who have never read any of Weatherhead's sermons, but are only familiar with him through his writings, may be surprised at his homiletical ability. The sermons included in

---

14. Ibid., p. 83.
15. Davies, p. 160.
16. Macleod, p. 83.
17. Davies, p. 162.

this study are all readable, well illustrated, and thought-provoking. "The Bondage of the Free" employs illustrations from every direction, from Francis Thompson to football to Tagore — quite a span for anyone. In this sermon Weatherhead discusses such practical modern problems as the "new morality" and the experiences of young people who have left home for the first time. His language is free-swinging:

> I shan't have to heed my father or mother saying "Be sure you are in bed by ten, Bob" and "I wish you wouldn't smoke cigarettes in bed. You will have the house on fire one of these days." I shan't be told, "You shouldn't attend this or see that show." Now I can do what I like. I am free at last. One is only young once. One only has one life to live. To hell with all those stuffy old conventions of my parents. Youth has a right to freedom.[18]

The sermon "Thou Shalt Love Thine Enemy" was written during war time and is a particularly courageous treatment of that subject — in contradiction to the criticism of Weatherhead's sermons as "more soothing than challenging." The Jesus of *that* sermon is certainly not a "sweet companion of the road." The other sermons are just as good, each in its own distinctive way.

In characterizing the total contribution of Leslie Weatherhead, the student of preaching must be careful to avoid a one-sided view. Whatever weight is given to various criticisms of his preaching — and they have some merit — it would be unfortunate if any criticism were lifted from its context and made into a blanket judgment of his work. His preaching is not worthy of such caricaturing, and those who would be fair in their evaluation cannot be content with this kind of easy pigeonholing.

The temptation to oversimplify the facts is strong in every field of study, but such a superficial approach destroys factuality and fairness. The excellent work of many a preacher has been ignored by succeeding generations because his contribution was reduced by critics to only one of its qualities, and as a result looked unbalanced or even foolish. The sermons of Weatherhead deserve better treatment than that.

---

18. Leslie D. Weatherhead, *The Key Next Door, and Other City Temple Sermons* (London: Hodder & Stoughton, 1960), p. 191.

Sermons

THE SUNDAY *AFTER* EASTER

Mark 16:12

SOME of you may remember Dr. Montgomery Campbell who, when he was bishop of London, took part in the service, attended by the Queen Mother, at which we dedicated this new City Temple. He was a man of great learning but also of great wit, and he had a chaplain who, devoted as he was, retained his northern accent. When the bishop was to be enthroned as bishop of London, he arrived at the west door of St. Paul's Cathedral attended by his chaplain and sought entrance by knocking three times on the door with his pastoral crook, according to the prescribed ritual. Something had gone wrong and the great doors did not open. The bishop knocked again, and once more there was no response. Whereupon the bishop whispered to his chaplain, "We must 'ave come to the wrong 'ouse."

If you had gone to the Upper Room at Jerusalem on Good Friday night you would have found, we read, the door shut and barred "for fear of the Jews." Inside were eleven despairing, humiliated, trembling men. Life was over for them. Their world had crashed in upon them. They had hoped Jesus would have been the Messiah to redeem Israel. He had promised so much. His words had been so fair, his deeds so gracious. They had believed him. And now he was dead and they were stuck there, deluded, frightened fools, and in real danger from those who had put their Master to death.

But suppose you had gone back to the same house a week later. The windows would have been open, the doors unbarred. Through them you might well have heard laughter and the singing of joyous psalms, and, had you listened closely, you might have heard the plans of those who, within a few weeks of the murder of Christ, were preaching his gospel and declaring his risen glory. You might have said to a friend, "We must have come to the wrong house!" But no, something had happened. Almost everything in the world was different. It was *after Easter.*

Previously unpublished sermon, by kind permission of Leslie Weatherhead.

The purpose of the whole service this morning is to make us ask ourselves a question and honestly to answer it. "Am I living on the wrong side of Easter?" If a bereavement has reduced you to unquenchable sorrow; if you have given up all hope of solving your particular problem; if your frustration has made you feel that life has no meaning for you; if the world situation has made you believe that God is dead, or indifferent, or careless; if the problem of suffering has made you ascribe to cancer the power to silence Providence, then you are living on the wrong side of Easter. I want to tell you to lift up your hearts today. This is the Sunday *after* Easter.

"Did that resurrection really happen?" you ask. It was all a long time ago and the accounts vary.

I am not going to attempt, this morning, to answer the question "*How* did it happen?" I've attempted that in my book *The Christian Agnostic*, but in my mind I am certain that Christ survived death and proved his survival to his followers, appearing to them repeatedly in what the New Testament calls "another form" (Mark 16:12). And the fact that accounts differ seems to me to authenticate the story. Streamlined identity of story would make one suspicious of collusion. Livy and Polybus, the two chief historians of the day, give completely irreconcilable accounts of Hannibal's crossing the Alps, but no one doubts that he did so; and why in the world should eleven cowards, locked in a room for fear, go out and preach the Resurrection to those who could have made them look bigger fools than ever and ended the Christian religion? Why should they go and die for their belief if it were a cooked up story? But, you may ask, what has this story to do with us? What is the significance of the Resurrection today?

1. *First of all, it throws light on our survival.*

We must be careful here. The resurrection of Christ does not *prove* our survival. Because something happens to a unique Person is no reason for believing that it will happen to us. Last Sunday we sang, "Made like Him, like Him we rise." Orthodoxy would question whether we were made like him, but certainly we do not rise in three days and leave an empty tomb.

I believe intensely in our survival of death, but on other grounds: the nature of God, the nature of man, the words of Christ to the dying thief, and a mass of evidence from the proceedings of the Society for Psychical Research.

But the Resurrection throws *light* on the question of survival in that it shows that there does exist another plane of being. Jesus, after Easter, could enter and reenter it at will. He could appear and disappear, and his promise, "I go to prepare a place for you," is better evidence of our survival than is his own unique resurrection. The universe is not just a phenomenon of matter, nor does it end at the point at which our senses fail to register its impact.

2. *Secondly, the Resurrection throws light on the apparent power of evil in the world situation.*

Now this is the emphasis the early church made. The first sermons—as you will find if you read the book of Acts—were not about the teaching of Jesus, but about his death and especially his resurrection. And they endlessly quoted it to prove, not their own survival, but the fact that God was not defeated by all the cruelty and violence of Rome or the jealousy and hatred of the Jews. Evil no longer had the last word.

Now this seems to me to have a most relevant bearing on our life today as we look at the world situation.

We look out on a world full of evil. Single phrases can almost overwhelm us with their burden of evil and misery. Vietnam, Rhodesia, racialism—and we think if only LBJ would talk to Ho Chi Minh! (Someone has said his greeting would be, "Hi! Ho!") If only Ian Smith would talk to Harold Wilson or, better still, Alec Douglas-Home. If only Mr. Carmichael in America would stop talking about "black power."

Well, let us follow every way of reaching world peace, but let us get our perspective right. The early church was persecuted and threatened for centuries with the power of imperial Rome, but listen to Paul just before he was beheaded: "Have this mind in you which was also in Christ Jesus, for the divine nature was his from the first but he made himself nothing . . . he humbled himself and in obedience accepted even death—death on a cross. Therefore God raised him to the heights and bestowed upon him the name above all names, that at the name of Jesus every knee should bow and every tongue confess 'Jesus Christ is Lord' to the glory of God the Father" (Phil. 2:5-10). Paul couldn't have said that before Easter. But he could say it after Easter. He knew then that evil never has the last word.

3. *The Resurrection throws light on the power of evil on our private lives.*

Few of us have escaped suffering, or sharing the suffering of others, disaster of one kind or another.

Before the first Easter this was looked upon as a punishment of God, and men still ask, "What have I done to deserve this?" The only answer as a rule is nothing except to belong to the human family and have to share its burden of ignorance, folly and sin—thalidomide, for instance—just as we share in its undeserved benefits—penicillin, for instance.

But whatever you do, don't live on the wrong side of Easter. Some people are even still living in the Old Testament, where religion was an insurance against all calamity. "A thousand shall fall at thy side and ten thousand at thy right hand but it shall not come nigh unto thee." Nonsense! You are just as likely to get cancer or arthritis or a coronary thrombosis if you are a Christian as if you are a pagan.

Christ never offered his followers immunity from disaster. He rather implied that they would not only have to face what others face, but face more for his sake. "Men will persecute you and chase you from city to city. Men will put you to death and think they do God service."

But he added, "He that endureth to the end shall be saved." He said he would be with us in all our sorrows and that if we plodded on in the Easter faith we should find the way home.

If God could weave a tragedy like the brutal murder of Christ's crucifixion into a plan called the redemption of the world by our Lord Jesus Christ—so that the Cross, once a symbol of shame like a hangman's rope, is now the symbol of triumph—he can take your cross and make that a triumph too. We must learn this lesson, for we live *after Easter*.

Mind you, we may have to wait for three decades or more, not just three days. "Be prepared to wait, my soul." A father opened the playroom door and beheld a war! There were two little boys and only one banana. (This is not part of my autobiography!) The father did not say, "What's the good of planning *your* future? What's the good of thinking of Cambridge or Oxford or a career? You can't even agree about a banana!" No! He waited. He had a plan greater than the boys could imagine.

But "eye hath not seen nor ear heard nor hath it entered into the heart of man to conceive the things God hath prepared for them that love him"—and for them that now hate him because they can't see far enough ahead. So, if you are living *after* Easter you will realise this most important truth. The *measure* of calamity, public or private, must be the *measure* of our faith.

One last word. I thank God for the saints. They are the great assets of the Church. I don't think of St. Augustine, St. Anselm, St. Thomas Aquinas. I think of saints I knew here. You see, I had the privilege of being minister here during the whole of the last war. I think of a little family, a man and his wife in business together, with an only son. In one week through the war they lost business and home, and their boy was killed. But like the Cross behind me their cross was lit up by their faith. They lived *after Easter*.

Have you ever said, "I'd give my right hand if . . ."? One girl-member had her hand blown off when she was setting off to save others from a burning house. Another, a nurse, came home after night duty to find her home a pile of rubble and all her loved ones dead beneath it. So I could go on. I don't remember one who gave up the faith that lives on this side of Easter.

When I look at the Cross, I watch him in imagination hanging there, his body tormented, his cause defeated, his soul deserted. If to those who gathered at the foot of the Cross he had cried from his anguish and said, "I was deluded. I was wrong. I hoped in God and trusted him, but he does not exist, or if he does, he is callous, careless and cruel.

I am sorry I asked you to follow me. Forgive me. I was mistaken. Go to your homes and forget all I have told you about God. There is nothing in it. . . ." Yes, if he had spoken thus we should have seen logic in the situation. For how can God be love if he lets down One who calls himself a Son and seeks only the Father's will?

Yet, as we listen we hear a low voice coming down through the years, with unspeakable assurance and without a quavering note of doubt: "Father, into thy hands I trust my spirit."

So on this Sunday after Easter, lift up your hearts. Take a look at Jesus risen and triumphant. Take a look at the saints and you will find that:

> And when the fight is fierce, the warfare long,
> Steals on the ear the distant triumph song,
> And hearts are brave again, and arms are strong.
> Allelulia!
> —WILLIAM WALSHAM HOW

BELIEVING

"Believe on the Lord Jesus Christ, and thou shalt be saved" (Acts 16:31).

WHAT a host of meanings is attached to the words "believe" and "believing"! "I believe in fresh air." "I believe the earth goes round the sun." "I believe the creeds." "I believe in God the Father." "I believe you are in love." "I believe in a vegetable diet." Sometimes the head speaks, sometimes the heart, sometimes the stomach! But they all use the same word, "believe."

When you think of the setting which was read to us in the lesson (Acts 16:16–32) what a strange thing for Paul to say to a jailer! The jailer had done his work. He had put Paul and Silas in prison. He had secured their feet in the stocks, locked all the doors and gone to his bed. Then at midnight there came an earthquake, and all his prisoners

---

Previously unpublished sermon, by kind permission of Leslie Weatherhead.

were free. Under Roman law his own life would be forfeit. He drew his sword to kill himself until Paul shouted that no one had run away. Then, surely thinking only of his own physical safety, he said, "What must I do to be saved?" It is incredible that it was a theological question. He *must* have meant, "How can I escape being put to death?"

A thousand questions rise to the mind. Did all the other prisoners go quietly back to their cells while the jailer discoursed with Paul about salvation? Surely what *must* have happened was that the jailer locked up the others and then took Paul and Silas to his own quarters where – we are told – the jailer's household had gathered. Then Paul twisted the jailer's question from its reference to physical safety to a far more important matter and gave his famous answer: "Believe on (or *in*) the Lord Jesus, and you will be saved, you and your household." Now here is a matter worthy of our meditation.

First, let us note the difference between the expressions "believe" and "believe *in*"; the difference between believing things about a person and believing *in* a person; the difference between agreeing with what a person says or does and believing in a person's integrity and character. I have one friend who is outstanding because I hardly agree with him about anything – theology, politics or literature – and yet I believe *in* him intensely. I don't believe what he says, but I believe *in* him. In a word, I trust him.

Now turn to the New English Bible and you find that our text supports this view. It reads, "Put your trust in the Lord Jesus, and you will be saved."

So, you see, we are delivered from the demand that we must get our theology right *first* before we can find our way in religion. I am greatly comforted to think that Pope John and Billy Graham and Albert Schweitzer and General Booth all deserve the label "Christian," yet no creed of any length could be devised to which they would all agree. But they all believe *in* the Lord Jesus. They all put their trust in him.

And what is meant by the word "saved"? Let us once and for all rid our minds of the idea that it means deliverance from some endless hell into which are plunged all those who do not "believe."

I won't go now into the long discussion of what Jesus meant by the word "hell" and the way the Church has distorted the meaning and filled it with terror. I will only say that the love of God and the compassionate understanding of the Saviour make me certain that no one is cast into torture because he could not make his mind accept certain theological propositions; because he did not believe what he was told.

Never once in all his ministry did Jesus demand such acceptance from those who would be his followers. It was a new way of life that he offered them. "Follow me." "Come into my fellowship." And men found there that loving God and loving one another were the two requirements. "Ye are my friends," said Jesus, "if ye have love one for another"; and I would define a Christian as one who loves Christ and seeks to meet every demand that life makes, in Christ's spirit.

Bernard Bosanquet, the philosopher (1848–1923), gives me a clue to what *I* mean by "saved." He says, "And now we are saved absolutely, we need not say from what, *we are at home in the universe,* and in principle and in the main, feeble and timid creatures as we are, there is nothing anywhere, within the world or without it, that can make us afraid." So we are saved from despair, from terror, from self-concern, from being finally defeated by anything that can happen.

This, then, is my message for you this morning: "Believe in the Lord Jesus, and thou shalt be saved," or rather, *"Put your hand trustfully in the hand of Christ and, whatever happens, you will be quite safe."*

One recalls words which King George VI used over the wireless in a dark hour of our nation's history. "I said to the man who stood at the gate of the year, 'Give me a light that I may tread safely into the unknown.' And he replied, 'Go out into the darkness and put thy hand into the hand of God. That shall be to thee better than light and safer than a known way.'"

I feel here that I must tell you about my own wife. In any case, I wanted to thank you for your prayers. They helped us all. A few days before I preached to you last, she and I faced a specialist who had studied our doctor's reports, x-rays, and a report from a pathological laboratory. My wife said to him, "It's cancer, isn't it?" "Yes," he said, "it means an immediate operation." But I was so proud of her. Not one tear, or whine, or whimper! She never asked what I am so often asked, "Why should this happen to me?" "We have done all *we* could," she said. "The rest is in God's hands."

Men and women, *that* is believing. Putting your hand in God's and going forward bravely knowing you are *safe* whatever happens. "They shall never perish," he said, "and no one shall snatch them out of my hand." "Believe in the Lord Jesus Christ and thou shalt feel safe in God's universe whatever happens to you." That is believing. That is far, far more important than believing in the Virgin Birth, or the Trinity, or the Athanasian Creed. The difference between that courageous faith and getting your theological orthodoxy correct is the difference between the snow-clad Alps and a mucky little molehill in your back garden.

But mind that believing, however courageous, doesn't mean doing nothing yourself. Someone wrote to us and told us not to go in for surgery but just to have faith. This doesn't seem sound to me. *Believing in a surgeon is part of my belief in God.* He is as definitely at work in a surgeon's skill—whatever the surgeon believes—as he is in a saint's prayers. One must turn, in all situations of calamity, to the *relevant* way of cooperating with God. In some situations it might be prayer alone, or faith, or suggestion, or psychiatry, or dieting, or massage or medicine. None is a cure-all. All are of God, and trusting the skilled help of those who have studied in those areas of therapy is an expression of our faith in God.

We talk of man's discoveries and we talk of a divine revelation. *But they are the same thing.* Man can only discover what God reveals, and God will not reveal anything until man uses all *his* resources and is in sight of using them wisely. If God had revealed nuclear energy a hundred years ago, man would have blown up the whole planet or else gone mad with terror at his own discovery. Man has only been allowed to discover facts about the universe when he has become capable of handling the situations which the discovery involves. In a sense, the whole universe has been made safe.

Paul sums it up in his famous sentence: "I am *convinced* that there is nothing in death or life, in the realm of spirits or superhuman powers, in the world as it is or the world as it shall be, in the forces of the universe, in heights or depths—nothing in all creation that can separate us from the love of God in Christ Jesus our Lord" (Rom. 8:38–39, NEB). Believe in the Lord Jesus and thou shalt be saved. Put your hand trustfully in Christ's and you will be safe, for nothing in the whole universe can hurt you or finally defeat God's purpose.

You will be able to say about cancer, about bereavement, about calamity, about *anything*, what Rupert Brooke said about war:

> War knows no power. Safe shall be my going,
> Secretly armed against all death's endeavour;
> Safe though all safety's lost; safe where men fall;
> And if these poor limbs die, safest of all.

FOLLOW THE DIRECTIONS

John 14:6

IN an American journal called *The Christian Century* (5 January 1966) an editor tells of receiving a small "assemble it yourself" instrument by post. After spending an hour of frustration in trying to

---

Previously unpublished sermon, by kind permission of Leslie Weatherhead.

put the pieces together, he discovered in the box a message from the manufacturer. Printed on a neat, white card were the words, "If all else fails, follow the directions."

That seems to me a parable very relevant to modern life and especially to modern youth, already described by one historian as "the lost generation." Puzzled, bewildered, confused, not knowing the way to worthwhile living.

Let us look, then, at this vexed question of following directions. Whose are to be followed? Men once took their directions from the Bible—even crudely opening it at random and believing that God would guide their finger. There was once a thing called parental guidance, but now the gulf between the generations is generally too wide. The attitude of an adult to youth, "This is what you ought to do," or "I'm telling you," does not any longer count for much.

We must accept this as a fact and not just wish it were not so. Perhaps it never was as true as we imagine, for I think I am right in saying that the oldest inscription in human possession, excavated from the ruins of ancient Babylon, when it was with great difficulty deciphered, ran thus: "Alas, alas, things are not what they were; children no longer obey their parents."

Be that as it may, I am sure it is far better *not* to pontificate with advice. If one is asked to help another with his problem, it is better to listen, to help the questioner to see the whole situation straightly, as one can see it who is not emotionally involved, and then to say, "What do *you* think is the best way through this difficulty?" The decision then is his, not yours, and his has the greater authority in most personal problems. It is better for the questioner to say, "I now see what to do," than to say, "I will do what you tell me, or what you think best."

But I think this attitude can be carried too far and can leave a person unhelped. From the lips of a marriage guidance counsellor himself, I heard this true story. He had talked aloud to his family, including his little eight-year-old daughter, about his counselling and about the danger of laying down the law. One Saturday afternoon he was cutting the hedge in his garden when a man got off his bicycle and spoke to him. The daughter of the counsellor, too far away in the garden to hear the conversation, said later, "Daddy, what did he want?" "Oh," said her father, "he wanted to know the way to Windsor." "Oh," said the daughter, "I suppose *you* said, 'Well, what do you think?'" The sequel to this story is even more intriguing. A few days later the daughter said, "Daddy, I've been counselling my school friend, Mary." "Oh, how did you do that?" said her father. "Well," said the girl, "I told Mary to tell me her story leaving nothing out." "Yes," said her father, approvingly, "and when she had finished what did you say?" "Oh," said his daughter, "I just said, 'Hmm!'"

I'm not just telling you that story to amuse you. The recent report on sex and morality is as noncommital. It says "Hmm." I think the *approach* of the report is excellent. I'm glad it doesn't launch out into too detailed a direction and I'm very glad it is not condemnatory and disapproving, but youth *could* have been given several reasons why sexual intercourse outside marriage is wrong, and I feel that those who buy the report may feel like someone who goes up to a signpost and finds it glistening with new paint, a great improvement on the old post which it replaces, but who finds no directions printed on it at all.

Some time ago, in a TV programme you may have seen, a questioner asked the plain question, "Is fornication sin?" To which an Anglican priest answered, "It depends what you mean by fornication and what you mean by sin." He might as well have said, "Hmm!" A lady asked, on the same programme, "What advice would you give to a young girl going up to the university for the first time?" The answer given was, "I should tell her she must find her own way." "Hmm!" again.

I believe there is a place for rules. Clearly those who arrange games believe in rules. "Thou shalt not," in a rugby scrum, "bite the ear of thine opposite number." Surely it is not feeble to suggest to young people who prepare to play the game of life that there are rules. And those rules are not the creation of a committee of both sexes who sit down one fine afternoon and, for lack of anything else on the agenda, say to themselves, "How can we stop young people having what we were forbidden?" There *are* some conventions which *are* outmoded, but many of them are rules for playing the game of life hammered out by people who, through many mistakes and failures, many disappointments and disillusions, have found how the game can best be played for the happiness of all concerned.

Even Dr. Alex Comfort, whom no one would regard as narrow-minded or religious, stated two rules for sex behaviour. (1) Thou shalt not risk bringing into the world an unwanted baby (that rule has value since no contraceptive is 100 percent safe), and (2) thou shalt not exploit another person for thine own selfish pleasure. I could add others on rather a higher plane since premarital intimacy makes nonsense of the marriage service, but my point is that even a pagan adviser like Dr. Comfort gives directions.

For five thousand years the Ten Commandments, which Moses borrowed from an earlier Babylonian philosophy, have stood as directions by which life can successfully be lived. Moses came down from the mountain and said to the people in other words: "Follow the directions." Isn't it a very serious thing to remove all the signposts and then blame youth for getting lost? Members of my generation were no better in their secret thoughts and phantasies than the present boys and girls, but there were railings at the side of the road and signposts at the crossroads, and though we often ignored them, *we knew that they were there.*

What then can we do? We can't pontificate. We cannot endlessly condemn. We can't quote the Bible. We can't wring our hands and moan that youth is going to the devil. Vast numbers of young people have splendid ideals and are doing some grand jobs in the world. If we label behaviour "wrong" we must know why it is wrong. We must show that anything is wrong if its widespread adoption would wreck society. If some modern attitudes were widely adopted no home would be secure and no wife happy. We must try to show—even by the disclosure of our own failures—that so many roads along which men and women are rushing today don't end in happiness and satisfaction and contentment and peace of mind. They end in remorse, in conscience distress, in unhappiness. I can see now in imagination a girl sobbing in my study and saying over and over again, "But he *promised* to marry me. He *promised*."

The last arrest of a train robber was not much of a triumph for the police. The man had changed his name and settled down on the south coast with his wife and little boy. He had plenty of money. Why couldn't he enjoy himself? When he was arrested he said, "I was going to give myself up. I couldn't stick it any longer." Couldn't stick what? He couldn't live with himself.

Are we not then to give directions? And is there not urgency in the matter? If I am in a nursery where children are playing at bedtime and I see a child in a flimsy nightdress walking backwards towards an unguarded electric fire, I don't say, "Excuse me, I hate to interrupt your game but there is a fire behind you." I shout, "Look out! Mind the fire!" Love and concern prompt urgency.

We lean over backwards to be "with it," not to be thought "square," to be thought broad-minded and so on, but Jesus gave pretty straight directions to people. "Sell all you have and come and follow me!"—not to be interpreted as a direction to all, but certainly to that one. "Leave the dead to bury their dead and come and follow me." Don't try to get right with God before you are right with men. Leave your gift on the altar steps and put things right with your brother and then come and offer your gift. One could think of dozens of occasions when Christ gave directions.

We haven't his authority to talk like that, but we can, within the loving fellowship, sit down and show that life will only work out happily in one way and that is his way. He made it like that.

And if we *can* get in a word on God's behalf we can help even more. Jesus told people to keep the commandments, and then he crowned them with his own emphasis. "Which is the greatest commandment?" they asked him. "Thou shalt love the Lord thy God with all thy heart and soul and strength and mind, and thou shalt love thy neighbor as thyself."

Margaret Knight, the atheist lecturer in psychology in a Scottish university, once claimed that humanists did just as much good in the world as Christians. I know that many of them are full of good works, though I know of no humanist who, for example, has sacrificed a career and gone as a missionary to, say, tropical Africa or India, to learn the language and offer a better way of life. However, when I had an hour with her in my own home, knowing that she was happily married, I asked her whether she would find it easier to do a thing for a beloved husband, or because a humanist ethical code regarded it as socially valuable. You can guess the answer. If I remember rightly she said, "I would do anything for my husband."

A love-relationship releases power to do, and to dare, and to die. "Love God and do what you like," was St. Augustine's direction; better translated, "Love God, and *then*, what you like, do."

It is agreed that we are living in a confused and bewildered age. Thousands of splendid young people are worried. Their generation has been called by a modern historian "the lost generation."

Well, thousands of people throughout the ages and right across the world have tried to follow Christ's way and have found peace of mind and a meaning in life. May I suggest that half an hour spent quietly alone with him, imaginatively behaving as though he were physically present with you, might give you the direction you seek? He said, "I am the way." Try it! A *way*, not the end of the road, but the end of a search for one, for a road that brings you out at last to worthwhile living, daily joy and inward peace. You won't feel so *lost*. For no one is lost who knows the way home. Just follow the directions.

SUPPOSING YOU MET JESUS

Luke 24:33

RELIGION, by the very meaning of the word, implies a bond. The second half of the word comes from the same Latin root, *ligare* 'to bind,' as our word *ligament*, the bond of fibrous tissue that holds the bones together or keeps an organ in its place.

The Christian religion, then, implies our link with Christ, that which binds us to him in a love-relationship.

Now such a love-relationship can hardly be maintained with a dead person who lived nearly two thousand years ago and now has passed

---

Previously unpublished sermon, by kind permission of Leslie Weatherhead.

entirely beyond all human contact. However difficult it may be for the modern to understand *how* the Resurrection took place, I am certain that Christ survived his death, proved his survival to his followers, and is still available to those who seek him.

Let us remember that all the earliest sermons in the church—those recorded in the book of Acts, for instance—were about the Resurrection. They were not expositions of his teaching. Nothing less would have turned runaways into missionaries overnight. If Jesus' death had been the end of him, it would have been the end of his religion. His friends might have venerated a tomb. His enemies would have exploded the "myth" of Resurrection if it had been possible to disprove it. The glorious gospel, "Jesus Christ is alive," was preached within six weeks of the Crucifixion in the very area where his death had taken place. Scores of people could have refuted the Resurrection if it had not taken place. Let us hold on to that fundamental fact, Jesus Christ is *alive*!

Let us then admit how hard it is to realise this fact. My feelings are often put into words when the children sing:

> I think, when I read that sweet story of old,
>   When Jesus was here among men,
> How He called little children as lambs to His fold,
>   I should like to have been with them then;
> I wish that His hands had been placed on my head,
>   That His arm had been thrown around me,
> And that I might have seen His kind look when He said,
>   "Let the little ones come unto Me."

If only we could have been in Galilee and listened and looked! How lucky were Peter and James and John! His friendship changed their lives! We feel it would change ours if we could be with him like that for a week!

Well, let's imagine it! Some of you have been to Palestine and you will remember the hills that slope down to the lovely lake of Galilee. Just imagine you are walking alone on those hills and you meet him. Imagine that you sit down together in the bracken and the heather, and with no one in sight and no sound but the birds and the bees and the light wind in the bracken, you talk together. Just you and Jesus. Just Jesus and you. What would happen?

1. Would a terrifying sense of sin descend upon you? Would you feel like Peter when he said, "Depart from me, for I am a sinful man, O Lord"? Jesus didn't depart. Peter didn't really want him to. Nor would you!

You know, Jesus said very little about sin. Judging by the words used in the New Testament, Jesus used the noun for sin on six occasions and the verb only three. Yet the noun and verb are used by

Paul ninety-one times! Jesus condemned hypocrites and people who made others suffer; especially those who made children suffer, and he did it unsparingly, but I am sure he would not drag your sins out of you and condemn them. Even if you started to relate them and confess them I think he would say, "Yes, I know, but now we've met things will be different." He wouldn't pronounce absolution but you would *know* you were forgiven and you would hate, at once, the things he hated and the things that, however desirable in low moments, robbed you of inward peace, that most precious of all his gifts. For ever after, if you wanted to know whether a thing was right or wrong, you would only have to recall the time you met Jesus, and ask yourself what he would think.

2. What else would it mean to meet Jesus? I am sure it would mean that you would want to put right anything wrong in your relationship with others. We can't be right with God if we are unwilling to be right with others.

Nothing is clearer in Christ's teaching than this. When he taught men to pray he included this: "Forgive us our trespasses, *as we forgive them that trespass against us.*"

And again, "If thou art bringing thy gift to the altar and there rememberest that thy brother hath aught against thee, go thy way. Leave thou thy gift before the altar. *First* be reconciled with thy brother and then come and offer thy gift."

And again, "If ye forgive not men their trespasses neither will my Father in heaven forgive yours."

I am sure if you met Jesus, one of the first things you would proceed to do afterwards would be to make it up with *anyone* with whom you had quarrelled, yes, even if you were sure you were in the right and they were wrong.

So, write that letter tonight, won't you? Offer to talk things over. Try to put things right. Be willing to swallow pride — even if you are sneered at, even if someone says, "I thought you'd climb down one day."

Believe me, an otherwise unattainable peace will flood your whole being when, for God's sake, you try to put things right with man.

3. Supposing you met Jesus, what else would happen? You would believe in yourself because Christ would believe in you. He would "see through you," no doubt. But we use those words as though they only meant seeing what is unworthy or despicable. He sees you at this moment as the man or woman you are capable of becoming. He sees the lonely path you have trodden, the battles you have fought, the conflicts you have faced.

When Michelangelo saw, in a builder's yard, a lump of marble, stained, misshapen, unattractive, cast aside, he said to the builder, "Take it to my studio. There is an angel imprisoned in that marble and I can set it free!" That is how Christ feels about you.

That is not just sentimental eyewash. Go to the records. See how he did react to people.

Men despised a woman because she was a prostitute. Jesus doesn't pretend she's an angel. He says, "Her sins, *which are many,* are forgiven for she loved much." No one is spiritually dead who can love, for love is of God. There was an angel imprisoned in Mary of Magdala and he set it free.

A woman was taken in adultery and was being tormented by the so-called righteous. He doesn't pretend she isn't a sinner, because he says, "Sin no more," but he says, "I don't condemn you." Guilt and shame and the crushing disapproval of men fall away. An angel is released. Her self-respect is given back.

So we could go on. Take a brief look at Zacchaeus, the dirty little profiteer, who extorted money from his own countrymen and paid it to Rome and took a big rake-off himself. But he meets Jesus. What happens? He immediately wants to put things right with others: "If I have defrauded any, I will pay him back fourfold." And beside this, his belief in himself is given back to him. Jesus *wants* to have supper with him. Jesus calls him, *him,* the outcaste, by what was to him the highest title, the loveliest label he could covet, "a son of Abraham."

There isn't time to quote further. You must read the record and you will meet Jesus. Don't be afraid. Even with a dying criminal he made a love-relationship. What did that criminal feel when Jesus said, "Today you will be with me in paradise"? Jesus Christ, the Son of God, went through the gates of death, if one may so put it, with his arm round the shoulders of a thief.

4. Another point I want to make is that if you met Jesus, you would go away to do his will; not to emphasise creeds, doctrines, liturgies, ceremonies, but to spread His loving spirit in the world.

That doesn't mean giving up what you are doing unless it is evil. It means doing the same job in a different spirit for a different Master.

No job is of itself secular. It is secular or sacred according to the way we do it and the One to whom we offer it. Christ was as much the Son of God when he made yokes as when he preached sermons. Indeed, before he had preached at all the Voice said, "This is my Son, my beloved, in whom I am well pleased." A preacher can make God and religion the means and himself the end, and his pulpit can be a platform on which he struts his pitiful ego hoping to win the praise of men. On the other hand, the humblest cobbler who puts in good leather where the cheat puts cardboard, can be the means God uses to answer the prayers of His people for health in wet weather. A certain epitaph runs, "Here lies the body of Martin Johnson who cobbled shoes to the glory of God in this village for forty years." At the end of the journey the important thing will not be what we've done. That is largely a matter of opportunity. It will be what all our doing has made us.

5. Finally, if you met Jesus you would go away with a new sense of

inward security because you would feel you belonged. Re*lig*ion: you would be bound to him who loves and cares, with a bond that naught could sever.

In a world in torment how badly we need to feel that anchor. Suicide, nervous breakdown, immorality, drug addiction all are on the increase — all of them attempts to escape from an apparently meaningless life, overshadowed by a nuclear bomb which could end all in a horrible death.

One *longs* to make men feel that they *belong* to God. "They are mine," he said, "and they shall never perish and no one shall snatch them out of my hand." Life is not meaningless; God is trying to work out a purpose and plan in each one of us. We are in the hands of a loving, undefeatable omnipotence, and if daily we try to do God's will as we perceive it we shall find mental peace. "In his will," said Dante, "is our peace."

I shall never forget a friend of mine, whose father was a very great man, telling me how, as a little boy, he so missed his daddy when public engagements took the great man away. One night, when his father was expected home, the lad wanted to stay up to greet him, but he had been rather naughty and was sent to bed. He awakened between ten and eleven and heard his father's voice, got up, dressed, and came down. He simply couldn't keep away, and yet he half feared a rebuke, for his act was one of disobedience. But his father took him into his arms and held him very close, and said, "My own little child." My friend says that he can remember the delicious sense of belonging to his father.

Supposing you met Jesus! You still can! He is here. He is anywhere where you will be quiet, and look, and listen. He will forgive. He will help you put relationships right. He will make you believe in yourself. You would find peace within his will and you would know that delicious, inward security which comes of knowing that you are *loved*. You can indeed go out singing:

> I am His, and He is mine,
> For ever and for ever.

WHERE *IS* THIS RISEN CHRIST?

"Oh that I knew where I might find him" (Job 23:3).
"She . . . knew not that it was Jesus" (John 20:14).

In those two passages separated in time by half a millennium we hear expressed both man's age-old quest for God, and the inability to recognise him when he *is* present.

In this sermon I want to make two assumptions.

1. The first is that the essential personality of Christ survived death and was able to convince his disciples, through their senses, of that survival.

I'm not going to take our time in offering you theories of the Resurrection, of what happened to his physical body and so on, however interesting. I've done that in my last book, *The Christian Agnostic*, which you can get on the bookstall.

Suffice it to say that if the Crucifixion had been the end of Christ it would have been the end of his religion. His followers, already in hiding, would have dispersed, and I doubt whether even his teaching would have survived.

To my mind, in a way we do not *yet* understand, his physical body dematerialised, and he manifested his presence "in another form" — as the gospel says (Mark 16:12) — but in a form which convinced his friends, who emerged from the hiding place to which terror had driven them, and preached about his risen power in the very place where he had been put to death.

2. The second assumption I want to make is that *in experience* — and let us underline those two words — there is no difference between the presence of God and that of Christ and that of the Holy Spirit. One man says he feels that God was near him. Another says he had an experience of the Risen Christ and the third says he felt possessed by the Holy Spirit. But the nature of each experience is the same. There is no qualitative difference.

So let us say that what we are seeking is an experience of the presence and concern of a loving Divine Being; and this experience we may call an experience of the Risen Christ, or of God, or of the Spirit as we like. In experience they are one.

Now many people say, "I have never had any experience of God. I have never seen a vision or heard a voice or known anything outside the ordinary." I want to do three things this morning. First, I want to prove them wrong. Second, I want to help them to recognise the impact of God upon them. And third, I want us all to have our experience of him deepened. We long for him, but so often when he is near we

---

Previously unpublished sermon, by kind permission of Leslie Weatherhead.

let an experience go unclaimed. We are like Mary, who "knew not that it was Jesus."

I claim that whenever we respond to beauty or truth or goodness we have an experience with the Divine Being whom some call God and some the Risen Christ and some the Holy Spirit.

Since Christ is the only divine being we can understand; since he is—as I believe—the Saviour of our world; since he is dedicated to it, as his willingness to die for love of it was exhibited at Calvary, I feel it is not far-fetched to call any experience of beauty or truth or goodness an experience of Christ. He was an incarnation of God. He is God's word to us. He alone is God's contact with us.

> God may have other Words for other worlds,
> But for this world, the Word of God is Christ.

1. Think of the strange impact beauty has upon us. For myself, mountains—of all Nature's loveliness—speak most eloquently. Yet what are they? Heaps of earth and stones. Why is it, especially if the sky is radiant behind them with dawnlight or sunset splendour, that they have this strange effect upon me? Why can heaps of earth and rock become the means whereby I have an experience of what I can only call the Divine? Not an experience of the man Jesus who lived in Palestine, *but an experience of that indwelling power that made Jesus the Christ of God;* the power that was expressed in the Risen Christ, whatever may have happened to his body.

Similarly with every form of beauty. I love to walk by the sea when the night is quiet and the moon is full, but why should a sheet of water lit up by the reflected light from our nearest planet do something to me, affect my whole nature, calm my spirit, make me want to worship? What *is* this presence that disturbs us all with "the joy of elevated thoughts"? And why "elevated"? Why do all our hearts, in Wordsworth's phrase, "leap up" when we "behold a rainbow in the sky"?

So it is with the beauty man creates. Architecture is so compelling that one could hardly stand on a chair in St. Paul's Cathedral and sing a comic song! Who was it said of a great painter that at one moment he stood with coloured oil on a hog's-bristle brush and a few hours later, having transferred the oils to stretched canvas, he had created something that all men would recognise as divine? Poetry can still move me to tears in a way, and for a reason, that I cannot understand. I cannot answer the American who said of a poet, "He could have said it all in prose." Above all forms of man-made beauty I put music. I am an ignoramus about it. All I can say is that some music brings God nearer to me in a unique way than anything else. I will make a confession to you. When I first drew up the City Temple service paper, I planned a period of silence after the anthem. It seemed fitting certainly, but the plain truth is that for a moment or two after some anthems I could not speak. A Latin poet once wrote of the *lachrymae rerum*, the tears of things. Indeed, there falls upon the spirit a sense of the numinous—the supernatural presence—which is "too deep for tears." That is an experience of God. Where *is* this Risen Christ? *There* in your heart when you respond to beauty.

2. It is similar in regard to truth. Have you never had moments when a truth, even a familiar one, one to which you have assented for years, suddenly shocks you by a new, penetrating sense of reality? Rupert Brooke spoke of "the hour of knowing."

I can remember in the First World War riding on horseback in the deserts of Mesopotamia from one Arab sheik to another on a government errand and hardly knowing which day of the week it was. Then, one part of my task completed, I rode into a camp where a service was being held in a Y.M.C.A. tent. I was tired and hot and dusty but, though I can't remember even the name of the preacher, I *knew* that Christ had forgiven my sins, that he was there and that he loved me. In a sense I knew all that before, but this was different. This deep perception of truth was an hour of knowing, an experience of Christ.

One is reminded of two lines of Browning in that long poem, "The Ring and the Book," discussing that wicked man Guido.

> So shall the truth be flashed out in one blow,
> And Guido *see* one instant and be saved.

Where *is* this Risen Christ? Wherever and whenever truth authenticates itself in your mind, for all truth is an expression of himself however we come by it and whatever it is about. Did he not say, "I *am* the truth" (John 14:6)?

Let a man follow the advice of Ruskin and read through the gospels imaginatively trying "to be present, as if in the body, at each recorded act in the life of the Redeemer," and almost certainly the reader will find he is not reading an irrelevant story, but some great truth about God will leap out of the printed page and capture a place in his mind. This is an experience of the Risen Christ.

3. Above all, wherever goodness is exhibited there is Christ. Years ago I attended a Roman Catholic service. Before he celebrated the Mass the priest preached to us about the "Real Presence." He said the wafer and the wine became the very body and blood of Christ. As the service proceeded, a little boy wandered into the aisle. He seemed lost. He began to cry bitterly. Then a man next to me rose in his place, gathered the little fellow in his arms and sat down. I can still hear, in imagination, the way he said, "There, there," as he comforted the child. Where *is* this Risen Christ? In the love of the man next to me who was comforting a little child. Where love is, God is.

We often disparage teenagers, but many are doing splendid work, some of them among the stricken people of Vietnam. If I had a teenage daughter, I would rather she went to *Vietnam* — yes, miniskirt, guitar, boyfriend, the lot — to minister to little babies, blinded, burnt, and mutilated by damnable American bombing, than that she went to Church here every Sunday; if by doing the latter, she identified the religion of the gay, royal Risen Christ, with the irrelevant nonsense frequently dished out in some churches, passing itself off as the Christian religion. I don't mean just the sermons, though they are poor enough. I mean chanting Psalms — because they are "set" — which express the very opposite of Christ's spirit, and using language in creeds, liturgies and hymns which makes no sense at all to the thoughtful youth of today.

The unreality and irrelevance in our day of what passes as the Christian message, and its apparent failure to meet men's needs, is due to the fact that we are seeking what is living in things that are dead: dead language, dead ideas, dead ritual, dead organisation. "Where is this Risen Christ?" we ask, and the angel of reality says, "Why seek ye the living among the dead? He is not here." He has gone before you. He has gone on into different forms of expression and beckons us to new spiritual experiences, new spiritual adventures, new patterns of organisation, new revelations of himself, new relationships with our fellows; and he offers us new meanings in life, new reserves of power, new depths of serenity.

Where love is, God is. That was the title of one of Tolstoy's loveliest stories. Let me tell it to you.

Martin, an old cobbler, is reading about Christ and half wishes Christ would visit him. He falls asleep musing, and is startled by a voice which says, "Martin, Martin, look into the street tomorrow! I will come!" The old cobbler cannot make up his mind whether the voice is real or whether it is just a dream. The next day he finds himself continually going to the window: "Will He indeed come, I wonder? It is too much to expect, and yet such things have happened." During the day the old man brings in a sweeper from the street, gives him tea, and invites him to warm his hands by the stove. Then he brings in a soldier's wife whom he sees from the window trying to wrap up her baby in a piece of old sacking, and he gives her food and drink and comfort. Then he brings into his little room an apple-woman and the boy who had run away with one of her apples. As he talks to her, her anger disappears, and, when he dismisses them, the boy is helping her to carry her load. The last scene shows Martin sitting at the table on which burns a solitary candle. "The day is nearly over and He hasn't been. It must have been a dream after all. Yet His voice seemed so real." But, as the old man sits there, the figure of the snow-sweeper rises up before his eyes, and a voice says, "Martin, Martin, do you not know me? This is I." Then the figure of the soldier's wife with the child in her arms appears out of the darkness, and the voice says, "And this is I." Then follows the figure of the apple-woman, and the voice says, "And this also is I." And the great truth dawns upon the old cobbler that God has come near to him in man, that in loving service to men and women he has actually served the Christ.

We all need to school ourselves to recognise the Risen Christ. How sad are the words, "She knew not that it was Jesus."

It is a good thing, when you finally put out your bedroom light and compose yourself to sleep, to let your mind run over the day that has gone. What has impressed you as beautiful? What has awakened you because it is part of the eternal truth? What have you recognised as good? For in all these things the Divine Companion has been near you, calling to you in all beauty, speaking to you in all truth, pleading in all you have seen of goodness, to get your sense of values right.

Hundreds of people, from a depth of desire often unguessed, are seeking for God and for an experience of him. He has his own secret way to every heart. Many times already he has been very near. When love came to you, he came. Do you remember? When you took your little one out of his arms into your own, he was there. You will remember that? When you stood by quietly while he took a life you loved back into his arms, though you so yearned to hold it longer in your own, you remember how close he was then? There have been thousands of times—in a child's laughter, in a woman's love, in the kindly ministries of nature, in music, in art, in literature, in the bread and wine, in the friends who help you. But, my brother, my sister, it may be that he is calling you to find him nearest in those whom you will go out to love for his sake. "There is thy footstool, and there rest thy feet, where live the poorest, and lowliest, and lost."

FOR ADDITIONAL INFORMATION ABOUT LESLIE WEATHERHEAD:

Carrier, John Pressley. "A Critique of Pastoral Care in the Ministry of Leslie Dixon Weatherhead." Th.M. thesis, Southwestern Baptist Theological Seminary, 1964.

Davies, Horton. "Psychological Preaching: Leslie D. Weatherhead." *Varieties of English Preaching, 1900–1960.* Englewood Cliffs, N.J.: Prentice-Hall, 1963.

Jones, Edgar DeWitt. "Leslie D. Weatherhead." *The Royalty of the Pulpit.* New York: Harper & Bros., 1951.

Weatherhead, Leslie D. *The Church and the New Order.* London: Epworth Press, 1941.
———. *Psychology, Religion and Healing.* New York: Abingdon Press, 1952.

FOR OTHER SERMONS BY LESLIE WEATHERHEAD:

The Key Next Door, and Other City Temple Sermons. London: Hodder & Stoughton, 1960.
The Significance of Silence, and Other Sermons. New York: Abingdon-Cokesbury Press, 1945.
Also: *That Immortal Sea* (1953), *When the Lamp Flickers* (1948), *Over His Own Signature* (1955).

FULTON J. SHEEN

1895–

FULTON J. SHEEN, photograph, courtesy of Fulton J. Sheen.

FULTON JOHN SHEEN

1895	Born May 8, El Paso, Illinois
1913	Graduated from Spalding Institute, Peoria, Illinois
1917	Received A.B. degree from St. Viator College, Bourbonnais, Illinois
1919	Received A.M. degree from St. Viator College; attended St. Paul Seminary; ordained a priest
1920	Received S.T.B. and J.C.B., Catholic University of America
1923	Received Ph.D. degree from Louvain University, Belgium
1925	Taught on faculty of St. Edmunds College, England
1926	Joined faculty of the Catholic University of America
1930	Became preacher for the radio "Catholic Hour"
1950	Became national director for the Society for the Propagation of the Faith
1952	Began "Life Is Worth Living" television program
1967	Named bishop of the Diocese of Rochester (New York)
1969	Resigned as bishop of Rochester to devote full time to writing and lecturing

FULTON J. SHEEN is noted for his famous converts: they include Henry Ford II, Fritz Kreisler, Louis Budenz—former managing editor of the Communist newspaper the *Daily Worker*—and Claire Booth Luce. In addition, thousands of less famous people have been converted to the Catholic faith under his influence. About this influence, Sheen is characteristically humble. Pope Pius XI once asked him, "How many converts have you?" Sheen replied, "I never count them, lest I should believe that I made them instead of the good Lord."[1]

---

1. *Catholic Digest* 23 (October 1959): 37.

FULTON J. SHEEN · 1895–

Life and Times

Fulton J. Sheen was born on May 8, 1895, in El Paso, Illinois. He was one of four sons. At his baptism he was named Peter; he took the name John at his confirmation. Sheen received his early education at Spalding Institute, Peoria, Illinois. After graduating in 1913 he entered St. Viator College, Bourbonnais, Illinois. He was on the debate team that defeated Notre Dame for the first time in the history of the school. He received both the A.B. and the A.M. degrees from St. Viator College and then enrolled in St. Paul Seminary in St. Paul, Minnesota. He was ordained a priest for the Diocese of Peoria (Illinois) in 1919. Next he enrolled in the Catholic University of America, where he earned two degrees. He completed his formal education in Europe, receiving the Ph.D. degree from Louvain University, Belgium, and studying in other European schools.

Sheen joined the Catholic University of America faculty as professor of philosophy of religion in 1926. He remained on the faculty for twenty-three years. Much of his time was spent in writing and lecturing outside of his normal classroom duties.

In 1930 he began preaching on the "Catholic Hour" radio program and his success was phenomenal. For twenty-two years he continued on the air. Largely as a result of his radio fame, he succeeded the Most Reverend Thomas J. McDonnell in 1950 as the United States director of the Society for the Propagation of the Faith. In this capacity he began the television programs in 1952 which were to make his name a household word throughout America. On his program, "Life Is Worth Living," Sheen spoke for thirty minutes without a choir or any other support, and without any interest-catching gimmicks. He spoke on spiritual matters without apology. Sheen bucked serious competition: he appeared opposite Frank Sinatra and Milton Berle when both were at the top of television ratings. His success was immediate. At one time his audience numbered between fifteen and twenty million viewers. The critics as well as the people liked his program. He was named the most outstanding personality in television in 1952 by the Academy of Television Arts and Sciences.

Sheen cares deeply about people and their spiritual condition; the number of converts attributable to him testifies to this concern. He uses all sorts of methods to reach people. At one time he advertised in the Washington papers for those interested in instruction in the Christian faith. As a result he had hundreds of people meeting under his guidance.

In addition to teaching, preaching, radio and television broadcasts, and personal contacts, Sheen utilizes effective writing to spread his faith. A prolific writer, he averaged over a book a year at the height of his career. He has been able to accomplish so much because of his natural abilities, his discipline, and hard work. One incident may illustrate his dedication. When Sheen was made a bishop, Pope Pius invited him to remain in Rome for a few weeks of vacation. Sheen replied, "I thought your Holiness had made me a bishop because there was a job to be done." He left Rome immediately and returned to America.[2]

In his writing and speaking Sheen deals with the issues confronting men in his time. Deeply spiritual in his approach to the Christian faith, he nevertheless attacks the problems and concerns of everyday life. He is particularly outspoken when discussing communism, humanistic psychiatry, and various moral issues such as divorce, sex, and war.

Even before the postwar tensions with Russia, Sheen directed a scathing attack on communism. Before World War II, he denounced any alliance of the Allies with Soviet Russia. During the war he opposed support to Russia and urged that Russia be barred from the conference tables. He insisted that his opposition was to communism and not to individual Communists as persons: he said that he hated communism but loved Communists.

Another major concern of the preaching of Sheen is the family. Some accuse him of sinking into shallow sentimentality when he speaks on the family. But he endeavors to make his approach practical and spiritual. He urges faithfulness and expressions of love in the family. He declares that sex should be treated as a holy gift. He encourages couples to have children early, and to have many of them. Sheen admits that large families, begun early in marriage, cause serious economic problems for family life, but he insists that the happiness which children bring is worth the sacrifices made for them.

Because of his effectiveness as a communicator, his church has chosen him for significant preaching positions. From 1930

---

2. James C. G. Conniff, *The Bishop Sheen Story* (Greenwich, Conn.: Fawcett, 1953), p. 30.

until 1952 he served as preacher at St. Patrick's Cathedral in New York City. His television preaching came as a result of his proven ability to relate the Christian faith clearly to a cosmopolitan audience. His many public appearances attest to his popularity.

His church, universities, and the public have showered him with acclaim and honors; the number of honorary degrees awarded him is too great to list. Honors, awards, and titles have been bestowed upon him by his church. In many ways, Fulton Sheen has become the best-known Roman Catholic in mid-century America—and probably the most admired and loved.

Sermons and Preaching

The "age of radio" was a short one, relatively speaking, and only a few men became known primarily for their radio preaching: Dick Sheppard and Studdert Kennedy in England, and in this country S. Parkes Cadman, Walter Maier, and to a lesser extent, Ralph Sockman. Others used radio effectively, though not as extensively as these men.

But only one man built his reputation as a preacher upon his use of both radio and television: Bishop Fulton J. Sheen. It is true that Billy Graham has appeared frequently on television, but only Bishop Sheen successfully sustained a continuing television series, competing successfully with the highest-rated American entertainers.

Sheen began his television program, "Life Is Worth Living" (originally titled "Is Life Worth Living?"), on a sustaining basis in February, 1952. When he began he had only three stations, but by the following May thirty-five stations were carrying his program. Nothing like it had ever happened before in television. The Admiral Corporation signed him to a two-year contract for a million dollars a year for each twenty-six-week series. From November, 1952, to May, 1953, the number of stations carrying his program increased to seventy-five.

In April of 1952 his program carried a Trendex popularity rating of 13.7, unequaled in the history of television by any other inspirational or intellectual program. By the time Sheen went on the air for the summer of 1953, he had an almost perfect Nielsen National Viewer rating of 19.0. The Videodex Report indicated an audience approaching ten million, and DuMont officials privately estimated it even larger. Harriet

BIOGRAPHY

Van Horne wrote in the *New York World Telegram and Sun*, "It's quite possible that he is the finest Catholic orator since Peter the Hermit."[3] Sheen was appearing opposite Frank Sinatra and Milton Berle, and when Berle's popularity rating began to drop a few points Berle said: "If I'm going to be eased off the top by anyone, it's better that I lose to the One for whom Bishop Sheen is speaking."[4]

The DuMont Network was overwhelmed by the mail response to the program (eighty-five hundred letters a week) and the five thousand requests a week for tickets to his half-hour show—most of which could not be filled, since there were only 1100 seats available in the Adelphi Theater, just off Broadway on Forty-fourth Street, from which the show was televised.[5] Eventually more than one hundred stations carried his program with an audience of fifteen to twenty million viewers.

Professional critics were as enthusiastic as the general public. One said, "As an inspirational spellbinder, there hasn't been anyone around like the Bishop, at least not during my lifetime."[6] The Academy of Television Arts and Sciences named Sheen the most outstanding personality in television in 1952. In 1957 Sheen dropped his show; he had suffered an attack of pneumonia. But he also said about his leaving the air, "One must occasionally retire from the lights of television to the shadows of the cross, where the soul is refreshed and strengthened."[7]

Those who had studied Sheen's radio career were not as dumbfounded by his phenomenal success as were most of the television officials. Sheen had been broadcasting for twenty-five years, twenty-two of them on the "Catholic Hour." He began preaching on the "Catholic Hour" on March 2, 1930, and the response to his preaching was overwhelming. Thousands wrote in each week for copies of Sheen's sermons. One little prayer book he devised and offered brought six hundred forty thousand requests for copies.[8] By the time Sheen began his television career, he was a seasoned veteran.

On his television program Sheen spoke for approximately

---

3. *Time*, 14 April 1952, p. 72.
4. Ibid.
5. Ibid.
6. *Catholic Digest* 23 (October 1959): 37–38.
7. Ibid., p. 39.
8. Conniff, p. 11.

twenty-three minutes, completely without notes. It was Sheen's custom to think through his sermons during the week prior to broadcast, gathering material and carefully structuring his ideas—but he did not write a manuscript, much to the mutual fascination and fright of television officials. Sheen correctly recognized the need for spontaneity in a program of that sort and flatly refused to run the risk of appearing stiff and unnatural by being tied to a manuscript. In the preface to his book of sermons, *Life Is Worth Living,* taken from his television broadcasts, he wrote: "Our telecasts were given without notes of any kind, nor were they written out prior to appearing before the camera."[9]

Sheen's naturalness was a great part of his success. Many writers commented on the "hypnotic" quality of his eyes—and there is no doubt that Sheen was possessed with a gaze as penetrating as any actor who ever graced a stage—but his greatest expressiveness was in the use of his hands. His gestures may have been calculated, but they were always graceful and somehow appeared entirely spontaneous. His voice added to the effect; it was deep and resonant—some members of the hierarchy spoke of him in private as "Full-Tone Jay"[10]—and his use of language was excellent. *Life* said of his delivery: "His language is vivid, his gestures are eloquent. His naturally hypnotic eyes look ever deeper under TV lights."[11]

Sheen's method in his televised sermons was basically uniform. He followed an inductive approach—one which began with the viewer, with material most acceptable to him—and proceeded only at the end of his sermon to those conclusions that would be less easily accepted by the audience. He demonstrated a superb ability to bridge the gap between the secular mind and Christian philosophy, even though he appeared in the lavish garb (purple cape, black cassock with purple piping, gold cross) of a Catholic bishop. He left the impression of a man who was so clearly right, so plainly reasonable on subjects well known to the average viewer, that when he revealed his final conclusions the skeptical viewer found himself faced with the unpleasant alternative of having to argue with a pleasant friend and an already demonstrated authority.

---

9. Fulton J. Sheen, *Life Is Worth Living* (Garden City, N.Y.: Garden City Books, 1953), p. vii.
10. Conniff, p. 24.
11. *Life,* 24 March 1952, p. 92.

Sheen won many listeners through his use of humor. He always insisted that he did not go in for humor deliberately and never told a joke as a joke. But he had a keen sense of wit and relied upon one particular "running gag" for part of his appeal. The joke concerned his "little angel," who supposedly erased the blackboard Sheen used to draw occasional sketches of things he wanted to illustrate. When the blackboard was out of camera range, a property man would run up and erase it; and when it again appeared on the screen erased, Sheen would pretend surprise and say, "That must have been my little angel." It began as a casual remark, but the popularity of the idea prompted Sheen to keep it in throughout his program. Actually he had no particular ability as an artist and knew it, and he took occasion to poke fun at himself about his own inability. Once when he drew a misshapen star he cracked, "That star looks as though it had a bad night."[12]

The popularity of Sheen's television program gave him many opportunities for lectures, and for the 1950s the fees he received for these lectures were staggering. Some of them ran as high as $2500, and others were rumored on several occasions to reach $5000, although he also delivered many addresses for nothing.[13] Sheen used much of the income from his speaking to support his various charities, principally the Blessed Martin de Porres Hospital in Mobile, Alabama, a 315-bed institution for Negroes, built almost entirely from royalties from Sheen's books and checks he received from lectures.[14]

Though Sheen invariably appeared relaxed and calm in the midst of the most trying broadcasting and televising demands, even while many of the professionals were in a state of near nervous collapse, he was an intense speaker and a man with a hectic, busy schedule. The pressure of his routine must have had some effect on his health; while still a graduate student at Catholic University he went to the Mayo Clinic at Rochester to be treated for ulcers. This condition gave him increasing trouble until at last he went to the Lahey Clinic in Boston, where the condition was corrected.

Even if he had not had ulcers before, the furor raised by his 1948 address on the subject of psychiatry should have given

---

12. Conniff, p. 7.
13. Ibid., p. 10.
14. Ibid., p. 29.

him ulcers. In March of 1948 at St. Patrick's Cathedral, Sheen delivered a vigorous sermon on psychiatry and confession that was extremely critical of psychiatry. The repercussions were swift. Dr. Frank J. Curran, chief psychiatrist at St. Vincent's Hospital in New York, resigned his post. Curran thought that Sheen's attack on psychiatry was an irresponsible, ill-considered condemnation of his profession. It was reported that many Catholics dropped badly needed psychiatric help, and soon other psychiatrists joined in the attack on Sheen. Sheen then made a statement to the effect that his words had been twisted—though he could never convince the psychiatrists.[15]

Sheen raised the ire of psychiatrists with such remarks as, "A complex is basically a conflict between what we ought to be and what we are." He also maintained that Freudian psychoanalysis is based upon four assumptions—materialism, hedonism, infantilism, and eroticism—and that it denies sin and would supplant confession.[16] Sheen wrote the book *Peace of Soul* to clarify his thinking on the subject, but it is doubtful that the book did much to soothe the psychiatrists. In it he said that psychiatrists are the enemies of man whenever they view the sense of guilt as an undesirable symptom and try to rid their patients of it.[17] Nonetheless, the book sold several hundred thousand copies and apparently capped the issue.

There have also been other criticisms of his work (besides the expected jealousies of those who envy his success), including the claim that Sheen has an "obsession" with the soul of man. One former associate expressed his disillusionment with Sheen by saying that he had made the mistake of thinking that he and Sheen were good friends, "but then I found out that to him I was just another *soul*."[18] It should be noted, however, that this comment is definitely a minority opinion, as evidenced by the adulation of the thousands of common people who have crossed his path.

Sheen also aroused the ire of many of his fellow priests at the consecration of a bishop in New Jersey when he lashed out at them in his sermon, saying, "For the love of Christ, stop being administrators and become shepherds of souls!" Some

---

15. Ibid., pp. 27-28.
16. Ibid., p. 28.
17. Fulton J. Sheen, *Peace of Soul* (New York: McGraw-Hill Book Co., 1949), p. 70.
18. Conniff, p. 3.

of those clerics who were present took his remarks personally and did not hesitate to say so.

Sheen's determined stance got him into conflict on another occasion when he got into a dispute over the amount of time to be allocated for music on the "Catholic Hour" program. It was reported that his encroachments on time alloted for choral rendition of hymns reached such proportions that the Paulist Choir threatened to withdraw entirely from the "Catholic Hour" unless Sheen changed his ways.[19]

Sheen is also deeply committed to the adoration of the Virgin Mary, repeatedly involving her name in his conversations, radio addresses, and television broadcasts. Conniff said of him, "He has never spoken in public on any subject without mentioning her name."[20] Naturally Protestant viewers or listeners were not as sympathetic with this stance as were his Catholic audiences. On his radio addresses he particularly depended upon a poem by Mary Dixon Thayer for his conclusion:

> Lovely Lady, dressed in blue,
> Teach me how to pray!
> God was just your little Boy,
> And you know the way![21]

In the preface to his book *Life Is Worth Living*, Sheen wrote: "Dedicated to our heavenly mother who stands behind me at every telecast and before whom I kneel in filial love, that these words borne on waves of light may bring readers to the Word and the Light of the World."[22]

Nevertheless, the modern figures who have been most exposed to broad public response in the United States—especially Harry Emerson Fosdick, Billy Graham, Norman Vincent Peale, and Bishop Sheen—have all received extensive criticism as well as adulation. Sheen has probably received no more criticism, and possibly less, than any of the others.

Perhaps the best conclusion to a study of the preaching of

---

19. Ibid., p. 30.
20. Ibid., p. 32.
21. Quoted in Conniff, p. 32. Reprinted with permission of The Macmillan Company from "To Our Lady," *The Child on His Knees*, by Mary Dixon Thayer. Copyright 1926 by The Macmillan Company, renewed 1954 by Mary Dixon Thayer.
22. Sheen, *Life Is Worth Living*, p. viii.

Bishop Sheen is to be found in his modest preface to *Life Is Worth Living:*

> On television, as well as in the arts and sciences, he who appears before the public may well ask himself: "What powers hast thou, that did not come to thee by gift? And if they came to thee by gift, why dost thou boast of them, as if there were no gift in question?" The talents of singing, painting, talking, teaching, are all gifts of God. No praise therefore is due to the author of these telecasts. If there be gratitude for putting them in print, the author accepts it as the window receives light, namely, to pass thanks back again to God, the Author of all good gifts. However, the imperfections, the failings, and the marring of the gifts are due to the window itself.[23]

---

23. Ibid.

Sermons

PAIN

"This day thou shalt be with me in paradise" (Luke 23:43, Douay).

THE FIRST WORD from the Cross tells us what should be our attitude toward unjust suffering, but the Second Word tells us what should be our attitude toward pain. There are two ways of looking at it; one is to see it without purpose, the other to see it with purpose.

The first view regards pain as opaque, like a stone wall; the other view regards it as transparent, like a window pane. The way we will react to pain depends entirely upon our philosophy of life. As the poet has put it:

> Two men looked out through their prison bars;
> The one saw mud, the other stars.

In like manner, there are those who, looking upon a rose, would say: "Isn't it a pity that those roses have thorns"; while others would say: "Isn't it consoling that those thorns have roses." These two attitudes are manifested in the two thieves crucified on either side of Our Blessed Lord. The thief on the right is the model for those for whom pain has a meaning; the thief on the left is the symbol of unconsecrated suffering.

Consider first the thief on the left. He suffered no more than the thief on the right, but he began and ended his crucifixion with a curse. Never for a moment did he correlate his sufferings with the Man on the central cross. Our Lord's prayer of forgiveness meant no more to that thief than the flight of a bird.

He saw no more purpose in his suffering than a fly sees purpose in the window pane that floods man's habitation with God's warmth and sunlight. Because he could not assimilate his pain and make it turn to the nourishment of his soul, pain turned against him as a foreign

---

Reprinted from Fulton J. Sheen, *The Rainbow of Sorrow* (Garden City, N.Y.: Garden City Books, 1938; reprint edition, 1953), pp. 25–34.

substance taken into the stomach turns against it and infects and poisons the whole system.

That is why he became bitter, why his mouth became like a crater of hate, and why he cursed the very Lord Who could have shepherded him into peace and paradise.

The world today is full of those who, like the thief on the left, see no meaning in pain. Knowing nothing of the Redemption of Our Lord they are unable to fit pain into a pattern; it becomes just an odd patch on the crazy quilt of life. Life becomes so wholly unpredictable for them that "a troubled manhood follows their baffled youth."

Never having thought of God as anything more than a name, they are now unable to fit the stark realities of life into His Divine Plan. That is why so many who cease to believe in God become cynics, killing not only themselves but, in a certain sense, even the beauties of flowers and the faces of children for whom they refuse to live.

The lesson of the thief on the left is clear: Pain of itself does not make us better; it is very apt to make us worse. No man was ever better simply because he had an earache. Unspiritualized suffering does not improve man; it degenerates him. The thief at the left is no better for his crucifixion: it sears him, burns him, and tarnishes his soul.

Refusing to think of pain as related to anything else, he ends by thinking only of himself and who would take him down from the cross. So it is with those who have lost their faith in God. To them Our Lord on a cross is only an event in the history of the Roman empire; He is not a message of hope or a proof of love.

They would not have a tool in their hands five minutes without discovering its purpose, but they live their lives without ever having inquired its meaning. Having no reason for living, suffering embitters them, poisons them, and finally, the great door of life's opportunity is closed in their faces, and like the thief on the left they go out into the night unblessed.

Now look at the thief on the right—the symbol of those for whom pain has a meaning. At first he did not understand it, and therefore joined in the curses with the thief on the left. But just as sometimes a flash of lightning will illumine the path we have missed, so too the Saviour's forgiveness of His executioners illumined for the thief the road of mercy.

He began to see that if pain had no reason Jesus would not have embraced it. If the cross had no purpose Jesus would not have climbed it. Surely He Who claimed to be God would never have taken that badge of shame unless it could be transformed and transmuted to some holy purpose.

Pain was beginning to be comprehensible to the thief; for the present at least it meant an occasion to do penance for his life of crime. And the moment that that light came to him he rebuked the thief on the left saying: "Neither dost thou fear God, seeing thou art under the same condemnation? And we indeed [suffer] justly, for we receive the due reward of our deeds; but this man hath done no evil" (Luke 23:40–41, Douay).

Now he saw pain as doing to his soul like to that which fire does to gold: burning away the dross. Or something like that which fever does to disease: killing the germs. Pain was dropping scales away from his eyes; and, turning toward the central cross, he no longer saw a crucified man, but a Heavenly King.

Surely, He Who can pray for pardon for His murderers will not cast off a thief: "Lord, remember me when thou shalt come into thy kingdom." Such great faith found its reward: "Amen I say to thee, this day thou shalt be with me in paradise" (Luke 23:42–43, Douay).

Pain in itself is not unbearable; it is the failure to understand its meaning that is unbearable. If that thief did not see purpose in pain he would never have saved his soul. Pain can be the death of our soul, or it can be its life.

It all depends on whether or not we link it up with Him Who, "having joy set before him, endured the cross." One of the greatest tragedies in the world is wasted pain. Pain without relation to the cross is like an unsigned check—without value. But once we have it countersigned with the Signature of the Saviour on the Cross, it takes on an infinite value.

A feverish brow that never throbs in unison with a Head crowned with thorns, or an aching hand never borne in patience with a Hand on the Cross, is sheer waste. The world is worse for that pain when it might have been so much the better.

All the sick-beds in the world, therefore, are either on the right side of the Cross or on the left; their position is determined by whether, like the thief on the left, they ask to be taken down, or, like the thief on the right, they ask to be taken up.

It is not so much what people suffer that makes the world mysterious; it is rather how much they miss when they suffer. They seem to forget that even as children they made obstacles in their games in order to have something to overcome.

Why, then, when they grow into man's estate, should there not be prizes won by effort and struggle? Cannot the spirit of man rise with adversity as the bird rises against the resistance of the wind? Do not the game fish swim upstream? Must not the alabaster box be broken to fill the house with ointment? Must not the chisel cut away the marble to bring out the form? Must not the seed falling to the ground die before it can spring forth into life? Must not the little streams speed into the ocean to escape their stagnant self-content? Must not grapes be crushed that there may be wine to drink, and wheat ground that there may be bread to eat?

Why then cannot pain be made redemption? Why under the alchemy of Divine Love cannot crosses be turned into crucifixes? Why cannot chastisements be regarded as penances? Why cannot we use a cross to become God-like? We cannot become like Him in His Power: we cannot become like Him in His Knowledge.

There is only one way we can become like Him, and that is in the way He bore His sorrows and His Cross. And that way was with love. "Greater love than this no man hath, that a man lay down his life for his friends." It is love that makes pain bearable.

As long as we feel it is doing good for another, or even for our own soul by increasing the glory of God, it is easier to bear. A mother keeps a vigil at the bedside of her sick child. The world calls it "fatigue" but she calls it love.

A little child was commanded by his mother not to walk the picket fence. He disobeyed and fell, maimed himself and was never able to walk again. Being told of his misfortune he said to his mother: "I know I will never walk again; I know it is my own fault; but if you will go on loving me I can stand anything." So it is with our own pains.

If we can be assured that God still loves and cares, then we shall find joy even in carrying on His redemptive work — by being redeemers with a small "r" as He is Redeemer with a capital "R." Then will come to us the vision of the difference between Pain and Sacrifice. Pain is sacrifice without love. Sacrifice is pain with love.

When we understand this, then we shall have an answer for those who feel that God should have let us sin without pain:

> The cry of earth's anguish went up unto God, —
>   "Lord, take away pain, —
> The shadow that darkens the world Thou hast made,
>   The close-coiling chain
> That strangles the heart, the burden that weighs
>   On the wings that would soar, —
> Lord, take away pain from the world Thou hast made
>   That it love Thee the more."
>
> Then answered the Lord to the world He had made,
>   "Shall I take away pain?
> And with it the power of the soul to endure
>   Made strong by the strain?
> Shall I take away pity that knits heart to heart
>   And sacrifice high?
> Will ye lose all your heroes who lift from the flame
>   White brows to the sky?
> Shall I take away love that redeems with a price
>   And smiles through the loss, —
> Can ye spare from the lives that would climb unto mine
>   The Christ on His Cross?"[1]

---

1. George Stewart, *God and Pain* (New York: George H. Doran Co., 1927), pp. 32-33. Used by permission of Doubleday & Co.

And now this final lesson. You and I often ask God for many favors which are never granted. We can imagine the thief on the right during his life asking God for many favors, and very especially for wealth which was probably not granted. On the other hand, though God does not always grant our material favors, there is one prayer He always grants.

There is a favor that you and I can ask of God this very moment, if we had the courage to do it, and that favor would be granted before the day is over. That prayer which God has never refused and will never refuse is the prayer for suffering. Ask Him to send you a cross and you will receive it!

But why does He not always answer our prayers for an increase in salary, for larger commissions, for more money? Why did He not answer the prayer of the thief on the left to be taken down from the cross, and why did He answer the prayer of the thief on the right to forgive his sins?

Because material favors draw us away from Him, but the cross always draws us to Him. And God does not want the world to have us!

He wants us Himself because He died for us!

THE WOMAN AT THE WELL

John 4

THERE is nothing more difficult in all the world than opening a conversation in the things of the soul. But in the Gospel of St. John we have a record of a complete conversation which Our Divine Lord had with a woman. Her lack both of culture and virtue does not hinder Our Blessed Lord making to her one of His greatest disclosures.

Reprinted from Fulton J. Sheen, *The Life of Christ* (Washington, D.C.: National Council of Catholic Men, 1952), pp. 43–49. Used by kind permission of Fulton J. Sheen. Scripture quotations in this sermon are from *The Holy Bible*, one-volume edition, translated by Ronald Knox, copyright 1944, 1948, 1950 by Sheed and Ward, Inc.

The scene takes place between Judea and Galilee, a strip of country inhabited by a mongrel, semi-alien race, the Samaritans. Between these people and the Jews there was a long standing feud. The reason was, the Samaritans were a hybrid race which was formed centuries before when the Israelites were brought into bondage in Babylon. The Assyrians sent some of their own people in among those who were left, to mix with them and thus create a new race called the Samaritans. Our Lord does not avoid these despised people, for as the Light of the World He must be the Missionary of Heaven to all the dark places of the earth.

The time is noon, and Our Blessed Lord is described in the Gospel as "being wearied with His journey," so He sat down at Jacob's Well. Footsore and weary in His work, not of it, He reveals that weariness can be put to a good purpose. Two of the greatest converts that Our Blessed Lord ever made, the woman at Tyre and Sidon, and this particular woman, were both made when He was tired.

The Gospel tells us: "A Samaritan woman came to draw water" (John 4:7). This was rather unusual, that a woman in the East would come at the heat of day in order to draw water. Usually women came early in the morning or late at night. The reason for her coming at noon will be discovered a little later. No sooner had she filled the pitcher when she saw the Stranger beside the Well. She would not look at Him, for she recognized in Him the features of a race which the Samaritans despised. But to her surprise, He addressed her with a request: "Give me some to drink." Whenever Our Lord wishes to do a favor, He always begins by asking for one. At Cana, He was the giver: here He is the suppliant. Instead of saying, as He might: "You need me," He says: "I need you." Her reaction to this request was quite natural, as she asked: "How is it that thou, who art a Jew, dost ask me, a Samaritan, to give thee drink?" Our Lord answered her: "If thou knewest what it is God gives, and who this is that is saying to thee, Give me drink, it would have been for thee to ask Him instead, and he would have given thee living water." "If thou knewest." Poor souls, how much they lose by the ignorance which comes of prejudice! "It would have been for thee to ask." How many blessings are lost for the want of the asking! Our Lord is here speaking of Himself as the gift of God, under the image of water which alone can satisfy the thirst of hungry souls. But the woman was incapable of understanding that as the body-thirst needs water, so the soul-thirst needs God. She saw only a race she hated, but she did not see the Son of God; the weary man, but not the Rest of weary souls; the thirsty pilgrim, but not the One Who could quench the world's thirst. It is the penalty of those who live close to the flesh never to understand the spiritual.

Continuing the conversation she asks: "Thou hast no bucket, and the well is deep; how then canst thou provide living water? Art thou a greater man than our father Jacob?" His answer implies that He was greater, for He said: "Anyone who drinks such water as this, will be thirsty again afterwards; the man who drinks the water I give him will not know thirst anymore. The water I give him will be a spring of water within him, that flows continually to bring him everlasting life."

There is a comparison between the natural waters of the world and the supernatural water of grace which He gives. He does not condemn the earthly streams or forbid them; He merely says that if you restrict yourself to the wells of human happiness, you will never be completely satisfied. As water never rises above its own level, so the best of earthly joys can rise no higher than the earth. They begin there and they end there. But the living water with which Christ fills the soul, springing from heaven conducts itself to heaven again. Flowing from the infinite, it elevates to the infinite.

There is a certain appeal about this Divine Water, for she had long slaked her thirst at one of the muddiest pools of sensual gratification. She who first addressed Him with some bitterness as "Jew," now grows in respect for Him and continues: "Give me water such as that, so that I may never be thirsty and have to come here for water again." There still is confusion in her mind, for she imagines that the water of which He speaks will exempt her from the toil of coming to the well in order to draw water. Our Lord was speaking from the top of spiritual apprehension, the woman from the bottom of sensuous knowledge. The windows of her soul had become so dirty with sin that she could not see spiritual significance in the universe. It is not so much the way men think that keeps them from God, but the way they live.

Our Blessed Lord seeing that she fails to comprehend the spiritual lesson, emphasizes the necessity of a good moral life as the condition of faith. With rather an abrupt turn of conversation He says: "Go home, fetch thy husband, and come back here." He means: "I know your soul wants this water, but before I can give it, there is something in your life that must first be set right." The words of Our Blessed Lord manifestly were intended to bring out her sense of shame and sin. The woman answered: "I have no husband." These words were an honest and truthful confession as far as they went, but they did not go far enough. She had asked for living water, but she does not yet know that the well must first be dug. The command: "Go home, fetch thy husband" is the first stroke revealing the foulness of her life. Sin must be confessed before salvation can be obtained. Conscience must be aroused. With master skill Our Lord was exposing her whole wanton career, like a lightning flash, and fastening upon her conscience with its guilt.

Our Lord answered: "True enough, thou hast no husband." Our Lord's commendation of the woman's honest confession deserves notice; it teaches us that we must make the best of an ignorant sinner's words. An unskillful physician of souls would probably have rebuked the woman sharply for concealing the truth. But Our Lord who knows all adds: "Thou hast had five husbands, but the man who is with thee now is no husband of thine; thou hast told the truth over this."

Our Lord was here saying that he with whom she was living now is not one of the husbands; that she had fallen into such degradation that she does not even go through the legal sanction, which in other times she would have done. Our Lord had touched her at a sensitive point. She now begins to feel that He is "meddling" into her life, probing her conscience. She must get out of this trap and away from a religion that demands a new way of living. "Didn't He know that everyone believes in divorce?" Her way of getting out of moral reformation was the same as millions of piteous feeble intellects who are always trying to escape the call of grace in their souls by pretending that they have intellectual difficulties, for example, that the Church is bent on raiding the Treasury or some equally diabolical lie. The woman, typical of those whose immoral life is challenged, changes the subject. Our Blessed Lord had brought the discussion to the moral order, namely the way she conducted herself personally before God and her conscience. But she drags it down to the intellectual level, in order that religion will be a subject for discussion and not decision, which it ought to be. She hopes to escape through flattery as she says: "Sir, I perceive that thou art a prophet." She who at first calls Him a "Jew," and then calls Him "Sir," and now she calls Him a "Prophet." So she presents the intellectual problem: "Well, it was our fathers' way to worship on this mountain, although you tell us that the place where men ought to worship is Jerusalem." The woman is making a wild attempt to get off the hook. She tried to draw a red herring across the path by bringing up the old religious squabble. But Our Lord now says to her: "Believe me, woman, the time is coming when you will not go to this mountain, nor yet to Jerusalem, to worship the Father. . . . the time is coming, nay, has already come, when true worshippers will worship the Father in spirit and in truth." Our Lord lifts up the whole debate into a higher sphere, and shows how in a little while the subject now in dispute will disappear altogether. He is saying to her: "To worship men must be honest. I have been trying to tear away your superficial ego, your mask and your pose, and compel you to see your life as it is in your conscience and before God. If you are prepared to do that, you can forget your local dispute!"

The words of Our Lord bring the poor sinner into deeper waters than she can conquer. But there was nevertheless one thing that He said that she could dimly grasp: Our Lord said something about the coming Hour of the Messias. The Samaritans themselves had some belief in the Messias. She said: "I know that Messias (that is, the Christ) is to come; and when he comes, he will tell us everything." For 1500 years the prophets had gazed across the fields on which they both stood and proclaimed the Messias! She even now dimly hints a new title for Him: "Christ the Messias."

These words were a cry of helplessness! Hidden in them is the cry of all Asia and the mission lands of the world at the present time to which we are dedicating ourselves and summoning souls to sacrifice. Buddha, Confucius, Laotze, all point to something beyond themselves. The people of Asia found their spokesman in the woman who has a presentment she yet dare not utter: "Thou perhaps are the one to whom we look." What she suggests is fulfilled as Our Lord tells her in answer to the aspirations of all the people of the world, and the yearnings of her heart, that He is the Messias. "I, who speak to thee, am the Christ" (John 4:26).

It is hard to imagine the shock the woman must have felt in suddenly realizing that a stranger Whom she meets at a well, affirms Himself to be the realization of all the dreams and hopes of every sinner of the world. In her excitement, she turns and runs into the city. But the Gospel with an exquisite touch of delicacy says: "She left her bucket." As Our Lord forgot His hunger in seeking a soul, as the Apostles left their nets in becoming fishers of men, so she forgets her thirst in finding the Fountain of Life.

Acting on the spur of the moment she goes into the city to tell the men, saying: "Come, see a man who has told me all things whatsoever I have done. Is not He the Christ?" Here there was a new title given to Our Lord, "Christ." She does not say that He has told her all the things that pertain to the worship of God, but all the things that she has done, even her own faults which she has shunned. The sun no sooner rises than it shines, and the fire is no sooner kindled than it burns, so grace acts as soon as it exists. She becomes one of the first missionaries in the history of Christianity.

It is interesting that she tells the *men*. Why not the women? It may very well have been that the women in the city would not allow her to associate with them because of her sinfulness. That is why she came to the well at noon; the others would come in the cool of the morning or the cool of the evening, but she had to come alone in the heat of the day. Now apparently because the women had shunned her, and refused to associate with her, she gives her first message to the men. It never pays to be unkind to sinners. Some day they may sit with Christ and we, their critics, may find ourselves without.

Picture this notorious woman, a few hours later, running across the fields, returning to the well, with men at her heels as usual, but this time in pursuit of salvation. The men prove, however, an ungrateful lot, for after they saw Our Lord they said to the woman: "It is not through thy report . . . that we believe now; we have heard him for ourselves, and we recognize that he is indeed the Saviour of the world." This is the first time Our Lord ever received that title.

Her spiritual growth is now complete. Human understanding is slow. At first Christ was to her a "Jew," then a Good Man, "Sir," then a "Prophet"—perhaps like all the other prophets, then "the Messias, the expected of the Nations," and now, at last, what He is in truth, the "Saviour of the world," the "Redeemer from sin." Conversion may be rapid as it is in some, but it is never complete until like the woman one sees in Our Lord, One Who came to save not the just, but sinners.

Like this woman, we are all like stricken deer, vainly trying to wrench the arrows of worries from our wounds. We are like sheep entangled in thorns, that make one more effort to escape from the pursuing shepherd who would rescue us. Our cry goes out in the words of the woman: "Give me this water." It is the cry of youth—"Give me this water, but not yet, wait till I reach the threshold of manhood." "Give me this water" is the cry of ripening manhood, "but not yet— disturb me not in the burdening heat of the day. Wait until I have breathing time and come to the evening of life, and the shadows are lengthening." "Give me this water," is the cry of old age, "but not yet," they say. "I want none until the sunset hour." "Give me this water," is the cry of the dying. And it was of that thirst that Lazarus suffered in hell.

"Give me this water," is the cry of the Communists as they hope to get from tractors and collectivized plunder, the real peace for which their souls yearn. "Give me this water," is the plea of every jaded lover of pleasure, as he mistakenly believes happiness is identical with distraction. "Give me this water," is the cry of the Hindus and Buddhists as they run in vain to slake their thirst in some vague impersonal pool of universal being. Everyone—everyone in the world is seeking God.

There are only two classes of people in all the world: those who have found God, and those who are looking for Him—and everybody is looking, thirsting, hungering, seeking. And the great sinners are closer than the proud intellectuals! Pride swells and inflates the ego; gross sinners are depressed, deflated, and empty. They therefore have room for God. God prefers a loving sinner to a loveless "saint." Love can be trained; pride cannot!

O Christ! Millions in this world have white grace in their souls; they feel Thy Presence, Thy Divine Life through the rebirth of Waters and the restrengthening of Thy Bread. Millions of others have black grace; they feel not Thy Presence, but Thy absence. They are lonely, unhappy, afraid of dying and weary of life. Did they but know! Make Thy Presence felt, as Thou didst to the woman at the well, assuring them that if they had never sinned, they never could call Thee Saviour! God love you!

TO CAESAR AND TO GOD

Luke 20:20-26

THERE are several things which good people rightly find hard to understand. One is: How can those who claim to be religious, hate others who are trying to be religious? Another is: How can men whose profession and calling is to religion, become defenders of Godless Communism, visit Moscow, associate themselves with Communist Fronts and even preach Communism from pulpits built from the pockets of those who believe in God! It is a scandal indeed, but Our Blessed Lord warned us against believing that those who mouth religion necessarily have religion in their heart. As He said: "The kingdom of heaven will not give entrance to every man who calls me Master, Master; only to the man that does the will of my Father who is in heaven" (Matthew 7:21). It is the practice and not the verbiage that makes a man Christian.

Our Lord suffered from such bigotry and wicked alliances. In His days there were two groups constantly at one another's throats. But they decided to forget their lesser hates, because they found a greater hate—Christ, the Divine Son of the Living God. They buried their hatchets alright, but they buried them in Him. These two groups were the Herodians and the Pharisees.

The Herodians were not a sect nor religious school, but a political party. Outwardly they were friends of Caesar and of the Roman Authority which had conquered Israel some decades before. As a few people in Albania or Estonia or China might be found who are favorable to the Soviets and the Communists, so they were friends of pagan Rome and Caesar because they favored Herod as the vassal of Caesar.

Perhaps in our language it would be best to describe them as a kind of fellow travelers. As some disloyal Americans join the Communists either because they hate God and morality and want to give their hatred collective strength, or else because their ill-gotten wealth worries their consciences, so the Herodians sympathized with the imperialism of Caesar. It is important to remember that the Herodians had no genuine affection for religion—no man does who is disloyal to his country.

There was another party which the Herodians despised, namely, the Pharisees, and they in turn reciprocated the hatred of the Herodians. They were not only anti-Caesar, but they believed themselves more religious than the rest of men, because they fulfilled the legal-

---

Reprinted from Fulton J. Sheen, *The Life of Christ* (Washington, D. C.: National Council of Catholic Men, 1952), pp. 65-71. Used by kind permission of Fulton J. Sheen.

istic code even to the smallest detail. They described themselves as puritans, keeping the law free from pagan infiltration, but being more concerned about its externals than its spirit; Our Blessed Lord said that they kept clean the outside of the cup while leaving pollution on the inside.

Perhaps the best way to understand the Pharisees would be to compare them to religious people in society, who are very much concerned with externals and social service, who go to Church Christmas and Easter, but who are not concerned with the Divinity of Christ or redemption from sin.

Both of these groups were enemies, because the Herodians sided with Caesar, and were willing to pay tribute to the conqueror, while the Pharisees despised Caesar and paid tribute under protest. Furthermore the Herodians did not believe in religion, while the Pharisees professed its externals, but did not accept the Divinity of Christ.

One day after Our Lord had cured a man on the Sabbath, the Gospel tells us that these two bitter enemies entered into an alliance: "The Pharisees began plotting with those of Herod's party to make away with him." Our Lord not only unites friends; He also unites His enemies. Anything less than the Divine leaves men with their petty divisions and quarrels. You will always find the Divine where you find the hatred of the world most united and concentrated.

That the Pharisees should have tolerated even such a temporary alliance with the Herodians, shows the virulence of the hatred against Our Blessed Lord. "And so, watching for their opportunity, they [the Pharisees] sent agents of their own, who pretended to be men of honest purpose, to fasten on His words; then they would hand him over to the supreme authority of the governor" (Luke 20:20). They "watched" Him, but not to learn the way of salvation, but rather to accuse Him and to deliver Him up to die.

The Herodians could not have come before Our Blessed Lord without arousing some suspicion of their base motives, nor could the Pharisees, always astute, come to Him in person. They sent some of their young scholars, as though in their guileless simplicity, they were merely seeking information. They gave Our Blessed Lord the impression that a dispute had arisen among them and the Herodians, as indeed would have been very natural, and they desired to settle it by referring it to Him as the great scholar. They began by praising Him, thinking foolishly that He might be won over by a little flattery.

They said: "Master, we know that thou art direct in thy talk and thy teaching; thou makest no distinction between man and man, but teachest the way of God in all sincerity." We do not know whether they really meant what they said, but they certainly did tell the truth. Then came the question, and a real trick question it was: "Is it right that we should pay tribute to Caesar, or not?" Remember that the Roman conquerors occupied their land, filled their superior courts, retained for themselves the right to put anyone to death. The question therefore was like asking whether or not they should pay any tribute to the invaders. This tax which we Pharisees so much detest, but the legality of which these Herodians support, ought we or ought we not pay? Which of us is right — we the Pharisees who loathe and resent it, or the Herodians who justify it?

They expected Our Blessed Lord to answer either "Herodians" or "Pharisees." If He answered, "No, it is not lawful to pay tribute to Caesar," then the Herodians would have delivered Him over to the Roman authorities, who in turn would order His death for conspiring to revolution. If He said, "Yes, it is lawful," then He would displease the Pharisees who would go before the people and say that He was not a Messias, nor the Saviour, for no Messias or Saviour would ever consent that the people should put their necks under the yoke of an invader. If He refused to pay the tax, He was a rebel; if He agreed to pay it, He was an enemy of the people. To say "No" would make Him a traitor to Caesar; to say "Yes" would make Him anti-national, anti-patriotic.

In either case it would seem that He is caught in a trap. In our language, the fellow travelers would condemn Him for being an enemy of Stalin; the demi-religious will condemn Him for being an enemy of His country.

To this trick question so maliciously proposed, Our Divine Lord gave a perfect simple reply. Seeing their malice, He said to them: "Hypocrites, why do you thus put me to the test?" Despite the fact that they began with a compliment, Our Blessed Lord heard the hiss of the serpent. Though they boasted that He was fearless and impartial, He blinds them with the flash of the one indignant word "Hypocrites." He then said to them: "Show me the coinage in which the tribute is paid." Our Lord had none. So they produced a silver piece and put it into His hand. On one side was stamped the features of the Emperor, Tiberius Caesar, with those evil lips seen in every image of him; and on the other side of the coin was stamped his title *Pontifex Maximus.*

A great hush came over the crowd at that moment as they saw the coin lying there in the hand of Our Blessed Lord. He was the true *Pontifex Maximus,* the real Bridge Builder between Heaven and earth; here He was the King of the hearts of men holding in his hand a silver coin. Very soon He Whose hands held Caesar's image would one day have those very hands pierced by the nails under the orders of the very man whose portrait He looked upon. Our Lord pointing to the coin asked them: "Whose likeness, whose name does it bear inscribed on it?" They answered: "Caesar's." Then came His answer: "Why then, give back to Caesar what is Caesar's, and to God what is God's."

Our Lord not only answered their question, but the question of all men for all times, by affirming that His Kingdom is not of this world;

that He is concerned with the eternal destiny, and politics is concerned with temporal prosperity; that what is God's and what is Caesar's no more contradict one another than the soul and the body in man. Our Lord is saying that the claims of civil authority and Divinity do not conflict. Human government has its rights, and God has His rights. The outer man is subject to the government, and the inner man is subject to God. To those who were so sensitive and tender-conscienced about Caesar's rights, Our Lord tells them to be even more cautious still about the rights of God. God must have His due as well as the State; He must have it more for He is the King of Kings and the Lord of Lords, and by Him all earthly kings and presidents, dictators and premiers hold their authority. As regards Caesar, He passed beyond all politics and parties by answering their question, "Is it right to give," by correcting them, saying, "give back," that is, "Pay to him as his due, what you have acknowledged." By producing therefore the coin, they were openly declaring that Caesar was their sovereign, at least for the time being. They themselves had settled the question whether it was lawful to pay the tax. If they are trafficking with Caesar's money they are in debt for the privileges created for them in the government under which they live.

Our Lord, in saying "Give back to Caesar what is Caesar's," was here asserting what Paul himself would say later on in his letter to the Romans, and he spoke of the very Caesar who would put him to death. "He is God's minister still, to inflict punishment on the wrong-doer. Thou must needs, then, be submissive, not only for fear of punishment, but in conscience. It is for this same reason that you pay taxes; magistrates are in God's service, and must give all their time to it. Pay every man, then, his due; taxes, if it be taxes, customs, if it be customs; respect and honour, if it be respect and honour. Do not let anybody have a claim upon you, except the claim which binds us to love one another" (Rom. 13:4-9).

Our Blessed Lord would not leave them with that lesson only. He added the deeper and weightier words: "And to God the things that are God's." To Caesar you owe the coinage which you have admitted is his. Our Blessed Lord after speaking of the first image of Caesar's, now spoke of a second image. The coin is from the mint of the Emperor, you are from the mint of God. The use of the coin is determined by its likeness, so too your use is determined by your likeness. Since you choose Caesar's coin, you are Caesar's subject. Give him his due. But also bear in yourself the image and likeness of God, as that coin bears the image and likeness of Caesar. Every faculty in you, your intellect, and your will, your soul, bears the stamp of the Divine. Render to God therefore your supreme and unceasing tribute. On your brow rests the stamp of Him Whose coinage and currency you are, but you are like lost pieces of silver from the Father's treasury. Search for that image in the mire of your lives, wash it with your tears, and burnish it back to brightness with your penance, and you will find on it the image of Him Who made you, and the superscription of His immortal Kingdom. You who are careful about politics, be equally careful about paying your taxes to God. Do not become nationalistic, that you become bigoted and irreligious and forget your duty to God.

And the gospel tells us they went away and left Him in peace: "They were full of admiration at his answer." The Herodians could not go to Caesar and say that He had rebelled against Caesar's authority; the Pharisees could not go to the people and say that He had betrayed their interests. To fellow travelers and to those who claim to be religious, Our Lord's words teach us peacefully to obey earthly powers while keeping inviolate our loyalty to God. But when people are base, there is no end to the lies that they will tell, for within three days, the Pharisees were stirring up the people charging that Our Blessed Lord had forbidden to give tribute to Caesar! That He is unpatriotic, a traitor! A betrayer of His people! Disloyal to Government! O Christ! Will these lies never cease?

Our Blessed Lord in saying to us: "Give back what is Caesar's" means: Pay your taxes; support public schools; when the government seeks enlistment of your life's blood to subdue the tyrannies of the world, give that blood; when it summons you to public service, obey, for the authority of the government is from God. "Give back to Caesar what is Caesar's." If you use American money, then be loyal, true Americans! Love it as one of the great earthly blessings of God Himself. And let no man challenge your patriotism. But on the other hand, while you are rendering a Caesar his due, while you are supporting public schools and paying taxes for those schools and for armies, do not forget either to "Give to God what is God's." Give unto God the little children; "Suffer the little children to come unto me and forbid them not, for of such is the kingdom of heaven." Build them schools, at your own expense, if you have to, in order to help them in God's name; fill them with consecrated teachers who will open the school day with prayer and close the day with prayer; instruct them in My Commandments. Teach them purity, obedience to parents, prayer, and regard for authority. Teach them as I have said: "What God hath joined together let no man put asunder." Give back to your Heavenly Father the material blessings you have received by feeding the hungry in the Missions and building chapels that the Memorial of My death may be re-enacted unto the consummation of the world. Give back to God the reflection of that image and likeness of your soul that is stamped there by grace! Give it back even when men persecute you, hate you, revile you for My name's sake, saying every manner of evil against you, that you are the enemy of Caesar because you worship Me.

If some of our citizens, Jews, Protestants and Catholics are trying to render to God the things that are God's and are taking it so seriously that at their own expense they build schools where the name of God will be taught, let there be no modern Herodian or Pharisee or a combination of both, arise to say they are disloyal to their country, or traitors, or subversive of American ideals! In the name of God, in the name of America, may we be honest and wise enough to see that he who prays is he who serves his country best. Because my knees bend to my God, my elbow does not refuse to unbend to salute my flag! It is because we love God and try to serve Him we are good Americans! God and Caesar are distinct, and we for one want to keep them distinct in their authority; we want no merging of Caesar unto God, of which there is little danger, and no merging of God unto Caesar, of which there is much danger.

In the name of God, in the name of America, let us be one! With the anti-God enemy at our gates, it behooves us to unite. The best way to be good Americans is to love and serve God. Let the spokes of a wheel represent Americans; the hub stands for God. The closer the spokes get to the hub, the closer they get to one another. The closer we get to God, the more united we are with one another! Destroy the hub and the spokes fall apart.

And if there is any country in the world which ought to understand these words of Our Lord, it is our own glorious country. Take in your hand a dime. What do you see? On the one side: "The United States of America," and the motto *E pluribus unum.* "Though we are many we are one." Then turn the dime over and you will see why we are one; for there is the word "Liberty" and under it, the name of Him Who gave us liberty, and to Whom we look to preserve our country: "In God we trust."

We can almost hear Our Lord speaking to us saying: "Give back to America what is America's, and give to God what is God's." And the vast majority of all of us are trying to do it, Jew, Protestant and Catholic! And if I have done anything in this broadcast to make one single person more charitable to a Jew, Protestant, or Catholic who is trying to serve God according to his conscience and the measure of his grace, then I have succeeded in making one better American! God love you!

TEMPTATIONS

Matthew 4:1-11

VERY FEW today believe in the devil, and that is exactly what the devil wants. He is always circulating the news of his death.

Satan never has to bother with those who do not believe in him; they are already his. He has used many in our Western world to convince us there is no hell — something rather hard to believe when there is so much evidence for hell around us. He has used the Communists to convince us that there is no God; they have failed to do this, but they have convinced us that there is a devil.

Satan tempts us in three areas of our life: our body, our soul and our relation to the world in which we live.

It was fitting that Our Blessed Lord Who is God in the form of man should suffer in some way, these three temptations of flesh, mind and worldliness to teach us to overcome temptations. Since He came to drive Satan from the earth, He must engage Satan in the greatest spiritual combat that ever took place on this our earth.

Immediately after His Baptism, when the Heavens opened and the Father declared Him to be His Son, hell opens, and the devil appears to Our Lord in the wilderness where, during forty days, He had eaten nothing. Scripture says simply: "Afterwards he was hungry." Satan, pointing down to the little black stones below that resembled round loaves of bread, said to Our Lord: "If thou art the Son of God, bid these stones turn into loaves of bread." Satan here strikes at the body — the weakest point of all and particularly because Our Lord was very hungry. Satan asks that Our Lord "do what comes naturally." If you have a libido, satisfy it; if you have an animal craving, give way to it; if you hunger, eat. Be self-expressive.

Do not think that Satan stopped tempting. He is still in our midst. He is in some of our universities, speaking through his stooges who tell the students: "You have a body, but no soul. Man is only a physiological bag filled with psychological libido. The only reason we live on earth is to have pleasures. Sex is the key to everything. Have you not read my Marx, who says that 'man is only an animal made for economic production,' and my sex-psychoanalysts who say: 'every desire is basically a sex desire'? Have you not heard my Molotov say: 'Bread is a political weapon — use it as power to win people to yourselves'? Forget the Divine! Turn religion into social service. Solve the food problem, the housing problem, the security problem; give man every-

---

Reprinted from Fulton J. Sheen, *The Life of Christ* (Washington, D. C.: National Council of Catholic Men, 1952), pp. 14-21. Used by kind permission of Fulton J. Sheen.

thing he needs for his body, for that is all he needs. Never let the U.N. take cognizance of what our missionaries are doing. Ignore them, because they are interested in souls. It is food only that matters. Turn your churches into social clubs; forget the supernatural. Does not my Stalin go into classrooms today and ask children to pray to God for bread; and when their prayers are not answered, Stalin feeds them? Stalin gives bread; God does not, because there is no God, there is no soul; there is only the body, pleasure, sex, the animal—and when we die, that is the end."

To that Temptation Our Lord answers: "Not in bread alone doth man live, but in every word that proceedeth from the mouth of God." Our Lord does not deny that men must be fed, or that social justice must be preached, but He asserts that these things are *not first*. He is saying to Satan: "You tempt Me to a religion which would relieve want; you want Me to be a baker, instead of a Saviour; to be a social reformer, instead of a Redeemer. Satan, you are tempting Me away from my Cross, suggesting that I be a cheap leader of people, filling their bellies, instead of their souls; you would have Me begin with security instead of ending with it; you would have Me bring outer abundance, instead of inner holiness. You and your Materialists say: 'Man lives by bread alone,' but I say to you: 'Not by bread alone.' Bread there must be, but remember that even bread gets all of its power to feed from Me. Bread without Me harms man, and I refuse to hold any theory about social security apart from the Word of God—even though I must go hungry. If I give bread alone, then even dogs shall come to My banquet. Those who believe in Me must do so even when they are hungry and starved and weak and in prison, and scourged and even rotting in your Soviet Buchenwalds.

"I am hungry! I have not eaten for forty days, but I refuse to become the ethical reformer by catering to the economic and pleasures and satiety. Say not that I am disinterested in social justice, for I am feeling now the hunger of India with its empty rice bowls; my stomach groans with the starving, crawling wrecks of humanity that go into the Uranium Mines in Siberia; I am one with My 100,000 missionaries who are hungry with the hungry, and thirsty with the thirsty in 603 missionary areas. Begone, Satan!"

Satan, having failed to win Our Lord away from His Cross and Redemption by turning Him into a Communist Commissar promising bread, now turns the attack upon His Spirit and His Soul. Seeing that Our Lord refuses to subscribe to the belief that man is an animal, or a stomach as he is for some economists, or sex as he is for some psychoanalysts, Satan now tempts Him to pride and egotism. As a symbol of that vanity, the devil took Him to a lofty pinnacle of the temple and said to Him: "Cast thyself down from this to the earth." Then, quoting Scripture, the devil continued: "For it is written, he shall give his angels charge concerning thee, to keep thee safe, and they will hold thee up with their hands, lest thou should chance to trip on a stone."

Satan is here saying: "Why take the long and tedious way to win mankind, through the shedding of blood, the mounting of a Cross, being despised and rejected, when You can take the short cut by a prodigy? You have affirmed Your trust in God! Very well! If You trust, do something heroic! Prove it, not by going to a Cross in obedience to God's Will, but by flinging Yourself down. It is the spectacular people want, not the Divine. People are bored! Relieve the monotony of life and their jaded spirits but leave their guilty consciences! How many times do You read in the press the words: Christ says? But when do you not read: Science says? It is the portents that people want. Science, machines, atomic fission, propaganda, publicity, anything that shows *outer power*—that our young minds crave, not Your pinnacle truths of sacrifice, grace, forgiveness and penance! If you want to convert minds today, do a miracle; not one that requires faith, but what we call the new miracle, the miracle of science.

"The children today in their so-called comics want not Thy miracles, O Christ, but the extraordinary feats of Superman; not One Who will teach their minds to be subject to God, but one who will teach them to be subject to power. My beloved Soviet Russia rightly calls religion a 'superstition' and what do they say has killed it? Science. Give up Your sublime truths about the mind needing the faith, the will needing grace, the mind needing hope, the whole being needing God. Power is below! Down in the depths! Jump from Your trust in God! Be a magician! Win the masses like my Communists are doing in China!"

The answer of Our Lord to Satan then and now is: "Thou shalt not tempt the Lord thy God." He means: "You tempt Me, when you see the wonders of science and forget I am the Author of the Universe. Your scientists are proof-readers, not the authors of the Book of Nature; they can come only to the edge of the picture, but not to Me the Artist who painted it. You would tempt Me to prove Myself Omnipotent to your feeblest test; you would pull watches on Me and say: 'I challenge you to strike me dead within five minutes.' Know you not that I have mercy on fools? You tempt Me by making atomic bombs explode against My Will and the pleas of My Vicar on earth, and when your cities are shambles you shriek out: 'Why does God not stop this war?' You tempt Me when you do foolish things which reason prohibits, like jumping from a steeple, and then when your minds are polluted with fears, anxieties and remorse, you expect Me to stop your flight to madness or your suicide. You tempt Me saying that I have no power unless I show it at your beck and call.

"I will never have many followers on the lofty heights of Divine Truth I know; I will never have the intelligentsia who are educated beyond their intelligence. I refuse now to do a stunt to win them. It is when I am lifted on the Cross that I will draw men to Myself; it will be by My sacrifice and not by science that I will appeal; I will win followers not with test tubes, but with My blood; not with power, but with love; not with celestial fireworks but by the right use of reason and free will. No sign shall be given to this generation but the sign of Jonas, namely, the Divine rising up from below, not the Divine plunging to hell. It is you, O Satan, who plunges to the depths below. I want men who will believe in Me even when I do not save them; I will not open prison doors where My missionaries are locked in China; I will not stay the red sickle that cuts off their heads; I will not halt the red hammer that batters down My tabernacle doors in Korea, for I want My missionaries and martyrs to love Me in prison as they go singing to their deaths. I never worked a miracle to save Myself; I will work few miracles even for My saints. Begone, Satan! Thou shalt not tempt the Lord thy God."

There is yet one area wherein man can be tempted and that is outside his body and soul, namely, in his relation to the world. "And the devil led Him up on a high mountain, and showed Him all the Kingdoms of the world in a moment of time. 'I will give thee command,' the devil said to Him, 'over all these and the glory that belongs to them.' " ... Then comes the most frightening words of Scripture: "They have all been made over to me, and I may give them to whomsoever I please; come then, all shall be thine, if thou wilt fall down before me and worship."

Satan is saying: "You have come, O Christ, to win the world, but the world is mine; I will give it to you, if you will compromise and worship me. Forget your Cross, Your Divinity, Your Kingdom of Heaven. If You want the world, it is at Your feet. There will be louder Hosannas than Jerusalem ever sang to its Kings: there will be no nails, Golgothas, crowns of thorns and crosses of contradiction. There is no ruler but me. Worship me and the world is Yours."

Satan is still tempting, saying to the followers of Christ: "You will never get ahead in the world unless you accept me; if you build schools to educate children in the ways of God, I will say that you are the enemy of public schools; if you oppose divorce, fight against the strangulation of the fruits of love, I will say you are reactionary. Your books will not be reviewed by Communist reviewers; I will flood the nation with lies that you are the enemy of the State and I will add to that the bigger lie for fools who will believe it, that you want your Church to dominate the State, and that you are disloyal; I have already told your missionaries in China that they can live if they join my independent church and deny the Vicar of Christ. Why does my Mao Tse-tung hold Bishops for ransom in China? Why are the dungeons of Hungary and Czechoslovakia, the prisons of Canton, Shanghai, Hankow, filled with the bleeding bodies of your priests and nuns, if it is not because they refused to do my bidding? See how my Soviet Russia advances. 37 out of every 100 people in the world are subject to it; the Soviets know the world is mine, that is why they are getting it! Forget heaven, and grace and sacraments and God; no shedding of blood, no martyrdoms, no self-denials are necessary in my way. Just worship me under any name, I care not, except not as the devil. Call me 'power'; call me 'religion,' provided you leave out your Divinity of Christ; call me 'patriotism,' provided you use it to malign those who believe in the spirit; just worship me and the world is yours."

Our Lord, knowing those kingdoms could be won only by His suffering and death said to Satan: "Away with thee, Satan; it is written, 'Thou shalt worship the Lord thy God, and Him alone shalt thou serve.' Satan, you want worship, but to worship you is to serve you, and to serve you is slavery. I do not want your world so long as it has on it the terrible burden of guilt. If I had all your kingdoms, all the hearts in them would still long for something you could not give, namely, peace of soul. Even now as you boast that Russia is yours, I tell you, there are millions behind your Iron Curtain that are awaiting My Redemption. I do not want your world at your cheap price. I am a revolutionist too, as My Mother sang in her Magnificat. I am in revolt against you. But My revolution is not by the sword thrust outward in imperialism, but inward against sin and all the things that make war. I will first conquer evil in the hearts of men, and then I shall conquer the world. I will conquer your world by going into the hearts of your dishonest tax collectors, your false judges, your Commissars, and I will redeem them from guilt and sin and send them back clean to their professions. I shall tell them it profits them nothing to win the whole world if they lose their immortal soul. You keep your kingdoms for the moment. Better the loss of all your kingdoms; aye, better the loss of the universe by splitting it with your bombs, than the loss of one single soul! It is the kingdoms of the world that are to be elevated to the Kingdom of God, not the Kingdom of God that is to be dragged down to the level of the kingdoms of the world. All I want of this earth is a place large enough to erect a Cross, then I will let you unfurl Me before the cross-roads of your world; I will let you nail Me in the name of the cities of Jerusalem, Athens and Rome, but I will rise from the dead and you will discover that you who won the battle, lost the day as I march with victory on the wings of the morning! Satan, you are asking Me to become anti-Christ. My Divine patience now gives way to Divine indignation. 'Get thee behind Me, Satan!'"

O Christ, Thou Who art the Son of the Living God, look with mercy on the millions in our land whose stomachs are filled with bread and yet are starving because their souls are empty; look with pity on the millions in Asia who have both empty stomachs and empty souls. Inspire them to knock at every tabernacle door until they find Thee the Bread, the Food of our souls – the end of the hunger of searching.

Look down in pity on our land which is becoming a nation of mental cripples by denying guilt and the need of pardon. Thousands have plunged from the pinnacle of belief in God down to psychoanalytic couches where their sin is explained away. Give them the grace to get down on their knees to receive the real Power that forgives sin, creates a new spirit of love within and enables them to start life all over again with Thee, Our Redeemer and Our Saviour.

Finally, O Christ, have mercy on all those who for the sake of a second or third marriage, or a social or political advantage have given up their holy faith! Teach them in their sleepless nights, their uneasy consciences, their fears and anxieties, that if love will not draw them to Thee, then let restlessness throw them back again to Thy Sacred Heart! This is not Thy Hour in the world, O Christ! It is the devil's! The hour of darkness when Thou art once more crucified. As the red cobra slithers and coils his way around the whole world, send to us the Woman to whom Thou didst give the Power to crush the Head of the serpent! O Mary! Mother of God! The Woman who conquers the Beast, who saw the Red Star fall from heaven like lightning, throw thy blue veil about the Reds, that they who now hate may love and those who love not may be on fire for Thy Divine Son, our Bread, our Power, our King! God love you!

For additional information about Fulton J. Sheen:

Adams, Henry Babcock. "Selected Sermons of Fulton J. Sheen and Harry Emerson Fosdick." M.A. thesis, Stanford University, 1956.
Conniff, James C. G. *The Bishop Sheen Story*. Greenwich, Conn.: Fawcett Publications, 1953.
Larkin, Juanita J. "Fulton J. Sheen's Career on Radio and Television." M.S. thesis, University of Wisconsin, 1954.
Malone, Henry. "The Radio Preaching Art of the Right Reverend Monsignor Fulton John Sheen." M.A. thesis, Catholic University, 1949.
Noonan, Daniel P. *Missionary with a Mike: The Bishop Sheen Story*. New York: Pageant Press, 1968.
Sheen, Fulton John. *God Love You: The Best of Fulton J. Sheen*. New York: Maco Magazine Corp., 1955.

For other sermons by Fulton J. Sheen:

Life Is Worth Living. Garden City, N.Y.: Garden City Books, 1953.
The Rainbow of Sorrow. Garden City, N.Y.: Garden City Books, 1938.
Also: *The Life of Christ* (1952).

JAMES STEWART

1896–

JAMES STEWART, photograph, courtesy of James Stewart.

JAMES STUART STEWART

1896	Born at Dundee, Scotland, July 21
1917	Received M.A. with first-class honors in classics from St. Andrews University in absentia while in service in France during World War I
1921	Received B.D. degree from St. Andrews University and studied at the University of Bonn
1924	Became pastor in Auchterarder, Perthshire
1928	Assumed pastorate of Beechgrove, Aberdeen
1935	Became pastor of North Morningside Church, Edinburgh, Scotland
1947	Became professor of New Testament language, literature, and theology, New College, University of Edinburgh
1952	Appointed as a chaplain to the queen
1953	Delivered the Lyman Beecher Lectures on Preaching at Yale
1963	Elected moderator of the General Assembly of the Church of Scotland
1966	Retired from professorship at New College

SCHOLAR, PROFESSOR, AUTHOR, PREACHER — the life of James S. Stewart has touched millions around the world. His ability and dedication took him to the heights as a preacher in Scotland during the middle portion of the twentieth century. Through his writing he made an impact for Christ on every English-speaking country in the world.

LIFE AND TIMES

James S. Stewart was born in Dundee, Scotland, July 21, 1896. He attended school in Dundee and then studied at St.

Andrews University in Scotland. From this university he received both the M.A. and the B.D. degrees. As a student he excelled in scholarly gifts. In further work at New College of the University of Edinburgh, and in Germany at the University of Bonn, he continued to display great intellectual talent.

His scholarly achievements passed from the schoolroom to publishing in 1928 when he was appointed to the joint editorship of the English translation of Schleiermacher's great work, *The Christian Faith*. In 1935, while still less than forty years old, he published *A Man in Christ*, a superb biblical and theological study of Paul. Prior to this he had written *The Life and Teaching of Jesus Christ*, a Bible study course for Church of Scotland youth. Both books enjoyed wide circulation.

Stewart also attained fame as a preacher. After completing his formal education, he served as pastor of St. Andrews Church in Auchterarder, the Beechgrove Church in Aberdeen, and the North Morningside Church in Edinburgh. While in the North Morningside Church, his popularity grew to the extent that people lined up for blocks early on Sunday morning waiting for a seat in the church. His books of sermons were eagerly read by preachers and laymen all over the English-speaking world.

In 1947 he was invited to become professor of New Testament language, literature, and theology at New College, University of Edinburgh, Scotland. He accepted this position and moved from the pastorate into the classroom. He immediately gained wide favor among students. Americans particularly were attracted to him and flocked to New College in large numbers in the late 1940s and the 1950s; they were often referred to as the "disciples of James" by the Scottish students.

His podium often became a pulpit and his class a congregation; his classroom presentations were frequently more like sermons than lectures. In a crisp accent—a cross between German and Scottish—he would enthrall the students with vivid descriptions of New Testament events or stirring challenges to Christian devotion. Class members sometimes were so caught up in his discourse that they failed to take notes. At times Stewart would pause in the midst of a lecture, whip off his glasses, and stand gazing above the heads of the students, as if looking into heaven itself; then he would plunge on, refreshed from a visit to some private spiritual oasis.

His classes were packed. Even in the largest lecture rooms students coming late often had to sit on the floor and on tables — all the seats were taken. Stewart was not content to have contact with students only in class, however. In spite of a busy schedule, his office was open to anyone who cared to visit with him. And each year he invited the students in his classes to come to his home in small groups. There they enjoyed tea, cookies, a cozy fire, informal discussion, and singing hymns and Scottish folk songs — with Stewart playing the piano.

Stewart's pietistic nature and evangelistic spirit caused him to be something of a controversial person in Scotland. He encouraged the Billy Graham crusades in Scotland while numbers of Church of Scotland ministers opposed Graham's meetings. A churchman of the Free Church stripe, he refused to back down from his stance in favor of evangelism. His writings indicate his deep concern about the proclamation of the gospel. He centered his preaching on central themes of the faith such as the incarnation, crucifixion, and resurrection of Jesus Christ.

Stewart also displayed deep concern for social problems. In *Thine Is the Kingdom* he wrote:

> If with the New Testament we believe that the eternal Word took upon Himself a body of flesh, we have no right to preach a disembodied Gospel dissociated from material and mundane concerns. The indicative of the incarnation carries with it a revolutionary imperative. It implicates us inextricably in history. It compels us to see the circumstances of man's corporate life as the raw materials of God's eternal purpose. The mysticism which would bypass earthly conditions it brands as a nauseating irrelevance. "As the Father sent Me into the world," said Jesus to His men, "so send I you."

He added:

> The proclamation of Christ lays the axe to the roots of the tree of serfdom and superstition, of racial discrimination and social injustice. From the hour when the Word became incarnate and the love of heaven struck down into the plagues and confusions of the world, the Church received the marching-orders of its mission. Like its Master, it was to take upon itself the burden of

the plight of men, and to involve itself in all the conditions of their life on earth.[1]

His ability as a preacher and his gifts as a scholar have been widely recognized by numerous honors given him. In 1952 he became a chaplain to the queen. He delivered the Lyman Beecher Lectures on Preaching at Yale in 1953. In 1963 he was elected moderator of the General Assembly of the Church of Scotland; taking a leave of absence from the University of Edinburgh, he gave a year in denominational service. Churches of various denominations, seminaries, and universities have sought him as a preacher.

His mystical, earnest manner wins admirers and friends wherever he goes. Shy and reserved, he never consciously displays his great learning. He prefers to minister in concerned simplicity as a herald of God with a faith to proclaim.

Preaching and Sermons

James Stewart has been called "one of the glories of the Scottish pulpit."[2] His preaching is marked by assurance and definiteness; he announces good news rather than petty moralisms. Horton Davies has said, "The only appropriate term for his preaching is 'heraldic.' " John McIntyre, in his book *The Shape of Christology*, said:

> If one were to try to track down in human terms the secret of the power of the preaching of Professor James S. Stewart, he might first mention the carefully chosen descriptive language, his constant practice of interpreting Scripture by Scripture, but the secret, I feel, lies in the way in which Professor Stewart so presents the biblical situations, so reconstructs the motives, attitudes, reactions of our Lord to those whom he confronts, that we ourselves are drawn into these self-same situations, ourselves confronted, challenged, judged, forgiven.[3]

---

1. James S. Stewart, *Thine Is the Kingdom* (Edinburgh: Saint Andrews Press, 1956), pp. 42–43.
2. Horton Davies, *Varieties of English Preaching, 1900–1960* (Englewood Cliffs, N.J.: Prentice-Hall, 1963), p. 231.
3. John McIntyre, *The Shape of Christology* (Philadelphia: Westminster Press, 1966), p. 128.

Stewart believes in an honest interpretation and exegesis of the Scripture. Interestingly enough, many have accused him of allegorizing Scripture, or at least of spiritualizing it. Stewart himself urged honest exegesis:

> There are some sermons which, starting out from a word of Scripture, proceed quite flagrantly to violate the intention of the original writer.... To say this is not, of course, to suggest that allegorizing is necessarily bad; nor does it imply a rigid and excessive literalism distrustful of all spiritual lines of interpretation. There is no reason why you should not, occasionally at least, extend the reference of a text beyond its immediate setting.... But the strongest and most helpful preaching is that which expounds a text or passage in dynamic relationship to its actual setting in Scripture. Loyalty to the Word of God demands scrupulous care in exegesis.[4]

Stewart's notable sermon "Anchors of the Soul" has been criticized frequently as an example of allegorical preaching. Stewart describes the four anchors of Acts 27:29 as hope, duty, prayer, and the cause of Christ. Technically, this is not allegory: it is true that allegory does focus on an *object* in the text—such as the anchor—rather than on the *truth* of the text; but allegorical preaching always believes that its interpretation is the true and deep significance of the Scripture. Stewart obviously does not. In this case he is guilty of nothing more serious than using a text as a literary device, from which he gains an interesting stylistic device. The sermon itself is actually not a development of that text at all, but rather a development of four great themes of the Scripture as a whole. But at best the matter is questionable, and it is easy to see why some have accused him of allegory.

Stewart believes that the best method of preparing a sermon is to begin by visualizing the congregation:

> When you sit down to write in your study, you must visualize a gathered congregation. This will give your work those qualities of directness, liveliness, verve and

---

4. James S. Stewart, *Heralds of God* (New York: Charles Scribner's Sons, 1946), pp. 155–56. Used by permission of Charles Scribner's Sons and Hodder & Stoughton.

immediacy which are so essential.... It will constrain you to clarify your own ideas. It will urge you to translate abstractions into concrete terms. It will embolden you to use personal forms of address.... It will keep the dominant notes of urgency and reality, of appeal for a verdict, sounding unmistakably.[5]

In most of Stewart's sermons he begins by reading his text, which is usually very short, and then plunges directly into the message. He follows the usual pattern of introduction, body, and conclusion, but he uses many different methods of developing his messages:

> Is the time-honored use of divisions—"heads" as they have been called—to be recommended? My advice would be to avoid any slavish bondage to tradition at this point. It is certainly not necessary that all sermons be divided into three parts. Sometimes your discourse may have six heads, sometimes none. Vary your methods deliberately. Cultivate flexibility. It is bad to cast all of your sermons into one mold, so that people will know in advance what shape they will be.
> The value of heads is, of course, that they drive home to your hearers' minds the truth for whose acceptance you are pleading. They focus the issue, and so help towards obtaining a verdict. They may stick in the memory when all the rest has been forgotten.[6]

Stewart regards it as bad psychology to announce all of the main divisions of the sermon at the beginning:

> It gives everything away. It holds no surprises in reserve.... But whether you formally announce any divisions or not, you must have them clear in your own mind. It is quite fatal to embark on a sermon without having a plainly charted course to follow.[7]

On at least one occasion in his published sermons Stewart gave his outline in the introduction in direct violation of his own principle; but he is not the first preacher, and certainly

---
5. Ibid., p. 119.
6. Ibid., pp. 131-32.
7. Ibid., p. 134.

not the last, to prove one of his own rules by practicing an exception to it.

Most of Stewart's sermons contain a discernible outline. Some of his sermons flow freely and the development is difficult to detect, but his theme moves smoothly in any case. Examples of his outlines:

"The Lord God Omnipotent Reigneth"
    I. The liberation of life.
        1. Release from petty worries.
        2. Release from fear of life.
        3. Release from self-contempt.
    II. The doom of sin.
    III. The comfort of sorrow.

"The Universality of Jesus" (Luke 23:38)
    I. As seen in the Greek title written over the cross.
    II. As seen in the Latin title written over the cross.
    III. As seen in the Hebrew title written over the cross.

"The Spirit of God" (John 3:8)
    I. The ceaseless action of the Spirit of God—"the wind bloweth."
    II. The sovereign action of the Spirit—"where it listeth."
    III. The indisputable evidence of the Spirit—"thou hearest the sound thereof."
    IV. The incredible origin of the Spirit—"but canst not tell whence it cometh."
    V. The incalculable destiny of the Spirit—"nor whither it goest."

Stewart is a master of the English language. He excels at painting descriptive word pictures, but he despises elevated language:

> Shun everything stilted, grandiose, insipid, or pedantic. . . . In your business of bringing the Christian religion decisively to bear upon the needs and problems of a twentieth century congregation, the language of Nicaea, or even of the Westminster Divines, may be a hindrance rather than a help. It is sheer slackness to fling at your people great slabs of religious phraseology derived from a bygone age, and leave them the task of

retranslation into terms of their own experience: that is your task, not theirs.[8]

He believes in simplicity and directness of expression:

> Have something to say, and when you are saying it, avoid . . . over-elaboration. . . . But artificial eloquence, like sham emotion, is a very dreadful thing. Learn to prune your language. . . . Prefer simple and even homely words to those that are abstract and difficult. . . .[9]

The sermons of Stewart give every indication that he is aware of the needs of the people to whom he preaches and the relevance of the gospel to his own day and time. In his Warrack Lectures he wrote:

> The Gospel is not for an age, but for all time: yet it is precisely the particular age—this historic hour and none other—to which we are commissioned by God to speak. It is against the background of the contemporary situation that we have to reinterpret the Gospel once for all delivered to the saints; and it is within the framework of current hopes and fears that we have to show the commanding relevance of Jesus.[10]

Stewart's sermon titles generally lack imagination and creativity, but there are some notable exceptions. Some of his better ones are "Clouds and Darkness and the Morning Star"; "O, Come, O, Come, Immanuel!"; "The Magnetism of the Unseen"; "Love's Last Appeal"; "The Transformation of Tragedy."

Most of the introductions to Stewart's sermons are interesting and direct. In his lectures he recognized that most of the older preachers began by describing the textual setting for their sermons, and he acknowledged the usefulness of that approach:

> For one thing, it provides a corrective of that arbitrary treatment of Scripture which, breaking all the canons of exegesis, imports meanings into texts in complete disregard of what the original writer meant to say.

---

8. Ibid., pp. 38–39.
9. Ibid., pp. 150–51.
10. Ibid., p. 11.

For another thing, the historical setting, if briefly and vividly sketched, will illuminate and make doubly relevant the message of the text itself.[11]

But Stewart recommended another method with certain advantages:

> There is, however, another method which is better adapted to grip your hearers' attention and secure their interest at the very outset. . . . That is to start from present-day experience. Begin where your hearers are. Meet them on their own ground. . . .[12]

A study of forty-nine of Stewart's sermons reveals that he followed closely his own theory of sermon introduction: twenty of these sermons begin by describing the historical background of the text or relating to the text in some fashion; twenty-nine of them begin in a contemporary fashion, either by referring to a contemporary situation or by beginning with a quotation, question, or story.

All of Stewart's sermons are well illustrated, particularly with English literature. His quotations, poems, and stories are taken from wide reading over a great span of history. Nevertheless, Stewart believes that illustrations and quotations should be used carefully. He said, "Do not scorn the aid of illustration, but use it sparingly in your sermons, and with discretion."[13] One of his most helpful rules with reference to illustrating is this suggestion: "No matter how vivid it may be in itself, if it does not immediately light up the particular truth under discussion, exclude it ruthlessly."[14] He warned that illustrations dragged in at random and needlessly multiplied reveal a careless mind.

The conclusions to Stewart's sermons are quiet rather than dramatic; he believes that the day of the florid, self-conscious climax has passed. People are rightly suspicious of sermons culminating in a blaze of literary fireworks, "like a sonata with a noisy coda." He wrote:

---

11. Ibid., p. 124.
12. Ibid., p. 125.
13. Ibid., p. 145.
14. Ibid., p. 143.

> *Diminuendo,* not *crescendo,* ought to be the rule as you draw near the end. Much better conclude quietly and even abruptly than indulge in any declamatory pyrotechnics.... You will never weaken the force of your final appeal by keeping it restrained. In nine cases out of ten, quiet notes are better there than crashing chords. No doubt there are exceptions.... Let your last words of appeal have in them something of the hush that falls when Christ Himself draws near.[15]

One of his favorite devices is to conclude with a poem: seven out of twenty-five sermons in *The Gates of New Life* end with a poem, and ten out of twenty-four in *The Strong Name* do the same. Only two sermons out of forty-nine do not contain a poem somewhere in the sermon.

Stewart's delivery is appealing; his voice is well modulated and shows a pleasing variety of pitch, quality, and articulation. There is no evidence of breathiness or nasality in his speech. His rate is varied and there is never a touch of monotone. In his lectures Stewart warned against speaking too slowly:

> The orthodox attitude would be to warn you against the errors of a too rapid delivery, and to beg and beseech you to go slow.... Common sense will teach you to regulate speed in accordance with the acoustics of the building in which you are speaking.... Preaching ought to resemble a purposeful, rhythmic march rather than a slow-paced saunter.[16]

Stewart frequently uses a change of pace within his sentences. He usually slows down toward the end of paragraphs, and the sermon ending itself is characterized by both a slowing down and a softening of tone. His delivery complements his message and has been rightly regarded as a great part of his communicative skill.

---

15. Ibid., pp. 137–40.
16. Ibid., p. 183.

Sermons

SACRIFICE AND SONG

"And when the burnt offering began, the song of the Lord began also with the trumpets" (2 Chronicles 29:27).

THERE must be few people in this world who can say that life for them has turned out exactly as they planned. There must be very few, perhaps none, who have seen everything working out according to the time-table and schedule of their dreams.

It is one of the commonest experiences of life, that men set their hearts upon the achievement of some strong desire or hope, and then providence says "No," or at least gives something totally different.

Here is a youth who wanted to be a doctor; but his father died, and he had to leave school and go out and earn a wage to help to keep the home going—and there will be no university now for him. Here is a business man who hoped to make his business a triumphant success; but the competition was fiercer than he had bargained for, and he began to find himself being left behind in the race; and the years are passing, and the burden and heat of the day are telling upon him, and he has lost some of the old resilience and buoyancy, and knows that he will never make much of that business now. Here is a man who wanted love and a home and children; and he has been given a road that will be solitary to the very end. Here is a woman who wanted to be a nurse in India, and she has got an office-desk in the town in which she was born. Here is some one made for art and music and all lovely things, yet tied to a life of drudgery, twelve hours in the day and seven days in the week.

It is a queer, incalculable thing, this life; and for few, for very few, does it work out in detail just as they had planned. Sooner or later, one fact confronts every pilgrim on the road, the fact of the discipline of hopes denied and plans defeated. Something in us, something in our hearts and hopes, has to be the burnt offering on the altar: life de-

---

Reprinted with the permission of Charles Scribner's Sons and T. & T. Clark from *The Gates of New Life*, pp. 32–41, by James S. Stewart. Copyright 1940 Charles Scribner's Sons and T. & T. Clark, Edinburgh.

mands it, providence decrees it. And what happens then? Is it not often this, that when the burnt offering begins, the song finishes, and all life's music is gone?

But look—it was so different here in Israel! "When the burnt offering began, the song of the Lord began also with the trumpets."

This was a memorable hour in the nation's history. Read what precedes this in the story, and you will see that for half a generation, right through the reign of King Ahaz, there had been a disastrous slump in morals and religion. But now Ahaz was dead; and a man after God's own heart, Hezekiah, was on the throne. He purged the land of its abuses; then summoned his people to a solemn service of rededication in the Temple. And the climax of that service was the moment which this text describes.

Can you picture it? Yonder stands the high altar, with the sacrifice laid upon it waiting for the fire. A vast concourse crowds the temple courts: they stand there, hushed and eager and expectant—for they know what that burnt offering on the altar represents. It represents themselves. It signifies their own life-dedication, as they offer themselves, body and soul, a willing sacrifice, to the God whom for years they have forsaken. Now before the waiting throng, a solitary figure moves forward to the altar, carrying the lighted brand; the fire leaps up, and the offering on the altar goes up in flame. And suddenly in that dramatic moment, the tense silence is shattered, and from the packed throng rises a great burst of jubilant music, peal after peal of triumphant melody. "When the burnt offering began, the song of the Lord began also, with the trumpets."

To-day I want to say that, if you and I belong to God, this story can happen all over again, at altars more personal and private and individual. That the sternly disciplining touch of pain and disappointment is an almost inescapable element in life we have already seen: life will not always run our way. But here is the great discovery—that these sore and difficult things, instead of impoverishing, can positively enrich; that the hard self-denials we have to make, and the frustrations which our hopes endure, can actually, under God, put into our life something of tremendous value which was not there before, a deeper tone, a finer touch, a nobler music; and that, when in our experience the burnt offering begins, then for us—perhaps not until then—the song of the Lord may begin also with the trumpets.

Do you remember the old familiar legend of the German baron who built his castle by the Rhine? From crag to crag and from turret to turret he hung wires, hoping that the winds, as they blew upon this great Aeolian harp, might make sweet music. Long and patiently he waited, and round his castle winds from the four corners of heaven blew: and still no music came. But one night there arose a hurricane, tossing the Rhine to fury; the black sky was stabbed with lightning and the thunder rolled, the earth trembled, and the winds were mad and shrieking. The baron went to his great castle door to view the terrifying scene—when hark! the sound of music, like angels singing through the storm. And suddenly he realized what had happened. His harp, strung from crag to crag, had come to life at last. The tempest had given it a soul. That oft-told tale goes down to the heart of life's deep mystery. How often it is only when trouble comes that a man's true quality stands revealed! When the burnt offering—the sore, costly thing—begins, the song of the Lord begins also.

Here, let us say, is a man who in his youth dreamed a dream: he set his heart on attaining success and distinction in his profession. But success and distinction, as the world counts them, have never come to him, no plaudits of the crowd, no glare of flattery or fame. Has he then failed? If he is no longer searching for the world's applause, if he has grown content to work on quite obscure, if he has seen issues that lie deeper far than human praise or blame, if he has learnt to live by the faith that life's true values are spiritual—character, and kindness, and cheerfulness, and humility, and compassion—has he really failed? Failed! The man is a most triumphant success. And round the altar of the burnt-offering, that daily immolation of himself, there is the music of the trumpets.

Or here is a girl who was once, to all intents and purposes, utterly frivolous, living for pleasure and for self and nothing else; and then she got married, and God gave her a child; and one day her child fell ill, and there was a great hush in the home, and for days and nights the angel of death was hovering there, and the dark valley of the shadow seemed closing round her little one. Then, marvellously, the shadow receded, and the knock of death's angel at the door of the home was heard no longer, and healing came, and restoration; and from that hour, people have noticed something in that woman's life which was never there before—a new poise and dignity, a deeper tone, a tenderer and more radiant serenity. What has happened? Simply this—that when the burnt offering began, the song of the Lord has begun also.

I am not suggesting, mark you, that this always or inevitably happens. It is quite obvious that it does not. Sometimes trouble and disappointment and heartache produce a purely negative reaction. Sometimes the burnt offering leads only to bitterness and self-pity and resentment. It all depends on whether your life, at some point, can be laid open towards God.

One of the bravest, most poignant letters ever written tells of the death of Dr. Edward Wilson, Scott's companion in the Antarctic. Scott himself, dying in his tent, was the writer. "If this letter reaches you, Bill and I will have gone out together. We are very near it now, and I should like you to know how splendid he was at the end—everlastingly cheerful and ready to sacrifice himself for others, never a word of blame to me for leading him into this mess. His eyes have a comfortable blue look of hope and his mind is peaceful with the satisfaction of his faith in regarding himself as part of the great scheme of the Almighty. I can do no more to comfort you than to tell you that he died as he lived, a brave, true man—the best of comrades, and staunchest of friends." Will you think of that—for does not the secret of spiritual victory in the day of sacrifice lie there—"his eyes with a comfortable blue look of hope, and his mind peaceful with his faith that he is part of the great scheme of the Almighty"? It is on that kind of faith—for each and all of us—that everything in the last resort depends, the faith that our own life, with all its difficulties and problems and hard self-denials and defeated hopes, has nevertheless a place in God's great plan, and that even in the most hurting experiences love almighty is in control. Without that faith, life is bound to lead to bitterness. But with it, the sacrifice becomes the signal for the song.

And so I repeat, it all depends on whether our life is open to God, whether we are ready under all circumstances to say, "O God, not my will, but Thine be done!" Can you look up from your knees, when you are at your prayers, into the face of God the Father, and say—"Lord, ask anything Thou choosest, anything at all, and if it is Thy will for me, I will accept it! Even if it means some terribly difficult denial of my own plans and dreams, even if it drives me down a lonelier, harder road than I ever thought I should have to travel—if it is Thy will, O God, for me, with unwavering heart I will accept it"—can you say that, and mean it?

You see, we have gone deeper now. The burnt offering we are thinking of now is something more than the inevitable discipline life puts us through. It is the surrender of our will to a higher will. It is the crushing down of our personal inclinations that our duty to God may be supreme. It is the dedication of every dream and desire to the mastery of Christ. It is the consecration of life to the religion of the cross. And that is the costliest burnt offering of all.

And that is why on many altars, and perhaps upon our own, it has never yet been offered. "I refuse to make such a surrender of myself," we say. "I will not have my inclinations thus overridden. I will not hand over the planning and controlling of my life to a higher authority. I will not bring myself to say:

> The dearest idol I have known,
>   Whate'er that idol be,
> Help me to tear it from Thy throne.

I will not do it! For if I did, what would be left to me? It would spoil everything. The zest of life, the liberty, the keen edge of its most thrilling pleasures, would all be gone. That burnt offering would stifle all the music!"

If only something or some one could convince us that that is the profoundest of mistakes! Cling to those inclinations, refuse to have

God interfering, plan out your heart's desire—does happiness lie that way? Surely life has taught us enough to make us see that that way only restlessness lies, and a dreadful unsatisfied feeling, and a hunger for something more than the poor prizes of this earth.

And if you are wanting happiness—and it is only natural that you should—if it is peace you are hungry for, and the ending of the strained, restless feeling which is like a fever in the soul and a shadow on the face, if you would like a heart not driven this way and that, but steady and satisfied and serene, will you remember what Dante said, the deepest, truest thing of all—"In His will is our peace"? I beg you to be sure of this, that however hard and difficult and sacrificial the road of that will may seem, it is down that thorny and unlikely road that there is waiting the great discovery, the very thing which has been sought everywhere else in vain—the peace of being able to forget oneself, the happiness of a heart content, and the serenity of God which passeth understanding. Our true life, our Christian effectiveness, our share in the joy which is the Spirit's most characteristic fruit, will always depend on the degree in which we surrender, or fail to surrender, our inclinations to the final control of God. Spiritual power will always vary in direct proportion to spiritual dedication. "In His will is our peace"; and in our burnt offering of ourselves on the altar of that will is the song of the Lord, with the trumpets.

I cannot ask any one to believe this, or to accept the truth of it, just by hearing it: it is far too different from our ordinary way of viewing things for that. But I can ask some one here to put his own life, her own life, into it, and to make the experiment at least. None who ever did that failed to find it true.

Think of St. Francis, who dedicated himself to the crucified Christ with such a passion of devotion that they said the very wounds of Jesus appeared upon his flesh: it was out of the throes of that experience that he composed his great Canticle of the Sun, one of the most glorious outbursts of praise that ever broke from human lips:

> All creatures of our God and King,
> Lift up your voice and with us sing
> Alleluia!

The stigmata in his hands, and the Hallelujah in his heart! The burnt offering—and the song! Think of Paul and Silas, and of their first experience of Europe—the Philippian dungeon, the lash, the rack, the torture, and then—"at midnight Paul and Silas prayed, and sang praises unto God." The burnt offering and the song! Think of Mary of Nazareth, called from her girlhood dreams to travel the road of a lonely destiny, to be the mother of Jesus; think of how she shrank back trembling from the call and from the sword that was to pierce her heart, until at last she bowed her head, and said, "Behold, the handmaid of the Lord; be it unto me according to Thy word." And then, immediately thereafter, the Magnificat! "My soul doth magnify the Lord, and my spirit hath rejoiced in God my Saviour." The burnt offering and the song! Best of all, think of Jesus. "Father, let this cup pass! Let this cup pass!" And His sweat was like blood. But then—the quiet acceptance. "If this cup may not pass away from Me, except I drink it, Thy will be done." And then, with lifted head, on like a conqueror to the cross and the victory—and all the herald angels singing to welcome Him home! The burnt offering and the song!

You cannot accept this until you have tried it; but none who ever tested it failed to find it true.

For God stands loyally to His word; and the one thing that can never happen is this—that you should make the sacrifice, and take the difficult road of consecration, and then find that God had let you down, and that there was no spiritual power, no inward happiness, no peace of heart as your reward. That, on the guarantee of Christ, will never happen.

And mark you, it is no broken melody, nor any plaintive minor cadence, that is the music born of self-sacrifice: it is "the song of the Lord—*with the trumpets.*" It is not only, said Paul, being a conqueror over yourself: it is being more than conqueror. It is not taking up your daily cross with stoic resignation: it is finding, as Samuel Rutherford found, that the cross is "such a burden as wings are to a bird, or sails to a boat." The joy that comes on the difficult road is real joy. The happiness that lies in putting God's will first is genuine happiness. It is no pale, wan, pious pretence, no forced cheerfulness, no making the best of a bad job. It is really being happy. It has red blood in it. It is positive, and eager, and magnificently alive. It is the song of the Lord—with the trumpets!

And the reason is, that in Christianity at least, you are not sacrificing for anything so cold or abstract as duty or dogma or the dictates of a code: you are doing it for the best Friend you have ever had. You are doing it for God's splendid Christ, the dear divine Lover of your soul. Oh, we need to get the note of adoration back into our religion! We need to recapture the thrill of the friendship of Jesus. We need to stand on the shore at break of day, and see Him coming back to us after the dark night of all our base denials, to hear the voice that says, "Lovest thou Me?" Once we have been there with Jesus, we shall not want to talk of sacrifices any longer; but we shall say—with David Livingstone and James Chalmers and many another—that any price we have to pay to make God's will our own is not really sacrifice at all, for we would rather be with Christ than anywhere else in the world. And then indeed the burnt offering will go up to God with the song of the Lord and the trumpets.

There is a very beautiful poem, which seems to me to sum up and express everything I have tried to say to-day. It is the story of a soul that shrank from the difficult road, but finally accepted it, and found there a happiness unspeakable.

> I said, "Let me walk in the fields."
>   He said, "Nay, walk in the town."
> I said, "There are no flowers there."
>   He said, "No flowers, but a crown."
>
> I said, "But the sky is black,
>   There is nothing but noise and din."
> But He wept as He sent me back,
>   "There is more," He said, "there is sin."
>
> I said, "But the air is thick,
>   And fogs are veiling the sun."
> He answered, "Yet hearts are sick,
>   And souls in the dark undone."
>
> I said, "I shall miss the light,
>   And friends will want me, they say."
> He answered me, "Choose to-night,
>   If I am to miss you, or they."
>
> I cast one look at the fields,
>   Then set my face to the town.
> He said, "My child, do you yield?
>   Will you leave the flowers for the crown?"
>
> Then into His hand went mine,
>   And into my heart came He,
> And I walk in a light divine
>   The path that I feared to see.

So it always is. And so it may be for some one here this morning. When the burnt offering begins, the song of the Lord will begin also, with the trumpets.

JAMES STEWART · 1896–

THE POWER OF HIS RESURRECTION

"Now the God of peace, that brought again from the dead our Lord Jesus, that great Shepherd of the sheep, through the blood of the everlasting covenant, make you perfect in every good work to do His will, working in you that which is well pleasing in His sight, through Jesus Christ; to whom be glory for ever and ever" (Hebrews 13:20–21).

THE MOST CHARACTERISTIC WORD of the Christian religion is the word Resurrection. If you had to choose one word to gather up and focus and express the very essence of the faith, would this not have to be your choice?

For this is what Christianity essentially is: a religion of Resurrection. This is what every worshiping congregation is intended in the purpose of God to be: a community of the Resurrection. And this is what the Gospel offers today to this dark and ruined world, where men peering into the future are daunted by the well-nigh impossible task of creating order out of chaos and life out of death: the power of Resurrection. In short, this is the essential Gospel. Rejoice that the Lord is arisen!

It is true, of course, that for us Christians the cross must ever stand at the very heart of things. If we bungling, sinful creatures lose sight of the cross even for a day, we are done for—and we know it. But a man may gaze at the cross, and miss the Gospel that saves—for he is still on the wrong side of Easter. This is Christianity's symbol—not the dead figure of the crucifix, but Christ risen, trampling a broken cross beneath his feet: "neither is there salvation in any other."

Far too often we have regarded the Resurrection as an epilogue to the Gospel, an addendum to the scheme of salvation, a codicil to the divine last will and testament—thereby falsifying disastrously the whole emphasis of the Bible. The fact is there would never have been a New Testament at all, apart from the burning certainty of all its writers that He whose mighty deeds they were recording had conquered death and was alive for ever. This was no mere appendix to the faith: this was, this is, the faith—the overpowering, magnificent good news. Rejoice that the Lord is arisen!

There is no darkness which this does not illuminate, no despair this does not smite with sudden hope. Test it and see.

For example, many in these tense, tumultuous days are trembling

---

"The Power of His Resurrection" by James S. Stewart from *Best Sermons*, 1949–1950 ed. Edited by G. Paul Butler. Copyright, 1949 by G. Paul Butler, pp. 97–101. Reprinted by permission of Harper & Row, Publishers, and James S. Stewart.

for the ark of God, haunted by the fear that the powers of darkness may ultimately defeat the dreams for which Christ died. Many are paralyzed by the terrible doubt. But Easter means that God has already taken the measure of the evil forces at their very worst and most malignant, that He has met the challenge precisely at that point and routed the darkness and settled the issue. Rejoice that the Lord is arisen!

Or the trouble may be more personal. Many are feeling strained and depressed and tired out, and quite inadequate for life, worried by the failure and the muddle of their own experience. But Easter means a living, radiant Christ walking at your side on the weariest Emmaus road. Rejoice that the Lord is arisen!

Or the burden of the mystery may be heavier still. It may be that some one whom you loved the best has left you and passed out of sight for ever across the river, journeying away to the country from whose bourne no traveler returns. But Easter means One *has* returned, to tell you of the glory yonder. Rejoice that the Lord is arisen!

Test it and see. Here is an evangel to scatter every darkness, and to exhilarate every broken spirit with strength and courage. This is the only Gospel the New Testament knows. He is risen indeed. O magnify the Lord with me!

Let us take one of the most moving and memorable expressions of the Easter truth ever penned. In Hebrews 13:20–21, we read: "Now the God of peace, that brought again from the dead our Lord Jesus, that great shepherd of the sheep, through the blood of the everlasting covenant, make you perfect in every good work to do his will, working in you that which is well pleasing in his sight, through Jesus Christ; to whom be glory for ever and ever."

Notice particularly how the writer puts it. He says, speaking of the Resurrection—"It was God who did this thing. It was God's mighty act that brought up the Lord Jesus from the dead."

This emphasis is characteristic of all the men of the New Testament. It is immensely significant that these first Christians never preached the Resurrection simply as Jesus' escape from the grave, as the reanimation of One who had died, or as the return of the Master to his friends. They always proclaimed it as the living God in omnipotent action. It was God's hands that had taken the stone which the builders rejected, and made it the head of the corner. "This is the Lord's doing," they declared, "and it is marvellous in our eyes."

Their insight taught them that it was what lay behind the Resurrection that mattered. And what lies behind it is this—God vindicating the dreams for which Christ died, God ratifying righteousness, justice and truth against the evil powers that hate these things and seek to crush and crucify them, God announcing His invincible divine determination to make Christ Lord of all.

It is at this point that the Resurrection fact strikes right into world history as it confronts us today. This is the dramatic relevance of Easter to our own confused, bewildered age. For if the power that was strong enough to get Jesus out of the grave, mighty enough to shatter and confound the whole hideous demonic alliance of evil, creative enough to smite death with resurrection—if this power is in action still (as the basic proclamation of Christianity declares), why then, you and I can lift up our heads, knowing and rejoicing that "God is in the field when He is most invisible." He shall not fail nor be discouraged till He have established truth for ever in the earth, and brought in the kingdom of heaven.

But the message comes home to us more intimately than this. For see how this writer to the Hebrews continues. "Now may God, who brought again from the dead the Lord Jesus, make *you* perfect in every good work to do his will, working *in you* that which is well pleasing in his sight." That is to say, the same divine creative energy which resurrected Christ is available for you, for me: and that, mark you, not only at death to raise us up, but here and now to help us to live.

Who could realize this, and not be thrilled by it? Here is the apostle praying for those Christians and for that Church, that the identical force which God had exerted in taking Jesus out of the grave might operate on a similar scale in their own lives, might go inwardly to work to make them strong and pure and brave and vital—to make them, in short, resurrected personalities, throbbing with new life!

I sometimes wonder if we have ever really comprehended that this—nothing less—is what the Gospel offers: the power which shattered death for Jesus, to help us now to live!

It is surely worth our pondering. Here was the Lord Christ, wounded and burdened and bowed down with human sin, cut off from the land of the living, with everything apparently lost, and all his hopes and dreams (so the world thought) dead and done for and defeated—and God by one mighty act of power, by the sheer energy of grace, had brought him through and set him on high: and now for ever that same power—not something different, but that identical energy—available for you, for me, for all who will receive it!

Too often we are like the man with the rake in Bunyan's dream, gazing permanently downwards, obsessed with such poor sticks and straws and dust as our own weak efforts of will, our own ineffectual resolves and insubstantial, wistful longings: never dreaming that the Lord God who resurrected Christ is standing there beside us, with that gift of supernatural power—ours, if we would have it!

It is this that explains the irrepressible excitement of early Christianity. They went, those followers of Jesus, to men who had been morally and spiritually defeated scores, hundreds of times, and they said—"Here is a way of victory! God has brought again from the dead the Lord Jesus. With such a power at work, what may not happen — for you?"

That was the message. And lest any of their hearers should think they were being merely rhetorical and romantic, always, these men of the New Testament went on to say — "We know it, for we have proved it. It has worked for us!"

The truth of that claim is apparent. How was it that a little group of men in an upper room — ordinary, fallible, blundering men — were able to go out and turn the world upside down? It was not that they were commanding personalities — most of them were not. It was not that they had official backing, impressive credentials, or illustrious patronage: of all that they had less than nothing. It was this — that they had established contact with the power that has resurrected Jesus, or rather, that this unearthly power had laid hold upon them.

And still today they accost us, saying — "It is abroad now in the earth, the power of the Resurrection. Why not for you?" And they look at us with absolute assurance: "Why not for you?"

But we are so slow to take it in. We are like our forefathers who lived all their days in a world containing the marvel of electricity and never guessed it was there. Dr. Johnson once said a striking thing about Oliver Goldsmith: "He would be a great man, if he realised the wealth of his internal resources." If only we Christians would come awake to that!

But we hesitate. "It can't apply to us," we say. "Our lives are not the stuff out of which God's Easter victories are made. And as for hoping to live on Christ's level, with that new risen quality of life, why, what's the use? All very well to talk like that, but we stopped trying long ago. It can't be for us — our problems are too many, our thwarting frailties too baffling, our chains of defeat too firmly shackled on our souls. We have toiled all night, and taken nothing." And so we go on our way with what Thomas Carlyle noted in Coleridge — "a look of anxious impotence in his eyes."

But those men of the New Testament will not accept that denial. "You surely don't imagine," they cry to us, "that the power which took Christ out of the grave is going to be baffled by you? That the God who did that terrific thing is going to find your little problem too hard for Him to deal with? That the God who in the mighty act of Easter broke through the last darkness of the universe is going to confess Himself impotent on the scale of your life, and say — 'No, I cannot work any miracles here: this is too intractable for Me'? But that just does not make sense," these writers say, "that doubt is utterly irrational! He that brought again from the dead the Lord Jesus, shall He not — today if you will ask Him — revive and quicken you?"

This, however, must be added: there is one condition. Before the creative God can come into our life, before this dynamic reality can lay hold of us, before our spirits can know the baptism of power and of eternity, one thing is needful. Self-surrender. Self-commitment.

And this writer to the Hebrews has very dramatically reminded us of that. For did you notice that even this magnificent, triumphant verse has a streak of blood across it? Did you hear, through this shout of Easter praise and the trumpets of victory, the diapason note of sacrifice? "The God of peace, that brought again from the dead our Lord Jesus . . . *through the blood of the everlasting covenant.*" There was no road to Easter for Jesus except by Good Friday; no way to that risen eternal quality of life except by life laid down. And that being so, this, too, is axiomatic: there is no road to the power of Easter for any of us except at the cost of self-commitment; no way to the experience of having God's energies loosed and set free into our life except through the discipline of self-surrender. That is the condition.

Here then, is the question each of us must face. With the supernatural force waiting to be used, this power that resurrected Christ and energized the Church and made life new for multitudes — with this available, why should my life ever be helpless and maimed and impoverished and defeated? Is it that I have been unwilling to travel the road that Jesus went and all the saints — the exacting road of consecration?

The ultimate secret of Resurrection power was given by William Cowper in the lines we often sing:

> The dearest idol I have known,
>   Whate'er that idol be,
> Help me to tear it from Thy throne,
>   And worship only Thee.

That is the streak of blood. That is the Good Friday sacrifice. And beyond it — all the power of Easter, all the efficiency of a conquering soul, all the thrill of being risen with Christ, all the marvel of life blossoming red from the dust of self's defeat.

THE DESIRE OF ALL NATIONS

"All the ends of the earth shall see the salvation of our God" (Isaiah 52:10).

PROLOGUE

THE HOPE OF THE WORLD lies in the Christmas message: Immanuel, God with us. Today some are looking to political machinery to fashion a new earth, some to social security, some to humanitarian sentiment and ethical endeavor. We need these things indeed; but unless there is a surer foundation we shall be heading straight for disillusionment. Not man's self-sufficiency but God's redemptive action, not mere human planning on the horizontal level but the inrush of a new power from the beyond—this is our supreme need now. In short, Christ is (albeit often unrecognized) the Desire of all nations, the Hope of the ends of the earth.

Now will you make an act of imagination? Imagine it is the year 1 B.C. We are going on a journey. We are about to visit three great cities: Rome, Athens, Jerusalem. We shall overhear three conversations—three groups of typical men discussing their hopes and fears for the world, just before the birth of Christ. Perhaps we shall find our own hopes and fears mirrored there.

I

The City of Rome. A room in an Officers' Club. Three junior Officers of Caesar's Army—Gaius, Cassius, Octavius—are discussing new postings for overseas which have just been announced.

GAIUS:
So you are going off, Cassius, with the next draft to Asia; and you, Octavius, to the forgotten legion in the wilds of Britain. I'm luckier than either of you! I'm for Carthage and North Africa. The gods only know when we three shall meet again. Do you like this overseas service, Cassius?

CASSIUS:
Like it? I hate it! But what can you do? It is the penalty of belonging to so great an Empire. It is the price of being a citizen of the master race. That's what we owe to Caesar. Have you heard the terms of Caesar's latest edict? "There has gone forth a decree from Caesar Augustus that all the world should be taxed." Those were the very words. All

---

"The Desire of All Nations" by James S. Stewart from *Best Sermons,* 1947-1948 ed. Edited by G. Paul Butler. Copyright, 1947 by G. Paul Butler. Reprinted by permission of Harper & Row, Publishers, and James S. Stewart.

the world—*that's* our Empire! That's why you have to go to Africa, Gaius, and you, Octavius, to Britain, and myself to Asia. Do you know what they are calling Caesar now? I heard them shouting it as he drove to the Colosseum yesterday. The air was ringing with it. They cried— "Caesar! Hail, Caesar Augustus, Saviour of the world!" Wasn't it fine?
OCTAVIUS:

Fine? I wonder. Saviour of the world Caesar? Oh, no doubt he has given us the Pax Romana: but what is that, when all is said and done? A subtle manipulation of the balance of power, and the legions massed on the frontiers. The thing looks secure, built to last a thousand years— but don't you trust it. The foundations are creaking. I tell you, the glittering civilization we are so proud of is disintegrating, and it will take more than Caesar to stop the rot. The recent revolt of the slaves, for instance—that was a symptom. Oh, I know they crucified the lot, and silenced them: but it showed what is coming. And I ask you, Cassius and Gaius, is it right that there should be a million slaves? Is it right that with all the resources of civilization at our disposal, there should still be those subhuman conditions? Is it right that life should be so cheap? There was Quirinus the other day. They wanted a son in the family, and when that baby was born it was a girl; and they threw the child out to die. Is *that* right? Surely you must see it—this shining civilization of ours has in itself the seeds of its own corruption and death. What do you say, Gaius?
GAIUS:

I say, Octavius, you're mad to talk like that! Don't you know that if Rome relaxed its hold, the world would fall to pieces? Don't you know that if you liberate the slaves, you wreck the State? Am I not right, Cassius?
CASSIUS:

Of course you are, Gaius. Don't you get playing with these revolutionary ideas, Octavius! In any case, you won't find any support— unless it is from some of those meddling Jews. Pompey was a fool ever to bring them here to Rome, but Caesar will look after them. Caesar knows what he is about. He has this cosmopolitan crowd under his thumb. Bread and circuses—that is all they want. As long as they have bread to eat, and circuses to amuse them, they ask no more. Can't you see that, Octavius?
OCTAVIUS:

No, Cassius, I can't. Bread and circuses! Do you think man can live by that? He wants more. He wants life. He wants freedom. I tell you, Cassius, he wants God!
CASSIUS:

Hark, Gaius, to our very religious Captain! He tells us we need God. Well—that, too, Caesar has given. Has not Caesar himself been raised to the rank of divinity? You and I, of course, don't believe it. We know it is just political expediency. But the man-in-the-street does believe it—and it hoaxes him all right. This Emperor-worship keeps men quiet: and what else is religion for? Do you agree, Gaius?

GAIUS:

Yes, heartily. That crowd at the Colosseum was right. Caesar *is* the Saviour of the world. And if you want peace on earth, good will among men, power politics will give it—nothing else!

OCTAVIUS:

You're wrong, Gaius! I know you're wrong. I had a dream one night. It was when I was away last year with the Fifteenth Legion building the great new military road across Macedonia to the East. One night I dreamt another army was using the road we had made—an army coming out of the East to match its power with Caesar. A strange army it was—peasants and artisans and fisherfolk and slaves. And on their banners they had—what do you think? A gallows-tree! A cross! And they spoke of another Emperor, both God and man in one, both dead and alive forever. And nothing could stop them. I saw them reaching Rome. I saw them casting down the throne of Caesar. I saw their strange new Emperor taking his place. Then I awoke, and it was a dream. But—Gaius, Cassius—I think God sent it. I think it meant that power politics has had its day. I think the strange new Emperor will be the Saviour of the world.

II

Now we leave Rome, and pass on to Athens. Three dons of the University of Athens, members of the Hellenic Academy of philosophy and the sciences, are having a walk together on the Areopagus, conversing as they go. Their names are Aristo, Leonidas and Dionysius. It is still the year 1 B.C.

ARISTO:

I hear you had a famous triumph in the debate last night, Leonidas. What was it all about?

LEONIDAS:

It was about the ideal society—the new order we have all been talking about for the last four hundred years, ever since Plato wrote his *Republic*. The actual title of the debate was "Can Culture Save the World?" I led for the affirmative.

ARISTO:

And who took the negative?

LEONIDAS:

It was Thrasymachus. You know him. He's a melancholy dog. His argument amounted to this—that if Culture could have saved the world, then why didn't Plato and Pericles save it, four hundred years ago? A fallacy, of course.

ARISTO:

Indeed, Leonidas, a glaring fallacy. And what did you say?

LEONIDAS:

Oh, I took the line that Plato and Aristotle laid the foundation, but the new knowledge has to permeate the general mind—which means universal education. I pointed out that we are moving in that direction: witness the fact that we have a universal language now—the Greek tongue will carry you anywhere in the world today. What a chance, by the way, for the missionaries of a new religion, if one should ever appear! I pointed out that little by little we are banishing ignorance, that we are translating knowledge into practical resources for living, that indeed there is no limit to what scientific enlightenment and intellectual energy may achieve. And with the last words of my peroration, I quite brought down the house!

ARISTO:

I'm sure you did, Leonidas. What were your last words?

LEONIDAS:

They were these: "The mind of man the only Saviour of the world!" Oh yes, it was a good debate; and when they took the vote, a splendid triumph—one hundred and seventy votes to forty-five—no doubt about it! You should have been there, Aristo; and you too, Dionysius. You're very quiet today, Dionysius. You don't challenge my argument, do you?

DIONYSIUS:

Yes, Leonidas, I do. You say knowledge—Culture—can save the world. I say it can't—not ever! You say knowledge is power. Yes, but power for what? Suppose a man is dominated by self-interest, what is to prevent him using his power for selfish instead of benevolent ends? Nothing. What is to prevent him making intelligence, Culture, truth itself the accomplice of evil? Nothing. All your argument in the debate last night, Leonidas, goes to pieces on one rock—the fact of evil, which not all your logic can rationalize away. You're a philosopher. You must see that!

LEONIDAS:

Yes, I think I do. But what is the alternative? If you rule out Culture and enlightenment as the Saviour of the world, what are you to put in their place? Force—like those imperial masters of ours at Rome?

DIONYSIUS:

No, Leonidas, certainly not force!

LEONIDAS:

Well, then, if salvation can come neither from the war lords at Rome nor from the Academy at Athens, where is it to come from? You are not suggesting we should look to Olympus, are you? We have a whole Pantheon of gods there to choose from—Zeus, Athene, Artemis, Apollo, and all the bickering hierarchy of heaven. Why, our very Acropolis is stuffed full of their statues: I hear that the latest—in case any deity should have been inadvertently overlooked—is inscribed "To the Unknown God"! This multiplicity of gods is the satire of every cheap comedian. You are not suggesting we should be credulous enough to make our prayer to them? Are you, Dionysius?

DIONYSIUS:

No, Leonidas, I don't mean that. But listen. You have read your Homer. You have heard Homer tell of gods like Apollo coming down to earth in human form. That's myth, of course. There is no salvation there. But just think, Leonidas – think, Aristo – what if the Great Spirit Himself, the First Cause and Creator of the universe, took flesh and came amongst us, and shared with us His being, His infinite power, His eternal life? Would *that* not be salvation?

LEONIDAS:

Oh, Dionysius, if only it could be! The great God . . . walking this very earth . . . the Healer and the Saviour of the world!

III

Once again we move on. From Rome and Athens we pass to Jerusalem. Let us enter one of the porches of the Temple. There three men are talking: a priest, a scribe, a Rabbi. They are Abner, Baruch and Joseph. The time is still 1 B.C.

BARUCH:

I love that psalm we had at morning prayers – the longest and the greatest of them all. Its words keep ringing in my heart: "O how I love Thy law! It is my meditation all the day." If men would only keep the law, and practice its precepts of brotherhood and good will and mutual kindliness, all our troubles would be solved. Salvation is such a simple thing: keep the law, and earn God's favor – do good works, and merit heaven. And if you fail, there is all the ritual of the sacrifices to put you right again. That's your part, Abner. You're a priest.

ABNER:

Yes, Baruch, if your lifework is the law, mine is the sacrificial system. Our fathers gave us everything when they gave us these. The law and the sacrifices – the salvation of the world! Why are you frowning, Rabbi Joseph? Don't you agree?

JOSEPH:

Listen, Abner – and you, Baruch. You've got the law and the sacrifices: are you content with the result? I certainly am not. Here am I, a Rabbi, a religious man: but I know my life, my character, are far short of what they ought to be. And you? Are you never disappointed? Never frustrated? Is the good always victorious – in you? Can you say that honestly? Oh, why are we all so impotent? Tell me that, Abner, priest of God!

ABNER:

Speak for yourself, Rabbi Joseph. I don't admit the impeachment. I am a righteous man. I thank God I am. I fast twice in the week. I give tithes of all I possess. I am quite satisfied with my record.

JOSEPH:

Are you really, Abner? Are you sure you are not running away from the truth about yourself? Have you ever faced yourself with all pretenses down? You're so proud of your good works. That's precisely the trouble: good works and pride—always hand in hand. And pride is the cardinal sin. So that our very good works, our very obediences to the law, are our undoing. That's the vicious circle, Abner; and neither your sacrifices nor Baruch's law can break it. Don't you see that's true?

BARUCH:

I see, Joseph, that you are becoming much too subtle. Besides, you're forgetting something. What about the Messiah? You don't imagine that Messiah, when He comes, is going to trouble about your bits of sins—or mine, or Abner's? He will have more to do than that! He is coming to deal with those Roman usurpers of our liberties, coming to consign the whole hateful crew to Gehenna. Down with Rome and up with Jewry! That's what I say. That's the kind of Saviour Israel needs. Rabbi Joseph, face the facts!

JOSEPH:

But I do! And the more I face them the more I see that your kind of Saviour will never save the world. Not through that sort of Messiah will man's inward spiritual nature find renewal. Above everything else man needs forgiveness. He needs cleansing. He needs the power of a new nature. And I tell you, Abner, all your religious observance can't do it. Baruch, all your moral effort is hopeless. If the human predicament is ever to be resolved, God alone must do it. But just think, Abner, when you talk about sacrifice—what if God should make the sacrifice? Remember, Baruch, when you quote your psalms about the law, what another psalmist says: "If I make my bed in Hell, behold, Thou art there!" If God were in very truth to come and meet us there, the great eternal Maker of us all humbling Himself for our sakes to the lowest depths, nothing could stand against that! It would be the routing of the darkness and the ending of the night. All things would be made new. O come, Redeemer of the race! Come now, O Saviour of the world!

EPILOGUE

Our journey is over. We have visited Rome, Athens, Jerusalem in the year 1 B.C. The hopes and fears we have encountered there—are they not just our own hopes and fears today? For still some look to power and government for the saving of the world; and some to knowledge and enlightenment; and some to the self-sufficiency of the morally religious man. But through it all, the human heart, unhealed, stands crying for a better deliverance. And at this holy Christmas season Jesus comes again. He comes—the Desire of all nations. He comes—your everlasting Hope.

Our glad hosannas, Prince of Peace,
Thy welcome shall proclaim;
And heaven's exalted arches ring
With Thy most honoured Name.

GENEROSITY WITHOUT LIMIT

"You know how generous our Lord Jesus Christ has been: he was rich, yet for your sake he became poor, so that through his poverty you might become rich" (2 Corinthians 8:9, NEB).

HERE in one trenchant concentrated sentence, interjected as it might seem almost casually into the midst of a severely practical discussion of church finance and Christian liberality, Paul has summed up the very heart of the evangel. "You know how generous our Lord Jesus Christ has been" — and then follow the four points of the compass of salvation.

1. *The wealth of Christ:* "He was rich." This points to the fact that the Christian religion does not start on earth: it starts in heaven. It does not begin with the stable and the manger: it begins at the throne of God. Our faith has in it the dimension of eternity, the mystery which flashed out in that startling word of Jesus — "Before Abraham was, I AM."

What Christians worship is not a human life that climbed up to God by some vague process of deification: it is a God who came down into humanity by an act of incarnation. We shall never really understand the faith, nor realize why it was that early Christianity hit the Roman Empire like a thunderbolt, until we have seen Bethlehem and Calvary against their proper background, which is that terrific background of the eternal world. This is what Paul was driving at when he said, in tones of breathless wonder, "He was rich."

Don't think this is remote theology, irrelevant in a world of strikes and nuclear weapons and inflationary spirals and jet propulsion. That is precisely what it is not. The fact is, it is the one faith realistic enough,

Reprinted from *Expository Times* 76 (October 1964): 32–34. Used by kind permission of James S. Stewart and T. & T. Clark.

down-to-earth enough, to make an impact either on the Roman Empire in the first century or on the problems of the world in the twentieth.

Do let us be clear that what we celebrate in church is not the life and death of a religious genius who taught wonderful lessons about the Fatherhood of God and the brotherhood of man, and held views on ethics and international politics far in advance of his time. That would never have crashed into the throne of Caesar and routed the darkness of the world. What the New Testament bears witness to on every page—what in point of historical fact carried the gospel like flame across the world—was not any such timid, reduced, desupernaturalized version of the faith. It was the stupendous conviction that in Christ Jesus the ultimate and eternal had struck down into history and broken right through into the life of man.

Behind Bethlehem and Calvary is the throne of heaven: which means that behind all the sufferings and tragedies and terrible mysteries of earth is the magnificent availability of infinite grace to help in time of need.

"You know the generosity of our Lord Jesus Christ," writes Paul, "that though he was rich—you know it!" Well then, he means, live by it, exult in it. For the hope of the world is there.

2. *The poverty of Christ:* "for your sake he became poor." Look at the record of that life: born in a stable; toiling at a joiner's bench; He fought no battles; He wrote no books; the applause of listening senates was never His to command; a man of sorrows and acquainted with grief; a real man, not an archangel or demi-god, a real man knowing the ache of weariness and the sweat of toil and the disenchantment of human ingratitude; the victim of bigotry, political opportunism, legalized murder; buried in a borrowed grave; leaving behind Him one legacy only— "My peace I leave with you." And all the time—this is the endless amazement of it, the thought that thrills those men of the New Testament—at the back of that humiliation, the splendour and glory of God! That glory was His true home. There He rightfully belonged. And now He had been stripped of every atom of glory, every shred of power, every rag of reputation. He had fathomed the fearful pit and the miry clay. He endured the Cross, and despised the shame. He descended into hell.

And, says Paul, writing to those Corinthians and writing still to you and me, it was "for your sake." For the great principle that runs through life is this: you can't help a man unless you get right alongside him. Caring for others is always linked to sacrifice. If you really care, it drains the virtue out of you—for it means you feel others' burdens as your burden: their troubles and defeats and complications become your own.

It is here that the Christian revelation breaks in with a trumpet-toned "how much more God!" God, to help this broken world, came right alongside its misery and frustration. "He was made sin for us," says Paul of Jesus in words that startle and shock, "He became a curse for us." The hope of this confused, bewildered earth is that in its deepest darkness God is veritably present. And whatever our personal predicament—fighting with loneliness, battered by temptation, wrestling with doubt, half-paralysed by the uncertainties of the future—is it not mightily reinforcing to know that the great Helper of men is really there at our side?

"You know how generous our Lord Jesus Christ has been," writes Paul, "he was rich, yet for your sake he became poor." You know that generous grace—it has been the theme of every Christian hymn you have ever sung, and of every Christian prayer you have ever said: and you know it is not myth or delusion, but a magnificent, triumphant reality in the strength of which you can live and die. For He who spared not His own Son, but delivered Him up for us all, how shall He not with Him also freely give us everything else besides?

3. Now the third point in this compass of salvation: *our poverty apart from Christ.* "So that through his poverty you might become rich"—this implies that in ourselves we are as poor as beggars.

Suppose that by some unthinkable calamity the revelation of God in Christ were suddenly taken out of your life; suppose you were left to fight your battle beneath the banner of materialism and to live by bread alone; suppose it were finally demonstrated that Jesus' teaching had been illusory and the truth for which He died a lie—would anything else, anything the wide world could offer, compensate for a loss so shattering and terrible?

This applies not only to individuals, but to nations, cultures, and civilizations. All the riches of human intelligence, skill, and planning, all the passion for a nobler justice on the earth, will not rescue the race from chaos and destruction, unless God first meets man at the level of his sin. If there is no superhuman factor in this fight, the dream is hopeless, and secular optimism just a tinkling cymbal: we are of all men most miserable.

And what of those who have been cradled in the love of Christ from their mothers' arms, to whom life's most moving experiences of joy and sorrow, marriage and parenthood, and the hush that falls when death is in the home, have come all haloed with the love of heaven? Take away God's mighty act in Christ, and what is left? Dust and ashes and emptiness and regret. It was to save us from this impoverishment that heaven stooped down to earth at Bethlehem and Nazareth and Calvary and the empty tomb. You know this grace of Christ, cries Paul, you know it and have proved it; and you know you are bankrupt without it!

4. Finally, *our wealth in union with Christ:* "so that through his poverty you might become rich."

Our dull and doubting minds are terribly slow to grasp it—the fabulous wealth that Christ our Lord holds out to us, the colour He can bring to life, the strength, the healing, the confident serenity.

What does it mean to find the Kingdom? Jesus once drew a picture of it. A poor farm labourer was out ploughing the field. His wages were a mere pittance; the family in the cottage could never made ends meet. And then one day suddenly, out there in the field, this man's plough struck something—buried treasure! He dashed home, broke in babbling almost incoherently, cried—"It has happened! Our troubles are over, we are rich beyond our dreams!" Something of that order, said Jesus, is what it means to find the Kingdom.

But we don't believe it, do we? Not really? St. Teresa in her day believed it. "With five shillings," she said, when they were scoffing at her for planning to build a new orphanage, seeing that five shillings was all she possessed, "with five shillings Teresa can do nothing: but with five shillings and God there is nothing Teresa cannot do!" Samuel Rutherford in his day believed it. He was writing from prison a letter to a friend. "Jesus Christ," he wrote, "came into my cell last night, and every stone flashed like a ruby!"

Do let us believe our own faith. "All things are yours in Christ," cries Paul—forgiveness yours, hope and peace and courage yours, the very power in which Jesus and the apostles lived yours; so that there is no trial you can't meet like a conqueror, no clamorous besieging perplexity you can't master with the glory of God in the here and now, no piercing thorns you can't wear as a kingly crown—through the grace of Jesus.

You know that grace. Thank God with all your heart that you know it. Thank God for Him who though He was rich for your sake became poor, that through His poverty you might become rich.

So Paul's words have taken us round the four points of the compass of our faith. As we saw at the outset, the words themselves seem interjected almost casually into a strictly practical discussion on Christian liberality and stewardship. But in this the apostle's intention is plain. "You know," he urges those Corinthians, "that Christ did this colossal, overwhelmingly generous thing for you. Will you not do a very minor thing for Him?"

It is this practical challenge that matters for us all. There is something God is asking each of us to do for Him—some gift we have been holding back, some sacrifice we are disinclined to make, some personal interest we will not surrender. But—we know the stupendous generosity of God, the heights and depths of Christ's self-sacrificing grace. And knowing it, can we hold back? Must we not lay our offering, ourselves, at Jesus' feet?

THE DIVINE STRATEGY

"It is not possible that the blood of bulls and of goats should take away sins. He has appeared to put away sin by the sacrifice of himself" (Hebrews 10:4, 9:26).

THE HISTORY of mankind has been the record of an age-long endeavour to answer one stubborn question, to deal with one radical dilemma. Where is real security to be found? How can the twist of evil in the world be straightened out? Can its jarring discords be resolved, its fierce tensions overcome? Can some strategy be devised to save man from the chaos of his own contriving, some expedient to take away sin?

It is the ever-recurring question which has haunted the thoughts of men since the dim ages of the distant past. To-day, more acutely than ever, it is forced on us. For twentieth-century man sees the glittering civilization he has laboriously constructed disintegrating before his eyes. He feels that his magnificent achievements of secular knowledge and invention may be working out to his own destruction. This is the desperate predicament which humanity seems powerless to heal. "O wretched man that I am, who shall deliver me?" Can anything deal redeemingly with this situation? Can anyone save us here?

It is the old perpetual question, with a new cosmic urgency to-day. But beside all this, each of us individually, if we are honest at all, knows that it is our question too. For in our own lives there appears the same predicament. Our best attempts to master our fate and captain our souls and work out our destiny are damaged by the same contradiction. If only we could eliminate the hard core of self, and conquer the estrangement and distortion, and achieve true spiritual harmony! It is the inarticulate demand of multitudes. "How can I be right with life and God? What will take away sins?"

Think for a moment of some of the great classic answers to that question down the centuries.

There was the answer of the Jew. "The blood of bulls and of goats" —as the writer to the Hebrews expresses it—in other words the whole elaborate sacrificial system, this was the device to purge the evil and break the vicious circle and set men free.

Now we all have something of the Hebrew in our constitution, and in some degree that kind of answer—modified and brought up to date—has been ours. Thus, when I trust to the externals of religion to secure me in the sight of God, my inner life still remaining unchanged; when, for example, my membership in a church has never made me

---

Reprinted from *Expository Times* 72 (July 1961): 304–6. Used by kind permission of James S. Stewart and T. & T. Clark.

acutely concerned for the refugee, the racially disinherited, or even for that un-churchy family down my own street, I am simply perpetuating the blunder of those in every age who have thought to save themselves by external ordinances, failing to see that all the religious observance in the world without a changed heart matters to God not one iota.

There came a time when the Jew himself began to doubt his own solution. "Wherewith shall I come before the Lord," cried one of his greatest prophets, "and bow myself before the high God? shall I come before him with burnt-offerings? ... Will the Lord be pleased with thousands of rams, or with ten thousands of rivers of oil?" The writer to the Hebrews is bluntly emphatic in his retort: "It is not possible that the blood of bulls and of goats should take away sins." There is no healing there.

So we turn to a second classic answer to the human predicament: *the answer of the Greek*. The Greek mind owes a double allegiance — to art and to philosophy. Hence the answer the Greek gave to the question about healing the hurt of humanity had two sides to it — one aesthetic, one intellectual. Over against the radical evil of the world the Greek sets the apprehension of beauty and the logic of thought. Why vex your soul about evil? The loveliness of Nature would charm it away; or alternatively, the wit of the philosopher would rationalize it away. Nothing else was needed.

To-day we all have something of the Greek in our constitution, and to some degree his answer has been ours. We, too, have thought to find our freedom aesthetically and intellectually.

Now admittedly the beauty of Nature is a thing to revel in. But as for "breaking the power of cancelled sin," will the perfumes of Arabia work that cleansing miracle? And what of our attempts to rationalize the mystery of evil away? With Hamlet, we may tell ourselves — "There is nothing either good or bad, but thinking makes it so." All the troubles of humanity could be solved by the application of a little logic and intelligence. So we say: until God silences that trifling, and out of the silence comes a voice — "Ye must be born again." It is not possible for man's intelligence, or his sense of beauty, to take away sin.

The third classic answer to the quest is *the answer of the Roman*. This can be expressed in a single word: moralism. The Roman Empire in the heyday of its power had an extraordinary genius for law and order. *"In disciplinam Augustorum"* — reads an inscription on a monument erected by Roman legionaries — "To the discipline of the Emperors." Certainly if discipline, the codification of law for the ordering of life, if that could have brought salvation, the Roman Empire would have done it — and Christ need never have died.

We have all something of the Roman in our constitution. How often we have trusted to man's political ideals and social labours for the saving of the world—yes, and to our own self-discipline and moral achievement to secure us in our status before God!

And where have they landed us? Is it not written devastatingly clear on the page of history that man cannot be his own redeemer? And for ourselves—can't we see that reliance on discipline, moralism, good works, call it what you will, tends inevitably towards that self-centredness and satisfaction and pride which, more than any weakness of the flesh, is the basic human sin?

The answer of the Roman, like the answers of Jew and Greek, fails us.

> Not the labours of my hands
> Can fulfil Thy law's demands.

"It is not possible."

What then? Then, rising out of the midnight of man's despair, smiting the darkness like a sudden dawn, comes the solving word: and all the classic answers of Jew and Greek and Roman fade before the glory of it.

> All for sin could not atone:
> *Thou must save, and Thou alone.*

Every other experiment fails: over every one of them is written the judgment of frustration—"It is not possible." Only Christ's experiment—the experiment of the Cross—triumphantly succeeds. "*He* hath appeared, to put away sin by the sacrifice of Himself."

I am deeply concerned that no one should imagine that this answer —the Christian answer to man's desperate predicament—is just archaic language, doctrinal theorising, vague, rhetorical, irrelevant. In point of fact, it is the most terrific thrust of absolutely shattering realism this world has ever seen. All our words and theologies stagger before the mystery of the Cross; but that is because the Cross itself is *the* eternal word, dynamic and explosive enough to turn the world inside out and set its cosmic dislocation right. It is more than a word— it is the supreme deed, God's deed, the dramatic break-through of the world beyond into this world of time and history. If you call the Cross history's blackest crime, the trumpeting triumph of concentrated naked demonism, you will be right: but God has got His hands on that demonic thing, and by a superb divine irony—like David using Goliath's own sword to behead the giant—has turned it into the Devil's irrevocable defeat. If only the world to-day would align itself with Jesus in His victory, we should see the powers of darkness discomfited again.

Do you see where this touches your life and mine? Suppose you get your life face to face with that Cross, that alchemy which turns the curse into a blessing and the iron of bitterness into the gold of peace. If it is going to heal the whole world at last, don't you think it could perhaps begin to heal you — even now with all the monotony of defeat, all the paralysis of ethical disenchantment? It is worth taking Jesus at His word.

The answer of the Cross succeeds where Jew and Greek and Roman failed. Is it possible that *this* should take away sins? Back comes the answer, a great shout from ten thousand times ten thousand voices: "Possible? It is proved, experienced fact!"

> Thou hast redeem'd us with thy blood,
>   and set the pris'ners free;
> Thou mad'st us kings and priests to God,
>   and we shall reign with thee.

These last two words are the crux of it: *"with Thee."* For as Christ identifies Himself with us in our weakness and defeat, so now we have to identify ourselves *with Him* in His power and victory.

The Cross may mean nothing to us — or it may mean everything. If it elicits no response in personal surrender, it will mean nothing: and the tedious, disillusioning struggle will go on unrelieved. If on the other hand we respond with every atom of our being, it can mean everything: and we shall know the joy of being made more than conquerors through our victorious Redeemer.

For additional information about James Stewart:

Davies, Horton. "Expository Preaching: Campbell Morgan, W. E. Sangster, and J. S. Stewart." *Varieties of English Preaching, 1900-1960.* Englewood Cliffs, N.J.: Prentice-Hall, 1963.

McDow, Malcolm Ray. "A Study of the Preaching of James Stuart Stewart." Th.D. dissertation, New Orleans Baptist Theological Seminary, 1968.

Stewart, James Stuart. *A Faith to Proclaim.* London: Hodder & Stoughton, 1953.

―――. *Heralds of God.* New York: Charles Scribner's Sons, 1946.

FOR OTHER SERMONS BY JAMES STEWART:

The Gates of New Life. New York: Charles Scribner's Sons, 1940.
The Wind of the Spirit. London: Hodder & Stoughton, 1968.
Also: *The Strong Name* (1941).

NORMAN VINCENT PEALE

1898–

NORMAN VINCENT PEALE, photograph, courtesy of the Foundation for Christian Living.

NORMAN VINCENT PEALE

1898   *Born May 31 in Bowersville, Ohio*
1920   *Received B.A. from Ohio Wesleyan College*
1924   *Received M.A. in social ethics and S.T.B. from Boston University; became pastor of Kings Highway Methodist Church in Brooklyn*
1927   *Became pastor of University Methodist Church in Syracuse, New York*
1930   *Married Ruth Stafford*
1932   *Became pastor of Marble Collegiate Church in New York City*
1952   *Wrote* The Power of Positive Thinking
1969   *Elected president of the Reformed Church in America*

EACH SUNDAY during the peak of his career, Norman Vincent Peale preached to more than four thousand persons in Marble Collegiate Church in New York. His sermons were published and distributed to a mailing list of over four hundred thousand. His books sold millions of copies. Foundations, magazines, newspaper columns, and radio programs flowed from his creative mind and were made concrete by his boundless energy. Few preachers have been more widely heard or better known than Norman Vincent Peale.

LIFE AND TIMES

Peale was born on May 31, 1898, in Bowersville, Ohio. His father, Clifford Peale, served as the town's Methodist minister. His mother provided enthusiastic warmth in their home. She instilled in her children the ambition to do great things for God.

Peale's home and church alike profoundly influenced him.

He idolized his father as the embodiment of strength and leadership. Sunday after Sunday he witnessed the power of Christ as it worked in human life. One of his most vivid memories was the conversion of the town tough. As he knelt down in the front of the church, the man was not ten feet from the family pew. The wide-eyed young preacher's son watched as the man surrendered his life to Jesus Christ. Afterwards the man was different, and Peale never forgot that experience.

Though a bright child, he was exceedingly sensitive and shy. Frequently he would hide in the attic rather than be available to recite for visitors. On at least one occasion his Uncle Will dragged him from his hiding place to the living room where he was ordered to do his part. His first public speech was a catastrophe. He rehearsed before mirrors and memorized his speech, but when he stepped on the stage, panic drove memory from him. According to the account in his biography, the event occurred like this:

> As he tottered to the front of the stage in the auditorium, his eye fell upon a little girl in the second row. She seemed to be regarding him with interest, and so in the awful hush that preceded his first words he looked directly at her in a mute and anguished appeal for sympathy.
>
> Her response was instantaneous, "Gosh!" she said in a whisper audible for half a mile. "Look at his knees shake!"[1]

Peale was small and unable to participate in rough and tumble athletics. He recognized that if he were to achieve recognition it would have to be with his wits and with his tongue. As a high school student he threw himself into the development of his writing and speaking ability; in college he further developed these abilities. Still bothered by some shyness, he frequently froze when called upon by a professor to recite. One day a professor called him aside after class and said: "Why don't you stop thinking about yourself? . . . Why do you think you freeze up the way you do when called on in class? . . . Because you're stupid? No. Because you're lazy? No. It's because you're so full of you that there isn't room for anything else."[2] Young

---

1. Arthur Gordon, *Norman Vincent Peale: Minister to Millions* (Englewood Cliffs, N.J.: Prentice-Hall, 1958), pp. 35–36. Used by permission.
2. Ibid., p. 53.

Peale determined to think less of himself and more of the needs of others, and this became a theme in his later preaching.

After receiving his B.A. from Ohio Wesleyan College in 1920, he took a job as a reporter on the *Findley Morning Republican* in Findley, Ohio. His editor pounded into him the journalistic writing style. He was told to use simple Anglo-Saxon words and to keep his sentences short. Later he followed this advice in his verbal reporting of the gospel. But reporting did not fill his vocational needs; more and more he felt that he was headed in the wrong direction. In 1921, at the Methodist Conference in Bellefontaine, he felt called into the ministry, and he entered Boston University to study theology and ethics.[3] At Boston University he applied himself diligently. In 1924 he was awarded the M.A. degree in social ethics and the Bachelor of Sacred Theology degree.

His preaching ministry began on the same shaky legs as his public speaking career. His first sermon was preached at Walpole, Massachusetts. He was so petrified with fear that he wired his father for help. His father replied by wire: "Prepare your own sermons. Just tell the people that Jesus Christ can change their lives. Love, Dad."[4] After preaching in the New England area during his seminary training, Peale took his first pastorate after graduation in Brooklyn, New York. The church grew rapidly, and in 1925 the new Kings Highway Church was dedicated. Under Peale's leadership the membership rose from forty-six to a thousand in three years. Called to the University Methodist Church, Syracuse, New York, in 1927, he enjoyed another successful pastorate. There he began to work with physicians and psychologists; increasingly he became concerned about communication and motivation.

In 1932 Peale moved from Syracuse to New York City to become pastor of Marble Collegiate Church. It meant a change in denomination, but he felt God leading him into this unique situation. When he arrived the church was averaging two hundred fifty people in an auditorium that would seat 1,450. The city was in the grips of the depression. Despair reigned. Fear and anxiety plagued almost everyone. In the midst of this situation Peale developed his approach to positive thinking. Nevertheless, he did not immediately develop the emphasis

---

3. Peale has stated that he believes in a divine call. In a letter he wrote, "The ministry is more than a profession; it is a calling" (Peale to James E. Carter, 18 March 1960).
4. Gordon, pp. 78–79.

that would be his hallmark. For two years he preached with little results. In evaluating his sermons, he discovered that he had been preaching primarily intellectual sermons. Finally he realized the people needed more than that. As he changed his approach the people responded in a phenomenal way.

Peale led the church to organize in a unique manner. He and Dr. Smiley Blanton established the Foundation for Christian Living, which specialized in Christian counseling. The staff of the church approached one hundred in number. The total congregation on Sunday morning averaged approximately five thousand.

In addition to preaching in his own church, Peale has been a prolific writer: his books have been best sellers; his newspaper columns have wide readership. His best-known book, *The Power of Positive Thinking*, has sold three million copies. Peale has given much time to radio and television. He has also engaged in frequent lectureships, speaking from eighty to ninety-five times each lecture season. Active in church-related organizations, he served as president of the Protestant Council of New York and of the Reformed Church in America.

Peale constantly emphasizes the positive approach to Christian faith. Many of his sermons and books center on personal religion. He urges men to trust in God and live abundantly. He points out again and again that faith in Christ can change human life. Although he does not use the technical terms of theology, his writings and sermons are largely Christ-centered.

Social concerns also grip him; the alcohol problem especially draws his attention. As a young man, Peale often went with his father and his brother, Bob, to the local cemetery where his father pointed out the graves of men killed by alcohol. Once he reprimanded Mrs. Eleanor Roosevelt from the pulpit for her stand on the drinking issue. He served as the president of the American Temperance Society.

Race relations also occupy Peale's attention. His church welcomes Negro members. As president of the Protestant Council of the City of New York, he took a more active stand on race than he had as a pastor. In his first sermon after taking office he proclaimed that Christianity must be taken out on the streets to do battle against social discrimination and hatred. He sent a telegram to President Johnson urging protection for those who demonstrated in Selma, Alabama.

Politics, another concern, at one time had been in Peale's

plans for vocation. Early in his ministry he became involved in political issues and supported specific candidates. From time to time he repented of this position and pulled away from active participation in politics. But frequently after a short recess he was back in the midst of political activity. One of the biggest furors of his life resulted from his opposition to the election of John F. Kennedy as president. Peale spoke before a conservative group known as Citizens for Religious Freedom. The resulting uproar was so great that Peale offered to resign his church. The congregation refused to accept his resignation and gave him a vote of confidence.

Controversy attended not only Peale's involvement in politics but also his theology. Many questioned his orthodoxy. Stung by the criticism hurled at him after *The Power of Positive Thinking* was published, Peale considered resigning from the ministry. His father sensed his discouragement, and shortly before his death he gave to Mary, Norman's stepmother, a message to pass on to his son:

> Mary's voice shook a little; she took a deep breath and went on: "He said, 'Tell Norman I've read every word he's ever written. I've read it all, and I've heard him preach for years, and his message is right. It's in harmony with the basic truths of Christianity and the teachings of Jesus. Tell him I know his message is designed for everyday people, not for scholars, and that I consider him one of the most effective teachers of Christianity in the world today.' And then your father said . . . he said . . ." The tears were running down Mary's face; she no longer tried to stop them. "He said, 'Tell Norman I said they were just a bunch of jackasses, and to pay them no heed—just put his trust in Jesus Christ, and never quit! The Peales never quit. It would break my heart if he should ever quit!' "[5]

Peale tore up his resignation.

In a statement which summarized his life goal and his theology, Peale declared:

> [I am] . . . a loyal minister in the oldest church in this land, the Reformed Church in America. I always was and still am an orthodox Christian. I believe in the Bible

---
5. Ibid., p. 276.

as the word of God as sincerely as the most dyed-in-the-wool fundamentalist, apart from the stilted vocabulary and mechanistic approach some of them insist upon. I accept completely the plan of salvation. I believe that Jesus Christ is the Divine Son of God and our Lord and Savior. I believe in the Holy Spirit, the Virgin Birth of Christ and, indeed, in all the statements of the Apostles' Creed.

I go right down the line with the historic doctrines of the Christian Church but I also believe that this ancient faith can be taught in new and fresh thought and language forms and applied scientifically and with creative power in people's lives; that it can solve the toughest problems of human nature and society, too.[6]

Preaching and Sermons

The sensational reception of Norman Vincent Peale's *The Power of Positive Thinking* catapulted him to national prominence—not only among church groups, but among people who don't even recognize churches when they pass them on the street. Among American preachers of this century, only Billy Graham, Bishop Sheen, and Harry Emerson Fosdick have had as wide an audience; it is equally significant that only these preachers have received as much praise and criticism as Peale.

Peale's message has been bitterly attacked and soundly denounced as "Pealism" and "the cult of reassurance." In an article in the *Saturday Review of Literature* entitled "Pitchman in the Pulpit," one writer described "Pealism" as "a puerile, vitiated, shallow revival of Pelagianism."[7] He further described it as a message appealing to "sick and sinking people" who mistakenly commit themselves to "this waterlogged life preserver." Among his many critics have been Paul Hutchinson, editor of *The Christian Century*, Reinhold Niebuhr, Donald Myer, Liston Pope, G. Bromley Oxman, and Franklin Clark Fry.

Others have been just as quick to defend him. Samuel Shoemaker, minister of the Calvary Episcopal Church in Pittsburgh, recognized some limitations in Peale's approach but defended

---

6. Norman Vincent Peale, *The Tough-Minded Optimist* (Englewood Cliffs, N.J.: Prentice-Hall, 1961), pp. 29–30. Used by permission.
7. E. Fuller, "Pitchman in the Pulpit," *Saturday Review of Literature* 40 (9 March 1957): 29.

him nonetheless. Grove Patterson, in an article in *Christian Herald* entitled "What Motivates Peale's Critics?" said:

> These critics ... leave out ... the crux—the very fundamental—of the Peale message. Over and over he demands spiritual conviction, the confession of sins, the plea for forgiveness, the sacrifice of evil habits, the surrender of the whole man to God and the service of one's fellows. Along with this, he demands the abandonment of negative thinking, the elimination of fear.[8]

But Patterson's most important criticism is that those who have evaluated Peale's "religion of assurance" have given no careful attention to his sermons. Ignoring for the moment whatever emphasis Peale has made in his books or through his special addresses, what has been the nature of his preaching?

In contradiction to his critics, Peale insists that his preaching is in agreement with the message of the Bible.[9] In a letter he stated that the purpose of his preaching was "to clarify the message and the teachings of Jesus so that people will understand and accept Him as Saviour."[10] He does not provide expositions of the Scripture in his sermons, nor can it be said that he usually develops his sermon in any textual way. Whatever agreement with the Scripture exists in his sermons is an agreement in theme—a message derived from the Scripture as a whole, rather than from specific texts.

Allen Broadhurst, professor of communication theory at the University of Connecticut, became interested in Peale and tried to discover the nature of Peale's preaching through thematic analysis. He analyzed two hundred forty-nine of Peale's sermons preached in his church between 1946 and 1960. Broadhurst discovered seven prominent themes with the frequency of their occurrence: (1) the God-Christ theme, 97 percent; (2) the thought theme, 65 percent; (3) the prayer theme, 63 percent; (4) the faith theme, 58 percent; (5) the problem theme, 57 percent; (6) the interpersonal relations theme, 50 percent; (7) the defeat-fear theme, 50 percent.[11]

---

8. Grove Patterson, "What Motivates Peale's Critics?" *Christian Herald* 79 (January 1956): 25.
9. Gordon, p. 228.
10. Peale to Carter, 18 March 1960.
11. Allen R. Broadhurst, *He Speaks the Word of God* (Englewood Cliffs, N.J.: Prentice-Hall, 1963), p. 76.

Broadhurst concluded that only the "positive thinking" or "thought" theme differentiated Peale from the average Protestant minister:

> In other words, this theme, which constitutes one of the basic messages of Dr. Peale's sermons, appears to be different from themes which one might expect to hear in a typical Protestant church. This theme is the message that thoughts and mind attitudes determine the situation of a person's life. Thus, a person becomes what he "thinks." The person whose thoughts are positive gets positive results, whereas the negative thinker leads a negative life characterized by doom, gloom and failure.[12]

Broadhurst insists that Peale's critics isolate his "positive thinking" theme from the main body of Peale's preaching. The theme itself is actually embedded in what can only be described otherwise as a primarily conservative Protestant theology.[13]

Whether or not Peale's emphasis is a distortion of the Christian message is open to question. Many reputable theologians deny that the "positive thinking" emphasis can be found in the Christian gospel at all; they feel that it has absolutely no place in proclamation, whether that emphasis be 100 percent of a man's preaching or 10 percent. Those who defend Peale are equally strong in insisting that he does not "water down" the message of the gospel nor its sterner demands; and that his message, if correctly understood and studied, reveals plainly the central truths of the gospel.

It does seem fair to say that Peale emphasizes more themes than just variations on the "positive thinking" theme in all of its aspects. But in the long run, anyone's final evaluation of Peale will have to be based upon that individual's personal approval or disapproval of the "positive thinking" theme itself. If that emphasis is judged to be a corruption of the Christian faith, then obviously Peale's preaching, with its great emphasis on that subject, cannot be appreciated. If, on the other hand, that thesis is not regarded as a corruption of the message of Christ, but an application of it to confused and baffled humanity,

---
12. Ibid., p. 83.
13. Ibid., p. 91.

then Peale's preaching can be regarded as a helpful ministry to millions of people.

As for his sermons themselves, Peale emphasizes simplicity: he does not believe in using words or ideas that cannot be understood by the man in the pew. Broadhurst says of his simplicity:

> His over-all sentence structure seems to be direct and simple and the words are assembled and related so as to convey thought with an economy of effort. . . . His sentences appear to be designed to communicate thought, and there is little or no embellishment that might get in the way.[14]

His sermons are short, averaging about twenty-five minutes in length of delivery. Peale lays great stress on understanding the personality of an audience; he believes that every group of listeners has its own mood, and that the speaker must shape his message to meet its particular needs.[15] He believes that a speaker can literally radiate love out across a congregation until he has enveloped them in a feeling of good will.

Peale always speaks extemporaneously. He believes that reading or memorizing a sermon blocks spontaneity and interferes with the audience empathy. He believes in leaving the exact expression to the inspiration of the moment:

> Yes, I believe that I am merely the agent of God's will and that He will give me effective expression. . . . Since I preach an optimistic religion, my delivery must be animated, vital and positive. I try to communicate with my audiences in a style as close to conversation as befits the occasion.[16]

In the January, 1969, issue of *Christian Living Today*, Mrs. Peale described her husband's sermon preparation. This account is reproduced in full because of its historical value:

> *How does Dr. Peale prepare his sermons?*
> This question is often asked, and by all kinds of people.

---

14. Ibid., pp. 88–89.
15. Ibid., p. 43.
16. E. E. White and C. R. Henderlider, "What Norman Vincent Peale Told Us about His Speaking," *Quarterly Journal of Speech* 40 (December 1954): 415.

They are particularly interested in knowing when my husband has time to prepare his sermons in the midst of his busy schedule of making speeches, serving as president of the New York City Council of Churches, heading the American Foundation of Religion and Psychiatry, overseeing the publication of *Guideposts* magazine, tending to his pastoral work at Marble Collegiate Church, and writing books and newspaper and magazine articles.

Fortunately, he is a very well-organized person and devotes a good deal of time to thinking about his sermons while traveling by train, airplane and automobile. Dr. Peale selects his sermon topics several weeks in advance. He always keeps a "sermon folder" with him. Into this go notes of all kinds: thoughts that occur to him about the various topics he has selected, illustrations that might apply, anecdotes, letters from people who have solved their problems and tentative outlines for the development of each theme.

In other words, sermon preparation is a continuous, never-ending process.

By Thursday of each week, the serious preparation begins, and it continues through Friday and Saturday, and right up to the moment Dr. Peale enters the pulpit at Marble Church on Sunday morning.

I have never known Dr. Peale to write a manuscript for his sermons, but he always prepares an outline. Usually it consists of an introduction and three points, which are put down in such a way that he has freedom of selection as he speaks. Depending on how much time he devotes to the first section, he decides as he is preaching whether to use all three points or only two, and which point he will eliminate.

It has never ceased to amaze me that Dr. Peale always delivers his sermons without notes of any kind, and that both sermons are as nearly identical as it is possible to make them. He never takes his outline into the pulpit; nor does he memorize it. Instead he photographs it on his mind in such a way that he can visualize clearly its point-by-point progression as he speaks.

He gives special care to the opening of each sermon, using statements or illustrations designed to capture attention instantly. The introduction also clearly states the objective of the sermon and the essence of the argument. In fact, the structure is somewhat like that of a newspaper story, with the basic thesis being capsulized in the first few statements and then elaborated on through the sermon.

A Biblical text, usually from the New Testament, is always the foundation for the sermons. Seldom if ever is the text stated at the outset, being introduced instead as a supportive element after the theme of the sermon has been stated in the introduction. From then on, throughout the sermon, the text is referred to often, and all of the material is closely related to it.

Dr. Peale uses picturesque, dramatic descriptions and true-to-life illustrations, which he selects on the basis of their direct application to the needs of the members of his congregation.

The sermons usually run about 25 minutes.[17]

Peale makes extensive use of illustrations in his sermon; usually illustrative material constitutes about one-half of his sermon. Occasionally one illustration will require three minutes to tell. Most of his illustrations come from his personal experience: "He feels that the minister should be able to justify everything he says in the pulpit through laboratory experience."[18]

Peale's sermon titles are not particularly creative, but they do attract attention because they appeal to self-interest and are a definite and concise statement of his theme. Examples of his titles include "The Magic Formula of This Life," "Three Sure Ways to Get Along with People," "Certainly a Happy Life Is Possible," "How to Relax Tension," "Peace and Quiet in a Noisy World."

There is seldom a discernible outline in Peale's sermons, but his development is always logical. His formula: state the issue, show its importance, relate it to the audience, illustrate it, and apply it. Peale is more interested in inspiring self-confidence than in conveying a body of information, and if his audiences are any judge he usually succeeds. His applications are brief, sometimes abrupt. He depends upon his illustrations to convey his thought. But his meaning is unmistakable and his enthusiasm contagious.

By any standard of measure, Peale's preaching is unique in

---

17. *Christian Living Today*, January 1969. Used by permission of the Foundation for Christian Living.
18. Broadhurst, p. 89.

the history of the Christian faith. Only a few other preachers of any century have ever commanded such audiences in a lifetime as Peale reaches weekly. In all of the swirl of controversy about him, one thing can be said with absolute certainty: Peale's preaching has uncovered a profound need in the hearts of millions of people.

Sermons

BE GLAD YOU'RE ALIVE

Philippians 4:4; John 15:11

THE GREATEST of all experts in the art of living tells us to be glad that we are alive—to be joyful. One of the statements in which He makes this assertion is: "Rejoice in the Lord alway: and again I say, Rejoice." Furthermore, He tells us how to be glad we are alive. He gives us a formula, a blueprint: "These things have I spoken unto you . . . that your joy might be full." To what things does He refer? The simple, understandable statements made in the course of His earthly ministry and which were written down in the New Testament. In other words, He wants us to be glad we are alive, and He tells us how we can have this joy.

We must not interpret His message to mean that joy is the ultimate end and aim of life. I could not convince myself that that would be a worthy motive for living. We are urged to be joyful that we might become what God intended us to be; namely, effective people. We have a mission in life. We have a function to perform. And Jesus wisely realized that a joyful spirit helps one to be effective.

The human being, to be effective, must be in harmony, and joy is just another word for harmony. All elements of one's life must, first of all, be in harmony with God, and then he must be in harmony with his fellow men. After that he must attain inner harmony. When a man is in harmony, his whole being works together, his mind, his body, his soul operating as one unity. When that happens there is joy and efficiency.

I was riding on a great DC-6 airplane with an engineer who had helped to build the engines. It was a radiant day, and we fell to talking about the beauty of the day and the joy of swift flight. I began to develop this theory about harmony and I could scarcely get the words out before he said, "I am an engineer, and the secret of making an effective engine is the degree to which we get harmony into that engine. Stress and resistance must be reduced to the lowest point. The parts

---

Previously published by Marble Collegiate Church, New York, and reprinted by kind permission of Foundation for Christian Living.

of an engine, being component parts of a dynamic universe, all work in harmony, and the engine actually sings for joy." He paused for a moment and then said, "Listen to the roar and throb of those mighty engines, each delivering twenty-five hundred horsepower. There is harmony."

Prior to that time the sound of an airplane engine had been only noise to me. Now, when I read that they are going to perfect cabins so that there will be heard in them no engine noise I am not sure that I am pleased. I shall never forget the feeling I had at that moment of space and beauty and glory and harmony. I want to hear those engines sing.

But, even this is nothing when compared to the beauty of a human being when he becomes harmonious. In preaching the Gospel we are dealing with powers and forces much greater than ourselves. We cannot diagram what happens to a human being when the Gospel reaches him. But we know that when a man gets in harmony with God, something great happens to him, whereby he is relieved from the conflicts and stresses that previously defeated him.

I spoke to the National Convention of the American Association of Television and Radio Broadcasters, and I told them that their organization was the most powerful group of people I had addressed in many a day. Every home that has an aerial is a mute invitation to these men to come into that house and to condition the minds of the men and women and children who live there. That group is being given the opportunity to create the America of the future.

One of the members came to me and said, "We had an employee who was in conflict with everybody, including himself. He fought with his wife, with his associates, and we almost thought we would have to let him go, though he was an old hand and we didn't want to. Of course his main conflict was with himself. Then we assigned him to religious programs. I don't know why we did it for he was the least religious man on that staff. Week after week that man had to pipe those programs out to the audience listening to that station. He had to listen, too, and it was painful for him. He resisted the message, criticizing those who gave the talks.

"Finally," said this radio executive, "God penetrated his consciousness. I saw this man lose his conflicts and become an harmonious personality. Today he is one of the happiest men of my acquaintance, and a very efficient worker."

It is amazing and pathetic how many people are not harmonious. They struggle along having no gladness in them at all. Imagine not being glad you are alive! Do you wake up in the morning hardly able to wait to be up and at the job? Do you go to bed at night regretfully, for fear of missing something? If not, do you want to know how to become glad you are alive?

I saw a newspaper advertisement not long ago which certainly represents the way a lot of people feel. A man of about forty-five was pictured sitting, his head in his hands, the picture of utter despair and lethargy. The caption read, "Have you that gray sickness? Half awake, half asleep; half dead, half alive?" Now, you know what that man needs – spiritual vitamins to make him come alive.

Briefly, how do we become glad that we are alive? The answer is in the teachings of Jesus. He is very astute. He says to get outside yourself. So many people are sick as a result of self-centeredness. When you lose yourself in something greater than yourself you become filled with joy. In other words, fight for something in human welfare; fight for somebody else; fight for the underprivileged; fight for the downtrodden; fight for the good. This makes people glad, makes them sing for joy even though they get into conflicts.

Two of the greatest orators of American history were Henry Ward Beecher and Wendell Phillips. Those men fought for abolition in a day when men were stoned in the streets of New York City and Boston for being abolitionists. These men won their battle for human freedom. Slavery was abolished.

One night after the war they met in a city where Wendell Phillips was delivering a lecture. Beecher went to hear him. After the meeting Beecher went back to the hotel with Phillips and lay down on the bed while Phillips paced the floor. "Henry," he said finally, "how did I do tonight?"

"I never heard a more brilliant speech," was the guarded reply.

"I felt dead," said Wendell Phillips. "I didn't feel happy about it. Something has gone out of me. You are my friend. Tell me what it is."

"Wendell," said Beecher, "it's all words: beautiful, magnificent, artistic words. But you aren't fighting for anything any more. The joy, apparently, has gone out of your speech."

If you aren't alive with happiness, go out into the community in which you live and find a group of people who are fighting a battle – juvenile delinquency, for example. Or get into the cause of developing good will between people of differing races, or creeds. Get into the fight for freedom. Get into the fight to spread Christianity, not only throughout this country, but throughout the world.

Why is it that some people have such a tremendous time living and other people get no thrill out of it at all? Take Branch Rickey, for example, who has been in baseball now for over fifty years. A mutual friend told me of an incident that took place at spring training after Mr. Rickey had been in baseball fifty years. A reporter from a New York paper came up with one of those questionnaires and said to him, "Mr. Rickey, you've been in baseball fifty years. Think back and tell me what was the greatest thrill you ever got out of baseball in fifty years?" Rickey lowered those big eyebrows of his, and his eyes flashed as he quickly answered, "My greatest thrill? I haven't had it yet." Now there is a man who is alive.

I went to the circus one night with a friend of mine by the name of Beverly Kelly. He has been with the circus for many years and I never knew a man to work any harder than Beverly Kelly does. As we were sitting there watching the circus I said, "Beverly, how long have you been with the circus?"

He said, "Twenty-seven years."

"Well," I said, "do you like your job?"

He said, "Why, Norman, it's a hundred percent better than working." I tell you, anything that you love is wonderful.

People are miserable who live only with and for themselves all the time. I've lived with myself for fifty-seven years and I've had my troubles, but not as bad as those of a man I met in Florida. He thought he was sick. His chauffeur brought him South in a big car with three nurses to do round-the-clock duty. But he really did not need them.

He asked to see me and the first thing he said when I went around to him was, "I am sick." And he kept repeating it at intervals throughout our short call.

I talked to his doctor about him. "Yes," said the doctor, "he is sick all right. But I haven't any medicine that will heal him. If you could just get him outside of himself he would be well and happy."

So, I decided to see what I could do. I saw an old lady trying to pull a chair onto the hotel porch. It was too big for her to handle and it got hooked under the railing.

I was sitting beside this man and I said to him, "Go over there and help that woman with the chair. It will make you feel better."

"You are younger than I," he said. "You help her."

But I insisted. So, groaning, he went over and helped the old lady who gave him a nice smile in return.

"How do you feel?" I asked him when he got back.

"Do you know," he said, "I got a kick out of that."

Then I reminded him of what Jesus said: "He that findeth his life shall lose it: and he that loseth his life for my sake shall find it" (Matt. 10:39).

"Why," he said, "I've heard that all my life, but I never understood it before."

When I went back to that hotel last winter I saw a man come striding down the corridor toward me, standing straight and walking with firm steps. I was passing him when he grabbed my arm. Then I recognized him, but he was so different now, for health radiated from him.

"Where are the nurses?" I asked.

"I don't need any nurses," he said. "I'm completely well."

That is a simple sort of illustration of the thing Jesus is trying to teach us—that we can be glad we are alive. But, we must get out of ourselves and give ourselves to other people, to our jobs, to some great cause, to something bigger than ourselves.

Jesus teaches us something else: "He that overcometh shall inherit all things" (Rev. 21:7).

A person who is the victim of some inner defeat can never be a happy person. If you are the victim of fear and carry anxieties all your days, you cannot be full of joy. If you are the victim of some sour cynicism, some skepticism about life and its goodness, sincerity and simplicity, if you are constantly rationalizing your own failures, you cannot be happy. If you have old sins from which you have never been freed, or some temptation to which you are constantly yielding, you cannot be happy. Jesus Christ, that greatest of all experts in living, says you can be glad you are alive only if you are master of yourself.

Every man can become master of himself. *Guideposts* magazine tells a story about a man who ran a little grocery store in the Bronx. He was a gentle old man to whom all the kids in the neighborhood came for comfort, whom people of all faiths loved. One night hoodlums came, stole $6.50 from the till, shot and killed the owner. Milton J. Cohen, the man's son, found the body. And the young man's grief soon became a steely hatred. He vowed, "I will find those hoodlums and I will shoot them dead."

He made application to the New York Police Force and, after long training, received his appointment as an officer. He roamed the Bronx night after night, his hand on his gun. For twenty-one months he did this, hatred in his heart. His wife was grief-stricken, seeing the light dying out of this fine, young husband of hers.

One night he caught a man and instinct told him this was one of the hoodlums he had vowed he would kill. He leveled his gun at the frightened eyes, but his trigger finger could not move. He seemed to hear the gentle voice of his father speaking. With his stick he knocked the knife from the boy's hand, took him to the Police Station and booked him. Then he went home to his wife.

"I had that guy," he told her, "but I couldn't shoot." He hesitated, then spoke again. "Father's hand was on the gun. And do you know, Honey, I feel free again, and happy."

"You are now worthy to be your father's son," she said brokenly. "You have been set free."

It is a great thing to be set free. Perhaps you have been haunted all your life by something that has kept you in conflict. Life is a battle field where two opposing forces meet and struggle constantly. The person who wins that battle, who rises above himself, who gains a victory over his spirit, becomes glad that he is alive. "These things have I spoken unto you . . . that your joy might be full."

Come alive. Be Glad You're Alive.

Our Heavenly Father: we ask Thy blessing upon every person and pray that Thou wilt communicate to every one the fact that life can be magnificent, wonderful, glorious if, by Your help, we conquer ourselves and give ourselves to the world. Through Jesus Christ, our Lord. Amen.

NORMAN VINCENT PEALE · 1898–

TRY PRAYER—
AMAZING THINGS WILL HAPPEN

James 5:16

SOME TIME AGO on a moonlit night I came into New York on a plane from Chicago. No matter how many times one approaches this great metropolitan area by air and sees it spread out below him, with lights like millions of jewels, it is still a fascinating experience.

On this particular night the plane was headed for La Guardia. In its gradual descent toward the airport it came straight over the very center of Manhattan Island. I computed that it was perhaps directly over Lexington Avenue. At any rate, seated on the left side of the plane looking out the window, I suddenly beheld Marble Collegiate Church down below. The gilded cock on top of the steeple was shining resplendently in the light of the moon. I could see the old church very plainly.

It occurred to me that Marble Collegiate Church is situated almost exactly at the geographical center of this vast, sprawling urban area. Some thoughts about our day and age went through my mind: the conflicts, the tensions, the stresses of our time. What a very different day it is from that in which this church was built back in 1854 when Fifth Avenue was only a mud street. The contrast seemed to impose a challenge upon this church, and all present-day churches, to say something meaningful and say it in a way that would be relevant to the life of our time.

Now I feel, and I believe the members of Marble Collegiate Church will agree, that the first objective of the Christian church, the fundamental reason for its existence, is to help people, human beings who, God knows, stand in need of help. The second objective is to get those people so to relate themselves to the life of our time that they will be a creative influence in building a better world that will reflect in some degree the radiance of the Lord Jesus.

It is impossible to understand why some people think there is something unimportant about helping people individually. Certain present-day religious leaders depreciate the individual. I fail to follow them. For example, the other day I saw a statement credited to the man who is head of the department of evangelism of a Protestant denomination, saying in effect—although I cannot quote his exact words and hope I am not being unfair to him—that from the evangelical point of

---

Previously published by Marble Collegiate Church, New York, and reprinted by kind permission of Foundation for Christian Living.

view helping an individual is an inane irrelevancy and that the proper purpose and function of the church is to evangelize masses of people and change society. But I have always thought it is changed individuals who change society.

And I got to thinking about Jesus. He went about everywhere, so the Scriptures tell us, doing good, helping people. He sat with a woman by a well one day—an immortal encounter—and He helped her. A poor man came to Him one night and said his daughter was sick unto death. And He helped that man. There was a man who was blind and He helped him. Is this an inane irrelevancy? He also promulgated an idea having to do with societies and empires, an idea known as the Kingdom of God on earth—a new order. Both these ideas are imbedded in the Scriptures.

Somehow for my part I never get away from the pathos of human life. Everybody in our congregation needs help of one kind or another. I can tell you for sure that I, the poor soul talking, need help very badly. Take, for example, a man who has been hounded by fear all his life—does he need help? Is it an inane irrelevancy to help him? Take an individual who is struggling with dishonesty, with lusts of the flesh, with temptation of all kinds—he needs help. If you can help him build himself up and become a strong man, is that an inane irrelevancy?

Or here is a couple whose marriage is about to break up. They can't seem to make a go of it; they are fighting each other and the home is about to collapse, which is a tragedy. They need help, a lot of help. Is it irrelevant to help them? Of course they are just two individuals out of the mass. Are we concerned now only with masses? Don't we see the pain on a human face? Don't we see the stooped shoulders of an aged person? Have we no longer compassion for heavily burdened human hearts? What has come over us, that helping the individual should seem an inane irrelevancy?

This is by way of saying that churches that handle both aspects of the Gospel as one deserve your support and your dedication. We must help the world and we must also help individuals, the poor souls who live in it.

One of the ways in which an individual gets help is by learning to use the great technique that Jesus gave us called prayer. In the Book of James, the 5th chapter, 16th verse, are these words: "The prayer of a righteous man has a powerful effect." That is how the text reads in a new translation of the New Testament called *Good News for Modern Man*. The King James Version says, "The effectual fervent prayer of a righteous man availeth much." You can take your choice. I rather like the older version myself, but this newer one has drive to it. "The prayer of a righteous man has a powerful effect."

Have you ever really had a powerful effect in your life as a result of prayer? If you haven't, you have not yet learned to pray in depth. Most of our prayers are on the surface. Lowell, the poet, in "The Cathedral" wrote:

> I, that still pray at morning and at eve, . . .
> Thrice in my life perhaps have truly prayed,
> Thrice, stirred below my conscious self, have felt
> The perfect disenthralment which is God.

Three times he prayed in such depth that he was thrust beneath his everyday self and experienced a "perfect disenthralment which is God." When that happens, there is a powerful effect. That is praying in depth.

You may be wondering, How do you pray in depth? You do it by keeping at it. You do it by giving it all you've got. You do it by completely turning your life over to God. You drive prayer down deep. That is where powerful results come from. When you pray in this manner, a changed person results. And changed people change situations.

How does God change a situation? By handing down some beautiful solution on a silver platter? Usually not. God changes people, and changed people change situations. Would you like to have something in your life changed? Maybe you think the situation in which you find yourself has become that way largely because of other people. This may be true. But it could also be true that you, yourself, need changing in order to change the situation. We may not be able to do very much about other people, but we certainly can do a job on ourselves. So, if any situation in which you find yourself isn't satisfactory take a good look at yourself and ask, "What is there in me that needs to be changed?"

Take the case of a woman who wrote me a letter. Her home had become a place of turmoil and unhappiness. She was full of resentment and self-pity and so nervous and irritable that she was constantly nagging and finding fault with her husband and her children. Her mind, as she describes it in a classic phrase, "was full of unhappy thoughts, miserable little devils floating in the stream of my subconscious." All happiness had gone out of her home. Finally her husband said to her, "Why don't you leave us long enough to find yourself and then come back to the children and me?"

Now maybe he was the one who should have gone away—I wouldn't know. But at any rate she assumed that he was right in what he said, although it made her very unhappy.

She went to the bedroom and flung herself across the bed and started to cry. She thought, How unfair that my husband wants me to go away and get changed. As she cried she reached to the night table for a box of Kleenex tissues to dry her eyes. And she writes, "Under the box I saw your book on positive thinking. (Her mother had lent it to her, telling her it would help her.) I thought, How can this help me? What does my mother mean? Nothing but death will help me. But I began to read and got the conviction that I did need changing and that God could change me."

Then she describes how it happened: "I began improving my thoughts and practicing discipline. I kept at it and one day was surprised to find myself and my home happier than ever before, and yet with less money.

"We all began giving. The children quit fighting among themselves and played good together. My husband began to play with the kids. We laugh now, go places and look to the future, and that's unusual in our home. How did me changing myself with God's help change every member of my family? And yet we all feel better."

She adds that she has now become a champion bowler in their area. This has no relation to the main thing, but I mention it because it just shows that when great things start happening a lot of things happen. She also adds that those miserable little devils floating in the subconscious are no longer there. Things change when people get changed. It doesn't always happen easily—not at all. Sometimes it is extremely difficult to make changes that have this effect, but it does happen and the text is true: "The prayer of a righteous man has a powerful effect."

The question is often asked, "Does prayer have any effect on materiality, or does it apply only to spiritual matters?" I believe that the prayer of a righteous man has a powerful effect even on materiality. If you really pray and put your life in the hands of God, He can lead you, step by step, so that your material condition changes. Why shouldn't He? He has power over everything, hasn't He? And materiality is nothing that is purely material. All materiality is infused with spirituality. It is only when you think of it as merely material that you form this cleavage.

At Marble Collegiate Church we have a group known as The Young Adults. It is a wonderful group, with a membership of several hundred modern young men and women who, through deep spiritual experiences, find newness of life and answers that answer. This year they put out a Lenten booklet called *Tune In on Life*, filled with individual accounts of thrilling spiritual experiences. One of their members, a young man named Harvey F. Guerin, writes in this booklet that in August 1967 he lost his job. Some months prior to this his wife had given birth to a baby daughter, Cathy. She was a blue baby and had to have a serious heart operation when only six days old. Later she developed mysterious high fevers, and this condition had persisted, worrying the life out of Harvey and his wife. Weeks passed, and Harvey couldn't find a new job. All he and his wife had to subsist on was the small unemployment checks which he received. On the 15th day of October, he reports, he had exactly $47 to his name, and he didn't know where he was going to get another nickel. And the rent was due. Sick baby, rent due, no job, $47.

He was feeling pretty bitter about this predicament, he says, and in his prayers had been pleading for God to give him some sign of a plan for his life before he was obliged to take some low-paying, stopgap job. But nothing happened. "Finally," he writes, "on the morning of October 16th I swallowed my enormous pride for a moment and cried, 'Take my life, Lord, and do with it what You will! I let it go!' Suddenly I felt a great peace and knew that I had finally turned myself over to God."

Well, a few days later he received from a lawyer—now get this—a letter telling him that a distant relative of his had left him a little money. Sounds almost melodramatic, doesn't it? And it shouldn't happen. It shouldn't happen, but the strange thing is, it did happen.

Then the next Sunday Harvey Guerin by mistake—or was it a mistake?—opened the employment section of the newspaper to the wrong page—and there he saw an advertisement which led to his obtaining a position as a social worker, where he is now engaged in exciting work with a future to it. And on January 1, 1968 little Cathy's temperature suddenly went down to normal and has stayed there ever since.

All right, you struggle with this all you want to. But do you know how you ought to come out? Not parading your doubts, but praising the Lord that amazing things will happen to people who are willing to turn their lives *completely* over to God: they will be guided, they will be sustained, they will be cared for. "The prayer of a righteous man has a powerful effect."

Finally, the amazing thing that prayer does is to fill your life with joy. This does not mean that your life will be all sweetness and light. Life is never all sweetness and light. But the great thing about Christianity is that, no matter how much trouble you have, if you pray in depth you will also have a constant flow of joy. It is like the oil gushers they have in Texas. I was watching one time when they struck oil in such a well. I'll never forget it. All of a sudden there is this mighty rumbling and from the depths of the earth a torrent of oil comes shooting up high into the air. That is what happens when you drive way down deep in prayer. Joy comes up.

A college freshman writes me: "I am so at peace with myself I've practically forgotten what it was like to be frustrated and unhappy. For a long time I had sensed that we in our family were growing apart from each other, and it bothered me deeply. And just lately I had felt pressure from implications that I should make something of myself. I felt obligated to go to college, although I wanted first to test and sample things for myself and go into something with my eyes open. [Parents shouldn't press young people too much, but let them live their own lives.] From these pressures I turned to boyfriends, hoping to find support and guidance from them, but many of them did not know how to help me, and things fell apart." In other words, the boyfriends didn't come through.

"I prayed to God to help me," she continues. "I am sure it was somehow meant for me to read your book *The Power of Positive Thinking*. It started me thinking. I tried a few spiritual methods and to my amazement they worked, but I was still uncertain as to whether the whole thing wasn't a big joke. Then I had a long confidential talk with my parents. We found a new understanding between us, and the world seemed to begin settling back to the way it had been when I was younger. I felt empty of disturbing emotions. I was at peace, which made me so happy.

"So I have rediscovered my parents and myself and most of all I have discovered God. Now my faith in God has multiplied several times over. I sit in my room in pitch darkness, happily contemplating, praying and jamming His wonderful strength into my heart and soul. It is really great. I simply can't express the feeling of contentment. It is overwhelming, enjoyable, and the close developing relationship with God is such a wonderful, uplifting experience. It's really a groovy way to go and if all the kids could see what they are missing they would know they are really out of it!"

You see, Jesus Christ still has the marvelous power to come into the lives of members of a confused generation and help them to find inexpressible joy. So the prayer of a righteous man has a powerful effect. Try prayer in depth – amazing things will happen.

Our Heavenly Father, we give Thee thanks for the amazing power of the spiritual in our lives, the spiritual which flows through the material and has power to change all our activities of mind and body. We pray that every one of Thy children may have a marvelous experience of Thy power. Through Jesus Christ our Lord. Amen.

NORMAN VINCENT PEALE · 1898–

BELIEVE YOU CAN AND YOU CAN

Philippians 2:5, 4:13

You know, friends, it occurs to me that preaching is a rather strange business. A man stands on a platform or in a pulpit and is supposed to communicate with the minds of the people sitting out in front of him. He is also supposed to give them a message that will help them. Well, that is what we try to do. Whether we succeed at it or not is another question.

It is so easy for church-going to become a formality. Just consider what happens. The same things are done the same way each Sunday, month after month, year after year, and maybe this gets a bit dull after a while. A Scripture passage is read, the preacher offers prayer, hymns are sung and at a certain point in the service a sermon begins.

Anyone who preaches or writes or engages in any activity over a long period of time develops routine ways of doing it. How to make things different enough to get through to everybody is the problem.

It might be a good idea for me, for instance, to stop wearing a pulpit gown and just show up in a business suit. That would at least be different. It might make people sit up and take notice. Or we might take all the pews out and put chairs around and have everybody sit in a circle. I read about one minister who sits crosslegged on the floor. I couldn't very well do that: I could get down, but I might have a hard time getting up! Or we might make everybody stand through the sermon. I do. Why not everybody? I sometimes think we make the whole thing too comfortable.

The purpose of these rather rambling remarks is to stress the fact that we preach for a purpose. The purpose is to reach you—and myself as well. I sometimes wish I knew what goes on in the mind and in the life of each person in the congregation. But that would be difficult to find out.

So about the only thing a preacher can do is to predicate his approach on the law of averages. There are only so many human problems in this world, and we all have to deal with them, no matter what our color, or our race, or our nationality, or where we come from. So the thing to do is to hit at those problems.

There is also one other means by which I can regulate what to say, and that is by taking a good look at myself and my needs. Perhaps I have as many varied problems as anybody—certainly as many difficulties with myself. If you are more in need of preaching than I am, I'd like to meet you sometime. So I figure if I just preach to myself, in

---

Previously published by Marble Collegiate Church, New York, and reprinted by kind permission of Foundation for Christian Living.

the presence of the congregation, I will very likely manage to reach a lot of people.

We are all in this together, friends. One thing that is pretty true of all of us is that we have problems and difficulties, troubles and sorrows, weaknesses and frustrations. Sometimes we feel very overwhelmed by them. Sometimes we even think we might just as well give up and say "So what! There is no use anyway."

Today we hope to reach you, really reach you, with one basic fact, and that fact is this: You never need to be overwhelmed or defeated by anything in this world. "Well," you say, "that is a big order." Sure is. The Christian Gospel deals in big orders. You have within you the capacity to handle anything. You may not think you have much capacity, for we all have a great tendency to minimize ourselves. But we must learn to stop that minimizing. It is an affront to Almighty God who created us.

Let me read you two quotations. The first one is from a gentleman by the name of Thomas A. Edison, who had one of the most astonishing inventive minds in the history of mankind. Many of the modern conveniences we have today came into existence through the fertile brain of this remarkable genius. Early in life he became deaf, which probably was a good thing: it meant he didn't have to listen to all the twaddle of the world and consequently he could think. And he sure came up with some tremendous things. I saw Edison once and shook hands with him, but didn't really get to know him. Later, I did know his wife very well, and his son Charles, who was at one time governor of New Jersey, a brilliant man in his own right. One day I had lunch with Mrs. Edison in her home in East Orange, and she showed me through her husband's laboratory and study.

But the greatest experience I ever had with the Edison family was the day they opened the inventor's old-fashioned roll-top desk, which had been closed and locked the night he died. They allowed it to remain locked until the 100th anniversary of his birth. On that occasion the desk was opened and a number of people were invited to see what the great man had left. Many reporters were there.

When the desk was opened I was interested to see that it was as mussy as my desk ever was. That comforted me. He had letters there, family letters; he had pictures, et cetera. Also lying on the desk was a pad where was scribbled, as though the great man had a premonition of his passing, a sentence saying that he was grateful for the work he had been allowed to do. This was followed by a comment, which I can't remember in its exact wording, expressing his conviction that we have only scratched the surface of this marvelous universe of which we are a part.

Now here is another statement Edison made one time, the one which I especially want to quote to you: "If we did all the things we are capable of doing, we would literally astound ourselves." Have you ever in your lifetime astounded yourself? If you haven't, it is a pity. Have you ever in your lifetime really felt that you had done all you were capable of doing? Have you ever felt the surge of a mental power beyond anything you had ever exercised? Have you ever felt the upthrust of something in you greater than you've ever been? This is a tremendous thought. "If we did all the things we are capable of doing, we would literally astound ourselves."

Edison would approve of my sermon topic of today. *Believe you can and you can!* That is exactly what he is saying here. Once in a while you hear the expression, "Get next to yourself." Why not? Be bigger than you've ever been. That is what Edison is saying.

You may object that this sounds all right, but just how do you go about doing it? We have the answer to that too. It is found in Philippians 4:13. I will quote from the new English version of the New Testament called *Good News for Modern Man:* "I have the strength to face all conditions by the power that Christ gives me." Here is the reason Christianity lives on when other philosophies die.

There is a tendency today on the part of some to make Christianity a small thing, and for that reason untold multitudes of people have turned away from it. But without hesitation I stand here as a preacher of the Christian Gospel and tell you, and tell myself, that "I have the strength to face all conditions by the power that Christ gives me." So be glad to be reminded who you are and what you are and what you can be and what you can do. Pull yourself up straight and look at that condition, that situation or that circumstance. Remind yourself that you have never half tackled the problems that life has laid before you. And say, "I have the strength to face all conditions by the power that Christ gives me."

Many young people today feel the need of deeper insight into life, but do not realize that Christianity has the answer. So a lot of them are running after Indian mystics, figuring they've got something. I went one night to a swami's place. He told us all to sit quiet. Everybody fidgeted. He said if we would sit quiet he would get a revelation. I sat there quiet for one solid hour, never even twitched a muscle. Once I had an enormous desire to scratch the end of my nose. But I said to myself, "I won't do it; I won't do it." And pretty soon the itch went away. While I was there I got an idea—like a flash. But I never went back to the swami, for Jesus Christ is my answer. He is the One who has the insights in the deeper silences and who, at the same time, is the greatest life-changing activist the world has ever known. Jesus doesn't retreat from the world. He wades into the world.

Just think of the import of this text. Just think of it. "I. . . ." That is a great old pronoun, you know? I! "I have the strength to face all . . ." (every one of them) "conditions by the power that Christ gives me." And how do you activate this strength and start overcoming difficulties with it? It is not easy. The reason it isn't easy is that you have to do something with this thing called your mind. The mind is a great thing. It is what makes you immortal. It is what gives you victory over circumstances. The Bible says, "Let this mind be in you, which was also in Christ Jesus." You have this mystical perceptive mind; you have this mind full of strength. If you take charge of your mind, you will take charge of your body and of your emotions; you will take charge of your environment and of your circumstances. A Christ-motivated mind has limitless power.

In a Chicago newspaper was an article about an interview with my good friend W. Clement Stone. Mr. Stone is a rare personality. He started out on Chicago's South Side with a widowed mother, no money, nobody for him. He was poor—and when I say poor I mean poor! He just didn't have anything! When he was six he was standing outside a candy-store window one day looking through it. There was an old man who used to buy peppermint candy there every day. The boy thought how wonderful it must be to be rich and buy peppermint candy every day—and a dill pickle. There wasn't anybody to buy candy or dill pickles for him. So the next thought that came to him was that the way to get them was to go to work. That is a curious, old-fashioned American idea. It used to have some currency around here, but now it is almost a thing of the past—the idea that you go to work for what you want. Then it occurred to the boy that he'd better think. So he figured out a way—and earned his first money selling newspapers in a restaurant. Today W. Clement Stone is worth one-third of a billion dollars.

The writer of the article calculated that Mr. Stone could now buy 1,233,000 candy canes every day for 20 years and 40,000 dill pickles a day for 20 years. Well, the last time I saw him he was on a diet—so he didn't want the candy canes any more. And Mr. Stone is not in life to make money. Dr. Arnaud C. Marts, who is a member of Marble Collegiate Church and head of Marts and Lundy, fund raisers, says that W. Clement Stone is the most generous human being he ever met. He has given millions of dollars to help boys through the Chicago Boys Clubs and other organizations. He has given over a million dollars to our religio-psychiatric clinic. A marvelous man! Money is just something to be used to help people. He is one of the most inspirational characters I have ever met—one of the greatest salesmen, one of the greatest businessmen and one of the greatest Christians.

Mr. Stone, according to this article, maintains that you can do anything with yourself if you take charge of your mind. He says you can control your body with your mind and control your emotions with your mind. He says that is why he never gets headaches. Apparently he has told his head that he doesn't want to have a headache, that he has no time for headaches. And he hasn't had a headache in years. He told me this three years ago, and I tried the same approach and I haven't had a headache since.

You see, the point is that there is so much you can do with yourself. "What the mind can conceive and believe, the mind can achieve," says Mr. Stone. It is worth struggling through this whole sermon just to hear that one statement. What do you want out of life? Something little? Okay—you'll have it. Something weak? You can have it. But whatever the human mind can conceive and can believe, it can achieve. "I have the strength to face all conditions by the power that Christ gives me."

Take another man I was reading about just recently: Glenn Cunningham. Probably very few members of today's younger generation know who Glenn Cunningham is. But I remember him well. I have always been a sports fan and go back to the days when all the newspapers in the United States had Cunningham's name in big print, with pictures showing his flashing feet. He broke the world's record for the mile run in 1934 and again in 1938. He was one of the greatest runners this country ever did produce.

When Glenn Cunningham was twelve years old he and his brother were starting a fire in an oil stove in an old-fashioned Kansas schoolhouse one day with what they thought was coal oil, but was actually gasoline. When they threw it on, the stove blew up. Glenn's brother was burned to death and Glenn was so horribly burned that he almost died too. Weeks went by and gradually he began to recover. But the burns left his legs terribly scarred and with many of the muscles in a kind of atrophy, somewhat like a form of paralysis. He was faced with the miserable prospect of probably being an invalid all his life.

But fortunately the boy had a mother who was a mother and no fooling. Glenn's mother had gone to school to the Lord Jesus Christ and she believed that you could do just about anything if you believed. She practiced the principle that if you believe you can, you can. She told her son, "The Lord made you whole and He wants you whole now. You'll not only walk, Glenn, you'll run and play. I believe it and if you believe it, it will happen."

And day after day she massaged his scarred, lifeless legs for hours on end. When she had to stop to do other things, she would get him to take over and continue the massaging himself. And after a while the boy's mind took control of his legs. I'll never forget the night in the old Boston Garden when I saw Glenn Cunningham run—when he could outrun any man in the United States. Tears were in my eyes. And the shouts of the multitude reflected admiration, not only for a great athlete, but for more than that—for a great man who believed that he could and who did!

"I have the strength to face all conditions by the power that Christ gives me." So take a long look at yourself, take a long hard look at your situation, take a good thrilling look at what you want to do and what you want to be—and DO IT, BE IT. Take charge of your mind. Enormous power is there. Don't ever think of yourself as weak, little, unfortunate, pushed around, victim of this or that. Don't be the victim of anything. Take charge of your mind in the name of Christ. Believe that you can and you can. Have that wonderful thing called faith — faith in the goodness of God, faith that God will help you, faith that God will see you through anything — for He will if you believe.

To me, there is nothing more thrilling in life than the great people we meet. One morning not so long ago a taxi picked me up at my door and I liked the driver the minute I got in. He gave me a big smile and said, "Good morning! A really great morning!" Well, for a moment I wondered if he had something wrong with his eyesight, because it was foggy and starting to rain. "A really great morning," he repeated.

"Yes, sir," I agreed, "a great morning."

We drove along, talking about this and that. Finally, as he stopped for a red light, he looked around and asked, "What's your name?" When I told him he said, "I thought so. I listen to you on the radio and thought I recognized your voice."

"Well, I am pleased that you listen," I said. "You don't turn it off?"

"No," he said, "I stick with you most of the time."

"I'm glad to meet a friend like you."

"I'm glad to meet you too," he replied. "Funny, your getting into my cab at this time." And slowly, with effort, he told me, "You see, my wife died. The funeral was just yesterday. We were married almost 30 years. You never saw a sweeter woman in your life. She was an angel. There was nothing but good in her. She loved everybody and everybody loved her. She was so kind to me all those years. I can't imagine living without her."

As gently as I knew how, I affirmed my own faith: "I don't believe you really will be without her. She will be thinking about you. She will be with you in spirit. You will feel her love comforting you."

"Thank you. Thanks a lot," he said feelingly. "She was so wonderful. I wish you could have known her."

He was silent for a moment, then spoke again: "Life is full of trouble, isn't it? I've got five children. Four of them are real good, but one sure is a problem. He has taken to drugs and runs around with a bad crowd. He is full of hate and meanness. I am worried about him. Can't seem to do a thing with him. It broke his mother's heart. Now I've got to be both mother and father to this kid."

I started to sympathize, but he interjected, "I know what you're going to say." And he assured me, "I have the same faith you do. Don't you worry about me."

Then he got off a tremendous statement. It sounded familiar to me, as though I had heard it before. Maybe he had picked it up somewhere. But it could be that he figured it out himself. What he said was, "You can be greater than anything that can happen to you."

Here was a brother. I felt that way toward him. Here was a Christian who knew that you can face any condition through the power that

Christ gives you. "You can be greater than anything that can happen to you." And that is a fact.

Our Heavenly Father, help us to know that within us is something greater than has ever shown; that we have capacities and abilities which, if released, would astonish us; and that we are greater than anything that can ever happen to us. Help us to know that when we believe we can, we can. Through Jesus Christ our Lord. Amen.

PROBLEMS ARE GOOD FOR YOU

Job 5:7; John 16:13, 33

A TALL, graceful American girl stood before the Royal Box in Wimbledon Stadium in London amidst cheering thousands. It all seemed unreal, for there advancing toward her, to bestow upon her the tennis crown of the world, was Her Majesty Queen Elizabeth II of England. The girl's mind went back in that flashing moment over her life.

Born in the city of New York of very poor parents, she had had to struggle all her life with one problem after another. When quite young, her family had lived for a while outside the city. During that time she was very ill, and her convalescence was slow. She was weak, and didn't seem to recover her strength. But she had a wise mother. One day her mother said to her, "There's a stone down by the barn. Can you see it?" The child said she could. Her mother then added, "I want you to go down and bring that stone up here so we can put it as a step by the kitchen door."

"Mommy," the child protested. "I'm so weak that I can hardly walk down there, let alone move the stone."

But her mother insisted, "You go down and if necessary move it only a half-inch in this direction, but move it."

So day after day the little girl pushed and tugged at that stone, mov-

---

Previously published by Marble Collegiate Church, New York, and reprinted by kind permission of Foundation for Christian Living.

ing it now an inch, now three inches, now five inches. It took her two months to do what any normally healthy girl her age could have done in fifteen minutes! But as she tussled with the stone she lost her weakness; she grew strong. And from this she learned a wonderful thing— namely, if we feel weak we can grow strong by struggle.

In the years that followed she had other frustrations and troubles. She became a champion at paddle tennis among the youngsters on the streets of Harlem, and in time she won the coveted tennis championship trophy of Wimbledon. Her name is Althea Gibson. She, I am sure, would readily agree with the proposition that problems are good for you. They were for her; they made her strong. They will be for you; they will make you strong.

A curious change appears to have occurred in our national philosophy with respect to problems. Our heritage as Americans is that of a people with courage and resourcefulness aplenty for tearing great problems to pieces. Indeed, we hewed this tremendous nation out of great problems. Then there arose among us the notion that ideally nobody should have a problem; that a part of the function of government and of civilization is to relieve us of all problems. This is because we are humanitarians. We don't want anyone to suffer. We want to alleviate pain. That is as it should be, and we all have this compassion. But there is a great danger in assuming that the *summum bonum* is the elimination of problems altogether. In the first place, it can never happen. If anybody comes along—politician, preacher or what not— and tells you that you are someday going to be free of problems, just don't believe him. It is not so. Problems are inherent in the nature of the universe.

It is written in the Book of Job that "man is born unto trouble, as the sparks fly upward." Jesus said: "In the world ye shall have tribulation: but be of good cheer; I have overcome the world." There is no escape from problems, but the idea is to struggle to overcome problems. In other words, I must tell you that you are going to have problems until the day you die. And, heaven help us, some are going to have problems after they die. So we may as well learn to handle problems.

How do you go about doing that? Well, there is a great text in the Gospel of John which says, "When he, the Spirit of truth, is come, he will guide you into all truth." The Christian religion is built upon perception, upon insight, upon understanding, upon wisdom. And there is a wisdom about problems. One of the basic elements of this wisdom is the deep philosophy which sees a problem as creative.

If we didn't have problems, we'd have to invent them, because our directional facility would be lost without problems. Problems help to steer a course through the years. I was traveling one day on a 707 jet plane. I'm always impressed with the marvelous operational facility of these craft: their force, their speed, their power. I was sitting by the window, with a vacant seat next to me. The captain came back through the plane, walking in a nonchalant manner. He sat down beside me and we had a little visit, in the course of which I said to him, "Captain, I've often noticed on these planes that out on the wing are a series of blades. And the same thing is repeated on the tail section. What function do they have?"

"Oh," replied the Captain, "those are what we call vortex generators."

"You'll have to elucidate that one," I said.

"Oftentimes the air is entirely too smooth," he explained. "Smooth air presents a problem. We can steer this plane better when we have a certain amount of turbulence. So when it is too quiet we have to manufacture turbulence by the flow of air through blades catching the tail section's blades and generating a sort of vortex." Applying this to a human being, may we not surmise that his directional sense might be impaired if he had no trouble, no difficulty, no problems? Fortunately, the good God when He created us installed, if you please, a vortex generator. Problems are good for you; and you know this when the Spirit of truth guides you into all truth. So let's never fall into the superficial assumption that the total elimination of problems would be just the greatest thing that could happen. Wisdom about problems is what we need.

One of the wisest human beings I ever knew—a man eighty years of age, I guess, or thereabouts, when I knew him—had never been to college, never went to high school, went through only three grades of grammar school. I often wonder what he would have been had he gone to high school and college. Perhaps he wouldn't have been half as wise as he was. They would have educated it out of him by the standardization process! But this man had a natural perceptiveness of the truth in God and the truth in people. I never knew anybody who knew the Bible as he did. He remarked to me that he was educated in the university of the Book. He was a wholesale grocer by trade—and a good businessman. One day I went to him—I was very young then— and said, "I've got an awful problem."

"I never saw an awful problem," he replied. "Let me see yours. I've always wanted to see an awful problem."

I ignored this and repeated, "I've got an awful problem."

But after taking a look at it he remarked, "This is a pretty good problem. Congratulations!"

"What do you mean, Congratulations?"

"Don't you know anything about God, son? God just has the time of His life. He has a sense of humor. You know, God actually has a lot of fun with people. He plays games with them; games like we used to play as children. God plays hiding games. He takes some wonderful thing and puts it down in the middle of a great big trouble. Then He gives you the trouble and says, 'Let Me see you find what I put in there.' He just chuckles while you hunt around in this trouble. When you find it, He laughs out loud, He's so happy."

"Well," I remarked ruefully, "He's sure going to get a big laugh out of this one."

"All right, son," my friend then said, "let us take this problem and just tear it to pieces." I had never seen a man dismember a problem. I've watched a Thanksgiving turkey being carved, and that's quite an art, but it is nothing compared with the way my wise friend carved up this problem. Finally he exulted, "Look, son, there it is! There is that wonderful thing God put in this problem for you!"

I never was so thrilled in my life. I never forgot the wise philosophy of this marvelous old man who had the perception of the truth that leads to all truth. So if you've got a great big difficulty, I tell you what you do. Go to your dining room table. That is probably the biggest unencumbered flat surface you've got in the house. Sit down there with your wife or your husband or somebody else and just tear that problem all apart, looking for the good that is in it. That is the way God devised it.

Bear in mind, too, that God wants to make us strong people. I've often asked myself, "Why does God have us here anyway? What is the purpose of living through all these years? What is He trying to accomplish with us?" Well, I've always felt that what He is trying to do is to make strong people of us, so that eventually He can say of each of us, "Well, there he is. He is as strong as this world can make him. Now I'm going to give him a bigger job with Me up here."

Nobody in this world has ever truly found himself until he got a philosophy of problems and trouble and realized that the way to handle a problem is to handle it spiritually.

I was told one time by a great businessman, whose name I will not mention, that he wouldn't think of handling a problem unless he handled it spiritually. By that he meant that always he would pray about it, try to find God's answer about it. I became so interested in his elucidation of the process that I want to give you his eight points for handling a problem spiritually. I have showed this list to many people, and I have used it myself in solving problems. It really works. I'll run through it quickly for you:

First: Don't panic. Keep calm. Even though you have to discipline yourself, keep calm. That is the only way to start handling a problem.

Second: Don't be overwhelmed by your problem. Don't get dramatic about it. Just tell yourself, "Well, it's a problem. But I am here and God is here and I can handle it."

Third: Practice de-confusion, because a problem generally becomes surrounded by confusion. So de-confuse it. A good way to do that is to take a paper and pencil and write every element of the problem down. That will help you see it freed from the blurring effect of emotional upheaval. De-confusion works wonders.

Fourth: Don't engage in post-mortems. Don't nurse regrets, thinking "Why did I do that? Why didn't I do this? Oh, I wish I hadn't done that!" Forget all that. Take the problem from where you now are.

Fifth: Seek a solution, not for the whole problem, but for the next step. If you deal with a problem in sequence of proper steps, you will see it completely solved after a while. One step leads to another and so on to the complete solution. Be content to see the next step.

Sixth: Practice creative listening. This idea was practiced by a friend named Harry Bullis, who is now deceased. Harry was president of one of the big flour mills in Minneapolis, a marvelous man, a great Christian. When he found himself faced with a big problem he would call his dog and go out in the woods. He said his dog had more understanding than a lot of people. He would walk until he found a stump, then sit down, and the dog would lie at his feet looking up at him. He would describe the problem out loud to the dog, to the air, and to God. Every once in a while the dog would seem to be thinking, "What's the matter with you, Harry? Why are you so stupid?" Then all of a sudden Harry would hear—not by the outer ear, but by the deep inner ear—the voice of God. He and the dog would then go home. Creative listening . . . you don't have to have a dog or go into the woods to practice it, either.

Seventh: Always ask what is the *right* thing to do in the given situation. If what you do isn't the right thing, it is the wrong thing. And no wrong thing ever turned out right. So if you insist on doing the right thing, you'll come out right.

Eighth: Keep on praying, keep on thinking, keep on believing.

There you have an eight-point program for the spiritual handling of a problem. If you will set yourself this standard, that you will handle every problem spiritually, then over the long term you will have high results—I can guarantee it—because you will be operating on a right principle.

Let me conclude with the example of a friend of mine who died in December, 1965. When he died a giant fell, for he had been without any doubt one of the greatest baseball men of all time. He had an intellectual, philosophical, spiritual understanding of the great American game such as no other man possessed. When he walked off the diamond for the last time, baseball's most colorful figure went to the eternal clubhouse and took off his uniform and hung it among the immortals. His name was Branch Rickey.

Several weeks before his death he was being inducted into the Hall of Fame in Missouri. Following his induction, he made one of his inimitable speeches. Presently he said, "Now I want to tell you a story of spiritual courage." And those were his last words. With that, he slumped over into unconsciousness, was in a coma for twenty-six days and then went home to the God and the Lord he had served so faithfully. Branch was a great Christian, of the sturdy, old, he-man type. Clean, honest and straightforward, he was a paragon among men for decency. I shall miss him all the days of my life. So will lots of other people.

Branch's manner of tackling a problem tended to be one of direct spiritual attack. I remember one case among many. He had a pitcher who wasn't doing too well—and he should have been doing very well. But he was behaving in a peculiar way. He would pitch his half of the inning and then rush into the clubhouse and phone his wife. He could hardly wait to get to the telephone to make this call. As a result, he was tense, nervous, high-strung. He wasn't putting the balls in the right place, he was getting hit. He just wasn't living up to what was expected of him. And potentially he was a brilliant pitcher.

Rickey came one Sunday to Marble Collegiate Church (he came often, as a matter of fact), and on this occasion came to my study after the service and, pacing the floor, asked me, "Norman, what am I going to do about this pitcher? Haven't you got some psychiatrists and psychologists around here? Can I send him over?"

"What's the trouble?" I asked. Branch told me about this rushing to the telephone. "What's his wife like?" I asked.

"She is as good as gold. She's a beautiful Christian girl. She is sweet and honest and clean and upright. And she is having a hard time with this boy."

"He's suspicious of her, eh?"

"I guess so."

"Well now, look," I said, "we might make a mistake, but why don't you call him in and in a very delicate way see if you can find out what goes on in his own moral life? Because it just could be that if he isn't straight himself he is trying to project a lack of straightness onto his wife and ascribe double dealing to her. If he is double dealing her, that could make him fear she is double dealing him. So he rushes in from the field and calls her up to see if she is there, not out with some fellow."

"I never thought of that," Rickey admitted. "I'll handle it just like you told me."

Actually there was no delicacy in the way he handled it. He called the pitcher in and said, "Okay, boy, let's have it straight. Who are you running around with?" And he hit it right on a sore spot.

The boy said, "Well, Mr. Rickey, you know how it is. When I'm out on the road with the boys the pressures are pretty tough. Now, my wife's a wonderful girl. I love her. I wouldn't double deal her for the world. But you know how it is, Mr. Rickey, the pressures...."

"Yes, I know how it is," said Rickey. "If you're any kind of a man at all you'll have some pressures on the inside that will handle those pressures on the outside. Don't give me that pressure business."

"Well, Mr. Rickey," the young man said, "I don't know what I'm going to do."

"I do," said Rickey. He shut the door. "Now listen, son. You just forget that you're a pitcher hired by me. We're both Christians and I'm your friend. We're going to pray to Jesus Christ, and we're going to ask

Him to clean you up and make you strong on the inside. Are you willing to do that, son?"

"Yes, Mr. Rickey."

So Rickey prayed. Now I've heard him pray, and I'll never forget it. He knew God and he knew Jesus and he knew how to talk to Them. I'm sure They loved him and that on some great green baseball field today he is leading other men. Then the boy prayed, and they settled the matter there. The wife never knew; nobody knew. You don't know. The pitcher reversed himself. He gained his strength, he gained his skill back again, and he finished his baseball career in a very creditable manner.

A lesser man would have edged around this problem, tried to handle it in some oozy way. But not Rickey. He came at the problem with a direct spiritual approach and got a spiritual answer. So whatever your problem is, bring spiritual wisdom to bear upon it and you will get a right answer. You will find in the long run that problems are indeed good for you.

Our Heavenly Father, when You created this universe You permitted problems to be here. We assume that You did so for a real and salutary purpose. Help us therefore to know that out of the handling of problems comes wisdom and by Thy help and guidance, if we determine to handle a problem right, we will get a right and a proper answer. For this we give Thee thanks through Jesus Christ our Lord. Amen.

NEW STRENGTH OVER OLD WEAKNESSES

Hebrews 11:34

I WANT to make an amazing statement to you. It is so astonishing that I have weighed it carefully before making it to be absolutely sure that nothing is being promised that cannot be delivered. For it would be a

---

Previously published by Marble Collegiate Church, New York, and reprinted by kind permission of Foundation for Christian Living.

cruelty to any human being to assure him of something which cannot be fulfilled. But this thing can be, and it is this: you do not need to remain as you are.

This is on the authority of the most reliable Book ever written, where it says in the Epistle to the Hebrews, ". . . Out of weakness were made strong." The passage where these words occur is sometimes called the Westminster Abbey of the Scriptures, because it is filled with people who overcame weaknesses—heroes and heroines of life. Also, our authority is the statement that "If any man be in Christ, he is a new creature: old things are passed away; behold, all things are become new" (2 Cor. 5:17). That, without doubt, is one of the greatest statements ever struck off in the history of human thought. "If any man be in Christ, he is a new creature." It means that you and I can become new. All these old weaknesses that have plagued us for years can be done away with. And everything becomes new.

If you have a feeling of inferiority; if you are torn by inner conflict; if you are borne down by depression; if your mind is riddled by sin; if you are a victim of weakness—you can become strong. You can gain new strength over your old weaknesses.

Yet, again and again people have come to me and said, "This is what I am. This is the way I was made. I just can't help myself. I'm weak in this way, and that is the way it's always going to be." Or somebody will say to me, "This is my weak point." But who made it weak? Why does it have to be your weak point? Why do you accept the idea that you have to be weak at this or that point? God never built weakness into anybody. If weakness has developed, it is because we have developed it.

I want to tell you, my friends, there is a power available to us whereby we can overcome our weaknesses. How do I know this? Because somebody told me? Oh, no, because I have seen it at first hand time and time again. I am enthusiastic about the Gospel. Why? Because I have seen it work so many times in so many people. And what it has done for other people it can do for you and for me. I have seen people whom you might have written off as absolutely hopeless, who have become wonderful, controlled, victorious individuals.

I had a reminiscence along this line the other day. During the last two or three weeks I have been making trips with a writer to my birthplace and places I lived as a boy and as a college student, sort of a foray into the past. Well, one day we took my wife along and went back to the city where I found her originally and where we were married—Syracuse, New York. We went over the old drive on which we did most of our courting. It was about a 35 mile drive from Syracuse to Canastota to Chittenango to Chittenango Falls to Cazenovia and back to Syracuse. The only thing I could find changed after 30 years was that the roads were better. The stream still surged over the Falls with the same old power and sparkle. And the lady by my side was just as sweet and pretty as ever, if not more so. In Cazenovia we went to the old Lincklean House where I had taken her to our first lunch. We stood by the same table, perhaps a foolish thing to do, but we got a lot out of it. We said how much we loved each other and what a happy time we had had and so forth, one of those conversations which I refuse to describe in detail. Then, in Syracuse, we went to various places we had known, including the University Methodist Church where I was pastor for 5 years before coming to the Marble Collegiate Church in 1932. I walked around through the various rooms, each one a memory, and as I passed through one room I remembered one of the greatest experiences of my life.

There I had seen the power of God change a man out of weakness into strength. I had been noticing, for a good many Sundays at the evening service, a young man who would come in and slink into a back seat. After the service he would slink out, without ever coming down to speak to me. I use the word "slink" advisedly because that is exactly what he seemed to do. I got to wondering about him.

Then, one Sunday night as I was shaking hands with people, all of a sudden there he stood in front of me. "I've got to see you right away," he said. "If you don't see me now maybe I'll leave. It has taken me months to get down to the front to speak to you and now that I'm here I still want to leave. But I've got to be here. So, see me quick, will you?"

Well, naturally I saw him. He said, "I am one of those miserable individuals who knows what is right, but doesn't have the strength to do what is right. I'd be better off if I didn't know what was right, because I'm caught in this dilemma. People tell me what is right, but they don't tell me how to do what is right. I'm weak, but nobody tells me how to be strong. I'm in misery, and something's got to be done about it."

"What have you been doing?" I asked.

"Well," he said, "for one thing, I'm living with a woman not my wife. We have lived together for several years and have two little children. And every time I look at them I can't tell you the terrible feelings that come over me. I haven't got the strength or manhood to do anything about it. Furthermore, I lie and I cheat and I drink too much. I gamble and haven't any control over myself. I'm in misery. Now, don't stand there and tell me I'm a sinner and weak and all that. I know it. I'm a dirty dog," he said, "and I admit it. What I want to know is how can I be strong?"

Well, I just got out the Bible and said, "Listen, son, I don't know exactly how God works in a human life, but I do believe in the Bible, don't you?"

He said he did.

"It says here that 'If any man be in Christ, he is a new creature.'"

The man looked at me. "That's what I want to be. How do I do it?"

I remembered what I had heard years before in the old revival preaching out in the Midwest, that only by the Grace of Jesus Christ can persons be changed of weaknesses like these. "I guess we had better get down on our knees and pray. We are both sinners. I, too, in a different way. Let us just ask Jesus Christ to come into your heart and mind and take out this weakness."

So, we knelt down and he prayed and I prayed. He came back a few days later and said, "Something has happened to me. I don't know what it is, but I feel differently. Mary and I want to be married. Will you marry us?"

"Of course, I'll marry you," I replied.

They came over to the church, knelt humbly, and the woman said to me, "I have wanted this for so long. I love him and it was the only way I could get him, so I did. But I didn't like it."

Nobody likes the wrong they do. You don't. I don't. Nobody does.

Well, I saw that man get hold of himself, live a decent family life, become powerful in his own nature. So I know I am telling you the truth when I say that no matter what weakness a human being has within himself, he can become strong through the Grace of God and be one of those who through weakness won strength. We can, by self-discipline, by self-management, take hold of our weak points and bring them up to Christ and make them strong.

"You can become strongest in your weakest place," is a statement given me one time by John R. Mott. This is a powerful thought. Try applying it to yourself right this moment. Say to yourself, "I can become strongest in my weakest place." Think now what your weakest place is and then bring this truth up against it.

They tell me that the point where two pieces of metal are welded together is stronger than anywhere else. If the metal breaks it will likely not break at the welded point. This is because to weld metal you apply an intense heat which drives the particles and molecules together in such a way that this becomes the strongest point. Spiritual heat has the same effect when applied to a point of weakness in a human being. So, if you have a weak place in your own character, apply the profound heat of faith and surrender and rededication and prayer, and that will be the point in you that will be the strongest.

A certain man told me the other day that his greatest weakness is anger. Isn't it strange how people get so mad? I saw a man in a telephone booth. Apparently he was talking to his wife, and at first he called her sweetheart. But then the tone of the conversation changed. The man got so mad he let loose a string of profanities. Finally, he threw the receiver at the telephone instrument so that it bounced all around the booth. And he came out mumbling and grumbling, his face red. His blood pressure must have been 200. Why does anybody get so mad?

I got to talking one day with a golf pro. He said that some people ought never to play golf: it does them more harm than good. He told me about one man whom he called a "captain of industry," a great executive. This executive got on the green in two on a par 4 hole. Now you know the perversity of inanimate objects. He putted the ball, and it went up around the hole then curved off to the right. He putted it again and it hung right on the edge, poised. You could have blown it in the cup, but that isn't according to the rules, so it took another stroke to get it in. What did this great captain of industry do? He picked up the ball, regarded it ferociously, walked over to the edge of the green, put it in the grass, and drove it into the dirt. Mad! Weak point.

The man who said his greatest weakness was anger decided to take it in hand. Now, every time somebody makes him mad and tensions begin to rise in him, he stops and applies what he calls the scrutiny of cold, analytical reason. You know, there is nothing that will take the heat out of anger like deliberate reason. Seneca said that the greatest cure of anger is delay. My friend says he waits 24 hours to see if he ought to be angry. And then he usually isn't. Also, he has devised what he calls a "mad scorecard." Every time he avoids being mad he writes it down, and he keeps this scorecard in his pocket. It is a game with him now. He told me that at first he managed to go 24 hours without getting mad. Then he made it for a week, and finally a month. When I saw him three weeks ago he proudly told me, "I haven't been mad for two months. And I decided I couldn't do this by myself, so I brought Jesus Christ in as my partner." I will venture the assertion that before this man gets through with himself he will be one of the best controlled human beings I ever knew. You can become strongest in your weakest place.

Recently I was in Houston, Texas, where I met a most inspiring human being, a man named Elmer Cary. He is one of the most alive individuals I have run up against in a long time. Kindness and geniality are written all over his face. He told me he had been working on his personality to make it responsive to his will. Every day he goes to the gymnasium where he takes good care of his body. Every day he goes into a church where he takes care of his spirit. Every day he goes out among people trying to do good. All this he told me while driving to the airport. And I want to tell you I took altitude long before I got on the plane, just simply by being with this man.

I said to him, "Elmer, did you ever have any weaknesses?"

"Oh, yes," he said. "As a boy that is all I did have. Look at my height." He stood about 5' 4".

Don't you remember what Winston Churchill said, that the measure of a man's height is how much he has from the bridge of his nose to the top of his head? I have seen fellows 6' 3" who had it all below the bridge of the nose.

"Well," he said, "I had an awful inferiority complex, and besides, my name was Elmer. Why," he said, "would anybody ever name a boy Elmer?"

"What's wrong with Elmer?"

"Well," he said, "I thought there was plenty wrong with it."

I told him about my name — Norman Vincent. I detested that name when I was a boy. The other day I visited the courthouse where I actually went to the judge when I was about twelve and asked if he would change my name. The judge asked me, "What do you want to change it to?" Well, that was during a certain presidential campaign and I said, "I'd like my name to be William Howard."

The judge said, "All right, hereafter your name is William Howard Peale." And I still have old school books where my name is written William Howard Peale.

Elmer continued, "And so, in order to overcome this inferiority complex, I found how to take this weakness and make it strong."

Elmer's method is so wonderful that I want to conclude this sermon by giving it to you. He tells me that every day — it doesn't make any difference how busy he is, how many appointments he has — he spends forty-five minutes with the Bible, soaking its great passages down into his brain. He reads and prays and meditates forty-five minutes with the Bible. "Then," he says, "I am ready to go and I put on the whole armour of God. I put on the whole armour because I don't want any room left for chinks or weaknesses to get in. Then I put on the helmet of salvation, for I want to keep my thoughts right, to keep truth instead of error in my mind. Next I put on the breastplate of righteousness, so that my heart will be right and nothing can get into my heart that isn't good. Then," he concluded, "I take the bright and shining sword of the spirit, and I go out and smash to pieces anything that is bad or weak."

By this time we were at the airport and Elmer was standing there telling me this. My friends, he stood before me six feet tall, every inch a man, a tremendous figure.

Incidentally, you will be interested to know that a year or so ago Elmer won a gold watch for being the world's greatest salesman of cemetery lots. Elmer says everybody needs one, and before I got on the plane he tried to sell *me* a cemetery lot. He almost had me believing I could go to Heaven quicker from Texas than any place in the world.

I looked back at Elmer when the plane took off. There he stood, his face alight; a man who, through weakness, became strong; who was a living example of the promise that "If any man be in Christ, he is a new creature: old things are passed away; behold, all things are become new."

You can become strong in your weakest place through your faith in Christ. So why not do it? Do it now. Leave your weakness on the altar of God, and go forth, having won strength over weakness.

Our Heavenly Father, we ask Thy blessing upon all Thy children. You built no weakness into us. We have cultivated it. With our cooperation You can take it away. Help us to yield it to Thee now, in this closing moment of prayer. Help us really give it up and then, day by day, hour by hour, minute by minute, living with Jesus Christ, become strongest in our weakest place. For this wondrous gift we give Thee thanks, through Jesus Christ our Lord. Amen.

For additional information about Norman Vincent Peale:

Broadhurst, Allan R. *He Speaks the Word of God.* Englewood Cliffs, N.J.: Prentice-Hall, 1963.
Davis, Elizabeth Logan. "Charles Clifford Peale." *Fathers of America.* Westwood, N.J.: Fleming H. Revell Co., 1958.
Gordon, Arthur. *Norman Vincent Peale: Minister to Millions.* Englewood Cliffs, N.J.: Prentice-Hall, 1958.
Oates, Wayne E. "Cult of Reassurance." *Religion in Life* 24 (Winter 1954-55): 72-82.
Peale, Norman Vincent. *The Power of Positive Thinking.* New York: Prentice-Hall, 1952.
Westphal, Clarence. *Norman Vincent Peale, Christian Crusader: A Biography.* Minneapolis: T. S. Denison & Co., 1964.
White, Eugene E. and Henderlider, Claire R. "What Norman Vincent Peale Told Us about His Speaking." *Quarterly Journal of Speech* 40 (December 1954): 407-16.

For other sermons by Norman Vincent Peale:

He has no sermon books. His sermons come in pamphlet form from the Foundation for Christian Living, Pawling, New York 12564.

MARTYN LLOYD-JONES

1899–

MARTYN LLOYD-JONES, photograph, courtesy of Martyn Lloyd-Jones.

DAVID MARTYN LLOYD-JONES

1899	Born on December 20 in Cardiff, South Wales
1921	Received M.B., B.S. degrees from University of London; began practice of medicine serving as chief clinical assistant to Lord Horder, royal physician, both in hospital and private work
1923	Received M.D. degree from University of London
1925	Became member of Royal College of Physicians of England (M.R.C.P.)
1927	Became pastor of a congregation affiliated with the Presbyterian Church of Wales in Port Talbort, South Wales
1938	Became associate minister with G. Campbell Morgan at Westminster Chapel, London
1943	Became minister at Westminster Chapel
1968	Retired from pastorate

MARTYN LLOYD-JONES began his career as a healer of men's bodies; he ended it as a minister to men's lives. The famous expository preacher and successor to G. Campbell Morgan earned his M.D. degree from the University of London, but after six years of practice he felt the call to the ministry and left the practice of medicine.

LIFE AND TIMES

Martyn Lloyd-Jones was born on December 20, 1899, in Cardiff, South Wales. He earned a B.S. degree and then an M.D. degree. His work as a student was noted by Lord Horder, one of the royal physicians, and by Sir Bernard Spilsbury of the British Home Office. He was headed for a significant career in medicine as a heart specialist. At the time of his decision to enter the ministry he was serving as chief clinical assistant to Lord Horder. He had received excellent training and was well regarded by his colleagues. But whatever success he could have enjoyed in medicine was certainly eclipsed by his stunning career in the ministry.

For eleven and a half years Martyn Lloyd-Jones served a congregation affiliated with the Presbyterian Church of Wales in Port Talbort, South Wales. He earned early fame as a preacher; conservative in theology and biblical in approach, his sermons were received enthusiastically. His reputation spread beyond South Wales; in London, G. Campbell Morgan heard of him. Morgan invited Lloyd-Jones to come to Westminster Chapel to serve as his associate. The former medical doctor accepted the famous preacher's invitation and moved to London in 1938.

From 1938 until 1943 he served as associate minister at Westminster Chapel. His preaching won the admiration of his London hearers. When G. Campbell Morgan passed from the Westminster scene in 1943, Martyn Lloyd-Jones became the minister of the congregation.

He assumed his new responsibility in difficult days for London. The city was racked by death and destruction under the pounding of Nazi bombing. Life for all was disrupted, and many experienced the grief of loved ones lost in combat and bombing. Throughout these tumultuous times he kept his preaching anchored to the biblical record.

During Lloyd-Jones's ministry in London, Westminster Chapel was second to none in attendance at worship services. People thronged to hear his sermons. Throughout these years he always preached in Westminster on Friday night and twice on Sunday, except when he was away on vacation. But he did not limit his preaching ministry to London. Throughout the week he preached in all parts of the British Isles. He became one of the best-known conservative ministers in England.

His fame spread beyond the shores of the British Isles to the United States, where his sermons were enthusiastically received by a widespread reading audience. The newly founded *Christianity Today* recognized his ability by printing one of his sermons, "His Kingdom Is Forever," as the Christmas sermon for the December 9, 1957 issue. After twenty-five years at Westminster Chapel, Martyn Lloyd-Jones retired August, 1968, from the active pastorate.

Preaching and Sermons

Martyn Lloyd-Jones continued the tradition of expository preaching in Westminster Chapel as successor to the illustrious G. Campbell Morgan. Successors to famous preachers generally find themselves in a difficult situation; they are often hard-pressed to fulfill the expectations of the congregation. But in the case of Martyn Lloyd-Jones the congregation had no cause for disappointment. For twenty-five years he preached to Sunday audiences of more than a thousand, many of them faithful members of the congregation and others who were visitors to the famous chapel. Crowds of that size would be significant in any age. But Lloyd-Jones succeeded in attracting and ministering effectively to such numbers in a day when expository preaching was said to be passé, and when other ministers were struggling to retain the interest of the most faithful.

During his lengthy and distinguished ministry Lloyd-Jones published many of his sermons; perhaps the most notable among these were his *Studies in the Sermon on the Mount,* a two-volume set of sixty sermons preached on successive Sunday mornings at Westminster Chapel. These studies have been well received on both sides of the Atlantic, both for their sermonic values and for their penetrating insights into the profound significance of the Sermon on the Mount.

As in the case of all of his printed sermons, these sermons were reproduced virtually as preached. Some of his published sermons were taken down in shorthand; others were transcribed from a tape recorder. This method was a deliberate attempt to preserve the oral quality of the sermons. Lloyd-Jones regards the sermon as a form of communication designed for an oral medium, and he believes that most attempts to prepare sermons for publication rob them of their true nature:

> A sermon is not an essay and is not meant, primarily, for publication, but to be heard and to have an immediate impact upon the listeners. This implies, of necessity, that it will have certain characteristics which are not found and are not desirable in written studies.
> To prune it of these, if it should be subsequently published, seems to me to be quite wrong, for it then ceases to be a sermon and becomes something quite nondescript. I have a suspicion that what accounts for the

dearth of preaching at the present time is the fact that the majority of printed books of sermons have clearly been prepared for a reading rather than a listening public. Their flavor and form are literary rather than sermonic.[1]

These observations are entirely in agreement with oral communication theory as to the differences in oral and written communication; and no other modern preacher says it so well, or so pointedly, as Martyn Lloyd-Jones.

Traditionally, historical studies in preaching have leaned heavily upon firsthand observations for the truest understanding of a man's work. In order to obtain an immediate impression from someone who had observed his preaching firsthand for more than twenty years, an evaluation of the pulpit ministry of Martyn Lloyd-Jones was requested from James I. Packer, warden of Latimer House, Oxford. Dr. Packer graciously submitted a significant evaluation based on his personal acquaintance with Lloyd-Jones, his repeated impressions of him in the pulpit, and his participation with him in numerous conferences on Puritan thought. Because of the significance of his remarks, they are included in full:

"Dr. Lloyd-Jones' sermons are on the grand scale—forty minutes at least, often sixty, sometimes more. Their form is austere: they consist of long chains of unrelieved biblical reasoning about God and human life. Rarely, however, do they feel like more than twenty minutes' length, whatever the clock may say. What is their secret?

"It is not just that this slight Welshman with the large domed head has a striking personal presence and command of language, although in fact he has both. Nor is it simply that he has a natural talent for advocacy and debate, or that he talks with great liveliness and passion, using all his body and the full range of an expressive and compelling voice; nor, again, is it that his line of argument (every Lloyd-Jones sermon is a cumulative argument) is superbly organized and magically clear; although all these things are true too.

"The secret lies, rather, in the fact that he communicates so vivid a sense of the presence of the God of whom he speaks—

---

1. Martyn Lloyd-Jones, *Studies in the Sermon on the Mount*, 2 vols. (Grand Rapids: Wm. B. Eerdmans Publishing Co., 1959), 1:vii. Used by permission.

the fact, in other words, that he has so much of what used to be called *unction* in his preaching. When he talks about preaching, he constantly stresses the need for an anointing of the Holy Spirit upon the preacher; when he preaches, you see what effect such anointing has. 'As men of sincerity, as commissioned by God, in the sight of God speak we in Christ' (2 Corinthians 2:17, RSV) – this is exactly the impression that Lloyd-Jones gives: hence the authority and power of his preaching, and hence the electric and often awesome impact it makes. I have never heard another preacher with so much of God about him.

"Phillips Brooks' definition of preaching as truth through personality is in point here. When Lloyd-Jones preaches, he becomes transparent: you see with complete clarity what manner of man he is. You see him as a dedicated professional in his ministry, though no man was ever freer of the facile professionalism of the pulpit. You see him as an intellectual aristocrat, though without any taint of intellectual snobbery. You see him as a gifted teacher who is absolutely certain that the greatest service he can do to any man is to instill in him the liberating truth of the Bible, and the amazing ways of a gracious God. You see him as an unrelenting realist, alternately impatient and scornful of shallowness in its many modern forms and compassionate towards its hapless victims. You see him as an honest man, who will never think a thing out less than thoroughly, or dodge an issue, or pull a punch. You see him as a true spiritual radical, a man tackling the problems of disordered lives at their very roots. You see him as a true physician, a man wise enough to insist on a complete diagnosis of the trouble so that he may be able to prescribe for a complete cure.

"But above all, you see him as a humble man, a man concerned to bring glory to God, as well as health to his hearers, by demonstrating the adequacy of the biblical message. . . . It is not his intellectual and theological strength, but the authority with which he speaks of the living God, and the sense he conveys of the glory and grandeur of life when one knows this God, that leaves the deepest impression.

"How does he preach? He first announces his text, usually with some variant of the formula: 'I should like to call your attention to. . . .' The formula means just what it says. Lloyd-Jones is an expository and textual preacher, and the whole concern of his sermon will be to make us attend to the message which his text contains. Next, he begins to talk around some problem of life or thought today, or some issue arising from the congregation's circumstances, on which the text will in due course be heard to speak; or perhaps he will point to the way in which some feature of the text or context exposes and questions us today, and enlarge for a little on that. At this state, a theme is being established and a train of thought started. The preacher is arousing interest and engaging the mind; not by the often frivolous devices of anecdotes, jokes, or a quaint use of words, which would only gain casual attention at surface level anyway, but by opening up an enquiry which all thinking persons must see is immensely relevant and important to them. The initial invitation, in other words, is to be serious about our own humanity, and to be willing to use our minds on our problems.

"To start on this level is, for Lloyd-Jones, a matter of principle: he never tires of insisting that the method of God's grace is first to make us think, and that the faithful preacher who looks to God to use his sermons must begin in the same way, by provoking thought. The style of these opening minutes is conversational, informal, and unstudied, yet at the same time serious and businesslike: you are made to feel at once that Lloyd-Jones knows exactly where he is going, and that his perception of life's issues is such that he will be well worth accompanying.

"Now, having set the stage, he brings his text to bear on the human condition he has been discussing. His approach is habitually Isaianic: having surveyed man's pretensions, his fancied greatness and adequacy, moral, religious, cultural, intellectual, he punctures them, humbling man and exposing his weakness, futility, and sin, in order then to exalt God as the only Saviour. The thrust of Lloyd-Jones' sermons is always to show man small and God great. He makes his point by stages, extracting from the text a climactic series of principles which progressively resolve the issue that was first raised. One issue per sermon is the rule; if a text raises two issues, Lloyd-Jones will preach two sermons. The exposition is paced with skill. The words flow quickly, in plain pointed sentences, but the preacher, so to speak, walks us round each thought before moving us on from it, and this both gives us time to think it ourselves (as distinct from just hearing him state it) and ensures that our minds are not outrun.

"As the argument nears its climax, Lloyd-Jones is likely to

become more animated and dramatic in style (this was most strikingly so when he was younger). These touches are not, however, pulpit tricks; they are simply another example of Lloyd-Jones' transparence in the pulpit, as we see what he himself is actually feeling about the things he is saying. If his voice rises to a Welsh 'hwyl' (an ecstatic falsetto), it is because he is saying something about God that strikes him as surpassingly wonderful while he says it. If he shouts, it is not because his argument is weak, but because he is saying something about God that strikes him at the moment of utterance as surpassingly strong. The most memorable of his sermons are those in which he is most completely caught up in his own declaration of the mighty works of God, and you see and hear this tremendously vital person saying these things in a way which shows him powerfully feeling them.

"Then from these moments of climax Lloyd-Jones takes us downhill to a calm, intensely earnest, yet wholly self-effacing conclusion. The argument will always end in sight of Christ, and his cross, and his covenant faithfulness, and his saving power. The whole aim of the argument will, indeed, have been to enable us to see these things more clearly than before, by making us realise more vividly than before how much we need to see them: for this, Lloyd-Jones would say, is how the knowledge of God, which sermons are preached to set forward, is actually brought about.

"Application has been going on throughout the sermon; in one sense, it has all been application. In the direct tradition of the Puritan 'physicians of the soul,' Lloyd-Jones has been bringing everything to bear on his hearers from the start. He will have shown that the problem with which the sermon began is essentially a problem of our relationship to God. He will have searched us, analysed us to ourselves, diagnosed us into self-despair, shown up sin and weakness and failure and need in vivid form. Now, in conclusion, he points us to the God of all grace. He does not *appeal,* for that would be asking for a response to himself. Rather, with intense compassion, he urges us to cast ourselves on the mercy of God in Christ, and his last words are likely to be an assurance about the life and glory we shall find when we do. Thus the preacher slips out of the picture, and leaves us with the God whom he would have us know.

"Lloyd-Jones is essentially a doctrinal preacher, teaching and applying systematically biblical principles and truths. His mental make-up reminds one in many ways of John Calvin, and his doctrines are recognisably those of evangelical Calvinism, developed in the manner of the Puritans, with their emphasis on regeneration, and of the eighteenth-century revival preachers, with their stress on the joy and exaltation of the knowledge of Jesus Christ. Historically (Lloyd-Jones, like most genuinely perceptive men, has a deep sense of history) his inspiration seems to come chiefly from Calvin, Owen, Whitefield, Spurgeon, and the Welsh Calvinistic Methodists of the first hundred years, men like Rowlands, Harris, and Williams.

"The individual flavour of his preaching is due, not to the presence of new doctrines, but to the fact that he presents the old ones, those of his theological mentors, in the way in which, as he believes, the twentieth century most needs to hear them — from a perspective controlled by repeated emphasis on the primacy of the intellect, the wholeness of revealed truth, the mental shallowness of modern culture, and the fact that there is no higher end in life than to know God."[2]

From the enthusiastic response of his congregation and his reading audience, it is apparent that Lloyd-Jones has succeeded remarkably in communicating to the twentieth century through expository preaching. It is significant to notice, however, that Lloyd-Jones does not mean by "expository preaching" that dreary, continuous parsing of Greek or Hebrew words or that aimless, meandering commentary on successive phrases that has been passed off as "expository preaching" by many lazy or inept modern preachers. For Lloyd-Jones, "expository preaching must always be *preaching* and not merely mechanical exposition."[3] In the preface to volume 1 of *Studies in the Sermon on the Mount*, he wrote:

> Another characteristic of expository preaching is that it is not merely an exposition of a verse or passage, or a running commentary on it; what turns it into preaching is that it becomes a message and that it has a distinct form and pattern.

---

2. The material above is from an unpublished paper graciously provided by James I. Packer.
3. Lloyd-Jones, 2:vii.

Furthermore, it must always be applied and its relevance shown to the contemporary situation.[4]

The sermons included in this selection differ slightly from the others in the set: they are continuous sermons from one passage of Scripture, rather than sermons based on various texts throughout the Bible. The purpose here is to show the *kind* of expository preaching practiced by Martyn Lloyd-Jones.

It will become evident from a reading of these sermons that he does examine the Bible in a most careful and meticulous way. He does not fail at contemporary application, nor does he lack for colorful illustrative material. It is obvious that Lloyd-Jones does not labor to include illustrative material, nor would that be altogether consistent with his philosophy of proclamation. But the material is there, welling up from the preacher's wide reading and from his acute observation of personal experience, adding the essential note of genuine involvement with his subject. Never does this material seem to have been forced, but there is a rather surprising amount of it — perhaps even surprising to Lloyd-Jones, if he were to analyze it carefully — with a great variety of sources and style.

In one group of thirty-five sermons printed in the *Westminster Record*, Lloyd-Jones used eighty-three illustrations, not counting the biblical illustrations. Fifteen of these illustrations were personal. Twenty-eight were literary, including references to Shakespeare, Kipling, Matthew Arnold, Browning, Tennyson, Watts, H. G. Wells, and Macauley, as well as several quotations from religious figures such as Spurgeon, Fénelon, Moody, Bernard of Clairvaux, Baxter, Wesley, Chalmers, Goodwin, Martyn, Bunyan, and John Fletcher. (The contribution of the Puritans to his thought is obvious in these names.) Fifteen illustrations were historical, including references to Hitler, Alexander the Great, the Clapham sect, the Locarno Pact, and the Spanish Civil War. There were twenty other brief references to various aspects of the contemporary scene, and four illustrations were derived from Lloyd-Jones's extensive knowledge of medicine. Hymns were frequently quoted, and occasionally other bits of poetry. News items were the rarest form of illustration used by Lloyd-Jones: in this group of his sermons

---
4. Ibid., 1:vii.

only one such illustration was used, taken from the tenth anniversary of the founding of the United Nations.

These illustrations are always skillfully employed and they never dominate. That is, the biblical materials remain in the forefront, and the illustrations function as servants of the Scripture. Lloyd-Jones did not begin any of these sermons with illustrations, choosing instead to begin with the biblical materials. That method of introduction is entirely in keeping with his philosophy of preaching. His own convictions on the subject are revealed in the sermon "The Christian Message to the World" (an exposition of Ephesians 2:4). The statement serves to summarize well his entire philosophy of preaching:

> The many who do not think in a Christian and biblical manner believe that the business of a Christian church on a day like this is to announce, for instance, a subject such as — "The Geneva Conference — Possibilities," and then go on to say what we think the statesmen should do.
>
> That, it seems to me, is entirely false and contrary to the biblical method. The biblical method, rather, is to display its truth, and then see the relevance of that to any given situation. You do not start with the situation, you end with the situation.
>
> The Bible invites us at the very beginning to stop looking on the horizontal level, as it were, to stop just looking at the world and at men; it invites us at the very beginning to lift up our eyes and to look at God. In other words, the whole case presented in the Bible from beginning to end is this: that life and man and the world simply cannot be understood until we see everything in the light of, and in the context of the truth about God. Therefore we must start with the truth of God and only then go on to the immediate situation.[5]

---

5. *Westminster Record*, July 1959, p. 74.

Sermons

THE IMPORTANCE OF SPIRITUAL THINKING

Psalm 73:16–20

WE PROCEED with our analysis of this 73rd Psalm. Let me summarise what we have already said and considered. In this Psalm we have the relating of an experience through which this man had passed. He had found himself in terrible distress, and in a position in which he says that his "feet were almost gone, his steps had well nigh slipped." What was his trouble?

It was a very old problem, a problem which is still with us; he had begun to observe the prosperity of the wicked; he had just made the observation that ungodly people seemed to be having a wonderfully good time in this world whereas he himself, a godly man, was having a very hard and difficult time. Nothing seemed to go wrong with the ungodly, they were always enjoying prosperity; but as for himself, he says: "All the day long have I been plagued and chastened every morning." He just began with that observation – he was having great trouble and these people were having none – and he began to think about it and meditate upon it and ponder over it until it had become a veritable obsession with him and he could not get rid of it. And he had almost come to the conclusion that he himself had cleansed his heart and had washed his hands in innocency in vain. He was on the point of saying that, but then he didn't say it. That was the slippery slope he found himself on – the position in which his feet had well nigh slipped. He was on the point of saying: "Is there anything in religion after all, is there any point in living the godly life? The prosperity seems to be entirely on the side of the ungodly, and people like me seem to be constantly in trouble and in difficulty."

Now that was his position. We pointed out that the good man did not say a word about it to anybody until he went back again and was able to start with the first verse of the Psalm: "Truly God is good to Israel,"

Previously published by The Bookroom, Westminster Chapel, London, in *Westminster Record*, and reprinted by kind permission of Martyn Lloyd-Jones.

which means "God is always good to Israel." He does not say anything until he can say that—"God is always good to Israel even to such as are of a clean heart."

We have looked at that and have seen how subtle temptation is, and how powerful it is. It comes to us through our circumstances; the devil seizes his opportunity and he comes as a would-be friend and he says: Is your God a righteous God to behave like that, is He a God of Love? He insinuates doubts. And then we went on last time to show how this man was saved from this terrible position, from this terrible danger of uttering those thoughts. He says: "If I say I will speak thus (verse 15) behold I shall offend against the generation of Thy children." That was the thing that held him; there he was on this slippery slope—I compared it to climbing a mountain, a glacier if you like, there is nothing but a sheet of ice. But suddenly he gets a foothold and he stays on the foothold—so that when he was on the point of saying something terribly wrong, he said: I cannot say that, I shall be an offence to God's people. He did not understand the main problem, but he said: I know that is right. So he stood on what he knew to be right and that held him and arrested the fall. It pulled him up for the time being.

We elaborated that and deduced certain positive principles which we should observe in our spiritual life. There are certain things which are unthinkable; and part of our trouble is due to the fact that there are certain back-doors in life which have not been barred and bolted. Most of the moral troubles are due to the fact that people are still considering things that have been answered, they are looking back. There are certain things that are beyond dispute, they are definitely wrong. This man acted on that principle, and it held him. I ended by saying that it does not matter at all at what low level you arrest yourself as long as you arrest yourself. Do not be one of those superior spiritual persons who seem to disdain the lower level. In spite of the low level, stand there. It is better to have your feet on the lowest rung of the ladder than to be on the ground. It is by climbing from there that you will find yourself eventually at the top.

But now we must proceed, because this man did not stop there, obviously. If he had stopped there he would never have written his Psalm at all, and he could not have said: "God is always good to Israel." That was only the beginning. When you are slipping the one thing is to stop, and having stopped you are in a position to go up again. That is exactly what this man did, and I am taking you through the various steps in this marvellous process, because even after having got his foothold he was still very unhappy. He said: "Behold if I speak thus I shall offend against the generation of thy children." But still he says: "When I thought to know this it was too painful for me." You see, though he is no longer slipping he still does not understand his main problem. But he is no longer going down, he is no longer in danger of uttering those terrible blasphemous thoughts. However, that does not mean for a moment he is clear about his problem. He is still an unhappy man. He says: "It is too painful for me." He was in great anguish of mind and heart, he still had his perplexity about God's ways with him — it was as great at that point as it was before.

I do want to emphasise that, because it is a very vital matter. The great thing, I say, is to stop slipping, but that does not mean that you are all right and that you are quite clear about your problem. This man was not clear, he was in real trouble still. Thank God, he knows enough to prevent his going down, but still the problem is as acute as it was before. Do you know that spiritual position? Have you ever been there? I have been there many a time. It is a strange place to be in, but in many ways it is a wonderful place to be in. You have something vital holding you, but still your original problem is as definite as it was at the commencement.

Well, now, what he tells us is this. He was standing there, he was no longer slipping, his mind was going round and round in circles, and he was in great anguish in his mind and in his heart; and he tells us that it continued until he went "into the sanctuary of God." "Then understood I their end." Now there is one point which I must make clear before I go on to expound this. If you look up the various translations of this Psalm you will find that some of them suggest that this should be translated like this: "It was too painful for me until I entered into the secret of God." They say it should be that instead of "until I went into the sanctuary of God." But the reasons for saying "sanctuary" seem to me to be quite overwhelming.

There are many reasons for that. One good reason is that all the Psalms in this section of the Psalter deal with the literal place, the sanctuary. Read the next Psalm and the Psalm that follows and you will find that each of them has reference to the tabernacle, the literal, physical, material sanctuary. It seems to me that this is conclusive, quite apart from other evidence which can be produced. However, it is a point which is quite immaterial, because what happens, among other things, when the man goes into the Temple of God is that he does enter into the presence of God. The people under the old dispensation when they went to the Temple went there to meet with God. It was the place in which God's honour dwelt, it was the place where the Shekinah glory of God was present. This man was entering into the presence of God, but as I say I think it is important to remember that sanctuary means literally the building. However, I just say that in passing. "Until I went into the sanctuary of God, then I understood it." He was unhappy, he was perplexed, it was an awful problem; but once he went there everything became clear to him. He was put right, and he began climbing up the ladder again until eventually he reached the top and said: "God is always good to Israel" — without exception.

There are certain very vital lessons for us in this particular section.

Here is a man who has gained a foothold and now he is beginning to ascend. What are the lessons? The first lesson I would suggest is this one—the vital necessity in the Christian life of spiritual thinking or of being able to think spiritually. Now let me show what I mean. The whole trouble with the Psalmist at this point was that he had been thinking of and approaching his problem solely in terms of his own thoughts and his own understanding. That, he tells us, was a complete failure. You see, there he was, he had these two positions in front of him—the prosperity of the ungodly, the troubles and problems and miseries of the godly, especially himself. This was his way of proceeding. He said: "This problem is quite plain, it is not complicated at all, there is no need to be involved about a thing like this. Facts after all are facts, and you cannot eliminate fact; and what a practical common-sense man of the world does is to look at facts. Very well, here am I. There is no need to argue, the thing is obvious, there is something wrong, I know all about the promises of God but where are they? How can I possibly be like this, and how can they be like that, if the message of God's word is right and true?" And he came to the solemn conclusion that it was wrong.

Now he had been reasoning like that, and he had gone back to it time and time again. You all know the process, don't you? You start with it and you go round and round in circles. Then you try to forget it by plunging into business or pleasure or something else. Then you go to bed at night, and you start all over again: "Things are going badly with me and well with the ungodly," and you go round and round the same circle again. You say: "Am I making a mistake? No, I am not, it seems perfectly all right, the fact is obvious." That was his position. What was the matter? I say that the whole essence of this man's trouble was that he was thinking rationally only instead of spiritually. Now this is a tremendously important principle. It is very difficult to put into language the difference between purely rational thinking and spiritual thinking, because someone may be tempted to say: "Ah, yes, that is it, I have always said that Christian thinking is irrational."

But that is a very false deduction. While I draw a distinction between rational thinking and spiritual thinking, I am not for a moment suggesting that spiritual thinking is irrational. What I am suggesting is this, that the difference between merely rational thinking and spiritual thinking may be put in this form, that it is a matter of plains and levels. Rational thinking is on the ground only; spiritual thinking is equally rational, but it takes in a higher level as well as the lower level. It takes in all the facts instead of merely some of them. I am going to develop that later, but I state it like that now in order that it may make clear what I mean by merely rational thinking and spiritual thinking.

Now I want to enunciate certain principles. The first is a statement, and it is this. There is a constant danger, Christian people, of our slipping back to merely rational thinking even in our Christian life.

It is a very subtle thing this, but without realising it at all, though we are Christian, though we are born again, though we have the Holy Spirit in us, there is the constant danger of our reverting to a type of thinking that has nothing to do with Christianity at all; and we can settle down to that without realising we have done it. This man was a very devout and godly man, a man who had had great experiences at the hand of God, but quite unconsciously he reverted to that merely rational type of thinking. Perhaps I can put that still more clearly by saying that we have to learn that the whole of the Christian life is spiritual and not merely parts of it.

Now let me elaborate that. Every Christian, of course, will agree, and will recognise at once, that the beginning of the Christian life is something which is altogether different from the rational way of looking at life. Let me put it simply like this. Take what Paul tells us in that 2nd chapter of the 1st Epistle to the Corinthians. He asks, in effect, why is it that some people are not Christian, why was it that the princes of this world did not recognise the Lord Jesus Christ when He was here. And he says the answer is this, that they had not received the Holy Spirit. They looked at Him only on the rational level. They saw nothing but a peasant; they saw nothing but a carpenter; they saw someone who had not been trained in the school of the Pharisees. They said: "This man cannot be the Son of God." Why? Because they were indulging in purely rational thinking. They were doing what I have suggested to you this Psalmist did.

The case of the princes of this world, and the case of all who do not believe in Christ, still is this. They say: "Jesus of Nazareth was only a man who was born, laid in a manger, lived, ate, and drank like other men and did work as a carpenter, was crucified in utter weakness upon a Cross." They say: "There are the facts, and am I asked to believe that that is the Son of God? It is impossible." What is wrong with them? They are only thinking on the rational level. They believe in the theory of evolution, and they say: "Things like that do not happen in the evolutionary process, things like that are impossible." That is rational thinking. You talk to them about the doctrine of the rebirth, and they say: "Of course things like that don't happen, there is no such thing as a miracle. We see laws in nature, but once you talk about miracles you are violating the laws of nature. As Matthew Arnold said, 'miracles cannot happen, therefore miracles haven't happened.'" That is rational thinking.

Now we all agree that before a man can become a Christian he has to cease to think like that. He has to have a new type of thinking, he has to have spiritual thinking. The first thing that happens to us when we become Christian is that we find that we are thinking in a different way. We are on a different level. In other words, as soon as we start thinking spiritually miracles are no longer a problem, the rebirth is no longer a problem, the doctrine of the Atonement is no longer a problem. We have a new understanding, we are thinking spiritually. Now everybody recognises that, all agree with that.

Our Lord was visited by Nicodemus, who came by night and said: Master, I have watched your miracles, you must be a Teacher sent from God, for no man can do the things you do except God be with him. And he was clearly on the point of adding: Tell me how you do it, what is the explanation? But our Lord looked at him and said: "Verily, verily I say unto thee, except a man be born again he cannot see the Kingdom of God" and "ye must be born again." What He was saying to Nicodemus was really this: Nicodemus, if you think that you can understand this thing before it has happened to you, you are making a real mistake. You will never become a Christian in that way. You are thinking rationally, you are trying to understand with your analytical mind, and you want to grasp it intellectually with your understanding. But you cannot. Though you are a master of Israel you must be born again. You have to become as a little child if you want to enter this Kingdom. You have to cease to rely on this power of thought which you have as a natural man, and you have to realise the nature of this new type of thinking which is spiritual. "You must be born again."

Now all who are Christian agree with that, and understand that. We say that the trouble with people who are not Christian is just that they will not surrender that natural way of thinking in which they have always been brought up, and in which they have been trained and to which given themselves. Yes, but the point I am making is this, that you have to do that not only at the beginning of your Christian life, not merely in the matter of forgiveness of sins and the rebirth and so on, you have to do it in the whole of the Christian life.

The whole of the Christian life is spiritual, not merely parts of it, not only the beginning. The trouble with so many of us is, as it was the trouble with this Psalmist of old, that we have come into the Christian life, we have started on a spiritual level, but we have dropped back to the rational with regard to particular problems. Instead of thinking of them spiritually we go back and think of them as though we were natural men and women. It is something that tends to happen to us all along the line. I have often listened to Christian people who are in perplexity, and as they have been stating their problem, at once as I have listened to them, I have realised that their whole trouble was due to the fact that they had dropped back to the rational level. For instance, when something happens to you that you do not understand, the moment you begin to feel a sense of grudge against God it is proof positive that you have already dropped back to the rational level. You say: It does not seem to be fair. Immediately you are on the rational level, you are bringing God down to your level of understanding. That is exactly what this man did. Everything in the Christian life must be regarded from the spiritual angle. The whole of this life is spiritual, everything about us must therefore be considered spiritually, every phase, every stage, every interest, every development.

Or let me put it like this, the problems and difficulties of the spiritual life are all spiritual, so that the moment we enter this realm we must think in this spiritual way and leave the other behind. That is especially true with regard to this whole problem of understanding God's ways with respect to us. That was this man's problem – Why does God allow these things, he says, why are the ungodly allowed to prosper? If God is God, why does He not wipe them off the face of the earth? And, on the other hand, if God is God, why does he allow me to suffer as I am suffering at the present time? That was the problem, trying to understand God's ways.

Now there is only one ultimate answer to that, it is the answer to be found in the 55th chapter of the Prophet Isaiah, verse 8: "For my thoughts are not your thoughts, neither are my ways your ways, saith the Lord." That is it. The first thing you have to realise, says God to us, is this, that when you come to consider Me and My ways you must not do so on that low level to which you have been accustomed, because My thoughts are higher than your thoughts and My ways are higher than your ways. But, even as Christian people, are we not constantly guilty of this? We will persist in thinking as natural men and women in these matters. We see that in the matter of salvation it has to be spiritual thinking, but if in the things that happen to us our thinking becomes rational thinking again, it is not surprising if we do not understand God's ways. His ways are altogether different, and the moment you begin to consider God's ways with respect to you, you must start with this basic postulate, that God's thoughts are not your thoughts, neither are His ways your ways. The difference between the two outlooks is the difference between heaven and the earth. So that as we come to look at ourselves and our spiritual experience when something happens which we do not understand, the first thing we have to say to ourselves is this: "Am I facing this spiritually, am I recollecting that this is a question of my relationship to God, am I sure my thinking is spiritual at this point? Or have I reverted unconsciously to the natural way of my thinking of these things?"

Let me give you a very obvious illustration. I have often known Christian people revert completely from spiritual thinking to rational thinking when in conversation they happen to take up the question of politics. When they come to talk about politics, they do not seem to be talking as spiritual people any longer. All the prejudices of the natural man come in, all the class distinctions, and all the worldly arguments – they bring it all out. You would not imagine that they are spiritual. Talk to them about salvation and they are all right; but talk about these things and they are guilty of all the prejudices of the natural man, the pride of life and the worldly way of looking at everything. As Christians we need to be told "not to love the world with its lust of the flesh, and the lust of the eye, and the pride of life." Our lives must be consistent; they must be spiritual everywhere; there must be no divergencies at certain points. The Christian must view everything from a spiritual standpoint.

A quotation from Spurgeon at this point will help. Alas, the history of the Church proves that what he said is but too common. He told his students that they would find that people who in prayer meetings prayed like real saints, and who usually behaved like great saints, in a Church meeting may suddenly become devils. It is true. You see, in praying to God they think spiritually. Then they come to the business of the Church and become devils. Why? Because they start off in an unspiritual manner. They have a party spirit within them and out it comes. It is simply because they do not know how to think spiritually in everything. The first principle we lay down therefore is that we must learn to think spiritually always. If we do not, we shall soon find ourselves in the same dangerous position which the Psalmist describes so graphically.

That brings me to the second principle, which is purely practical. How are we to promote and encourage spiritual thinking; how can we bring ourselves to think spiritually? Obviously that is our greatest need. Well, this man tells us. "When I thought to know this, it was too painful for me until I went into the sanctuary of God. Then understood I their end." What does it mean? Let me put it like this. We must learn how to conduct ourselves and all our thinking into the spiritual realm. Now it is very clear as to how this happened in the case of the Psalmist. Let us analyse it, let us analyse, if you like, the psychological process through which he went. Incidentally, there is such a thing as spiritual and biblical psychology, though it is not called that very frequently.

How did he do it? I think it happened like this. When he was on the point of saying that thing that should never be said, he thought of his fellow-believers. That pulled him up and steadied him, and held him. But fortunately he did not stop at that. "Ah," he says, "I have to consider my fellow-believers. Where do I meet them? I always meet them in the sanctuary." So he rushes to the sanctuary. He had been staying away from the sanctuary, as we all tend to do when we get into this kind of trouble. The trouble with this man was that he had been living with himself, and so got into that vicious circle. You start thinking about things like this, you become miserable and unhappy, and you do not want to see anybody. You do not want to mix with God's people, you are so consumed with yourself — you are having a hard time, God isn't fair to you — and there you are, going round and round in circles. You are miserable and feeling very sorry for yourself, and feeling that you are being treated very harshly. One's self is always at the centre of this problem. The first thing to do therefore is to get out of yourself. Get out of the vicious circle! Stop turning round and round in circles on the rational level! Get out of it!

But how does one get out of it? I suggest that there are three main things here. I would put first what this man puts first—literally going to the House of God. What a wonderful place God's House is. Often you will find deliverance by merely coming to the House of God. Many a time have I thanked God for His House. I thank God that he has ordained that His people should meet together in companies, and worship together. The House of God has cured me from "the mumps and measles of the soul" a thousand times and more—merely to come here. How does it work? I think it works like this. The very fact that there is a House of God to come to at all tells us something. How has the House of God come into being? It is God who has planned and arranged it. To realise that alone puts you immediately into a more healthy condition. Then you begin to go back across history, and you begin to remind yourself of certain truths. I am here at this present time with this terrible problem, but the Christian Church has been going all these long years. (At once you are beginning to think in an entirely different way.) The House of God goes back all through the centuries to the time of our Lord Himself. What is it? And immediately the cure is proceeding. And then you go to the House of God, and to your amazement you find other people there before you. You are rather surprised at that because you had come to the conclusion while you were talking to yourself that there wasn't perhaps anything in religion at all, and it wasn't worth continuing with it. But here are people who think it is worth continuing with; and you feel better. You begin to say: I think I am wrong, all these people must be right. The healing process is going on, the cure is being completed.

Then you go a step further and you begin to find something like this. You look round the congregation and suddenly find yourself looking at somebody whom you know has had an infinitely worse time than you have been having. You thought your problem was the most terrible problem in the world, and that nobody had suffered like that before. Then you see a poor woman, a widow perhaps, whose only child has died or has been killed. But she is still there. It puts your problem into a new perspective immediately.

The great Apostle Paul has a word for this as for all things. This is how he puts it: "There hath no temptation taken you but such as is common to man" (1 Cor. 10:13). Where the devil gets us is just here. He persuades us that nobody has ever had this trial before. It is my problem, nobody has been dealt with like this. But Paul says: "There hath no temptation taken you but such as is common to man." All God's people know something about this: and the moment you feel even that, you are better. We are such strange creatures. And sin has had a strange effect upon us. We are always helped when we are suffering by hearing that somebody else is suffering also! It is true of us physically, and it is true on the spiritual level also. The realisation that you are not alone in this helps to put the thing in the right perspective. You are one of a number: it seems to be something that happens to God's people – the House of God reminds you of all that.

Then it reminds you of things that go still farther back. You begin to study the history of the Church throughout the ages, and you begin to remember what you read years ago, perhaps something in the lives of some of the saints. And you begin to understand that some of the greatest saints that have ever adorned the life of the Church have experienced trials and troubles and tribulations which cause your little problem to pale into insignificance. The House of God, the sanctuary of God reminds you of all that, and immediately you are beginning to climb, you are going upwards, you have your problem now in its right setting. The House of God, the sanctuary of the Lord, teaches us all these lessons. People who neglect attendance at the House of God are not only being unscriptural – let me put it bluntly, they are fools. My experience in the ministry has taught me this, that those who are least regular in their attendance are the ones who are most troubled by problems and perplexities. There is something in the atmosphere of God's House. It is ordained that we should come to God's House to meet His people. It is His ordinance, not ours. He has ordained it not only that we shall meet each other but also that we might come to know Him better. Those who do not attend God's House will be disappointed some day, because on some favoured occasion the Lord will descend in revival and they will not be there. It is a very foolish Christian that does not attend the sanctuary of God as often as he possibly can, and grieve when he cannot.

The second thing that helps us to think spiritually is the Bible. Now in the days of the Psalmist they did not have a Bible like this, but you and I have the Book, God's Word. It is not only in the sanctuary, it is available everywhere. Turn to it in the home or in the Church, it does not matter where, and it will immediately make you think spiritually. It does so in almost endless ways. Why has God given us this Word? It is precisely in order to help us to deal with this problem we are considering. The mere History in the Bible is invaluable even if there were nothing else. Take a Psalm like this, and its story. Merely to read what this man went through puts me right, and all the histories do the same. But that is not God's only way of giving this great teaching. Begin to read your Bible and its great teaching and doctrines and you are again reminded of God's gracious purposes for man. And at once you begin to feel ashamed of your foul thoughts. This is how God has revealed Himself, and He is revealed right through the Scriptures.

Then it has explicit teaching on the question of the suffering of the godly. Paul writes to Timothy, who was ready to whimper and complain when things went wrong, and he says to him: "Yea and all that live godly in Christ Jesus shall suffer persecution." Timothy could not understand it. He was afraid because he saw that the servants of God were being persecuted: and many a servant of God has thought the same since. I have met men who have stood for the same Truth, but they were never persecuted, yet all that are godly in Christ Jesus shall suffer persecution. Paul speaking to the early Christian Churches said that it is "through much tribulation" we must enter into the Kingdom of God. If you grasp Paul's teaching to the early Christian Churches you will not be surprised at these things, indeed instead of being surprised at them you get to the stage in which you say: If I am not having this trouble, what is wrong with me? Why are things going so well with me? In other words, the whole atmosphere of the Bible is spiritual, and the more we read it, the more we shall be delivered from that rational level and raised to a higher level where we shall see things on the spiritual plane.

Just a word on the other essential aid – prayer and meditation. That is what happens in the sanctuary of God. The Psalmist did not merely go to the building, he went to meet God. The sanctuary is the place in which God's honour dwells, the meeting place for God and His people. It is when we come face to face with God and meditate upon Him that we are finally delivered from that low level of rational thinking and begin to think again spiritually.

I wonder whether there is someone who is surprised that I have not put prayer before this. I am sure there are some, because I know a number of Christian people who have a universal answer to all questions. It does not matter what the question is, they always say: "Pray about it." If a man like this had come to any one of them they would have said: Go and pray about it. What a glib, superficial, and false bit of advice that often is. I am saying that from a Christian pulpit. You ask: Is it ever wrong to tell men to make it a matter of prayer? It is never wrong, but it is sometimes quite futile. I mean this. The whole trouble with this poor man, in a sense, was that he was so muddled in his thinking about God that he could not pray to God. If you have muddled thoughts in your mind and heart concerning God's way with respect to you, how can you pray? You cannot. Before we can pray truly we must think spiritually. There is nothing I know of that is so fatuous as the glib talk about prayer, as if prayer is something into which you can always immediately rush.

If you doubt my word, let me quote one of the greatest men of prayer the world has ever known. I refer to the great George Muller of Bristol. George Muller, in lecturing to ministers especially on this question of prayer, told them this. He said that for many years the first thing he did every morning of his life was to pray. He had now long since discovered that that was not the best way. He had found that in order to pray truly and spiritually he had to be in the Spirit himself, and that he must prepare himself first. He had discovered that it was good and most helpful, and he now strongly recommended it to them, always to read a portion of Scripture and perhaps some devotional book before they began to pray. In other words, he found it was necessary to put himself and his spirit right before he could truly pray to God.

Now that is exactly what happened to this Psalmist. He was in this vicious circle, and thinking as he did, he could not pray because his whole thinking was wrong. Now in the steps I have enumerated his thinking was put right, and then he was in the right condition to pray. Very often we waste our time thinking we are praying when we are not really praying at all. It is often but some sort of desperation that is crying out. Our whole mind and attitude is wrong and we cannot pray like that. We must take time with prayer. We do not begin to pray to God until we realise His presence, and we do not realise His presence until our thinking about Him is right. Paul said again to the Philippians: "We are the circumcision which worship God in the Spirit and rejoice in Christ Jesus and have no confidence in the flesh." We must pray "in the Spirit," we must be spiritually prepared; and that means that your thinking is straight and true.

So the steps are perfectly right — the House of God, the Word of God, prayer to God and communion with God. Thus having realised that all those other thoughts were blasphemous and wrong, when your spirit is cleansed and bathed, you turn to God and you face Him, your spirit finds rest. That is the process, or, rather, that is the beginning. We haven't finished yet, but having got the foothold that is how the process continues. In trouble, "until I went into the sanctuary of God" — and found myself face to face with Him.

FACING ALL THE FACTS

Psalm 73:16-20

WE COME BACK once more to our consideration of this great Psalm, this 73rd Psalm. We have already considered it together three times,

---

Previously published by The Bookroom, Westminster Chapel, London, in *Westminster Record,* and reprinted by kind permission of Martyn Lloyd-Jones.

so let me hurriedly recapitulate what we have seen. The Psalm is a description of a terrible crisis through which this Psalmist passes. He had been in a very dangerous position, he tells us in the 2nd verse: "But as for me my feet were almost gone, my steps had well nigh slipped." What was the matter? The trouble was that he had started looking at the ungodly. He was a godly man who was having rather a difficult time. He seemed to be surrounded by troubles. He said: "All the day long have I been plagued and chastened every morning." In the meantime he saw that these ungodly people were flourishing; nothing seemed to go wrong with them; "there are no bands in their death but their strength is firm, they are not in trouble like other men neither are they plagued like other men." He had been looking at them, and he began to feel envious of them. He said: "I was envious at the foolish when I saw the prosperity of the wicked."

And as he had gone on looking at them, he was commiserating with himself and feeling very sorry for himself, and he was on the verge of saying this: "Verily I have cleansed my heart in vain and washed my hands in innocency." In other words, he was on the point of saying: "Is religion worth while after all, is there any point in my striving to live this godly life, is God's word true? I have been following it and this is what is happening to me. Those other people scoff and blaspheme His Name, but look at them!" And he was on the point of expressing himself and saying: "I have done it all in vain; I may as well retire and retreat out of the Christian life." He nearly said it, his feet had well nigh slipped; but he did not say it, and the whole point of the Psalmist is to tell us what it was that pulled him up and helped him to recover himself and eventually to arrive at the position he expresses in the 1st verse, which is the conclusion of the process through which he had gone: "Truly God is good to Israel." He had come to see that, although he was still suffering and being plagued — "God is still good to Israel." And it was only when he came back to that position that he spoke at all.

Well now, how did he recover himself? The first thing was that which he tells us in the 15th verse: "If I say I will speak thus, behold I should offend against the generation of thy children." That saved him. He still did not understand God's way with respect to himself; but he knew this, that to speak like that would be an offence to those other godly people. And he said: "That is something I cannot do, whatever God may be doing to me, I cannot do that. I must never say or do anything that is going to be an offence to someone who is looking to me. I cannot be a traitor. If I do not quite understand Christianity at the moment, I must at any rate be a gentleman; and if I haven't anything good to say, I will say nothing. Because I am in trouble that is no reason why I should put other people into trouble." The point I am stating is just this, that we must thank God for anything that holds us in time of temptation. It does not matter how low it is: anything that is going to hold us from falling, stand on it. When you are climbing that glacier and you begin to slip, if you can get your feet in anywhere, put your feet in lest you hurtle to destruction. That held him, but he did not stop there. That caused him to pause, and he began to think. He puts it like this in the 16th verse: "When I thought to know this, it was too painful for me."

That was our theme last time. Though this realisation that he would do harm to others had held him and prevented him from going further down, it did not explain his problem to him, he still did not understand God's ways. It was still painful; he was in agony of soul, and he continued in agony until he went into the sanctuary of God. Though he was a godly man he had dropped from spiritual thinking to rational thinking; but when he went into the sanctuary of God he was back again in a spiritual atmosphere and his whole thinking was re-orientated. We ended by pointing out that there are certain ways in which we can encourage ourselves to think spiritually; there are certain things which, if we do them, will promote spiritual thinking.

It may mean literally coming to a building like this. Every Christian thanks God for fellow Christians and for a public act of worship. I pointed out how this man before he went into the sanctuary thought only of himself and his troubles. He revolved around himself, he commiserated with himself; but then he went into the sanctuary of God, and to his amazement he found many other people in it. And already he began to feel better. It is a good thing to go to the sanctuary of God, it gives you a kind of mental and spiritual spring-cleaning. And the other thing is the Word of God. Men in those days were more or less dependent upon the spoken word; we have the Word of God in print also. Take your troubles to the Bible and it will help you. The ultimate thing was prayer. God dwells in the sanctuary, you meet with Him there. But wherever you find Him go to Him and meet Him.

We must now go on, because the man's process did not stop there. That is vital, and I must again emphasise it. We must learn to think spiritually in the whole of the Christian life. Our trouble is that we departmentalise ourselves; we live in categories and compartments. A man realises that he is a Christian on Sunday, but he seems to forget he is a Christian in business or in his profession. I reminded you of people who can be truly spiritual about salvation, but when they talk about other things they forget their Christianity and they talk as though they were men of the world. All our thinking must be spiritual. But that is not enough. This man went into the sanctuary of God. That alone put his thinking in the right atmosphere, but he went beyond that. What happened to him there? Well, he tells us: "When I thought to know this it was too painful for me until I went into the sanctuary of God, then understood I their end."

Now the first word we have to deal with is this word "understood." This is again one of those great fundamental principles of our faith which we can so easily forget. What he tells us is that what you find in the sanctuary of God is not merely a general influence, not merely a matter of atmosphere. When this man went into the sanctuary of God he was given understanding; he did not merely feel better, he was put right in his thinking; he did not merely forget his problem for the time being, he found a solution. I wonder how this can be put plainly and clearly. It is such a vital point.

Religion does not, and should not, act as a drug on us. There are people in whose case it does act like that. It may be a terrible thing to say, but to be honest I have to say it. There is often, far too often, justification for the charge that religion is nothing but "the dope of the people." To many people it is a form of dope and nothing else. What I mean is this, that their idea of the House of God, the sanctuary and worship is just somewhere where they can forget their troubles for the time being. That is why they may be interested in the aesthetic aspect—a beautiful service. They want some general effect. They are not interested in Truth—they want very short sermons for that reason—they are interested in some general effect, and while they are there they forget their troubles. "How nice, how beautiful," they say. But that is not the religion of the Bible—"then understood I their end." What happened to this man was not that he went to the temple and suddenly heard the strains of beautiful music coming from the organ, and then looking at the stained-glass windows and the beautiful lighting he gradually began to feel a little bit better and he forgot his trouble for the time being. No! It was something rational—"then understood I their end." True religion was never meant just to produce some general effect. The Bible is a revelation of God's ways with respect to man. It is meant to give "understanding"; and if it does not give us understanding, then it is something that may well do us harm and we would be better without it.

I am sure that I need not stress the vital importance of this. There are many things that we could do that would make us feel better. There are many ways of forgetting your troubles. Some go to the cinema, others run to the public-house or to the bottle of whisky which they keep at home. Under its effect and influence they feel much better; their problem does not seem so acute, all seems much better and happier. And there is no question about that. Others run to the cults, such as Christian Science, which is philosophical rubbish. But it makes people "feel better." There are many ways of doing it, but the question is: Does it give understanding, does it really help you to see through your trouble? "Then understood I their end."

Now that sort of thing can happen in the House of God. There are people who seem to think that what you should do in the House of God is just to go on singing choruses until you are in a state of intoxication. You come under some emotional influence and you do feel better. The world does that. It makes people sing comic songs to appropriate music, and they are wafted under its influence into a state in which they definitely feel better. All that may be of the very devil, because the test of the value of these things is, does it give understanding? – "Then understood I."

Let us never forget that the message of the Bible is addressed primarily to the mind, to the understanding. There is nothing that gives me such joy about this Gospel as this aspect. It enables me to understand life. It does not merely give me an experience. I have knowledge, I have understanding, I know. I can "give a reason" for the hope that is in me. I do not say only that "whereas I was once blind I now see," and I do not know why or how – I know, I can give reasons for the hope that is in me. Thank God that this man when he went into the sanctuary of God found an explanation. It was not merely some temporary effect that he received; it was not some kind of injection that was given to him to assuage the pain just a little for the moment, but which leaves the problem still there, and leaves him where he was, so that when he goes home the effect passes and he is back again where he was. Not at all. Having started to think in a straight manner in the temple of God he went home and continued thinking straightly. And it ended in the production of the 73rd Psalm! Understanding!

Do you "know in whom you have believed"? Do you know what you believe? Are you interested in Christian doctrine? What is your desire, is it simply to be happy or is it to know the Truth? It is the most searching question that can ever be put to Christian people. God forbid that we should ever be people who are simply out for entertainment, and whose religious services should be mainly entertainment. I speak advisedly because there is a very real risk of this.

I once had to speak in a very famous Bible Conference. I was there for four days. Every service was introduced by 40 minutes of music of various types. I did not hear the Scriptures read once during the entire time of that Bible Conference. A friend of mine visited a famous church in a certain continent. A number of people were being dedicated for the mission field that morning and there was also a Communion service. There were two anthems by the choir, three solos, a very brief prayer, but the Scriptures were not read at all. And that church has a very great reputation as a very evangelical church. You do not get understanding that way by having a musical entertainment and cutting down Scripture reading and cutting down the exposition of the Scriptures. You do not get understanding like that. That is a travesty of the biblical picture of a church. "Then understood I." It is because so many do not understand that they are always grumbling and complaining, and do not really have an insight into the times through which we are passing.

Very well, that is the first thing. It gave him understanding, it put him on his feet. But we must take that further. How was this man given understanding? The answer is that what happened to him in the sanctuary taught him how to think truly. In other words, I am saying that not only must our thinking be put right in its very atmosphere, not only must it become spiritual instead of being merely rational; it means a correction in detail also. That is what happened to this man.

Let us divide it up like this. He tells us that certain general defects in his thinking were put right, and then he goes on to tell us how certain detailed aspects of his thinking were put right. This time we shall deal mainly with the general. Now the first thing that is necessary is that our thinking should be whole and not partial. This man's fall had been arrested, but he was still unhappy. He was in agony of mind until he went into the sanctuary of God. "Then understood I their end." Ah, here is the thing he had forgotten! His thinking, he saw, had been incomplete. Let us develop that a little. I suppose in the last analysis that this is one of our central troubles, our thinking tends to be partial and incomplete.

You remember that line of Matthew Arnold's: "He saw life steadily and he saw it whole." You cannot pay a man a greater compliment than to say that he saw life steadily, yes, but also whole. I think it was the late Lord Oxford and Asquith who once said that the greatest gift a man could ever have was the capacity for what he called "cubical" thinking, the ability to see right round a subject. Truth is like a cube, and you must see all the facets – the power of cubical thinking. The failure to do that is, I think you will find as we analyse ourselves, the trouble with most of us.

Take this man, for instance. It was obviously his entire trouble. He was just looking at one side, and he saw nothing else, and it gripped and held him. What happened when he went into the sanctuary of God? He began to see the other sides, he began to see things as a whole instead of merely a part. Is not that the whole trouble with prejudice? We are all born into this world as creatures of prejudice; and all errors are ultimately to be explained in terms of prejudice. Prejudice is a power that pre-judges issues, and it does it in this manner – it shuts out all aspects of truth except one. And it will not allow you to see the others. People who are guilty of prejudice invariably expose themselves. They say: "I have always said this." Exactly. They will not see any other side – that is prejudice. Prejudice holds you to the one facet and it will never allow you to move. The result is that you are blind to every other side.

There it is, and it accounts for much of the tragedy of the world, and certainly most of our errors. I could illustrate this at great length. I must not do so, but I do want to suggest certain implications of this because they are so important at the present time. I am going to suggest that anyone who is not a Christian is really not a Christian because he does not see the whole situation. It is the thing that explains unbelief, it is the thing that explains most of the mistakes people make in life.

Take, for instance, materialism. The philosophy of materialism is not as popular as it used to be. Towards the end of the last century it was the controlling philosophy, everything was explained in terms of materialism. It is no longer popular because the new nuclear physics is really smashing the whole materialistic philosophy, because it says that even material objects have life and power. Nothing is stable and immobile. There are forces, mighty forces everywhere, and what is called matter is nothing but mighty atomic energy holding certain things together. If you had said this fifty years ago it would have been regarded as scientific blasphemy. The materialistic outlook was in control. Why? They were only looking at one side, they did not know all the facts. So materialism has had to go.

I can illustrate the same thing in the realm of medicine. The thing to do in medicine today—and let me remind you that there are fashions even in medicine—is to talk about psycho-somatic medicine. At long last the medical profession has discovered that the patient himself is important. Until recently their interest seemed to be in particular parts of a man's body, but the patient was ignored. A man went to a doctor and the doctor was only interested in the pains in his stomach. And they explained the pains in the stomach as due, as they thought, to local conditions in the stomach, acidity, etc. When I was a student if I had been asked what was the commonest cause of pains in the stomach and I had said: "Worry and anxiety," they would have thought there was something wrong with me and would have dismissed me as being unscientific. But by today they have discovered that that is really the answer. A man's body is not merely physical, mind does come in. Anxiety, worry, all these things cause messages to be sent from the mind to the local parts of the body. The body is not only matter and material. But still they will not bring in the spiritual. God grant that they may come soon to see that the spirit is as important as the psyche.

In the same way I could show you that the whole idea of man as an economic unit is based upon the same fallacy. The trouble is that they only see one aspect. When they say that it is everything, that it is all, they are simply prejudiced and have forgotten the other facts which are equally important. To people who believe in economics the whole problem of man is nothing but economics. No, says the other man, it is biology. They say the entire person and all his behaviour can be explained in terms of the balance of his ductless glands.

Others say that this is all quite wrong, and that man is intellectual. They seem to think of man as purely intellectual, sitting in a vacuum, entirely rational, and that nothing else matters at all. We must not be delayed by these things; but cannot you see that the trouble all along the line and in all these things is that they are only looking at one side, one aspect? What they are forgetting and what so many are forgetting is the sensibilities. They are forgetting life itself, and they are forgetting factors like emotion. These things are left out, and yet they are all a part of life, and they are central. Lusts, desires, sin, evil, all these things come in, all these facts make us what we are and make life what it is. "There are more things in heaven and earth, Horatio, than are dreamt of in your philosophy." That is what we should say to the modern man. That is how Shakespeare put it.

I am not sure but that Browning is even better. You remember that great poem, "Bishop Blougram's Apology." You remember the interview between the old Bishop and the young journalist who had become dissatisfied with the Christian religion. The young man was going to think life right through. He was going to break with everything he had been taught in the past, he was going to think things right through and make a new philosophy. The old Bishop said in effect: Do you know, I was once a young man and I did exactly the same thing. I thought I had it perfect, I assembled all the component parts, I had a complete scheme and philosophy of life, I thought nothing could upset it, but —

> Just when we're safest, there's a sunset-touch.

(Just when you think, to use the modern jargon, you have the whole of life taped, just when you think your philosophy is perfect.)

> Just when we're safest, there's a sunset-touch,
> A fancy from a flower-bell, someone's death,
> A chorus-ending from Euripides,
> And that's enough for fifty hopes and fears —
> The grand Perhaps.

You see what he means. With your rational mind you draw up your plan of life and think you can explain everything and have catered for everything. But just when you have done so, you may be taking a walk in the country. You see a sunset, a glorious golden sunset that moves you to the very depth of your being in a manner you cannot explain. Or it may be "A fancy from a flower-bell" or "someone's death." Your philosophy somehow does not cover it or explain it. There is a mystery about it which you cannot get at. "The grand Perhaps"! There is something else after all, beyond, above, behind all we can understand.

> And that's enough for fifty hopes and fears,
> As old and new at once as nature's self,
> The grand Perhaps.

Or, as Tennyson put it: —

> Our little systems have their day,
> They have their day and cease to be,
> They are but broken lights of Thee,
> And Thou, O Lord, art more than they.

That is what a man sees when he comes into the sanctuary of God. He begins to see things as a whole, he is reminded of things he had forgotten and ignored. The Apostle Paul put this in a marvellous phrase. There was a time when he hated the Name of Jesus of Nazareth and he persecuted His people. He thought he was doing God service by killing Christian people. But when he saw Him and came to know Him everything become new, and looking back on his old life he said: "I verily thought with myself that I ought to do many things contrary to the Name of Jesus of Nazareth." Precisely. He thought "with himself," instead of thinking with Christ. It was prejudice. "I thought with myself." As long as you and I think with ourselves we shall never see life truly. Is not this the whole trouble with life today?

I read a book which was designed to tell us how life should be ordered and run in this country. It is a very able book, the argument I felt was most convincing. Yet there was one radical defect. It was something that was not mentioned in the book. It was this. The scheme for the social and economic running of this country I felt was perfect but for one thing, and that was that the man who wrote it did not know anything about the doctrine of sin. If everybody in this country had been perfect that scheme would have been perfect, but what the author forgot was that men and women do not live by ideals but rather by desires, that we are governed by what we want and what we like. We have passions and lusts, we are creatures of greed and envy, of thirst and sexuality. These things are in our very constitutions. Man himself had been forgotten in that book; and it is the ultimate fallacy and the cause of the failure of every idealist system that man has ever proposed. You can plan to abolish war and to make a permanent state of peace in this world. Such plans are all perfect in theory, but they forget greed, they forget desire, they forget these failings that are in human nature, even in the very mind of man. You can produce a perfect scheme, then someone who happens to be in the conference will suddenly desire something, and your perfect scheme has gone once and for ever.

We must face all the facts. "Then understood I their end." Ah, there were facts that he had not considered, there were elements he had not taken in. Take in all the facts; think as a whole; think of yourself completely. Realise the corruptness of your own human nature. Realise also that you are not merely a body. There are other factors in life, and unless you have considered them you do not know life truly. These other things matter. Take it as whole. Lift up your eyes on the universe. See its mystery and marvel. Can you reduce it all to the material level only? Of course you cannot, the scientist cannot. Look at the "mysterious universe" and try to explain it. See how you fit into it. Look at it as a whole. Or take a book on history. See how it works, observe its processes. Can you really explain it all in terms of evolution? Face the facts. Oh, the folly of the man who says that men are automatically getting better and better! Can you, in the light of the things we read in the newspapers constantly, say that man is on the way to perfection, that he is better than he was?

Read history, look at it as a whole, and you will see that it is man, man in sin, who is still controlling. Then look at Christ. Look at His life, look at His record, look at what He has done. Stand before the Cross, face it, look at it, try to explain it. Then look at the story of the Church and the martyrs and the saints. Take it all in. Do not be content with anything less. Bring it all in. Then rise to the ultimate height, and stand before God. Lack of true thinking is our ultimate trouble, for if you do not think of all the aspects and phases, and face all the facts, you will inevitably go astray. If therefore you feel that you have a grudge against life and against God and are commiserating with yourself, I have but one word to say to you. Rush to the sanctuary, consider all the facts, remember the things you have forgotten.

There is, however, one further principle. Not only did this man see that his thinking had been incomplete, he saw in addition that he did not think things right through to the end. He says: "Then understood I their end." Oh, what a fallacy that is! Most of the troubles in life today are due to the fact that people do not think things right through to the end. This man only looked at the prosperity of the ungodly, but when he went into the sanctuary of God at once he saw their end. That is a great theme in the Bible.

James has a great word in his Epistle in the 5th chapter and the 11th verse about the case of Job. He says: "Ye have heard of the patience of Job and have seen the end of the Lord." Job had been having a hard time, and he could not understand what was the matter. He had not thought on to "the end" of the Lord. The end of the story in the last chapter of Job is that Job who had been bereft of everything ended by having much more than he had before. That is "the end" of the Lord. Go on to the end. Do not stop short.

Is not that the argument of the 37th Psalm? What that man says is that he had seen the wicked in great power and spreading himself like a green bay tree, but when the end came he had vanished off the face of the earth, and no one could find him. So he says: "Mark the perfect man, and behold the upright: for the end of that man is peace." That is the great theme in the Bible. Our Lord has put it once and for ever in the Sermon on the Mount. "Enter in at the strait gate for wide is the gate and broad is the way that leadeth to destruction and many there be that go in thereat. For strait is the gate and narrow is the way that leadeth unto life and few there be that find it." You see what He is saying. Look at the broad way, how marvellous it seems. You can go in with the crowd, you can do what everybody else is doing, and they are all smiling and joking. Wide and broad are the gate and the way. It all seems so marvellous. And this other seems so miserable—"strait is the gate." One at the time, a personal decision, fighting self, taking up the cross. "Strait is the gate, narrow is the way," and it is because they only look at the beginning that so many people are on the broad way. What is the matter with them? They do not look at the end. "Wide is the gate and broad is the way that 'leadeth' to destruction." "Strait is the gate and narrow is the way" – but – "it leadeth – (that is the end) – unto life."

The whole trouble in life today is that people only look at the beginning. Their view of life is what we may call the cinema or film view of life. It always attracts, and all who follow that way are apparently having a marvellous time. And, alas, so many young people are brought up on that kind of life. They think that that is life, and that it is marvellous, and that to live like that must be supreme happiness always. But look at the end of those people. Look at them passing to and fro in the divorce courts as they turn marriage into licensed prostitution, unworthy to have children because of their selfishness and because they do not know how to bring them up. But people are attracted by the appearance; they only look at the surface, they only look at the beginning. They do not look at this type of life in its end, they have no thought whatsoever as to the ultimate outlook. Nevertheless it is as true today as it has ever been, and the Bible has always said it, that the end of these things is destruction.

There is nothing so hopeless in the world, ultimately, as the bankruptcy of the non-Christian view of life. Do you know that poor Charles Darwin, the author of the *Origin of Species*, confessed at the end of his life that as a result of concentrating on one aspect only of life he had lost the power of enjoying poetry and music, and, to a large extent, even the power to appreciate nature. Poor Charles Darwin. He had looked so much in this microscopic way at life that whereas he used to enjoy poetry when he was a young man, now alas in his old age he found no pleasure in it, and music came to mean nothing to him. His trouble was that he had deliberately circumscribed his field of vision instead of allowing the glorious panorama to speak to him.

The end of H. G. Wells was very similar. He who had claimed so much for the mind and human understanding, and who had ridiculed Christianity with its doctrines of sin and salvation, at the end of his life confesses that he is utterly baffled and bewildered. The very title of his last book – *Mind at the End of Its Tether* – bears eloquent testimony to the Bible's teaching about the tragedy of the end of the ungodly.

Or take the phrase from the autobiography of a rationalist who was the head of a College in Oxford. He writes like this. "But to me the war brought to a sudden end the long summer of my life. Henceforth I have nothing to look forward to but chill autumn and still chillier winter, and yet I must somehow try not to lose heart." The death of the ungodly is a terrible thing. Read their biographies. Their glittering days are at an end. What have they now? They have nothing to look forward to, and like the late Lord Simon try to comfort themselves by reliving their former successes and triumphs. That is the end of the ungodly.

Contrast that with the godly life which seems so narrow and miserable at first and on the surface. Even a hireling prophet like Balaam, bad man as he was, understood something about that. He said: "Let me die the death of the godly and let my latter end be as his." He said: I have to say this, these godly people know how to die, I wish I could die like this. "The way of the wicked is as darkness but the path of the just is as the shining light, that shineth more and more unto the perfect day." What a glory. Let us come back to the 37th Psalm; there it is again: "Mark the end of the perfect man and behold the upright, for the end of that man is peace." And then listen to the Apostle Paul, in spite of all his tribulations and persecutions and trials and disappointments, listen to him as he faces the end: "I am now ready to be offered and the time of my departure is at hand, I have fought a good fight, I have finished my course, I have kept the faith: Henceforth there is laid up for me a crown of righteousness, which the Lord, the righteous Judge, shall give me at that day," and thank God for this — "and not to me only, but unto all them that love His appearing" (2 Tim. 4:6–8). That is the way to die, that is the way to end. One of John Wesley's proudest claims for his early Methodists was: "Our people die well."

"Consider thy latter end." Do not merely go to church to consider your present prospects; consider your latter end. "The end." How glorious it would be for all of us to be able to face it like that, and to be able to say: "Henceforth there is laid up for me a crown of righteousness which the Lord, the righteous Judge, shall give me at that day." The way to be able to say that, and to be certain that you will receive that crown, is this. Having looked at the two possibilities as a whole, go immediately to God and confess your blindness, your prejudice, your folly in trusting to your own understanding, and ask Him to receive you. Tell Him you accept His message concerning Jesus Christ His only Begotten Son, Who came into the world to die for your sins and to deliver you, and yield yourself to Him and rely upon Him and His power. Give yourself unreservedly to Him in Christ and you will see life with a wholeness and a blessedness you have never known before.

And the end will be glorious. Your path will be as the shining light that shineth more and more however black and blacker the world becomes and, even in the shadow of death, it will shine more and more unto the perfect day. "Then understood I their end."

MARTYN LLOYD-JONES · 1899–

BEGINNING TO UNDERSTAND

Psalm 73:16–20

WE RETURN to our study of how this Psalmist recovered himself when he was on the point of turning his back upon God and of saying things about the godly life which would have been an offence to all God's people. What saved him was that he went "to the sanctuary of God." There he discovered certain vital things. The first was that all our thinking must be spiritual and not merely rational. He found also that he had been guilty of thinking in a partial manner and of ignoring certain vital facts without which no right judgment can ever be formed.

The process did not stop at that point however. His thinking not only had to be put right in general but also in certain particular respects. We proceed now to consider these.

As we saw hurriedly last time, he discovered that his thinking about the ungodly had been most defective. Here he was in the temple. But what was the origin of the temple? That made him consider the whole history of God's people and all the enemies and opposition they had had to encounter and to overcome. And always the story was that God had delivered His people and routed their enemies. The history and the story of the Christian Church should do the same for us. Lord Macaulay once said, "No man who is correctly informed as to the past will be disposed to take a morose or desponding view of the present." If that is true in general, it is particularly true in the realm of the Christian faith. It is our ignorance of Church history, and particularly of the history recorded in the Bible, that so frequently causes us to stumble and to despair.

What then is the teaching of the Bible in this respect? The first thing we find is that it gives us the actual history. We can never remind ourselves too frequently of stories such as that of the Flood, of Sodom and Gomorrah, the Philistines, Assyrians, Babylonians and Belshazzar. They all teach the same thing. But towering above them all is the great fact of the Resurrection which shows God triumphing finally over the Devil and all his powers. The continuing victory is seen everywhere in the Acts of the Apostles, and a grand view of the End is given in the Book of Revelation.

The actual history of the Christian Church since the days of the Apostles continues the same story. We know what has happened to all powers that have attempted to exterminate the Christian Church,

---

Previously published by The Bookroom, Westminster Chapel, London, in *Westminster Record,* and reprinted by kind permission of Martyn Lloyd-Jones.

such as the Jews, Romans, etc. Likewise we know the epic stories of all the martyrs and early confessors, the Waldensian Church, the early Protestants, the Puritans and the Covenanters. Indeed, this very century in which we live has provided yet further evidence.

The Bible, however, does not merely record history. It helps us to understand the meaning of history. It teaches certain principles very clearly. The first is that everything, even the evil powers, are under God's hand. As the Psalmist puts it here in verse 18: "Surely Thou didst set them in slippery places." They are not free agents. Nothing happens apart from God. "The Lord reigneth." "By Me kings reign." It is of vital importance that we should grasp the biblical doctrine of Providence. It can be defined as "That continued exercise of the divine energy whereby the Creator upholds all His creatures, is operative in all that transpires in the world, and directs all things to their appointed end." God is over all and as we read in Psalm 76:10: "Surely the wrath of man shall praise Thee: the remainder of wrath shalt Thou restrain." In connection with this we have to remember God's permissive will. It is beyond our understanding, but it is clearly taught that He suffers certain things to happen for His own purposes.

Another thing we see clearly here is that the whole position of the ungodly is precarious and dangerous. They are in "slippery places." All they have is but temporary. The Psalmist suddenly saw clearly what Moses saw when he "chose rather to suffer affliction with the people of God than to enjoy the pleasures of sin for a season." Age and decay, death and judgment, are certain. The most terrible thing about sin is that it blinds men to the realisation of this. Their pomp and glory is but for a season. "The Lord reigneth, let the earth tremble."

The Psalmist saw this so clearly in the sanctuary of God that he not only ceased to be envious of the ungodly, but gives the impression that he even began to feel sorry for them as he realised the truth about their position. There is perhaps no better test of our profession of the Christian faith than just this. Do we feel sorry for the ungodly in their blindness? Have we even a sense of compassion for them as we see them as sheep without a shepherd? Thus the thinking of the Psalmist was put right with respect to the ungodly.

Now we proceed to consider the next step and to show how this man's thinking was put right also about God Himself. We have seen how his thinking about God had gone seriously wrong because he had started in the wrong way about the ungodly, and thus had got into the position of questioning and querying even God. He says: "Verily I have cleansed my heart in vain and washed my hands in innocency" – "I have been trying to obey God but it doesn't really seem to pay. Is God what He says He is?" Now that is a terrible thing to think; and that is, particularly, the thing on which we must now concentrate. This man shows us how his thinking was put right about God. In a sense he has already said it: "Surely Thou didst set them in slippery places." The moment he utters that word "THOU" one feels that the whole position is beginning to change.

What was it that was adjusted when he began thinking truly about God? I think the first thing he saw now truly and rightly was the character of God; because, after all, the thing that this man had been beginning to doubt was the very character of God Himself. Many of these Psalmists with strange and remarkable honesty confess that they were tempted along that line. For instance, in the seventy-seventh Psalm you find the same thing expressed very definitely. The Psalmist asks: "Will the Lord cast off for ever and will He be favourable no more? Is His mercy clean gone for ever; doth His promise fail for evermore? Has God forgotten to be gracious?" That is the type of question, and, as I pointed out at the very beginning, some of the greatest saints have sometimes been tempted to ask these questions when things have gone against them. Well this man in that way had been asking these questions: Does God care, and if He does care why does He not stop these things? Is it that He cannot do it?

How often have people asked these questions. How often did people say in the last world war: Why does God permit a man like Hitler to live? Why doesn't He strike him down; if He is God and has this power why doesn't He strike him? The question arises, can God perhaps not do it? Or have we been mistaken in our ideas about God, have we been wrong in our ideas about His mercy and compassion and goodness? Those are the questions that arise acutely. Why does He not demolish these people who are opposed to Him and His people? Now this man had been assailed by such questions; and here he finds his answer. At once he is put right on these questions by remembering the greatness and the power of God—"THOU hast set them in slippery places." There is nothing outside the control of God. Many a Psalm such as the fiftieth expresses it. It is indeed the great theme of the Bible. There is no limit to the power of God. He is eternal in all His powers and in all His attributes. "He spake and it was done." He created everything out of nothing, He suspends the universe in space. Read certain great chapters of the Book of Job and you will find it expressed in a most amazing manner. For instance read the twenty-eighth chapter of the Book of Job, and there are many other chapters in the Bible that proclaim exactly the same thing.

"In the beginning God." This is a fundamental postulate; the Bible asserts it everywhere. Whatever the explanation may be of all that is happening in the world, it is not that God is not capable of stopping it. It is not that He cannot arrest these things, because God by definition is illimitable. He is absolute, He is the everlasting, Eternal God to Whom everything on earth is but as nothing. He owns everything, He governs, He controls everything; all things are under His hands. "The Lord reigneth." Now that is the first thing about which this man was put right, and that very clearly.

But he was also put right on the second question about the righteousness and the justice of God, because that is the order in which these things arise. If God has the power, why doesn't He exercise it? If God has the ability to destroy all His enemies, why does He allow them to do the things they do? Why are the ungodly allowed to flourish; what about the justice and righteousness of God?

The answer is given by the statement made by Abraham of old: "Shall not the Judge of all the earth do right?" (Genesis 18:25). It is as fundamental a postulate as that concerning the greatness and the might and the majesty of God. God is eternally just and right. God cannot change. God cannot (I say it with reverence, it is a part of the truth concerning the holiness of God to say it) — God cannot be unjust. It is impossible. James put it like this. "Let no man say when he is tempted, I am tempted of God, for God cannot be tempted with evil, neither tempteth He any man." "He is the Father of lights, with Whom is no variableness neither shadow of turning." If it were possible for any change or modification to take place in God He would no longer be God. God, as He has revealed to us, is, from everlasting to everlasting, always, ever the same; never any difference, never any modification. So Abraham is obviously right when he says: "Shall not the Judge of all the earth do right?" He can do no other.

So let us realise that, so that, when we are tempted of the devil or by our own predicament or any position which the devil may use to query the righteousness of God, we may realise that what we are really saying is that it is possible for God to vary and to change. But that is impossible. He cannot, because God is God, and, because of what He is, there can never be any variation in His justice or righteousness, there can never be any question of injustice or unrighteousness.

But we must go beyond that. The Psalmist went beyond that and came to the point at which he discovered that the Covenant of God, and the promises of God, are ever faithful and ever sure. In other words God is not only just and right, but God has committed Himself to man, He has given certain promises. Therefore the next great doctrine of the Bible is that the promises of God are always certain and sure; what He hath promised. He will most surely and certainly perform. You will remember that word of Paul the Apostle to Titus; he refers to "God Who cannot lie" (Titus 1:2). And He cannot lie, again for the same reason. When God gives a promise, that promise is certain to be kept. All his promises are absolute promises, and whatever He has said, He is certainly going to do — "For His mercies aye endure, ever faithful ever sure."

Now that was all-important to this Psalmist, because as one of God's people he knew about the Covenant. He knew the promises God had made to His people, and how He had pledged Himself to them. He had told them that they were His peculiar people and that He would take a special interest in them, that He loved them and was concerned about their prosperity and happiness, and that He was going to bless them until eventually He received them unto Himself. Very well, the Psalmist had been tempted to ask, if that is so, why am I like this? But now in the sanctuary of God he finds that he was all wrong and that God works indirectly as well as directly.

He saw that in the sanctuary of God: if you read the verses that follow you will find how he elaborates all that. He says: "Nevertheless I am continually with Thee, Thou hast holden me by my right hand; Thou shalt guide me with Thy counsel and afterward receive me to glory." He sees it all and so when he came to write his Psalm he began by saying: "Surely God is good to Israel" – God is always good to Israel, He never breaks a promise. These are what we must always regard as fundamental postulates in all our relationships to God, and we must never be tempted to question or query anything along that particular line.

The Psalmist was put right in his thinking about God, first of all, with regard to the character of God. Well then, if that is so, we are still confronted by our main question. If I now know that God has all power and that nothing can limit it, that He is always just and righteous, that He is always faithful to His Covenant and promises, I therefore ask: Why then is it that the ungodly are allowed to flourish and prosper in this way, and why is it that the godly are so frequently to be found in a state of suffering? Now here is the heart of this question which has always troubled mankind and which is probably being asked by millions of people in different parts of the world at this moment: Why does God permit this kind of thing? The Psalmist discovered the answer in the House of God. He puts it in a very interesting and charming manner. You will find the same thing in several Psalms; it is an idea indeed that is to be found in many places in the Scriptures. The answer is given here in words which, if you like, we may describe as a very daring anthropomorphism.

The Psalmist says that the explanation is this, that God for the time being seems to be asleep. "When Thou awakest Thou shalt despise their image" he says in verse 20. Now that is an anthropomorphism. In other words, the Psalmist, in order to convey what he had discovered in the sanctuary of God, has to put it in human terms. That is because of the limit of our thinking and our language. It is a pictorial representation in terms of what is true of us as men. God cannot sleep, but He appears to be as one sleeping. It is not that He has not the power, but He is for the time being asleep. It is not that he has forgotten to be gracious, He is asleep – that is the argument. A similar statement is found in the next Psalm in the twenty-second verse, where, having described the desolation of the Church and the way in which the enemy has come into the Church and has reduced it almost to shambles, the Psalmist ends by a prayer. He says: "Arise, O God, plead Thine own cause," etc. It seems as if he turns to God and says: "God, why don't you awake, arise, O God." It is the same idea. In the forty-fourth Psalm in the twenty-third verse you get it more explicitly: "Awake, why sleepest Thou, O Lord? arise, cast us not off for ever." Here is a man in desperation, he sees the desolation produced by the enemy, he sees the success of the ungodly and the suffering of the godly; he is now right in his doctrine, so turning to God he says: "Awake, why sleepest Thou, O Lord?" Why don't you assert yourself? That is the idea, and that is the idea which we must now apply in detail.

Why does God thus appear to be asleep? Before I come to the spiritual answer to this question, may I indicate the gross inconsistency that is to be found in the argument of people who glibly speak like this about God. There are so many people who say: If God is God, and if God has the power, and if God is merciful and gracious, why did He not destroy a man like Hitler at the beginning of his regime, why did He not wipe him out, and all his forces, and thereby save suffering, why did He not intervene earlier, why did He not assert Himself? That is the argument they put forward, and yet they are generally the very self-same people who are loudest in their claim for what they call the free-will of man. If you begin to preach to them about the doctrines of salvation, if you should mention terms like "predestination" and "the elect," they say: I maintain I have a free will, I have a right to do what I like with my own life. Yet they are the people who say God should exert His power and His might over other people. You cannot have it both ways. If you want God to assert Himself like this, He must do it all along the line, not just in what you choose. There is an utter inconsistency in the argument. When such people are thinking about others they say: God should control them; but when they think of themselves they say: "It is very wrong of God to control me, I am a free man, I must be allowed to do whatever I like, I am a free person, I must have my liberty." Ah yes, but the other man must not have liberty. Let us leave it at that; but it is important.

But more seriously from our standpoint, why is it, do you think, that God does appear to be asleep, why is it that God does allow the ungodly to flourish like this? There are certain very definite answers in the Scriptures to that question. Here are some of them. There is no doubt at all that one of the reasons is this: that God permits these things in order that sin may be revealed for what it really is, that He may allow it to manifest itself and show itself in all its ugliness. If you want a classical statement of that you will find it in the second half of the first chapter of Paul's Epistle to the Romans where he traces the decline and fall in the history of mankind. Paul was writing about the civilisation, of society, as it was in his own day. He describes the terrible ugliness and foulness of life; he gives us that horrible list of sins, those sexual perversions and all those other things that were destroying life at that time. And he says that the real explanation of that is that mankind, having substituted the creature for the Creator, man having rebelled against God's holy law, "God has given them over to a reprobate mind," He has withdrawn the restraining power, He has allowed sin to develop into what it really is; and there it is.

Surely that is something of which we need to be reminded today. There is a great deal of attention being paid at this moment to the moral condition of this country, and very rightly. Why is this necessary? I suggest the answer is still precisely the same. Our fathers and forefathers increasingly turned their backs upon God. They queried the authority of the Scriptures — it was done even in pulpits — and man became the authority. What man thinks about the Bible, what man thinks about God, what man thinks about morality became the rule. Man put himself in the position of authority and turned down the authority of God; and we today are reaping the consequences of that. God, as it were, turns to mankind and says: Very well, I will just allow you to see what your views and your philosophies lead to.

Today we are beginning to see what sin really is: it is revealing itself in its ugliness; we are seeing it in all its utter horror and foulness and malignity. There is no question but that God, in order to teach mankind the exceeding sinfulness of sin, sometimes withholds His restraining power, and allows the ungodly to have their fling. He gives them rope and the whole thing appears in its true colours. It was ignored by the philosophers and the psychologists attempted to explain it away, but we are seeing it for what it is — this horrible foul perversion and lust. It is there in the heart of the educated as well as the illiterate.

That is one reason. But it is not the only reason, for there is no doubt that God permits this kind of thing also partly as the punishment of sin. Again, if you read the first chapter of the Epistle to the Romans you will find that point comes out also. In other words God withdraws His restraining power sometimes in order that people may reap some of the consequences of their own sins, and thereby He punishes sin. We are all one by nature in this that we want the pleasure of sin without the consequences, we desire to be able to sin and not to suffer for it. But you cannot, for "There is no peace, saith my God, to the wicked," and God has so made man, and so made life, that there are always effects that follow causes. If you sin, you will suffer, and sometimes God allows the world to get into a state of godlessness as part of its punishment. I do not hesitate to assert that that is the only real explanation of the two world wars. It is partly God meting out punishment to mankind for all its defiance of Him during the last hundred years, it is part of the punishment. God allows things to develop in order that mankind may reap the consequences of that which it has sown. If you "sow the wind" you may well "reap the whirlwind"; and we have experienced that in our own life-time.

What is the next thing? I believe that God allows the evil and the evil-doers to have this fling and this rope and this licence, as it were, in order to make their overthrow more complete and sure. Biblical history is really but an exposition of this principle. God seems to be asleep and the enemy rises, he blasphemes the Name of God. Think of it in the case of Assyria. They set themselves against the God of Israel, and God allowed it all to happen; they inflated themselves almost into the heavens and said: "Nothing can stop us." Then God suddenly pricked the bubble and the whole thing collapsed, and the final discomfiture was greater than ever. It is when the great big bully has made his final boast that he is always brought down. If God had brought him down at the beginning it would not have seemed so wonderful. So God allows evil and evil powers to do astounding things to the world, so much so that even the godly begin to ask: Can God ever stop this? Then, when the end has almost come, God arises and down they go. The discomfiture of the enemy is greater then and more complete.

Then again God allows it in order to display His own greatness and glory over all this great and mighty enemy. God arises and without a word He demolishes him, and all who see it turn to this Almighty, glorious God. All this is put in a very great phrase at the end of the twelfth chapter of the Book of the Acts of the Apostles. A king called Herod seated upon a throne made a great oration to certain people, and after he had delivered his oration the people cried out saying: "It is the voice of a god and not of man." Then God we are told sent an angel and smote this man. "And he was consumed of worms and gave up the ghost. But the word of God grew and multiplied." You see the contrast, the pomp and the greatness were demolished; but the word of the God Whom the foolish king was trying to destroy grew and multiplied, and so God's glory was manifested.

The last explanation I would put forward is this: That there is no doubt at all that God sometimes permits the ungodly to flourish for the sake of disciplining His own people. I am sorry to have to say that, but I must say it. We need to be disciplined. How often did God raise up enemies against the Children of Israel in order to discipline them. They, His own people, had become slack and were forgetting God. He pleaded with them, He sent them prophets but they paid no attention, so he raised up Assyria, he raised up the Chaldeans to chastise, to correct His own people. And I do not hesitate to assert that many of the things we have had to endure in this century have been partly because we, God's people, have needed to be disciplined. It was, alas, the Church herself that undermined the faith of the people in the word of God, and it is not surprising that things are as they are. Maybe we shall have to endure much more in order that we ourselves may be humbled and brought low and brought to realise that we are God's people and that we must rely upon Him and Him alone.

There, it seems to me, are some of the answers given in the Scriptures as to why it is that God seems at times to be asleep.

But that does not exhaust what the Psalmist learned about God's ways. The next thing he describes is what happens when God does awake. He has been put right about the character of God, and sees that the explanation is that God seems to be asleep, and then he ends with this – the things that happen when God does awake. "How are they brought into desolation, as in a moment! they are utterly consumed with terrors. As a dream when one awaketh; so, O Lord when Thou awakest, Thou shalt despise their image." What is he saying? The first thing he says is that God does awake. "When Thou awakest." It is going to happen. O, no, God is not permanently asleep. When it does come . . . ! There is a limit to what God allows the ungodly, there is an end to the latitude and the apparent licence that He gives to His enemies. He certainly allows them to do a lot, but there is an end to it, there is a limit. "My Spirit will not always strive with man." "How long is this to go on?" someone asks God early in history. The answer was: "Until the iniquity of the Amorites is full." There is a limit. "My Spirit will not always strive," and a day is coming when it will not. God does awake. God will awake.

What happens when He does awake? This man says very clearly what is going to happen to these successful ungodly people when God does awake. He says: "As a dream when one awaketh, so, O Lord when Thou awakest Thou shalt despise their image." What a picture! That ungodly man that seemed so great and marvellous, when God arises, vanishes like a dream. It is as if it had but been a phantom, an image, an appearance, and had never been a reality. The ungodly that seemed to be so powerful, so self-sufficient and almost indestructible, when God arises, are gone like a flash. The Bible is full of this. Read the fortieth chapter of Isaiah and you will see there that God says that to Him the nations are but "a drop in a bucket" and as "the small dust of the balance." These great nations with their atomic bombs and their hydrogen bombs, these mighty nations! But a drop in a bucket, and the small dust of the balance.

And not only that. Listen to the sarcasm and the derision. All the nations of the earth "are as grasshoppers," even Great Britain, the U.S.A. and the U.S.S.R. Ah, there have been other great empires and nations and commonwealths before, but they have all gone because they were not submissive to God. All the nations of the earth are but as grasshoppers – when God awaketh.

Let me give you one other example; it is one of the most notable in history. You have read of Alexander the Great, one of the greatest generals of all time, a great monarch and a mighty warrior. He conquered almost the whole earth. "Alexander the Great" he was called. Do you know what the Scriptures call him? Read your Bible right through and you will never find the name of Alexander the Great. It is not mentioned. But Alexander the Great does come into the Scriptures, and you will find the way in which God refers to him in the eighth chapter of the Prophet Daniel. As Walter Luthi has pointed out, he who to the world is Alexander the Great is to God "a he-goat." That is it. When God arises — Alexander the Great — a he-goat — a grasshopper. That is what happens when God arises, to nations, to empires, to individuals, to all. "When Thou arisest": and He has arisen. Read the history recorded in the Bible and you will find that God does arise, and has arisen, and His enemies have been scattered.

The final message, however, that comes to us out of all this is that these great events of history which have already happened are but a pale adumbration and a mighty warning of that which is to happen. The world is Godless, it is Christless; it ridicules the grace of God and the Saviour of the world and especially the holy Blood of His Cross. The world is arrogant and prides itself on its sin. But this is what is going to happen.

The Apostle Paul, who had been greatly persecuted, writing his second letter to the Thessalonians, says: "So that we ourselves glory in you in the churches of God for your patience and faith in all your persecutions and tribulations that ye endure: which is a manifest token of the righteous judgment of God, that ye may be counted worthy of the kingdom of God, for which ye also suffer: seeing it is a righteous thing with God to recompense tribulation to them that trouble you; and to you who are troubled rest with us, when the Lord Jesus shall be revealed from heaven with His mighty angels, in flaming fire taking vengeance on them that know not God, and that obey not the gospel of our Lord Jesus Christ; who shall be punished with everlasting destruction from the presence of the Lord: and from the glory of His power; when He shall come to be glorified in His saints, and to be admired in all them that believe in that day."

O yes, this is as certain as the fact that this is 1953 and as certain as the fact that we are alive at this moment. The Lord will come riding upon the clouds of heaven and all His enemies will be scattered and routed, Satan and hell and all opposed to God will be cast into the lake of fire and go to "everlasting destruction from the presence of the Lord." That is the end of the ungodly. That is the power and the glory of the God Whom we love and Whom we adore and serve.

If you do not understand what is happening, put it into that context. God is God, God is holy and just. He will keep His promise; what He has promised He will certainly perform. He is permitting these things for His own end. A day is coming when He will arise and scatter His enemies, and the Kingdom of Jesus Christ will stretch "from shore to shore" and all men shall confess in heaven and earth and under the earth that He is The Lord, to the glory of God the Father. Thank God that His promises are ever sure. God grant that we all may see and know and understand God's ways and be rid, once and for ever, of all sinful doubt and unworthy questioning.

SELF EXAMINATION

Psalm 73:21-22

HERE we come to yet a further step and stage in this man's account of the crisis through which he had passed in his soul and in his godly walk. You remember how he had been unhappy because he had observed the prosperity of the wicked and had contrasted that with his own troubles and trials and problems. He had meditated so much upon this that he had become very unhappy, indeed he was even beginning to wonder whether God was fair, whether God was true to His own word, whether there was any point in being a godly man at all because it seemed to lead to nothing.

Thus he was in a terrible condition; and he was on the point of expressing himself in public, he was on the point of asking a question which should never be asked, he was on the point of saying: "Verily I have cleansed my heart in vain." He was on the point of saying that, when he suddenly realised that to say that would be to discourage God's people and that, at any rate, he felt was something he could never do. So he did not do it. He tells us how he was very unhappy about it all. He still could not understand God's ways and he was very wretched until he "went to the sanctuary of God." Then everything was put right, and we have been tracing the steps in his recovery.

We have considered the way in which he was put right by going into the sanctuary of God. The essence can be put in this way, that he began to think in the right way. His thinking became spiritual again; he rose up from the natural, rational level to the spiritual level and he began to think spiritually. As he did so, he found he was put right in the three respects in which he had gone wrong. He had gone wrong in thinking about the ungodly, he had gone wrong in thinking about God and he had gone wrong in thinking about himself. We have already dealt with the first. He puts it in a graphic statement: "Until I went into the sanctuary of God, then understood I their end." He saw that the truth was this: "Verily thou hast set them in slippery places." Their whole position is most precarious: "Thou casteth them down to destruction; how are they brought into desolation as in a moment; they are utterly consumed with terrors." Then we saw last time how his thinking was also put right about God. He had been questioning God's power to deal with these ungodly, and God's desire to do so, but he had been put right. "As a dream when one awaketh so, O Lord, when thou awakest, thou shalt despise their image." God is as it were but asleep, He is

---

Previously published by The Bookroom, Westminster Chapel, London, in *Westminster Record*, and reprinted by kind permission of Martyn Lloyd-Jones.

allowing these things to take place. It is not that He cannot prevent and stop them, it is not that it is not His purpose to do so. He is choosing for some inscrutable reason to allow these things to happen, but a day is coming when God will awake and arise and His enemies will be scattered. They will be seen thus for what they really are, a phantom, an image, a dream. We ended by saying that this is but an adumbration, a prophecy of the great day when God will finally arise and all His enemies shall be scattered and Satan shall be cast into the lake that burns, and all that is opposed to God shall be destroyed. "When Thou awakest." He came to see that about God.

But now we come to a consideration of how he was put right in the third respect—his thinking was put right also about himself. This he describes in this striking and severe manner in these two verses that we are now looking at. At once I would call your attention to the striking contrast they present to what he has previously said about himself in verses 13 and 14, where he said: "Verily I have cleansed my heart in vain and washed my hands in innocency; for all the day long have I been plagued and chastened every morning." He is there very sorry for himself; there is nothing wrong with him; he is a very good man, he is being very hard pressed, he is being dealt with very unfairly and even God seems to be unfair to him. That is how he thought about himself outside the sanctuary; but inside the sanctuary it is this: "Thus my heart was grieved and I was pricked in my reins; so foolish was I and ignorant, I was as a beast before Thee." What a transfiguration! What an entirely different view of himself! Well, it is all the result of the fact that his thinking has been adjusted and put right and made truly spiritual.

Now this is a most important matter, and a most important point in the whole movement of the teaching and the doctrine of this Psalm; because, let us be quite frank and honest and admit it, we are very prone to stop short of this point and to end before we come to it. We are all quite happy to read about the ungodly—and I do not know anybody who has been upset about a sermon which shows how the ungodly have been set in slippery places. Then that great doctrine about God—"the Lord reigneth"—there is nothing so exalted as that, and we all like to hear about that. We like to read about the ungodly, and we like to read about God because that makes us feel that everything is going to be right for us. But the danger is to stop at that point and to go no further. This man, however, goes on, and as he does so he reveals not only his honesty and his sincerity and the truthfulness that was so essentially a part of his makeup, but he also—and this is the thing I want to emphasise—displays an understanding of the nature of the spiritual life. Now that is most important.

What we have in these two verses is this man's account of his repentance and what he said to himself about himself, and about his recent conduct in particular. It is indeed a very classical statement of this very point, and I am pausing with it, and inviting you to consider it with me, because it is one of those essential matters in connection with the whole discipline of the Christian life. This state in which a man pauses and looks at himself and talks to himself about himself, this repentance is one of the most essential and vital aspects of what is commonly called the discipline of the Christian life. Now I do not apologise for emphasising this because it is a matter which is being seriously neglected at the present time. How often do we hear about the discipline of the Christian life these days? How often do we talk about it, how often is it really at the centre of our evangelical living? There was a time in the Christian Church when this was at the very centre, and it is, I believe profoundly, because of our neglect of this discipline of the Christian life that the Church is in her present position. Indeed, I see no hope whatsoever of any true revival and re-awakening until we return to this.

As we approach this great subject let me start by saying that there seem to me to be two main dangers in connection with this subject, and of course as usual they are at the opposite extremes. We are always creatures of extremes, either at one end or the other. The difficulty is to walk in the right, correct position, avoiding all violent reactions. The true position, generally, in the Christian life is in the middle.

One danger that used to be fairly common was the danger of morbidity and introspection. Of course, it is still true of some people, but I would say that it is not the commonest difficulty with Christian people at the present time. There are certain people, however, who are still subject to this. I believe it is still true to say that in certain parts of this island of ours, for instance in the Highlands of Scotland, you will still find the thing to which I am referring. It certainly was at one time very common there and elsewhere amongst Celtic people. I certainly was brought up in a religious atmosphere in which it was very prevalent. There are still people then who are given to this tendency to morbidity and introspection. They spend much, if not all, of their lives in analysing themselves and in condemning themselves, in being conscious of their unworthiness and their lack of fitness. They become introspective and turn inwards on themselves. They are always feeling their own spiritual pulse and taking their own spiritual temperature, and they become almost immersed in this process of self-condemnation.

May I tell you the story of one of the most pathetic things I have witnessed. I was in the dying bed-chamber of one of the saintliest and most godly men I have ever been privileged to meet. In the room were his two daughters—both of them in middle age, if not over. The old man, the father, was dying, and he knew he was dying and he said that the one thing he was unhappy about was the fact that neither of his daughters was a Church member, or had ever taken Communion. It was a truly astounding statement because two more godly women and active women in connection with the life of the Church to which they belonged you would never find. But they were not Church members. Why had they never taken Communion? The answer was that they felt unworthy of it; they felt they were not fit to do so; they were so conscious of their failures and their sins and their shortcomings. There they were, two most excellent Christian women, but because of this introspection, because they turned in upon themselves, they felt they had no right to partake in the inner life of the Church.

Now that kind of thing was once very common. People would get up in Church meetings just to say that they were terrible sinners, and to stress how much they had failed. They hoped they would arrive in heaven, but they could not see how such worthless creatures could ever get there. You may be familiar with that in your reading. It was certainly a tendency in the lives of those saints, John Fletcher and Henry Martyn. They were not extreme cases, but they obviously had that tendency, and it was a feature of the piety of that age.

But that is not at all the danger today, and especially, if I may say so, here in London and in the circles in which most of us turn. Indeed, the danger amongst us is the exact opposite; it is the danger which the prophet Jeremiah expresses in these words, the danger of "healing the hurt of the daughter my people slightly saying peace, peace, when there is no peace." It is the extreme opposite of the other tendency. It is the absence of a true godly sorrow for sin, and the tendency to spare ourselves and to regard ourselves and our sins and shortcomings and our failures lightly.

Let me put it in a still more drastic manner. I believe there is a very real danger amongst some evangelical people in particular of misusing the doctrine of salvation, misusing the great doctrine of justification by faith only and assurance of salvation, and a consequent failure to realise what sin really is in God's sight and what it really means in a child of God. The idea seems to have gained currency, I know not why, that repentance should play no part at all in the life of the Christian. There are people who seem to think it is wrong to speak of repentance. They say that the moment you see that you have sinned and then have put your sin "under the Blood" you are all right. To stop and think about it and to condemn yourself means that you lack faith. The moment you "look to Jesus" all is well. We heal ourselves so easily; indeed, I do not hesitate to say that the trouble with most of us is that in a sense we are far too "healthy" spiritually. I mean by that that we are much too glib, and much too superficial. We do not take trouble in these matters; we, unlike the Psalmist in these two verses, are on much too good terms with ourselves. We are so unlike the men depicted in the Scriptures.

I am suggesting that this is due to the fact that we fail to go on to the step to which the man in this Psalm went. He was not only put right about the ungodly and about God but about himself, and you notice the way in which he deals with himself. Now we do not seem to do that these days, and the result is that there is this false appearance of health as if all were well with us. There is very little sackcloth and ashes, there is very little godly sorrow for sin, there is very little evidence of true repentance.

Let me show you that the need for and the importance of repentance is something that is taught in Scriptures everywhere. There is no more classical teaching about this, of course, than that which you find in the parable of the Prodigal Son. There is a man who sinned and in his folly left home, and then things went wrong with him. What happened? Well, when he came to himself what did he do? He condemned himself, he spoke to himself about himself. He dealt with himself very severely, and it was only after that that he arose and went back to his father. Or take that wonderful statement in the 2nd Epistle to the Corinthians in the 7th chapter, verses 9–11. What pleased the great Apostle about those people in Corinth was the way in which they dealt with themselves. You notice that he goes into it in detail. He says: "For behold this selfsame thing, that ye sorrowed after a godly sort, what carefulness it wrought in you, yea what clearing of yourselves, yea, what indignation, yea, what fear, yea what vehement desire, yea, what zeal, yea what revenge. In all things ye have approved yourselves to be clear in this matter." In other words, these Christians had committed a sin and Paul had written to them about it and sent Titus to preach to them about it.

Now there we have a definition of what is really meant by a true spirit of repentance. These Corinthian people had dealt severely with themselves and had condemned themselves, and because of that Paul tells them that they are again in the place of blessing. Then there is that wonderful example of it in the book of Job. You remember how Job throughout the main part of that Book is justifying himself, defending himself and sometimes feeling sorry for himself. Ah yes, but when Job came into the presence of God truly, when he was in the sanctuary and met with God, this is what he says: "Wherefore I abhor myself and repent in dust and ashes." There was no more godly man than Job, the most upright in the world, the most religious man. He no longer remembers the things that had happened to him and all the blessings he had enjoyed because of his adversity. Job had been tempted to think of God like this man in the 73rd Psalm, and he had said things he should not have said; but when he sees God he puts his hand on his mouth and says: "I abhor myself and repent in dust and ashes."

I wonder whether we know that experience. Do we know what it is to abhor ourselves, do we know what it is to repent in dust and ashes? Our prevailing doctrine does not seem to like that, because we say we have passed out of the 7th of Romans. We feel that we must not talk about sorrow for sin because that would mean that we are still in the very early stage of the Christian life. So we pass over it and turn to Romans 8. But have we ever been in Romans 7? Have we ever really said from the heart: "O wretched man that I am, who shall deliver me from the body of this death?" Have we ever really abhorred ourselves and repented in dust and ashes? This is a very vital part of the discipline of the Christian life. Read the lives of the saints throughout the centuries and you will find that they did it very frequently. Go back to Henry Martyn, for example, go back to those mighty men of God and you will find that they frequently abhorred themselves, they hated their lives in this world, they hated themselves in that sense. And it was because of that that they were so mightily blessed of God.

Nothing is more important, therefore, than for us to follow this man and to see exactly what he did. We can put it in this form. We must learn to turn upon ourselves and to deal with ourselves faithfully. It is a vital matter in this Christian life. What are the steps?

I have tried to divide them in this way. First and foremost we must really confess what we have done. Now we do not like doing that. We are aware of what we have done, and our tendency is to say: "I turn to Christ and at once I am forgiven and all is well." That is an error. We must confess what we have done. This man spent a lot of time in commiserating with himself, in looking at other people and envying them, he had spent a lot of time with these unworthy thoughts about God and His ways. But after his recovery in the sanctuary he says to himself: "I must spend an equal amount of time in looking at myself and looking at what I have done." We must not spare ourselves. We must really confess what we have done, which means that we must deliberately hold these things before ourselves. We must not shield ourselves in any way, we must not attempt to slide over it, we must not take a casual glance at it. No, no, we must hold the facts in front of ourselves and say: "This is what I did, this is what I thought and said." I must hold it in front of myself deliberately.

But not only that, I must analyse it, and I must work it out in all its details and consider what it involves and implies. This is something that by means of self-discipline we have to do quite relentlessly and resolutely. This man undoubtedly did so, that is why he ends by saying: "I was as a beast." He said: "I actually thought that about Thee, O God, and I was on the point of saying it — that is what I really did." He put it before himself and he held it there until he was crushed to the ground and felt he was a cad and a beast. We shall never really abhor ourselves unless we do that. We have to hold our sin before ourselves until we really see it for what it is.

Let me emphasise that we have to particularise and to descend to details. I know this is very painful. I am preaching as much to myself as to you. We have to particularise and that means that it is not enough just to come to God and say: "God, I am a sinner." You have to bring it down to details, you have to confess to yourself and to God in detail what you have done, you have to be quite particular. Now it is easier to say: "I am sinful" than it is to say: "I have said something I should not have said, or thought something I should not have thought, or I have harboured an unclean thought." But the essence of this matter is to get right down to details, to particularise, to put it all down on paper, to put every detail down before yourself, to analyse yourself and to face the horrible character of sin in detail. That is what the masters in the spiritual life have always done. Read their manuals, read the journals of the most saintly people who have adorned the life of the Church and you will find that they have always done that.

I have reminded you of John Fletcher. He not only asked twelve questions of himself before he went to sleep each night, but he got his congregation to do the same. He did not content himself with a cursory general examination; he examined himself in detail, such as: Do I lose my temper? Have I lost my temper? Have I made life more difficult for somebody else? Did I listen to that insinuation that the devil put into my mind, that unclean idea; did I cling to it or immediately reject it? You go through the day and you put it all before yourself and face it — that is the method.

Then we must view it all in the sight of God — "before Thee." We must take all these things and ourselves into the presence of God, and before we speak to God we must condemn ourselves. You notice Paul's word in 2 Corinthians 7, verse 11: "Yea what indignation." They were indignant with themselves. Our trouble is that we have ceased to be indignant with ourselves, and we are to be indignant with ourselves because we are all guilty of those sins that I have been enumerating. These are horrid things in the sight of God, and we are not indignant. We are on too good terms with ourselves; that is why our witness is so ineffective. We must learn to humble ourselves, we must learn to humiliate ourselves, we must learn to strike ourselves. Paul tells us in 1 Corinthians 9:27, that he "keeps under his body." He pummels it, he beats it until it is black and blue. And we must do the same thing with ourselves. We must learn again — I must not call it the art — we must learn again this discipline of self-humbling and self-humiliation. We must put ourselves down, we must strike ourselves, we must condemn ourselves. It is an essential part of this discipline. Undoubtedly this man did it, because he ends by saying: "So foolish was I and ignorant, I was as a beast before thee." It is only a man who has gone through the process of self-examination thoroughly who comes to that view. If we therefore are to come to that we must persist in the way I have indicated and truly search ourselves in order that we may see ourselves for what we really are.

The next point for our consideration is this. What is it we discover when we have done all that? There can be no doubt at all as to the answer given in this 73rd Psalm. What this man found when he examined himself and really began to think correctly about himself was this: That the great cause, if not indeed the only cause of all his troubles was "self." It is always the trouble. Self is the last enemy and our most constant enemy; and it is the most prolific cause of all our unhappiness. As the result of the fall of Adam we are self-centred. We are sensitive about ourselves, always selfish and protecting ourselves, always ready to imagine offences, always ready to say that we have been wronged and dealt with unfairly. Am I not speaking from experience? May God have mercy upon us. It is the truth about us all. Self, this enemy that follows the greatest saint to his death, this enemy that tries to make a man proud of his own humility. This man found that that really was the cause of all his troubles. He had gone wrong in thinking about the ungodly, he had gone wrong in thinking about God, but the real cause of all was that he had gone wrong in thinking about himself. It was because he was always revolving around himself that everything else seemed to be so terribly wrong and grossly unfair.

I want to introduce you to the psychology taught in this verse — true biblical psychology. I wonder whether you noticed it. When self takes control of us something inevitably happens and it is this, our hearts begin to control our heads. Listen to this man. He has recovered himself in God's house, he has been put right about the ungodly and about God and now he comes to himself and he says: "My heart was grieved and I was pricked in my reins" — again a part of the sensibility — "So stupid was I and ignorant, I was as a beast before thee." You notice the order. He puts the heart before the head. He points out that it was his heart that was grieved before his brain began to function wrongly — heart first and then head.

Now this is one of the profoundest bits of psychology we can ever grasp. The real trouble is that it is the self, when it asserts itself, that causes this reversal of the true order and of the right sense of proportion. All our troubles are ultimately due to the fact that we are governed by our feelings and our hearts and sensibilities instead of thinking clearly and facing things as we should. The heart is a very powerful faculty within us. When the heart gets into control it bludgeons a man; it makes us stupid, it takes hold of us and we become unreasonable and so cannot think clearly. That is the thing that happened to this man. He had thought that it was a pure question of fact — "There are the ungodly, look at them and look at me." He thought that he was very rational, but he discovered in the sanctuary that he wasn't rational at all and that he had been governed by his feelings.

Is not this the trouble with all of us? The Apostle Paul puts the whole matter in a great word in the 4th chapter of the epistle to the Philippians, verses 6 and 7. Observe the order of the words: "Be careful for nothing — be over-anxious for nothing — but in everything by prayer and supplication with thanksgiving let your requests be made known unto God." What will happen? This is what will happen — "And the peace of God which passeth all understanding shall keep your mind and hearts? Not at all! "The peace of God which passeth all understanding shall keep your hearts and mind through Christ Jesus." Hearts first, then mind. That is profound psychology.

The Apostle Paul was a master physician in connection with diseases of the soul. He knew that it was quite pointless to deal with the mind until the heart was put right, so he puts the heart first. The trouble with anyone in this condition who feels that he is having a hard time and that things are not going right is that he begins to question God; whereas the real trouble is that his heart is becoming soft and he is being governed and controlled by his heart. His feelings have taken possession of him and have blinded him to everything else. All the troubles and quarrels and disputes in life are ultimately due to this. There is no question about it — all family quarrels, all disputes between husbands and wives, all quarrels between relatives, all quarrels between classes and groups, all quarrels between nation and nation can all be put down to this — self is being controlled by feelings.

If we stopped to think we should see how wrong it is, because what we are really saying is that we are absolutely perfect and everybody else is wrong. But patently that cannot be true because all are saying the same thing. We are all governed by this feeling about ourselves and tend to say: "People are not fair to me, I am always being misunderstood, people are always doing things to me." And the other people are saying exactly the same thing. The trouble is that we are being controlled by self, we are living on our feelings, and in a most extraordinary way we are being governed by ourselves. We all know this from experience. It is the very devil, you cannot reason with it. We take our stand and we say: "I don't see why I should give in." We hold on to it. We even put an emphasis on it unconsciously — "I" — "What have I done? Why should I be treated like this?" "My heart was grieved and I was pricked in my reins" — yes, it is always the heart. The principle I would emphasise is that when self is in the ascendant it always plays on our feelings. Self cannot stand up to a real intellectual examination. If, as I say, we only sat down and thought about it we should realise what fools we are, how idiotic we are, because if you sat down and thought you would say: "I feel like this, but so does the other person. I say this, but he also says this. Obviously we both think we are right. It is both of us, and I am as bad as he is." "He that is down," says John Bunyan, "need fear no fall, He that is low no pride."

We must learn to keep a careful watch on our hearts. It is not surprising the Scripture says: "My son give me thy heart." It is not surprising that Jeremiah says: "The heart is deceitful above all things and desperately wicked." How foolish we are in our psychology. We tend to say of people: "Well, you know, he is not very intellectual, he does not understand very much but he has a good heart." That is quite wrong. However unintelligent we may be our minds are much better than our hearts. It is not because men think that they are wrong, generally speaking, it is because they do not think. "The heart is deceitful above all things and desperately wicked." This poor man in the 73rd Psalm was being controlled by his heart, but he did not know it. He thought he was reasoning out facts. The heart is deceitful, it is so clever and subtle; that is why we must watch it. "This is the condemnation," we read in John 3:19, "that light is come into the world and men loved darkness rather than light because their deeds were evil." It is the heart that is wrong, so we end with the advice of the wise man in Proverbs 4, verse 23: "Keep thy heart with all diligence for out of it are the issues of life." Watch your heart, watch yourself, watch your feelings. "Keep thy heart with all diligence for out of it are the issues of life." When your heart is sour everything will be sour and nothing will be right. It is the heart that governs everything and there is only one final treatment for this sour and bitter heart: it is to come to God as this man went, and it is to realise that God in His infinite love and grace and mercy and compassion sent His Son into the world to die upon the Cross that we should come to abhor ourselves, that we might be forgiven and once more have a clean heart, that David's prayer may be answered, "Create within me a clean heart, O God." That prayer is answered in Christ. He can cleanse the heart and sanctify the soul:

> 'Tis Thine to cleanse the heart
> To sanctify the soul
> To pour fresh life in every part
> And new create the whole.

Once a man gets to know himself and the blackness of his own heart and the deceitfulness of his own heart, he knows that he has to fly to Christ. And there he finds forgiveness and cleansing, a new life, a new nature, a new heart, a new name. Thank God for a Gospel that can give a man a new heart and renew a right spirit within him.

SPIRITUAL ALLERGY

Psalm 73:21-22

WE ARE CONSIDERING this man's analysis of himself, after he had come to himself as the result of going to the sanctuary of God. You remember that this man had gone sadly astray in his thinking in three main respects. He had completely misunderstood the position of the ungodly. He had regarded them as objects of envy because he saw their prosperity; he had been contrasting their condition with his own and so he had been guilty of being "envious at the foolish." Likewise, and as the result of that, he had been guilty of thinking very wrongly about God and God's attitude towards him and God's promises to His people. And as the result of that, of course, he clearly had been guilty of thinking in a very wrong way about himself.

In other words, this man having started with the simple observation of the apparent success of the ungodly had gone completely wrong in all his thinking, and he had been going round in that miserable circle where nothing seemed to be right. He was on the point of expressing himself about it, but he didn't for the reasons we have considered. But he still wasn't happy until he went to the House of God, where he began to think spiritually and to see that his thinking had been wrong, and especially in these three main respects. We have already considered the first, how his thinking about the ungodly was put right, how he saw that they were really objects of pity rather than of envy, because they were set in such slippery places and because their end was to be doom and disaster. So he ended by feeling sorry for them instead of envying them. At the same time he came to see the truth about God, about God's greatness and God's love, and about God's great power and what God is going to do.

Then here in these two verses he tells us how he came to see that he had been entirely wrong also in his thinking about himself. We began our consideration of that last time. The points we then made were these. The first big thing he discovered was that self after all is the real trouble, and it is because self tends to get into control that we have so many of our difficulties and problems and perplexities in this life. That is the key to everything. We emphasised that this man was very honest with himself, indeed he was quite brutal with himself. We are going to see that still more this time. He did not take a mere cursory glance at himself and then forget all about it and go on to something else; he just stood and looked at himself, he looked steadfastly into that mirror and faced himself down to the smallest detail. He flinched at nothing.

Previously published by The Bookroom, Westminster Chapel, London, in *Westminster Record,* and reprinted by kind permission of Martyn Lloyd-Jones.

That is absolutely essential. There is no possible growth in the Christian life unless we are ruthlessly honest with ourselves.

Self-examination is, perhaps, of all the aspects of the Christian life the one most neglected today. This is partly because of erroneous teaching, but also because we do not like doing anything that is painful to ourselves. There is no question about this teaching. Nothing is so characteristic of the true saint as the way in which he examines himself, faces himself, and deals ruthlessly with himself. This man did so, and he had to admit that self was really the source of his troubles. Then he discovered this other very interesting thing, that when self is in control in that way it generally happens that the heart takes control of the thinking. It is a very sad state of affairs when our minds are governed by our hearts. That was never meant to be the case. The mind, the understanding, is man's supreme gift; it is undoubtedly a part of the image of God in man. The power to reason and to understand and to think and to know why we do things, and whether or not we ought to be doing them, is one of the things that differentiates man from animals.

So when we find ourselves, if I may use such a term, thinking emotionally we are in a very bad condition. This man had got into that condition when the heart came before the head. The Bible is very concerned about this, and its teaching everywhere is that we should always guard the heart, because "out of it are the issues of life." That means that it shall be under the control of truth, so we are urged to "seek wisdom" and to "get knowledge." We must never give the impression that people become Christian by ceasing to think and by just responding to their hearts. A Christian is one who believes and accepts and surrenders himself to the Truth. He sees it, is moved by it and acts upon it. The term "heart" in Scripture does not mean the emotions only, but includes the mind, and repentance means a change of mind.

Let us now go on to consider what this man discovered about himself in detail. He tells us in these two verses. The first thing he discovered when he really saw the position truly was that he had very largely been producing his own troubles, and his own misery and his own unhappiness. He found in the sanctuary of God that it was not really the ungodly at all, it was himself. He found that he had, to use our phrase, "worked himself up" into this condition. Now let me give you the evidence for that. Verse 21 reads in the authorised version—"thus my heart was grieved and I was pricked in my reins." This translation rather suggests that something had happened to his heart, something had happened to his reins, his kidneys—another seat of the feelings and emotions according to ancient psychology. But actually what this man said was something slightly different. These words which are used in the 21st verse are reflexive. What he is saying is that he had done something to himself. He was saying: "I have soured my heart." He had done it himself, and as regards the reins you can translate like this: "I was preparing for myself a piercing pain." He had been doing it himself. He had been stimulating his own heart, he had been exacerbating his own trouble, he had been souring his own feelings. He himself had really been producing his own troubles and giving rise to this piercing pain which he had been enduring until he went into the sanctuary of God.

Now this is clearly a very important and vital principle. The fact is, and must we not all confess it in the presence of God at this moment, that we tend to produce and exacerbate our own troubles. We, of course, tend to say, as this man had been saying before he went to the sanctuary of God, that it is that thing outside us that produced all the trouble. But it is not that thing at all, it is us. I remember reading once a phrase which I think puts this point quite well: "It is not life that matters, but the courage that you bring to it." Now I do not accept that philosophy of courage, but I am quoting the phrase because, though it is wrongly stated, there is an essential of truth in it. "It is not life that matters" — well, what matters? It is you and I and the way we face it, the way we react, our behaviour with respect to it.

I can prove that quite simply. You may see two persons living exactly the same sort of life, facing the same conditions precisely, and yet the two persons are very different, one is bitter and sour and grumbling and complaining, the other is calm and quiet and quite happy and composed. Where is the difference? It is not in the conditions, it is not in what is happening to them; it is something in them, the difference is in the two persons.

Now this can be proved abundantly. There is that couplet that puts it so well: "Two men looked out from prison bars. The one saw mud, the other stars." Now the two persons were in the same cell looking out through the same bars, but one, you see, looked at the mud, the other saw the stars. It is not life, it is not the circumstances, it is not the ungodly, it is not these things, it is us. This man discovered all that, that he had been creating and exaggerating and exacerbating his own troubles. He had been soured in His own heart. God knows we all tend to be guilty of the same thing. It is not the thing itself that matters. The particular thing is there, of course, but it is very important that we should realise that it is the way in which we react to that thing that determines what is going to happen to us, not merely the thing itself. We have a phrase which I think puts this very well. We say a certain type of person: "He is always making a mountain out of a molehill." Quite right. That is exactly what this man was doing — making a mountain out of a molehill. There was something there, of course; even a molehill is something. There must be something to work on, but the thing itself was very small, it really was just a molehill. But this man was making a mountain of it, he had worked it up into a mountain. He therefore thought that he was confronted by a mountain of trouble, but he wasn't really. He has turned the molehill into a mountain. So it is that we bother ourselves and agitate ourselves and get into this condition.

We have another phrase which describes it. We say that "We become worked up" about something. Now that is not quite accurate, it is not so much that we become worked up as that we work ourselves up. In other words, the reaction is too big for the stimulus. That is obviously the case because we are not properly balanced, we are not in a right condition, we are hyper-sensitive.

I could illustrate this endlessly. Everybody today is talking about being allergic to things. That is one of the current phrases. Now what does that mean? It means that you are hyper-sensitive. There are some people for instance who cannot be in same room as a cat without having an attack of asthma; others cannot be near a field of hay without having an attack of hay fever, their eyes water, etc. You are familiar with all that. What is the matter? The authorities say it is the pollen in the air. But it is not simply the pollen of course, because other people can walk in the same field and nothing happens. The pollen is there, but the point is that these people suffer from hay fever not because of the pollen but because they are hyper-sensitive, they are allergic.

Now that is the kind of thing this man discovered. But he goes beyond that, and rightly so. He says that he worked up the sensitivity, indeed hyper-sensitivity. It can be done quite easily. You can make your heart hyper-sensitive, you can tend it and fondle it, and the more you do so the more your heart will like it, and the more sensitive and sorry it will be for itself. You can so work it up into this condition that the slightest thing will cause trouble at once. If you strike a match — just one match — in a barrel of gunpowder there will be a terrible explosion. It is not the match that counts primarily, it is the barrel of gunpowder.

That is the kind of thing this man discovered. He had been totally wrong in his thinking about the ungodly. He thought that they alone were the cause of his problem. But he discovered that it was not anything of the kind. He had worked up his heart into this foolish condition, he was hyper-sensitive. And so he was in such a state and condition that when the slightest thing went wrong it would cause an explosion. I am sure we all realise the truth of what I am saying, but the question is, do you see yourself doing that? Every time you talk to yourself about yourself do you feel sorry for yourself? If so you are doing this thing that this man had been doing to himself; you are increasing this morbidity and hyper-sensitivity, and you are preparing yourself for a painful experience. This is what is called masochism.

You are familiar with that kind of perversion of which we are all more or less guilty. It is a strange thing about human nature, it is one of the appalling consequences of the Fall, that we take this perverse delight, as it were, in hurting ourselves. It is a most peculiar thing, but we enjoy our own misery because, while we are enjoying it, we are also pitying ourselves at the same time. That is where the subtlety of it all comes in. While we are thoroughly miserable and unhappy there is a sense in which we hold on to it because it gives a kind of perverted enjoyment. We are still protecting self and magnifying self.

This man found all that in the sanctuary of God. He had been grieving himself; he had produced his own misery and he had kept it up. He had exaggerated the whole thing instead of facing it honestly. He was not in all this great trouble, he was not having a hard time; he was just looking at things in such a way as to give himself a hard time—foolish man that he was! Are we not all like him at times—foolish creatures that we are.

Now the opposite to all this is that blessed condition which is described by the Apostle Paul in the 4th chapter of the Epistle to the Philippians, verses 11 to 13. He puts it like this: "For I have learned in whatsoever state I am therewith to be content; I know both how to be abased and I know how to abound; everywhere in all things I am instructed both to be full and to be hungry, both to abound and to suffer need. I can do all things through Christ which strengtheneth me." In other words, he has arrived in a condition in which he is no longer hypersensitive. He is in a condition in which it does not matter very much what happens to him; it is not going to disturb him. "I have learned in whatsoever state I am therewith to be content." That is the position in which all of us who are Christians should be. The man who is not a Christian cannot possibly be there and is not there. He is like a barrel of gunpowder; you never know when there is going to be an explosion. The slightest pin-prick causes all the trouble—hyper-sensitive because of self. But the Apostle Paul had remembered what our Lord puts first to His disciples, namely: "If any man would be My disciple, let him deny himself." Self must be put out first. Then "take up the cross and follow Me." Because self is dethroned and put into the background, the disciple is not hyper-sensitive and these things do not cause troubles and alarms and explosions. He is balanced because self is put out and he is living for Christ.

Let us examine ourselves in the light of this. Think of all your grievances, think of all your hardships and all the slights and insults and all the rest of the things we think have been heaped upon us, and all the misunderstandings. Let us face them in the light of all this and I think we shall see at a glance that it is rather a miserable and sorry business. It is all worked up. There is nothing there really; it is just making a mountain out of a molehill. If we could but make a list of the things that have upset us how ashamed we should be. How small, how petty we can be!

Let us leave it at that, and let us go on to something else. For the next thing this man discovered was that he had become stupid. The authorised version translates verse 22 as: "So foolish was I." Now that word really means "stupid." A much better word is it not? He was like a beast, utterly irrational, behaving in a stupid, absurd manner. But this is always true of this condition that we are describing and analysing. What does it mean exactly? He says: "so stupid was I and ignorant." "I was"—he repeats the emphasis—"I was as a beast before Thee." Again let us note his honesty and truthful dealings with himself. He does not spare himself at all; he has seen the truth about himself and he states it—"I was as a beast before Thee."

What does it mean? Let us analyse it like this. It means first and foremost that he was behaving instinctively. What is the difference between a beast, an animal, and a man? I have already hinted at the answer, that surely God's supreme gift to man is understanding and reason and the power to think. The animal may be highly intelligent, but the animal lacks that true quality and faculty of reason, the power to stand outside itself, to consider itself and to consider what it is doing. It is man alone who can do that, and that is a part of the image of God in man. But the animal does not do that, the animal acts instinctively. There is no question about that.

I need not waste time in giving an illustration of what I mean, but take the question of the migration of the birds—swallows, etc.—that come to us in the spring and go to a warmer clime for the winter. There is very little doubt but that it has been proved quite scientifically that it is not so much intelligence as instinct that governs that. In other words, animal behaviour is a matter of instinctive response to a given stimulus.

Well, this man tells us that he had been behaving like that. In other words, he did not stop to think, he did not stop to ponder and reason about it. To be stupid means not to think logically and not to think clearly. You and I are meant to think logically, we are meant to think rationally, we are meant to think consecutively. But this man had not been thinking like that, he had been like the animal. The animal jumps to conclusions, he responds at once without any interval to the stimulus. The Psalmist had been doing that. And we all must see, when we begin to think about this, how subject we all are to this. It is very un-Christian, however.

One of the great differences between a Christian and a non-Christian should be that the Christian always puts in an interval between the stimulus and the response. The Christian should always put everything into another context. He should think about it, he should not jump to conclusions, he should work the thing out. In other words, and surely this is very vital and important, one of the hall-marks of the Christian should be the capacity to think and to think logically, to think clearly and to think spiritually. Now is not that the whole object of the New Testament Epistles? What do they say? They reason with us. These Epistles were given to Christian people like ourselves who had their problems and perplexities, and what they all say is just this: "Don't just react to these things; think about them, put them into the purposes of God; relate them to the whole view of salvation and the

Christian life: and having done that you will find that you will think about them in a different way." The Christian is a man who thinks in a different manner from the non-Christian. His thinking is logical, it is clear, it is calm, it is controlled, it is balanced, and above everything else it is spiritual. He thinks everything out in terms of this great truth that he has here in the New Testament. But the animal cannot do that. "I was as a beast before Thee, I was stupid." That kind of behaviour is not only like an animal's, it is more or less like a child's also. A child behaves like that because its reasoning faculty has not sufficiently advanced and developed. It jumps to conclusions, it reacts to stimuli like the animal. It has to be trained to think and to reason and not to be stupid.

Another way in which he found that had been stupid was this. He found that he had obviously held an idea of the godly life which was quite false. He desired pleasure the whole time and thought that his life was to be one long round of sunshine and happiness. That was what had made him complain and say: "I have cleansed my heart in vain and washed my hands in innocency" and "For all the day long have I been plagued and chastened every morning." Let me put this quite brutally and plainly. Is not this true of all of us? We tend to take all the gifts and the pleasures and the happiness and the joy without saying much to God about it, but the moment anything goes wrong we begin to grumble. We take our health and strength, our food and clothing and our loved ones, all for granted; but the moment anything goes wrong we start grumbling and complaining and we say: "Why should God do this to me, why should this happen to me?" How slow we are to thank, how swift to grumble. But that is like the animal, isn't it? The animal likes to be petted and patted, he eats and enjoys his food, but the moment you correct him he does not like it. That is typical of the animal, and it is typical of the child outlook. The child will take all you give it, but if you withhold something it wants it resents it. That is being stupid, that is the failure to think, that is the childish, stupid, beastly attitude. But how true it is; it was true of this man and it is true of us.

Let me put it like this. This man had been taking the blessings and the joys for granted. We all seem to assume that we have a right to these things and that we should have them always. Therefore the moment they are denied us we begin to question and to query. Now what the Psalmist should have done was this. He should have said: "I am a godly man, I believe in God. I am living this godly life and there are certain things I know about the character of God. There is no question about that. Now certain painful things are happening to me, and I see that the case of the ungodly is very different. But of course there must be some very good reason for this." Then he should begin to seek for reasons, and to look for an explanation. Had he done so he would undoubtedly have arrived at this conclusion, that God had some purpose in all this. We have already considered some of those reasons. He would have to come to the conclusion that even though he may not understand it, God must have a reason, because God never does anything in an irrational manner. He would have said: "I am certain of that, and, therefore, whatever the explanation is, it is not the thing I first thought of." He would have thought it out.

But how slow we are to do that. We seem to think that as Christian people we should never have any trouble. Nothing should ever go wrong with us, we should never have anything untoward happening to us at all, and the sun should always be shining about us, and all who are not Christian should know constant trouble and difficulty. But the Bible has never promised us that. It has rather promised that "through many tribulations we must enter the kingdom of God." It says also: "Unto you it is given in the behalf of Christ not only to believe on Him but also to suffer for His sake" (Phil. 1:29). So the moment we begin to think, we see that the idea that came to us instinctively is quite wrong and utterly false according to the Bible's teaching.

Let me sum it all up by putting it like this: "I was stupid, I was as a beast before Thee." It means this, that like beasts and animals, we always dislike discipline. We never see the need and necessity for it; and whenever we are disciplined by God we always tend to object and even to question and to query God's love and God's goodness. Now that is something which this man has described perfectly here when he says that that is to behave like a beast. No one by nature likes to be disciplined. He wants to go on responding to his instincts; he does not like to be controlled. Animals always object to discipline, and you have to train them and to be patient with them. Sometimes you have to be severe because they do not like discipline. Now this is characteristic of the immature Christian, the babe in Christ. Such a person resents discipline, and yet the answer to that is just this.

The author of the Epistle to the Hebrews does not hesitate to use a striking and almost surprising phrase. He says: "If you are not experiencing chastisement there is only one explanation for it and that is you are not children of God, you are bastards" (Heb. 12:8). That is what he says. If you are a child of God then you are certainly going to be disciplined, because God is preparing you for holiness. He is not an indulgent father who gives us sweets constantly and does not care what happens to us. God is holy, and He is preparing us for Himself and for glory; and because we are what we are, and because sin is in us, and because the world is what it is, we must needs be disciplined. So He sends us trials and tribulations in order to pull us up, and to conform us to "the image of His dear Son." But we do not like it, and like the animal we squeal because we dislike pain. But if we thought, if we were not stupid, we would even thank God for the pain. We would say with the man of the 119th Psalm: "It is good for me that I have been afflicted." I sometimes think that there is no better test of the Christian position than just that, that we can even thank God for trials and troubles and for chastisement, because we see that they have been used of God to bring us nearer and closer to Himself.

Let us hurry to the next thing this man found about himself. It is that he was ignorant. That is not the same thing. To be stupid and ignorant is not the same thing, but stupidity usually leads to ignorance. This man was ignorant about the true position of the ungodly, he was ignorant about God, he was ignorant about himself, and was ignorant also about the very nature of the life he was living. He had become ignorant about the whole purpose of godly living.

As I have just been saying, the trouble with us is that we do not see the whole purpose of the Christian life. Let me sum it up by putting it in this form. If you and I react as this man reacted to trials and troubles, in the last analysis there is only one thing to say about us, and that is that we are ignorant. What are we ignorant of? We are ignorant of everything the Bible says about the godly life, and we are especially ignorant about the New Testament Epistles, all of which have been written to enlighten this particular ignorance. So if we always grumble and complain about God's dealings with us and His chastisements we are simply making the confession either that we do not know our Scriptures at all, that we have never understood the New Testament, or else that we are wilfully ignorant, that we refuse to think and to apply what we know. We see these Books, but we refuse to listen to the arguments and we refuse to allow them to apply themselves to us. "Ignorant."

This man says: "I was behaving as an ignoramus, I was behaving as if I knew nothing about Thy purposes, I was behaving as if I were a mere tyro in these matters, as if I had never read or heard the history of the past." And it is perfectly true. The moment you allow your heart and your feelings to get into control you become hyper-sensitive, allergic in this sense; and you just behave as if you knew nothing and become ignorant and as a beast in the presence of God.

That brings us to the final matter, which is the worst of all. Listen: "Thus I exacerbated my own heart and I pricked myself in my reins and gave myself pain. So stupid was I and so ignorant, like an ignoramus; indeed I was as a beast before Thee." I think that that was the thing that broke this man's heart, and it is the thing that ought to break all our hearts. You see, what this man realised in the sanctuary of God was this, that he had been thinking all these horrible, foul, foolish, stupid things actually in the presence of God. "Before Thee." That is why he thought of himself as a beast. Fancy thinking these things, and being on the point of saying them, in the presence of God. What he had forgotten was this, that God is "the discerner of the thoughts and intents of the heart," and "Neither is there any creature that is not manifest in His sight but all things are naked and open unto the eyes of Him with whom we have to do" (Heb. 4:12, 13). If only we realised that, we should never behave again in the way this man had done and we, to our shame, have often done.

You and I are always in the presence of God. When therefore you are sitting in your corner and feeling sorry for yourself because you have been hurt, and because this or that has happened to you, just remember that all this is happening in the presence of God. And when you ask: "Is God fair to me, is it right that I should be suffering and the other person so prosperous?" remember you are doing that and thinking that thought about God in the very presence of God. "Before Thee." This man had forgotten the greatness of God. If you and I were only to remember the greatness of God always there are some things we should never do again. When you realise you are but a fly, or a grasshopper, or even less in the presence of the Almighty, and that He could remove you out of existence as if nothing had happened, you will no longer stand up and flout yourself in His presence and begin to question Him. We must realise, in the words of a wise man of the Old Testament, that "God is in heaven and you are on the earth." The greatness of God.

But, especially, we must remember the love of God. God is love. This man realised that he was a very stupid, foolish man questioning the love of God. He owed everything to the love and goodness and graciousness of God. So when you think these hard, unworthy thoughts of God, remember that you are thinking about the One who so loved you that He sent His Son into the world and even to the shame and agony of Calvary for you. Yet we think these thoughts of such a God even in His very holy presence. Just picture yourself sulking in the presence of God, sulking like a spoilt child. Look at the little child sulking, look at the animal. How ridiculous they look. Well, multiply that by infinity and think of yourself in the presence of this almighty, holy, loving God. Oh, no, there is nothing to be said for this condition. This man is right; he is not being unkind to himself, he is saying the simple truth — "I was as a beast, ignorant, utterly foolish."

What is the opposite of this? I can think of nothing better than the condition of the Prodigal Son after he came to himself. I have no doubt that up to a point that poor fellow thought he had been hardly dealt with. He left home in a huff. He was going to assert himself, but things went wrong and he thought he was being harshly dealt with. Then he came to himself and he went home and said: "Father, I have sinned against heaven and before thee and I am not worthy any longer to be called thy son." That is it, that is just another way of saying exactly the same thing. Nothing to recommend us, no excuses, we have just been unutterably stupid like beasts. We have failed to think and to reason, we have failed to apply these Scriptures. It is this horrible self that has been in control, and we are so hyper-sensitive that nothing and no one is right but ourselves. Let us face it, let us unmask it, let us analyse it and put it in front of ourselves. Let us look at it honestly and then be heartily ashamed of ourselves. Then let us go to that gracious loving God and acknowledge that we are as worms and less before Him, that we have no claim upon Him at all, and no right to His forgiveness. Let us tell Him that we do not wish to be healed quickly, that we feel that we do not deserve to be healed at all.

We began with that last time. I end with it now. The trouble with many of us is that we heal ourselves too quickly. We feel we have a right to be forgiven. But the teaching of the Scripture, and the teaching of the lives of the saints as they have faced life, is that like the Prodigal Son they have felt that they are unworthy of forgiveness. They felt that they deserved nothing but damnation, that they had been like beasts in their stupidity, and that they had no claim at all on God. Indeed, they were filled with amazement that God could forgive them. Let us examine ourselves in the light of that. Do we rush back to God feeling we have a right to forgiveness? Or do we feel we have no right to ask for forgiveness? That is how this man felt, and I suggest that that is how the true Christian always feels at first.

Paul after years of preaching looked back across the past and said: "I am the chief of sinners." He was still amazed that God could ever have forgiven him. Though he was an Apostle, he still felt as it were that he could receive something in an evangelistic service! He was still reacting as a sinner, he was still amazed at the wondrous Cross and the love of God in Jesus Christ our Lord. "So stupid was I, so foolish; I was as a beast before Thee."

For additional information about Martyn Lloyd-Jones:

Lloyd-Jones, David Martyn. *Truth Unchanged, Unchanging.* New York: Fleming H. Revell Co., 1950.

―――. *The Plight of Man and the Power of God.* Grand Rapids: Wm. B. Eerdmans Publishing Co., 1966.

―――. *The Presentation of the Gospel.* London: Inter-Varsity Fellowship, 1949.

FOR OTHER SERMONS BY MARTYN LLOYD-JONES:

Faith on Trial. Grand Rapids: Wm. B. Eerdmans Publishing Co., 1965.
Studies in the Sermon on the Mount, 2 vols. Grand Rapids: Wm. B. Eerdmans Publishing Co., 1959–60.
Also: *Spiritual Depression: Its Causes and Cure* (1965). The monthly *Westminster Record* available from Westminster Chapel, Buckingham Gate, London, has sermons in each issue.

W. E. SANGSTER

1900–1960

W. E. SANGSTER, photograph, courtesy of Paul E. Sangster.

WILLIAM EDWIN SANGSTER

1900	Born June 5 in London
1926	Ordained in the Methodist ministry
1939	Became pastor of Central Hall, Westminster
1950	Elected president of the Methodist Conference of Great Britain
1953	Made chairman of the Evangelical Committee of the World Conference of Methodists
1955	Appointed as head of the Home Mission Department of the Methodist Church of Great Britain
1960	Died of muscular atrophy

"SERVICE BEFORE SERVICES" was his motto. His own approach to preaching followed these words. In his book *The Approach to Preaching* he wrote:

> I have tried to make my own preaching part of my life. In the week preceding the Sunday, and during the days, therefore, when I have been preparing the sermons for delivery on that Sabbath, I have tried to make them autobiographical, to live in them, to incarnate in my own life the truths I was led to proclaim, to know the thing in experience before I uttered it in words.[1]

The ministry of W. E. Sangster was a living testimony to the effectiveness of his efforts to live up to his motto.

LIFE AND TIMES

W. E. Sangster was born in London, England, in 1900, the son of working-class parents. He attended Shoreditch Secondary

---

1. W. E. Sangster, *The Approach to Preaching* (Philadelphia: Westminster Press, 1952), p. 111.

School, then served in the First World War. In these early years, as he indicated in his writings, he definitely sensed a call into the Christian ministry. Sangster studied for the ministry at Handsworth College, Birmingham; Richmond College, London; and the University of London, where he earned the B.A., M.A., and Ph.D. degrees. The Methodist church ordained him to the ministry in 1926. After several charges, he became pastor of the Westminster Central Hall in 1939.

When he came to Westminster, Sangster was in his physical and preaching prime. A robust person, he had an active interest in athletics. Boxing was particularly a favorite hobby of his. In addition to his physical stamina, which he was to need during the arduous years in London during the bombing of World War II, he brought a lengthy pastoral experience to the work at Westminster. He had served as minister in Bognor Regis from 1923 until 1926, in Colwyn Bay from 1926 to 1929, in Liverpool from 1929 until 1932, in Scarboro from 1932 until 1936, and in Leeds from 1936 until 1939.

Sangster's activities took him beyond the bounds of his own church. He served on the board of the University of London. He was in charge of shelter welfare from 1940 to 1945. He wrote numerous books and articles, many of them dealing with the themes of prayer, evangelism, and preaching. In 1940 the bombing of London by the Nazis began. Sangster reinforced the basement of his church and opened it to those who had been blasted from their homes. Hundreds of persons used it as permanent quarters. Sangster and his family also made their home there; they lived in one cramped room for five years. His wife provided meals each night for those in the shelter. Sangster moved through the distressed people bringing comfort and hope. He told stories, joked, and encouraged optimism. He offered religion only when it was asked.

Soon after the basement became a home for so many, the people asked for evening prayers. These were followed by increasing numbers of religious services, as well as other activities. There was a weekly lecture on current affairs. A Saturday concert provided entertainment. On Sundays, Sangster preached to congregations that increased in size each week. In his congregations sat men and women of the lower and middle classes as well as university students and professional people.

Sangster believed in prayer, evangelism, and personal ministry. In many ways he was a pietist. But he was no gloomy, sanctimonious preacher; he radiated an infectious humor almost constantly. He had a wide range of interests, including a great concern for the social injustices suffered by the people around him. From his own early years he realized keenly the disabilities that adverse economic and social conditions could impose upon people. His concern for the total needs of men, and his effectiveness in meeting those needs, led to many recognitions and honors. In 1950 he was elected president of the Methodist Conference of Great Britian. Three years later he was made chairman of the Evangelical Committee of the World Conference of Methodists, and in 1955 he was appointed as head of the Home Mission Department of the Methodist Church of Great Britain.

Progressive muscular atrophy began to take its toll. By 1958 he was seriously affected. For two years he endured suffering with unlimited courage. One Easter day, in the grips of the disease, unable to walk or speak, he wrote to his daughter: "It is terrible to wake up on Easter morning and have no voice with which to shout, 'He is risen!'—but it would be still more terrible to have a voice and not want to shout."[2] In 1960, death finally ended his magnificent life.

Preaching and Sermons

Sangster approached preaching from a biblical perspective. In *The Craft of Sermon Construction* he defined a sermon as "a manifestation of the incarnate word, *from the written word,* by the spoken word." Sangster insisted that a sermon could be truly Christian preaching only if based upon the Bible:

> "From the written word!" It is all based on the Bible. Whether it is true to say that the Bible *is* the Word of God, or whether, as some believe, it is only accurate to say that the Bible *contains* the Word of God, we will not pause now to discuss. . . . There are legitimate forms of Christian preaching (so we have argued) which are not direct expositions of the Bible, but no preaching out of harmony with the Bible, and no preaching which could not honestly be related to the Bible, can establish its claim to be Christian preaching at all.[3]

---

2. W. E. S., *A Daughter's Tribute,* 1960, p. 13, pamphlet cited in Horton Davies, *Varieties of English Preaching, 1900–1960* (London: SCM Press, 1963), pp. 206–7.
3. W. E. Sangster, *The Craft of Sermon Construction* (Philadelphia: Westminster Press, 1951), pp. 34–35. Used by permission.

An examination of Sangster's sermons reveals that he was true to this principle. All of his sermons are careful developments of biblical texts. He does not indulge in lengthy expositions of Scripture as did G. Campbell Morgan; Sangster's expositions are brief, even abrupt. He does not get lost in the background of a text and wander aimlessly, trying to find his way out of Canaan into the twentieth century:

> Those who plead for life-situation preaching take the view that far too many sermons begin with a text, dawdle with it in Samaria or Jerusalem, and quite often never get the theme related to present-day life at all. The preacher takes a specialized interest in the flavor of a Greek verb, or gives a lengthy historical description of the precise circumstances of the Hebrew prophet he is discussing, but what it all has to do with the farm laborer in the transept or the harassed businessman in the back pew, nobody seems to know. Some worshipers even doubt if the preacher knows himself. He is just "preaching"—filling the twenty-five minutes allotted to the purpose with talk![4]

Sangster did not believe that life-situation preaching was a distinct sermon form in itself (he regarded it as a type of introduction or approach to a text, rather than a separate sermon form); but he felt that the life-situation approach was useful for gaining relevance in biblical preaching.

Sangster believed in doctrinal preaching and he resented the idea that it was necessarily dry. He admitted, "Some men, of course, could make any subject dry! Their capacity in dehydration is unlimited. But doctrine is not dry of itself."[5] He believed that people who "did not want theology" in their religion must be firmly corrected:

> In a northern city where I once worked, the local Unitarian minister plastered the walls of the town with a bill saying that he offered "religion without dogma." Standing beside one of his bills, I asked him next day if he believed in God. Friendly fellow though he was, he seemed to resent the question. "Of course," he said,

---
4. Ibid., p. 59.
5. Ibid., p. 43.

"I believe in God. You might have known that I am positive on that."

"Take care," I warned him, smiling. "It is dogma."[6]

Sangster was an effective doctrinal preacher; in fact, many commentators regard it as his strongest form of preaching.

Sangster regarded the evangelistic objective as the principal concern of Christianity: "Unquestionably, the great end of Christian preaching is to win men and women to a whole-souled committal to Christ and to their spiritual upbuilding in Him. Where the evangelical appeal is rarely or never sounded, an awful incompleteness hangs over the whole work."[7] He insisted that evangelism should not be narrowed to mere emotional appeal nor preached to the exclusion of the other themes in the Christian faith. True evangelistic preaching would inevitably lead to social reform beginning with the individual and spreading to the church and the community as a whole. In this way evangelistic preaching exercised an incalculable influence for the good: "In this indirect way, the evangelist may serve the explication of the social gospel beyond even his most ambitious dreams."[8]

But Sangster was equally fond of insisting that the gospel had its social implications:

> The congregation that never hears of the social nature of the gospel will be narrow in its outlook, small in its thinking, and spiritually debilitated. . . . It is less than the truth to say that the gospel has social "implications." It is social in its nature. That man is purveying skim milk who rigidly confines himself to what he calls the "personal gospel." And it is not even "personal," seeing that "person" implies relationship. It is merely *individual*, and engrossed with man in his separateness.[9]

Sangster believed that both evangelism and social emphasis had their place in the preaching of the gospel; but whenever one denied the rights of the other, confusion resulted. Evangelism must not be denied by the man with social concerns, but neither should the evangelist deny social emphasis: "But he

---
6. Ibid., pp. 43–44.
7. Ibid., p. 53.
8. Ibid., pp. 52–53.
9. Ibid., p. 49.

will not deny as an evangelist the right and the duty of preachers more able with social problems than he is himself to deal directly with economic questions on occasion, and he will bless God for the men who can do it with assured knowledge, penetrating insight, and unmistakable spiritual power."[10]

As for his preaching method, Sangster wrote a complete manuscript for one of his sermons each week and preached his second sermon from brief notes. He explained the reason for this method:

> By writing one sermon a week I hoped for precision, clarity, and terseness in expression; by preaching a sermon without writing every week, I hoped to develop the freeness and readiness of the true extempore style. Each method helped the other. The people never knew my methods, nor could they have distinguished any difference in the preparation by the preaching.[11]

He felt that the passing years brought a greater mastery of sermon preparation to the preacher, and that many men would feel less and less the need to write in full. These preachers might choose to write only the beginning and the end of their sermons, allowing a word or a note to suffice for an illustration. But if the preacher used a full manuscript, Sangster said that he should not read it:

> It needs hardly to be said that, because a man writes a manuscript in his study, he is not compelled to read it from his pulpit desk. On the contrary, one greatly hopes that he will do no such thing. . . . Every preacher should aim to be free of his manuscript, and not too tied to his notes. If you have got something from God to say to the people, it is better to look them in the face when you say it.[12]

Sangster believed that a congregation appreciated sermons spoken directly to them in a free style and that reading a manuscript interfered with communication from pulpit to pew.

All of his sermons show a careful, clear outline. He regarded each point of the sermon as "a minor whole in this faceting structure, with its own beginning, development, and inter-

---

10. Ibid., p. 53.
11. Ibid., p. 176.
12. Ibid., pp. 176–77.

mediate conclusion."[13] Each of these points should be servant to one simple theme, the thesis of the sermon itself. Sangster felt that many sermons failed because the listeners could not say at the close of the sermon precisely what it had set out to achieve.

The language of Sangster's sermons is direct, his sentences clean and uncluttered. He avoided theological jargon and hackneyed clichés:

> "Outpourings of grace," "the witness of the spirit," "washed in the blood," "toiling in rowing" — four phrases that I heard recently in one religious address, and a hundred similar phrases, mean very little to the people outside and whom we are particularly eager to interest when they make their infrequent visits to church.[14]

Sangster was a master of sermon illustration. His sermons reveal an incredible breadth of reading and variety of approach. His book *The Craft of Sermon Illustration* is a standard work on the subject. Sangster believed that illustrations should never be used as decorations, nor should a preacher ever build his sermons around illustrations. Illustrations which need explaining are hardly illustrations at all. Each illustration must throw light on the subject; if it does not, if it is obscure, then it does not illustrate.

Sangster concluded his book on illustrating with seven suggestions summarizing his thinking on the subject: (1) don't confuse illustration and argument; (2) don't make it a rule that each sermon must contain a given number of illustrations, and don't illustrate the obvious; (3) don't labor the moral; (4) don't forget the facts; (5) don't glorify yourself; (6) don't neglect the setting of the illustration; (7) don't use illustrations that steal attention from the sermon theme. In discussing that final thought, he reminded preachers to omit illustrations that *sound untrue*, no matter how true they may be. Wherever possible, and especially in the case of improbable illustrations, the preacher should document his stories.

The following sermonic works of Sangster will be appreciated by those who already enjoy him, and their excellent quality should create fresh interest in those who are not familiar with his work.

---

13. Ibid., p. 170.
14. Ibid., p. 184.

Sermons

DRUNK AND MAD

Acts 2:15; 26:25

IT IS WELL KNOWN that the earliest Christians had to defend themselves against the double charge of being drunk and mad. When Peter stood up to address the astonished population of Jerusalem at the Feast of Pentecost, he began his address with a reference to his friends, and said: "These are not drunken as ye suppose." When Paul faced Festus and Agrippa in the crowded court at Caesarea, he was compelled to counter a remark of the procurator by saying, "I am not mad, most excellent Festus." Odd as it may seem to us, apostles had to defend themselves against the honest belief that they were either inebriated or deranged.

Most modern Christians are not under the same dark suspicion, though it is hardly to their credit to stress the distinction. It may be, that if they lived nearer to the heart of their faith, they, too, would need to answer the suspicions their conduct aroused, and interlard their conversation with the assurance that they were neither tipsy nor unstrung.

What are the marks of a man who is drunk? — not dead-drunk and helpless, not conscience-stricken and quarrelsome; but just normally and vulgarly drunk?

He is gay, jolly, hearty, jocular, exhilarated, genial . . . exuberant! The Greeks have the best word to describe his feelings. They called it "euphoria," and euphoria means an immense sense of well-being.

There is, of course, a true, as well as a false, euphoria. One sees it, in its best expressions, in a puppy, who just turns over and over for the sheer joy of being alive. One sees it, also, in the gambolling of lambs, and the excited gallops of young colts. One sees it in healthy children, who never walk where they can skip, and who dance along the road with ebullient joy, and, in the phrase of Wordsworth, "feel their life in every limb." That is the real euphoria, a sense of health and well-being.

Reprinted from William E. Sangster, *These Things Abide* (London: Hodder & Stoughton, 1939), pp. 133–41. Used by permission of Hodder & Stoughton.

Alcohol gives a spurious euphoria. It "bucks a man up," helps him to forget his troubles, and fills him with a sense of expansiveness to his fellows. He overleaps the conventions, talks to people he does not know, and feels, for the time being, that the world is a wonderful place to be in, and that he is a rather important person in it.

The trouble with alcohol is simply this. The euphoria is a sham. It does not last, and the reaction is sharp and unpleasant. The night before is seldom worth the morning after, and every man with a remnant of self-respect, loathes himself for having sunk to that condition.

Nevertheless, while it lasts, the exuberance lives with it, and that all-embracing cordiality, and infectious gaiety, give us the clue that we seek. It was this that led the astonished people of Jerusalem to suspect that the Apostles were drunk.

I wonder if our religion makes us exuberant, cordial, infectiously gay? I wonder if cold conventionalities thaw in our presence? I wonder — dare I write it? — if, on such grounds as these, anyone ever decided that we were drunk!

Perhaps only the historian, with a taste for psychology, will ever give a satisfactory answer to that mysterious question as to how the infectious faith of Jesus became associated with gloom, and frowns, and mirthlessness. It was surely among the most tragic misrepresentations of the truth, when the lie went abroad that Christians were dejected melancholiacs. Those fine men we call "Puritans" had something to do with it, so far as England is concerned. Grossly misunderstood as they have been in some quarters, and denied the national honour that should manifestly be theirs, it is nevertheless true that they fostered a tradition of drabness, and stole the colour from common life. They even prohibited maypoles and mince-pies! They thought God frowned on mirth, and they made life, not merely serious (which, of course, it is), but always solemn (which it need not be).

So it is to-day, that any third-rate comedian in a provincial music-hall carries, as part of his stock-in-trade, not only a few jokes about dictatorial mothers-in-law, but a few jokes also about miserable Christians. If, in any way, we have contributed to this wide misconception, may God in heaven forgive us, because it is a travesty of our true traditions.

Christianity imparts the real euphoria. It gives, in the divine indwelling of the Holy Spirit, a witness within a man that it is well with his soul. It makes music inside him.

Consider the record of history. Whenever this fount of living water breaks fresh from the rock, it bestows this glad exuberance. The first Christians were accused of being drunk. The first Franciscans had to be reproved for laughing in church because they were so happy. The first convents of the Reformed Carmelites were most happy places, despite their austerities, because St. Teresa insisted on musical instruments, and a jolly time in the hours of recreation. The first

Methodists stole some of their hymn-tunes from operas, and set the songs of Zion to dance music.

> My God, I am Thine;
> What a comfort divine,
> What a blessing to know that my Jesus is mine!
> In the heavenly Lamb
> Thrice happy I am,
> And my heart it doth dance at the sound of His name.

The first Salvationists jumped with joy. General Booth always told them that if they felt the Spirit move them they could leap in a hymn or a prayer. They leapt! Dr. Farmer, the organist at Harrow, used to tell how he adjudicated once at a great musical festival, and heard a Salvation Army band in action. His musical soul was offended both by the drummer and the man with the French horn. He is said to have appealed to the drummer not to hit the drum so hard, to which the beaming bandsman replied, "Oh, sir, I'm so happy, I could burst the blessed drum." When Dr. Farmer turned with a word of similar appeal to the man with the horn, the enthusiast held up the much-twisted instrument and said, "But, sir, I'm so full of joy, I want to blow this thing quite straight."

And, it is so easy to hear these stories and feel rather superior. It is not a bit hard to purse the lips and think—if not to *say*—that exuberance and devotion *cannot* belong together. They can. Church history is witness. It is when the fires in the individual heart, or in the denomination, are dying down, that convention frowns on exuberance, and an air of superiority is affected towards those who cannot restrain the primitive joy.

Nor need this joy depart though the horror of war has come upon us. It can live with the tenderest sympathy towards those who suffer, and the most sensitive awareness of the evil of the times. Few men carried a more sensitive soul into the last War than that prince of Padres, Geoffrey Studdert-Kennedy. Asked for advice, before his own service in France began, by the Rev. Theodore Hardy, V.C., M.C., D.S.O., this is what Kennedy said: "Live with the men, go where they go; make up your mind that you will share all their risks, and more, if you can do any good. You can take it from me that the best place for a padre (provided that he does not interfere with military operations) is where there is most danger of death. Our first job is to go beyond the men in self-sacrifice, and reckless devotion. Don't be bamboozled into believing that your proper place is behind the lines: it isn't. If you stay behind you might as well come down: you won't do a ha'porth of good. Your place is in the front. The line is the key to the whole business; work in the very front, and they will listen to you when you come out."

He took his own advice, and was decorated for conspicuous gallantry in tending our own and the enemy wounded under heavy fire, but those of us who knew him personally knew how the horror of war had furrowed his tender heart.

Yet he was the soul of mirth in the mess. His fount of fun was irrepressible and, wherever the laugh was the loudest, Kennedy was the cause. The Colonel—who stammered a trifle—was perplexed by it all.

"I can't make the young b-b-beggar out," he said. "And he does it all on g-g-ginger beer!"

But a second charge was laid against the apostles too. They were accused of being mad.

What are the marks of a man who is mad?

They are, of course, varied and numerous. He may do strange things. His conduct is incapable of rational explanation. Quite often, he has some deep obsession, flies in the face of convention, and acts with what can only be called monstrous imprudence. Many men who are thought to be mad are thought also to be quite rational in the major part of their life, but clearly deranged in one special particular.

Nor is it hard to see how vital Christians have come under this dark suspicion. What could seem more completely obsessional to his old friends than Paul's utter devotion to Jesus Christ? Home, family, race, and everything commonly counted of worth, he tossed aside for his new Master. Much of it—such was his new contempt—he dubbed as "refuse." He said: "For me to live is Christ."

What could have seemed more foolishly imprudent than the action of C. T. Studd in giving away to the work of God nearly £30,000—almost his entire fortune—on the eve of his wedding? And what will seem more crass than the action of his young bride who, in order to "start clear," gave away immediately the little bit which was left over?

Or, if we test a man's sanity by devotion to a distinguished and useful career, what can we say of Albert Schweitzer and Toyohiko Kagawa? Schweitzer could have won the highest distinction in half a dozen fields: in music, in theology, in philosophy, in comparative religion, in pedagogy, and in medicine. He put it all resolutely aside to be a missionary for Jesus Christ.

The family of Kagawa decided, as his studies in middle-school terminated with such brilliance, that he must go to the University, and then into diplomatic service. When he refused, proclaiming himself a follower of the despised Jesus, he was promptly disinherited.

Clearly, it is not hard to understand why people should think these devotees mad.

But do they think *us* mad? Is our conduct so prudent and rational, so intelligible to their minds, and wise by their standard, that they have no difficulty in understanding us?

It is greatly to be feared that we cause them no perplexity at all. Our motives measure up to their standards. They see that we are as prudent as worldly wisdom requires. Selfishness, with a dash of benignity, seems to sum us up, and contact with us carries no challenge at all.

Yet, surely, it is the world that is mad, and not those vital Christians who scorn convention and selfish ease. Discerning men have seen the insanity of the world getting more chronic for years. We burn food while people starve. Is that sane? The factories have been crammed with garments while the poor have lacked protection from the bitter winds, and all their piteous need could do nothing about it until someone had made a profit on those clothes. Is that sane? We have drifted into war again though it is murderous, evil, wasteful, and the very essence of wickedness.

It is not the Apostles in any age who are mad: the world is mad. The world presumes to judge the men of God: the men of God have already judged the world. Their madness is heaven's sanity on earth. Worldly wisdom is so often the cunning of hell conventionalised. Perhaps no more complete condemnation could be uttered of us than just this: that men can explain us without any reference to Jesus Christ.

A "mad" story comes down the ages to us from Taiwan, a story now nearly two centuries old. It concerns the efforts of the Chinese to subject the wild inhabitants of that beautiful island, and stamp out their barbarous custom of head-hunting. Even yet the task is not complete. The Japanese, who are now the over-lords, have enclosed the fiercest tribes that remain within an electrified guard-line two hundred and thirty miles long, and within that enclosure the bloody work continues still.

But much of the island is long free of the practice, and free largely by the work of Gaw Hong. Many years ago this Chinese gentleman was appointed magistrate and, by just and kind dealing, he won the affection of the fierce people of his area. They came both to love and revere him.

Steadily, he stamped head-hunting out. The old blood-feuds between the Pe-pa-hwan and the Chinese disappeared, and an era of prosperous co-operation began. But a great religious feast approached, and the tribesmen were troubled because they believed the gods demanded human heads. They went to Gaw Hong about it, and pleaded for permission to placate their deity in the only way the gods desired. The Magistrate reasoned with them, postponed decision, pointed out that old feuds would begin again but, finally, worn down by their importunity, consented.

"Take *one* head," he said. "Only *one*. And take it when, and where, I shall appoint."

And when the day of the feast was at hand, Gaw Hong told them what to do. They were to take the head of the first man using a certain path in a certain wood, at dawn the next day. Nor did they fail to keep his instructions. The assassin, waiting in the grey light, saw a man come slowly down the path: the arrow found its mark, and the man had hardly fallen before his head was severed, put in a sack, and rushed to the waiting chiefs. And when the sack was opened . . . there was the head of Gaw Hong.

Even the Japanese are impressed by the fact that the vows the tribal chiefs took against head-hunting that day have been kept. When they look on that long electrified guard-line in the North-East, they half wish somebody would die for the Taiyal.

Mad, of course . . .

And yet . . .

GOOD WITHOUT GOD

Micah 6:6–8

THE OLD PROBLEM of the relation of morality and religion is assuming a new importance in these days. People who are constantly on guard against national bias, and who have an acute concern lest they claim a righteousness for their own nation which it does not possess, are nevertheless deeply impressed by the fact that respect for the rights and liberties of others, respect for truth, and, indeed, respect for most things precious, have been manifestly undermined in those countries where religion has been persecuted or destroyed. Protests made by preachers in the piping days of peace, come back with new meaning and, in the light of current events, no longer seem the puritan patter that once they did.

Is there a deeper connection between religion and morality than common thought has been willing to concede? Can one be good and not religious—or religious and not good? If one is both, is it an accidental and fortuitous connection, or a necessary and vital one; and is their separation to be regarded as a dreadful divorce?

Quite plainly, the question is not merely academic. It is practical

---

Reprinted from William E. Sangster, *These Things Abide* (London: Hodder & Stoughton, 1939), pp. 87–95. Used by permission of Hodder & Stoughton.

in its application to the individual life, and to national life as well. Men often claim to be good without religion. They say: "I know how a decent man should live, and I live like that. But I do not need a weekly diet of worship to do it. I can dispense with sermons and sacraments, prayers and parsons, churches and chants, hymns and amens. I can be decent without religion."

Nations make the same claim. Russia affirms that it has a tenderer social conscience than capitalist countries, and cares for the unprivileged people in a way unparalleled in lands where religion is not proscribed. The leaders in Germany would have us believe that it has added to the health and "dynamism" of their nation to imprison outspoken pastors like Dr. Martin Niemöller, and confine religion to a tepid personal piety.

Is it true? Are religion and morality so easily put asunder?

In ancient times, and among many peoples, the connection between morality and religion was not close. Indeed, both morality and religion were largely governed by tribal custom, and the distinction we are seeking to draw hardly existed in the primitive mind. Even among peoples of some ancient cultures, like the Babylonians, it can be shown that there was no necessary connection between the two. The gods had certain rights which had to be safeguarded. By ritual and sacrifice, human respect was shown to the deity, but, in ancient religion, the gods were thought of as being far more jealous for their own prerogatives than they were concerned in the moral habits of nations, or of individual men. I think it has been shown conclusively that the Israelites were the first people to conceive how close the connection was, and they made sin serious the moment they saw that God was holy. "Holy! Holy! Holy! is the Lord of Hosts," said Isaiah. "The sacrifices of God," said David, "are a broken spirit: a broken and a contrite heart, O God, thou wilt not despise." "Burnt offerings will not placate God," said Micah. No! Not even thousands of rams, or ten thousands of rivers of oil. "What doth the Lord require of thee but to do justly, to love mercy, and to walk humbly with thy God."

Now, it is insight into spiritual truth like that, that made the Children of Israel the great people they undoubtedly were. They were not great fighters: the Philistines proved that. They were not great farmers: their inability to squeeze from the soil as much as the Canaanites explains the seductiveness of the Baalim. They were not great philosophers, as the Book of Ecclesiastes bears witness. But, despite their waywardness and folly, they had among them men of great spiritual insight, and these men saw that the holy God required a holy people. "Religion and morality," said the prophets, "belong together." Mere ceremonies are as nothing to Him. Men must adore Him by the devotion of clean hearts and ordered lives. And, in the midst of our human dilemma, which the passing ages revealed—our utter failure to reach a height that was utterly necessary—God sent His only begotten Son, and grace was thrown like a bridge across the abyss, and the path to the highest was made possible by union with Christ. So religion and morality were bound together in the will of God. The way to the heights, not of mere respectability but of holiness, is only possible by Him. The witness of the New Testament and the claim of Christianity is this: that the higher reaches of morality are only to be achieved by true religion. Henceforth, they are joined together and, what God hath joined together, let no man put asunder.

But, it is just there that the critic intrudes. "I *can* put them asunder," he says. "I can deny religion, ignore the churches, and live like the best of you. It is absurd to say that religion and morality belong together because progressive nations have been atheistic, and some of the best men we have known have not been religious men—Sir Samuel Romilly, Sir Leslie Stephen, Edward Clodd, and many others. There are thousands of men to-day who have nothing to do with religion, and yet continue to live a high moral life, and to retain the respect of the whole community. Does that not prove that religion and morality can be divorced?"

Quite frankly, it does not. I think we can show why.

Almost everybody alive to-day owes an incalculable debt to Christianity, whether they embrace the faith themselves or not. For two thousand years the ethic of Christ has been percolating into the minds of the masses of people and, however far we may be from realising His ideals, it is undeniable that His influence has been the most cleansing and civilising force that this world has ever known. The chaos of the times is plainly due to the neglect of His teaching. Had His teaching concerning love been applied, we should not now be at war. Had His teaching concerning brotherhood been heeded, it is doubtful if any innocent and honest person would be hungry. Had His teaching concerning unselfishness been taken to heart, Europe to-day would not be a continent in arms.

But, even despite this neglect of His teaching, He has exerted such an influence on the world that it is probably no exaggeration to say that, without it, ordered existence would have perished long ago in anarchy and strife. Everybody born into modern civilisation owes Him, therefore, an unpayable debt. Though the origin of hospitals goes back to pre-Christian times, it cannot be questioned that Christianity gave an immense impetus to all work for the care and cure of the sick. Schools, orphanages, homes for the aged poor, have all come to birth by the power of His influence. The only holidays the poor had for centuries were begotten by Him, and are still enjoyed at the festivals of His Church: Christmas, Easter, and Whitsun, require Christ to explain them. When serfdom held the world in thrall, and the poor had no class-consciousness, they would have had no holidays at all but for His influence. To-day we call them Bank Holidays, but Bank Holidays were not instituted until 1871. These holidays are Christian festivals, and are meaningless apart from Him.

The belated emancipation of women was not delayed by any word of Jesus: they were never inferior with Him. National hatred He condemned. Slavery proved incompatible with His teaching. As His Apostle said: "There is neither Jew nor Greek: there is neither bond nor free: there is neither male nor female, for ye are all one in Christ Jesus."

If one were to sit down in a cool hour, and try to extract in thought from the world, all the sweetness and love which Christ has put into it, one would be left with a very dark picture indeed. Seeing that we are all made to some extent by our environment, no man alive (unless it be some unevangelised Negro from the heart of Africa, or Eskimo from the frozen north, or remote Chinaman beyond the reach of the gospel), can say that he has been utterly uninfluenced by our Lord's message, or has been good without His aid. The very ideals our critics boast about were shaped by Him. The community which nourished and educated them is, in its best manifestation, the product of that same holy power. When we add to this all the secret interior ministries of His grace which work on, even in the hearts of those who deny Him—the counsel of conscience, the warnings against evil, the quickened longing for higher things—and then make a sum of the outside influence and the interior constraint, it is astonishing that men should deny the debt they manifestly owe. And though they ignore or deride Him, the secret services of His grace continue still.

It is not impertinent to put these questions to the boasters who declare their independence of Christ: "Who whispered in your ear when you trembled on the edge of sin, and saved you from utter shipwreck? Who pleaded the truth and made reply to every argument of sin? Who built the Church you attended and made this land, with all its faults, a sweet land to grow up in? It was Christ—the Christ you affect to despise. All your life you have been indebted to Him, and in ways, direct and indirect, you taste His bounty still."

The men who are quoted as being good without religion are often, in a special sense, the product of the faith they profess to despise. It can be shown that the very foundation of their character was put in under direct Christian influence, and their love of truth, their clear demarcation of right and wrong, and their high idealism, run back to the Nazarene. Sir Samuel Romilly is often quoted as a great and good man who proves the independence of morality from religion. He rejected the Christian faith but did a remarkable work in humanising our national prison codes. He was a good man, though he was not a religious one. Yet his biographer makes clear that he was the grandson of Huguenot refugees, people who had fled from France for their faith, choosing rather to live as aliens in a strange land than to give up their vision of God. And he was brought up under the most definite of Christian and evangelical influence, in a home where Christ was put first, and the nobility and high moral quality of his character run back to that.

Sir Leslie Stephen is often quoted to similar purpose. He was once in Holy Orders, and resigned when he became an agnostic. He was a good man without religion. But his sister said of the home in which they grew up together: "To have been my father's child was like having been brought up in a Cathedral." The foundations of his character were put in under the definite influence of Christ.

And so with Edward Clodd. Clodd was so much opposed to religion that H. G. Wells humorously suggested that he went to sleep at night with a large pistol on his pillow for fear of a revelation, and looked under the bed every evening to make sure that the Deity was not there. He was a good man without religion, but he illustrates the same truth yet again. His parents were pious Baptists, and brought him up in their dearly-loved faith. He came to deride their devotion, but the strength of his moral life was drawn from the very source at which he sneered.

No one admires the "self-made" plutocrat who prefaces his boring accounts of how he succeeded by saying, "I owe nothing to my parents." Nothing indeed! Flesh of their flesh, and bone of their bone. Who gave him a fit body and a keen mind: a will of iron, and nerves of steel? Who held him to a warm breast, and nurtured him at life's tenderest time?

And it is not dissimilar with those men who were trained in the faith of Christ, nourished in His word, and afterwards boast that they can be good without His aid. Their moral stability, their desire for the best, the very frame of their character they owe to Him. Indubitably, their morality is in debt to His religion.

And that is one of the things that has made the wide neglect of religion so serious. It seems fantastic to some people to suggest that their personal neglect of spiritual values can have any effect on a nation's life. They doubt, as we have seen, whether it has any effect on their own life, but the evidence is all against them. Morality cannot survive its divorce from religion for three generations. A man can ignore his parents' religion while utilising their moral capital, but his own children and grandchildren will suffer an awful impoverishment. Indeed, the bill sometimes comes in sooner than that. Arnold Bennett sneered at the Methodism in which he had been reared, but his respect for accepted moral values seems not to have survived its severance from religion. Sometimes these critics plead intellectual doubts, and say that they have difficulty with the divinity of Christ. It would seem that a number of them have difficulty, also, with the ten commandments. The common neglect of the faith, even in this land, since the Armistice of 1918, will take its toll. The tinselled license which has been advocated as "new morality" has made many insensitive to the touch of God, and the eagerness with which certain "advanced" teachers have prated of "the rights of wrong," and been willing "to greet the obscene with a cheer" has dimmed the nation's spiritual vision.

Religion is more than a buttress to morality—but it *is* that. Our faith is not exhausted as a regulator of conduct—but it *is* a regulator of conduct. Without it, morality lacks achieving dynamic. In days of peace the protestations of the prophet seem morbid and irrelevant, but, in time of war, even the unwilling are forced to concede the pertinence of what he said.

And if this be true within the compass of an individual life, it is not less true in the life of nations. Stifle the religion of Christ, deny the pulpit liberty to apply the gospel to social and national questions, kill or imprison her pastors, and you have wounded the community in a vital place. If nothing is done to staunch the wound, it will bleed to death.

The manner of its death can be traced. Freedom dies. Opportunism supplants principle. Truth yields place to propaganda. Oppression and bad faith become too common to excite surprise. The right of might becomes axiomatic, and a nation belies its noblest past. Liberty of conscience is denied in the land of Luther. The austerity of the moral law becomes a jest where Kant expounded it. Jews are persecuted in the country which gave birth to Heinrich Heine, Jacob Mendelssohn, and Albert Einstein.

Is it only a coincidence that most things precious began to decay when Christian teaching was stifled, or is there evidence here that moral strength and rectitude depend upon the plain proclamation of the gospel? An old book said it long ago: "Righteousness exalteth a nation."

THE PLEDGE OF THOSE GLORIOUS SCARS

Isaiah 49

I THINK it was Dr. George Adam Smith—to whom all close students of the prophecy of Isaiah are in debt—who first gave me the clue to that elusive word in the forty-ninth chapter which declares that Zion is "graven" on God's hands, and her walls continually before Him.

Of course, the city was in ruins. It had been in ruins for forty or fifty years. When the Babylonians had swept down upon Jerusalem, they had utterly devastated it. They had wrecked its palaces, desecrated its great altar, ruined its homes, butchered its defenders, and dragged down, stone by stone, the walls that once engirdled the city of God. When they marched out they left only the dregs of the population, the undisputed owners of a pile of ruins.

Perhaps it is Warsaw which has brought the picture back into my mind. As day succeeded day of that stubborn siege, and every weapon of modern war was unleashed on those heroic citizens, I saw again the ruined cities of Northern France as I saw them in 1918. I saw, with special vividness, the first one my battalion entered on our journey to the occupied zone. The houses were all windowless, roofless and bare. The floors, and all that the floors had ever contained, had fallen in one hopeless mass of debris to the bottom of the shell. I remember the scattered inside of an old piano: a battered coal-scuttle: the twisted frame of a bed: a child's toy. I can see now the streets of that city filled with holes, and the holes filled with water, so that the troops could not march in any decent formation, but had to break rank and get through as best they could.

I recall a dog, emaciated beyond belief, nosing in the ruins for the food he could not find. I remember the shell of the church, the cloisters open and bare to the wind and rain, the crucifix smashed on the wall, and the works of the clock festooned down the ruined tower. I saw the rotting carcass of a dead horse.

Nor was this city of the dead entirely without inhabitants. Around the gaping holes in one poor shell of a dwelling, some pitiful mortals had dragged a tarpaulin, and were shivering on the other side and calling it "Home." All was desolation. Indeed, one tottering wall shook as we passed it, made a drunken effort to steady itself, failed, and fell with a gigantic thud, covering us with its dust.

Warsaw brought it back to my mind, and drove me again to the Book of God. Jerusalem was like that. It was only the setting that was different. When Isaiah spoke his paradoxical word, the city was one

---

Reprinted from William E. Sangster, *These Things Abide* (London: Hodder & Stoughton, 1939), pp. 99–108. Used by permission of Hodder & Stoughton.

unlovely mass of mouldering decay. The eye of dismayed imagination sees it as the Babylonians left it, plus forty, or fifty years, of utter neglect. And this is Zion, the city of which the Psalmist said: "They shall prosper who love thee: peace be within thy walls and prosperity within thy palaces. . . ." And there were no walls! There was barely one stone upon another.

Then God said: "Thy walls are continually before Me."

What did He mean? There were no walls. The walls were a memory of the past or a dream of the future. They had no being or substance, no foundation in fact. If we had been there, we could not have seen them.

"Thy walls"?

Ah! This, surely, was what He meant. Those walls *had* being: those solid buttresses of stone were not without ideal existence: reality (in its truest sense) could not be denied to those mighty battlements that once enclosed the city of God. It were as though He said: "I intend it. It finds place in the plan of your God. It is on the programme of the Almighty. Those walls are not ruined in My vision. *You* lose the view of the ideal when the actual is distorted—but not God. I see what *is,* on the background of what *will be.*"

God has a dual vision. He sees twice. We cling to what we are pleased to call the "facts," but He holds, with omnipotent firmness, what He divinely names "My plan." We lose the vision of the rose when the bud is perverted—but not God. Behind the poor perversion, He still sees the perfect flower.

This, then, is part of the art of life: to get the double vision of God: to stand at His side and see the world and men from His divine angle, and keep faith with ideals even when the devil seems to have won. I can believe more easily in some things I do not see, but which I know my God intends, than I can believe in things I *do* see, but which I know that He has marked for destruction. I see slums, but I believe in garden cities. I see besotted sinners, but I believe in sanctified saints. I see war, but I believe in peace.

Stand for an hour at God's side, and see the pageant of humanity. Look at that woman grown unwomanly, that daughter of shame: drugging her conscience, believing a lie, vending her body, selling her soul. Do you feel sick inside at the sight of such foulness? Do you?

But not God! He says: "Daughter, thy purity is ever before Me."

Or look at that man who has made mammon his God, and who lives consumed by one great passion of greed. He always interprets "success" in grossly material symbols, and is careless whom he treads down in his feverish striving for place. No single thought does he give to the need of his spirit, but seems rather to choke the last effort of his dying soul. His friends may have lost all recollection of his nobler nature—but not God! To this finished specimen of cultured selfishness, He says: "Son, thy soul's health is ever before Me."

A friend of mine has told how he was stopped one day by a tramp who asked for help.

"Excuse me, sir," said the tramp. "I know I've no business to stop you, and if I'm caught begging I'll be the guest of His Majesty for a bit; and I guess I'm not much to look at, but poverty don't help a man to look handsome, and there's no use denying I didn't live straight, sir, and I've paid the penalty to the full, but, by heaven, sir, you don't know the man I meant to be. . . ."

My friend gave him a shilling and watched him go. And as he gazed after the retreating figure of the poor, odorous, unshaven rag-bag, this phrase echoed in his ear: "The man I meant to be."

Everyone else may long since have forgotten it—even his mother. But not God! Behind a man debased like this, a mere pillar of the pubs, God still sees a redeemed and sanctified personality.

It is dubious if any equipment for Christian service could be more enriching than to share the double vision of God. It incites to effort, it nourishes faith, it fosters hope, and it deepens love.

One of the most distinguished sculptors in America is named Mr. Gutzon Borglum. He is a sculptor in "a big way." It is not unusual, in that country, for gigantic memorials to be shaped out of a mountain or from a huge escarpment of rock and, when the design has been agreed upon, Mr. Borglum arrives with an army of helpers and hews their wishes out.

But Mr. Borglum will not be remembered longest for the mountains he has moulded, but rather for a wonderful head of Abraham Lincoln which he carved for the Capitol at Washington. He cut it from a block of marble which had long been in his studio, and the transformation of which filled his Negro charwoman with superstitious dread.

It seems that she barely noticed the early work on the familiar block of stone, and went on dusting it as usual, but, one morning, she saw the unmistakable lineaments of the mighty President appearing in the marble, and she ran to Mr. Borglum's secretary in something near to terror, and said in an awed voice: "Am dat Abraham Linkum?"

"Yes," said the secretary. "That is Abraham Lincoln."

"Well!" said the old woman. "Well . . . How in de world did Massa Borglum *know* dat Abraham Linkum was in dat block ob stone?"

How did God know that Peter the rock was in Peter the unstable? How did God know that Paul, the Apostle, was in Saul the persecutor? How did God know that Augustine the saint was in Augustine the incontinent? How *did* God know?

Because He has a double vision, and sees the inwardness and possibility of things, and because that blessed vision is never dim.

Nor must we think that God only sees twice when He looks on the failures of life—the sots, and harlots, and skinflints. We sin in different ways. He sees twice when He looks on the pious. The souls that have come nearest the Divine intention have not achieved all that God wills.

Indeed, the rate of our progress may be measured by the steadiness with which we gaze on the ideal picture God holds in His heart of us all. Emerson said it years ago, and it is a sharp rebuke to the smug:

> Could'st thou in vision see
> Thyself, the man God meant;
> Thou never more would'st be,
> The man thou art—content!

Yet, that is His aim both now and in eternity: to make the ideal and the actual one. And to trustful obedience that ultimate identification is sure.

Yet, it is just there that the critic enters and raises an admonitory hand. He accuses us of the fashionable malady—"wishful thinking." It is said that the pulpit has long been prone to this disease. Indeed, it appears always to accompany the prophetic office. Our critics say its genesis is here: we image to ourselves an ideal picture of what we desire to happen, and believe that God wills, but we forget that this is merely the fruit of imagination, and we fall to asserting it as a fact. We pass from "we hope" to emphatic assertions that "it *will* be," and do it so often, and so easily, that we seem unaware of the transition. But people who are careful to make distinctions between dreams and realities have already parted company with us.

The objection cannot be lightly waved aside. The exiled Jews, to whom Isaiah first flung out the promise, might well have raised the point themselves. There was no immediate probability that their city would be rebuilt, nor that the spiritual values dear to the heart of Judaism at its best would survive in the welter of warring peoples. What made the prophet so confident that the walls of Jerusalem were always before God?

No prophet has ever given a satisfying analysis of His own self-consciousness. When he tries, it often amounts to little more than the explanation of the water-diviner who says, "I don't know how I know, but I know." And the water-diviner can, at least, call for spades to prove his point.

Nor could Isaiah have satisfied any contemporary psychologist with a keenly sceptical mind. He does not even try. He uses rather an odd figure of speech, and declares that God cannot forget His people because He has "graven" them (or printed them) on the palms of both His hands. Because they are indelibly marked where they cannot be overlooked, they need never fear that God has forgotten them.

The figure of speech is of more than ordinary interest. It suggests tattooing, a custom common both East and West. Yet this tattooing is not hidden away and known, perhaps, only to its bearer, but it is carried where all may see and none can overlook. The palm of the hand has passed into a proverb as a symbol of familiarity. If you doubt my knowledge of a neighbourhood, I might counter your doubts by saying: "I know it like the palm of my hand."

And that, says the prophet, is where God carries the reminder of His people's needs: where it cannot be overlooked. It is not a word to a ministering Spirit, or a mental note in the Divine mind: it is graven on the palms of God's hands.

Nor must we miss, in these days of hope deferred, the significance of the word "graven." To our Western minds, at least, it suggests something deeper than tattooing.

When I was in the Army my friends tried to persuade me to be tattooed. Our battalion included an expert in this somewhat obscure art, and most of the men succumbed to his seductions. One could have the regimental badge on one's chest, or the flags of the Allies on one's back: some preferred a cupid on one arm, shooting an arrow through a heart on the other arm, or (for an extra fee) a fierce boa-constrictor winding around the whole body. If I resisted temptations, it was not because it failed in pictorial attractiveness.

Yet, I have watched the process, and know as much as can be known from watching. It is a pricking and pigmentation of the skin. It is the work of a needle. It is not painful, or costly, or dangerous.

But let us leap the centuries and see the awful fulfilment of the prophet's word. It was not the work of a needle then: it was the work of a nail. It did not prick the skin: it went through. We were not tattooed on the palms of His hands: we were *graven* there.

> The dear tokens of His passion
> Still His dazzling body bears;
> Cause of endless exultation
> To His ransomed worshippers:
>   With what rapture
> Gaze we on those glorious scars!

Let us slip into that upper room, and make company with those frightened disciples who met behind locked doors "for fear of the Jews." And, presently, another Figure appears in their midst, regal, effulgent, and "with eyes majestic after death" and, turning to one of their number, He says: "Reach hither thy finger and see my hands...."

O blessed wound prints! Most precious evidence of everlasting love! Thou *hast* graven us upon the palms of Thy hands!

Here, then, is comfort for the most obscure, for His love runs down to details, and delights to minister to the separate ones. You, who find it so hard to believe that you are of consequence in heaven, when you are of such little consequence on earth, you are graven on the palms of His hands: the great God, Who sustains the universe, thinks upon you!

You, who are so nervous and panicky, living, perhaps, in daily dread of an aerial bombing, though as yet no danger has come nigh your dwelling, you are graven on the palms of His hands: the Lord of life watches over you.

You, whose dear one is in peril, and who wait the post in thrilling hope of a letter from him — or fearful dread of an official notification about him — you (and he) are graven on the palms of His hands. God made you, and His tender mercy is over all His works.

Think on your Lord!

> See where before the throne He stands,
> And pours the all-prevailing prayer;
> Points to His side, and lifts His hands,
> And shows that you are graven there.

AND AFTER DEATH — WHAT?

John 14:2

I HAVE a section of my library given entirely to guide books. They fascinate me. Many of them are thumbed and annotated from the happy days when I toured the countries they describe, but they all received preliminary study before I set foot on any of those distant lands. It has long been my conviction that, if the most is to be made of travel, one must learn as much as possible about new lands before the journey begins.

And some day God will give me leave to die — or a bomb may effect my swift dispatch before a week has sped. What is it like on the other side of the river? What happens when we die?

It is idle to deny that this old and hard question has returned with a new persistence. The casualty lists make such solemn reading. The losses already sustained have darkened a multitude of homes. Even

---

Reprinted from William E. Sangster, *These Things Abide* (London: Hodder & Stoughton, 1939), pp. 179–90. Used by permission of Hodder & Stoughton.

if one does hold by faith that death is a journey to our Father's more immediate presence—is there nothing to learn of life on the other side? And what of those who cannot believe in the continuance of life at all?

Some people believe that nothing happens when we die because the individual life no longer exists. They believe that, when the heart ceases to beat, and the body begins to decay, that the mind ceases also, and, as to the soul, they have never found cause to believe in its existence at all. Sir Arthur Keith, the distinguished anthropologist, took that view. He believed that life went out like a guttering candle.

Christian people resist this belief. They hold that there are cogent reasons for rejecting it, even apart from the New Testament.

Life on this earth is incomplete. We are not really men and women yet: we are only in process of becoming such. Some wider sphere of service is demanded by our unexhausted powers. Many others would say with Cecil Rhodes as their last words: "So little done: so much to do."

Moreover, the injustice and inequalities of life plead for recompense. This universe would have been made not by a good God but by a leering devil, or by some extraordinarily powerful idiot, if all its loves and hates, its achievements and its injustices, just ended in the passionless calm of death. The moral law, which is so deeply grounded in our nature, demands vindication after death.

Nor can we easily think of the annihilation of all consciousness. We can think of the end of our *own* consciousness, but not of *all* consciousness. One need not be a profound philosopher to realise that we only know things through our minds, and if there were no minds, how can objects as we now know them persist? On the idealist philosophy, it is, indeed, "inconceivable."

Finally, the almost universal desire for survival points the same way. From earliest times, as the contents of old tombs conclusively prove, men have desired continued life and believed in it. Among the moderns, there are some who say that they do not desire it. Mr. Pearsall Smith, in his reminiscences, *The Unforgotten Years,* plainly says, "For any other form of being I feel no longing," but, such a frank confession invites the rejoinder from Christians that no man who has known the thrill of life with Christ on this earth but *would* desire its continuance hereafter. In any case, such sentiments are not common to mankind.

Fun has been made of this argument on the ground that, because you desire a good dinner, it does not prove that you have one. But the fun is premature because the argument is misunderstood. Because you desire a good dinner, it may not prove that you have one, but if you, and almost everyone you ever met were conscious of *hunger*, it is a very strong presumption that there is such a thing as *food*.

There is.

And because the mass of mankind have desired and believed in survival, this argument is not unworthy to rank with the rest in its support.

But the confidence of Christians in survival does not base itself chiefly on these arguments. Their greatest confidence is grounded in the life of Christ. They hold that the God whom Jesus revealed would not fashion man through countless ages, encourage him to foster the loving relationships of life, and then utterly extinguish him at the last. I met a man the other day whose little child was killed ten years ago: a child (with an unformed personality)—ten years ago—(and they say time heals): but when the name of that little child rose to his lips, the tears started from his eyes and I turned my head away to spare his embarrassment. Is God less tender than a human parent? Has He nurtured our life through the ages, to cast us away at the last? Christians hold also that the resurrection of Jesus is plain evidence that the spiritual survives death and that, when sin had done its utmost in nailing Him to the wood and hiding His tortured body behind the sepulchral stone, it was still powerless to destroy the Life which used His flesh. Death was dead, not He.

Moreover, the teaching of Christ concerning the future life deepens Christian confidence. While it is true that He said very little about the *conditions* of life hereafter, the *fact* of survival underlies all He uttered. We have seen cause already to delight in His plain word: *"In My Father's house are many mansions: if it were not so I would have told you."* Nothing could be plainer than that, and it does not seem less precious to me because it is in John's gospel. He says in effect: "If seventy years of life, more or less, is all you could expect, I would be frank with you and urge you to make the most of it, but in My Father's house. . . ."

Notice also His use of the words "death" and "sleep." He used "sleep" where we use "death," and used it with such consistency as to exclude the idea that it was a figure of speech. To the mourners standing around the breathless body of a little girl, He said: *"She is not dead but sleepeth."* To His disciples, concerning a man already laid in the grave, He said: *"Our friend Lazarus is fallen asleep."* To a company of people met to hear His teaching, He said: *"If a man keep My saying, he shall never see death."* "Sleep," and not "death," was the word Christ always used to denote the end of physical existence, and He never spoke of it as though it were a thing of major importance. Life goes on. That is axiomatic in the teaching of Christ. What we call "death," and He called "falling asleep," simply marks the transition to another plane of life.

It must not be forgotten, of course, that the force of this reasoning will depend in any one's mind on what view they hold of Christ. We believe that He was God on earth, but, even to those who find that conviction hard, we would say this: "He is the best of whom you have ever heard, the bravest, kindest, purest soul, the world's supreme spiritual genius, the founder of a faith already accepted by a third of the world. His words cannot be lightly set aside. If His own resurrection were not the highly attested fact that it is, you would still need to give the closest scrutiny to what He said."

What happens when—in our use of the word—we die?

We go to another plane of being. It is hard to avoid spatial metaphors, even though it may be nearer the truth to insist that the continued life is a *state* rather than a *place*. But it is well to remember that we have no knowledge of personality apart from some "form"—and cannot easily conceive it.

What idea can one have of "spirit" without "form"? When one tries to conjure it up in the mind, one always thinks of it in some "form"—however rarified—even though it only be an "upright blur." Paul tells us plainly that there is a spiritual body. It is hard for mortal minds to see how personal identity could be preserved at all, except in some recognisable form. The view which Paul had of Jesus on the Damascus Road, was a clue to him of the "body" which would clothe believers on the other side of death: the body of our low estate will be transformed to the body of glory.

Now, the New Testament does not lift the veil on the conditions of life on that plane. Death is a toll-bar. At a toll-bar one has to pay "dues." This body is one of the "dues" at the bar of death. It belongs to this plane. We have lived here in a material world, and we could only correspond with our environment through a material form. But now we are going to a spiritual plane, and this "form" must be left behind. Let it rot. It has served its purpose. The question that confronts the released soul is this: "Can I correspond with my new environment? How will I fare when the spiritual is supreme?"

What did Christ mean when He used the word "death"? He did not mean our physical end. That was plain to us. He called that "sleep," and yet He used the word "death."

How did He use that darker word?

He kept it in reserve for something more awful and sinister than the end of physical activity can ever be. He spoke of a death of the soul, a process of spiritual decay at work in men, the consequences of which were so awful that nothing He could do was too much to save them. He saw them bound for a world where the conditions of life required soul health for its existence and He saw men enslaved to sin.

That was what broke His heart and laid Him on the Cross. Christ loved men and wanted to save them. He would never have said, as we might do, that a certain man was dying of T.B., but He would have said, as we hesitate to do, that a certain man was dying of sin. But that is the awful truth of it and, if this generation will not hear, so much the worse for this generation.

Think for a moment. Think of a really debauched man — the kind of man whose mind (as Montaigne said) was "a merry-go-round of lustful images," whose whole interest is in deep drinking and loose women. When that man loses his body, what is left? His life has almost wholly consisted in the stimulation of nerve. How can he correspond to a spiritual environment? Will he even *want* to? It was Cardinal Newman, I believe, who said, "Heaven would be hell to an irreligious man." It would. The barrier to heaven is not in God: it is in our bankrupt selves.

There is a sense, therefore, in which every day is judgment day. Every day the choice between good and evil is presented to us in simple ways. When we choose the higher, we fashion our character in harmony with our future environment, and, when we prefer the lower, we are making ourselves less capable of life where Christ reigns. God's laws work on immutably. "We are not punished *for* our sins, but *by* our sins." Yet God is at hand to aid the most helpless who will turn to Him for help. Devout souls are not made perfect in the instant of death by some stroke of power. Perfection can never be given: it can only be co-operatively attained. But that is God's ambition for us all, and the end He will pursue through all eternity. Theoretically, I must believe that some men may turn their back on Him for ever, but the resources of divine love are beyond the measurings of man's mind, and sin will be more cunning than I have seen it yet if it can defeat every artifice of Calvary love. We do not know. Yet, if our freedom is real, we must concede the possibility, and gather a new urgency in service from that sombre thought.

For the rest, we deprecate "descriptions" of heaven, and are sure that harm has been done by overpressing the imagery of scripture. Humorists have made much fun from the idea of mortals growing wings and being given a place in the orchestras of heaven. Some, who had no thought of caricature in their mind, have, nevertheless, regarded heaven as an interminable church service with the choir doing most of the work. Sir Walter Scott dreaded for himself "an eternity of music," and hoped for "some duty to discharge with the applause of a satisfied conscience." Mr. Lloyd George confessed to Lord Riddell: "When I was a boy, the thought of Heaven used to frighten me more than the thought of Hell. I pictured Heaven as a place where time would be perpetual Sundays, with perpetual services from which there would be no escape. It was a horrible nightmare . . . and made me an atheist for ten years."

The hard and overworked, not unnaturally, have thought of heaven just as a place of rest, and would find it hard to believe that, to many of us, endless rest would become endless boredom.

One cannot buy a map of the Celestial City. Perhaps it is half-childish to wish one could. Better, by far, to say with Richard Baxter:

> My knowledge of that life is small,
> The eye of faith is dim;
> But 'tis enough that Christ knows all,
> And I shall be with Him.

Yet these things can be said with positiveness. There is authority in the Bible for asserting, negatively, that in heaven there is no sin, no sorrow, and no pain: positively, that we shall be *employed*, that we shall *develop*, and that we shall have unspeakable *joy*.

Why do I say that we shall be employed in heaven? First, because I cannot conceive such personalities as ours finding joy in any survival which did not involve activity. Moreover, Jesus once replied to criticism of His actions by saying, "My Father worketh even until now, and I work." When John caught his blinding glimpse of heaven, he said of the saints: "They serve Him day and night in His Temple." The hint we get of heaven, in phrases like these, is not of life compounded of public acts of divine worship, but "of toil unsevered from tranquillity"; of God in action in continual works of providence, and in all the vast purposes of redemption. One of the sweetest joys I know on earth is to feel that I am working with God; to be conscious of the pressure of His guiding hand, and arise to do the tasks He sets me. If service ended with death, I think I should want to cling to earth, and husband the taper of life with miserly care.

When we think on our dear ones within the veil, many questions that leap to the lips remain unanswered. We do not

> Know to what high purpose God
> Dost yet employ their ripened powers.

But it is not profane to speculate.

Every day thousands of souls pass into eternity, many of them with a minimum of preparation. Some are from lands unlit by the light of the gospel, and some are from the dark slums of modern cities. Some are hurtled into eternity from the battlefield, and others sink to a watery grave in the wide ocean. God has not finished with them in the instant of death.

Is it fanciful to suppose that He makes glad use of His obedient and trusty servants to minister to these immature souls on the other side? And, if this be true, ought we to speak quite so confidently of "untimely death" because it comes to some of our friends before a ripe old age? If we knew all the "work" of God's wide Kingdom, we might be thrilled at the prospect of the creative and redemptive service which awaits us there.

When one looks on the dear dead form of a powerful and gracious friend, it is so hard to believe that all that beneficent strength has turned to dust. Matthew Arnold found it so when he pondered on his noble father. He said:

> O Strong soul, by what shore
> Tarriest thou now? For that force,
> Surely, has not been left vain!
> Somewhere, surely, afar,
> In the sounding labour-house vast
> Of being, is practised that strength,
> Zealous, beneficent, firm!

"My Father works," said Jesus. I believe that, across the river, we shall work with Him.

> And every power find sweet employ
> In that eternal world of joy.

I believe that in heaven we shall develop. No static life will be ours. God entertains the highest and holiest purposes for His children. He aims to bring us to perfection, to the "measure of development which belongs to the fullness of Christ"—and this task is not a task for earth alone. Busy in His royal service for others, by which alone the selfishness and pride of our nature is subjugated, He fosters our growth in all things good.

The word "mansion" in English ears denotes a rather large and ornate house. But the Greek word which lies behind this translation in John's fourteenth chapter carries no such implication. It normally referred to stations on a journey, places of comfortable accommodation for a night. Two ideas are implicit in it—rest and *progress*. A picture is given of a place where travellers rest and refresh themselves, before they continue their course. The fact of progress and development, therefore, lies hidden in this most treasured phrase of John's, and links itself in our thought with a word in his first Epistle: "Beloved, now are we children of God, and *it is not yet made manifest what we shall be*."

The road stretches on, but it never ceases to be the King's Highway.

I believe that heaven is the home of joy. How often heaven and joy are linked in the New Testament. We read that there is *joy* in the presence of the Angels of God. We hear the Master say in the parable: "Well done, good and faithful servant, enter into the *joy* of thy Lord." We are assured that, those who come out of great tribulation, have every tear wiped from their eyes.

Meteorologists tell us that in the stratosphere the weather is always fine: snow, fog, rain and frost belong, all of them, to the earth and its immediate confines. An aeroplane which mounts to the stratosphere can fly above all earth-born clouds. A soul which mounts to heaven soars above corroding care.

> It were a well-spent journey,
> Though seven deaths lay between.

Work, development—and joy also! Joy is not pleasure. Pleasure satiates—but joy rises to rise again.

There is no guide book to heaven, no wealth of detail, no answer to a hundred questions which frame themselves within the mind.

But if we know, on the highest Authority, that there is no sin, no sorrow, and no pain: if we know, on that same Authority, that there is service, growth, and bliss—is it not enough? Can we not journey through these dark days in cheerfulness and confidence, giving a word and a hand to others who will travel at our side, and not clutching too tightly at the things of earth?

Nor need any fearful soul wonder if we shall know each other there. To doubt it would make nonsense of almost everything the New Testament says upon the subject. We are the children of One "able to do exceeding abundantly above all that we can ask or think."

To meet my dear ones who have passed over before me is a constant theme of my thought, and will be all but the first of my requests.

"Above all that you can ask or think . . ."

Above!

WHEN HOPE IS DEAD—HOPE ON!

1 Corinthians 13:13; Hebrews 6:19

ALL OF US have seen copies of the famous picture by G. F. Watts called "Hope," and most of us have heard the absurd story told about it.

The picture shows a blindfolded woman sitting with bowed head on

---

Reprinted from William E. Sangster, *These Things Abide* (London: Hodder & Stoughton, 1939), pp. 63–71. Used by permission of Hodder & Stoughton.

a sphere, and she holds a lyre in her hand. Only one string of the instrument remains unbroken, only one star shines in the dark sky. Reaching out for some meaning not easy to grasp by people who do not think in symbols, the artist called the picture "Hope."

Two charwomen were said to be gazing at it once and were somewhat mystified. "Hope?" said one. "Hope? Why is it called 'Hope'?"

To which the other replied, gazing at the figure perched precariously on the sphere, "I suppose because she hopes she won't fall off."

Now, that is not merely absurd, it is illuminating. Many people think of hope as a poor precarious thing, an illusion, a vanity, a disease of the mind. The cynic has said, "He, who lives on hope, will die starving." Cowley said, "Hope is the most hopeless thing of all." The soldier is apt to turn bright promises aside with a despondent question, "What hopes?" Schopenhauer, the distinguished German philosopher, looked upon hope as the bait by which nature gets her hook in our nose and makes it serve her interests, though they may not be our own. That is the common assessment of hope in the world—a poor, vain, deceptive thing.

But hope is not so thought of in the New Testament. Paul makes Faith, Hope and Love, the cardinal virtues of Christendom. "And now abideth faith, hope, love." He speaks also of "the patience of hope," and of "hope that maketh not ashamed." All through the New Testament, hope is spoken of in that same high way. The author of the Epistle to the Hebrews bursts out into that daring paradox, "A hope both sure and steadfast."

Now, how did this sharp contrast arise? An illusion: a steadfast reality. A dream: a fact. A disease of the mind: a cardinal virtue. Hope cannot be both. Is the world right, or the New Testament? Is it a bit of folly, or is it precious beyond price? What is the solution of the dilemma?

The answer is not difficult. They are talking of different things. There is a higher and a lower hope. There is a genuine quality and a counterfeit. There is a real article and a substitute. There is gold and there is gilt.

Let us look at each of them in turn.

I think you will recognise the lower hope more easily if I employ its usual name. It is commonly called "optimism." Optimism is much praised. People love to boast that they are optimists, and they speak as though this quality conferred distinction on them. Sir Thomas Lipton said: "I am the world's greatest optimist. I am proud of the distinction. There is something buoyant and healthy in being an optimist. It is because of my optimism that I have gone through life smiling. I am always in good humour and good fettle. Dr. Optimist is the finest chap in any city or country. Just try a course of his treatment. It will work wonders, and this doctor charges no fees."

Nor need we deny the value of optimism. It is not full cream, but there is something to be said for skimmed milk. If the choice were pressed upon us, most of us would prefer to live with an optimist than with a pessimist. A friend of mine has set it out in this way. The pessimist says, "It will rain this afternoon." The optimist says, "There's a rift in the clouds," and he puts on his mackintosh and goes out. The pessimist says, "I suppose there is no milk in that jug." The optimist says, "Pass the cream, please." The pessimist says, "The country is bound to lose this war." The optimist says, "The outlook is dark, but we shall win through."

Of course, optimism is better than pessimism. Doctors know that. Professor W. Langdon Brown, of Cambridge University, addressing the medical students of Westminster Hospital some little time ago, sought to remind them that there are precious tonics not easily examined by biochemical analysis, and he concluded his striking address by saying that the best of tonics is hope.

Yet, all this concerns the lower hope, and, when everything has been said in its favour, it is a poor counterfeit of the real thing. If flourishes most where there is no depth of earth, and it soon withers away. It has no necessary connection with religion.

If every doctor knows that optimism is, as Professor W. Langdon Brown has said, a good tonic to the body, every doctor knows also that optimism is a constant concomitant of consumption. The disease may be making its last rapid moves to a tragic end but, normally, the patient seems blissfully unaware of it. Keen as the people in sanatoria normally and naturally are to get home, their cheerfulness is proverbial. I have been visiting such patients in all parts of the country for years, and have been impressed again and again by the hopefulness which they display.

But many of them are sick unto death, and optimism alone cannot save them.

Nor is it less pathetic when the optimism is displayed by the relatives.

"It is all right," said a cheerful fellow to me one day, when I had been visiting his wife who was gravely ill. "She is bound to get better. I am an optimist, you know. I always look on the bright side of things."

But I buried his wife before the week was out.

Of course, we appreciate optimism, and willingly admit its simple service to the community, but it has been immoderately praised and fully explains the world's cynicism concerning hope. Boisterous confidence which has no solid foundation looks pitifully ludicrous when crushing disappointment comes, and deepens the contempt in which it is widely held by the disillusioned. Looking on the bright side of things may seem both bold and brave, but if it involves also (as it so often does) a foolish neglect of facts which point the other way, it only adds to the bitterness of ultimate failure. A friend of mine, who used to be in the legal profession, tells me that he often wound up the business of people who *would* persist in looking on the bright side of their accounts!

But how different is all this from New Testament hope. It is as different as the gambler's dice from the proved results of accurate research. We go forward into this dark period in our nation's life, not inflated with the foolish optimism which seems to give buoyancy to those who do not know Christ, but with a quiet and unquenchable hope drawn from the deep sources of our faith. The language which comes easy to optimists, we cannot use. Confident boasting of a swift and not-too-costly victory, and wishful anticipation of speedy revolution in enemy lands, are not the grounds of our hope. It is deeper based than either of these.

It is based, first, on:

The indestructibility of truth. Some people would have us believe that truth is a fragile thing, the first casualty in any war. None would deny that we live in an age when scant respect has been paid to it, and propaganda put forward as something "rather better." Indeed, there have been times when words have almost ceased to have meaning. Aggression has masqueraded as "Protection." Wanton and wicked invasion has been described as though it were a pitying and sacrificial act of succour. Appeasement has been called "Weakness," and a confederation aiming at peace has been regarded as a team of gangsters bent on encirclement. The mind whirls in the midst of such vast misrepresentation, and truth seems a poor mangled thing.

But it only *seems* so. Truth is mighty. It does not achieve its victories by any lightning war. The lie wins all early engagements, and sometimes seems to be in secure possession of the field. The truth may even be nailed to a cross and taken down, a poor bleeding clod, to be hidden in a sepulchre, sealed with a great stone.

But it rises again! The life-principle in it cannot be killed. Somehow, it partakes of the life of God and, therefore, of God's eternity. Ultimately, its triumph is sure.

Did not our own Milton say: "Though all the winds of doctrine were let loose to play upon the Earth, so Truth be in the field, we do injuriously to misdoubt her strength. Let her and Falsehood grapple. Whoever knew Truth put to the worse in a free and open encounter? For who knows not that Truth is strong, next to the Almighty? She needs no policies nor stratagems to make her victorious. Give her but room, and do not bind her when she sleeps."

In a London Hospital, a few years ago, a small quantity of radium was lost. Though its bulk was quite inconsiderable, it was valued at £1,500, and an immediate and thorough search was made. By some means it was thought possible that it had been swept into a wastepaper basket, and taken to the destructor to be burned. So the dust and clinkers of the refuse plant were sieved and examined.

And there was the radium!—unharmed and unimpaired for all the fiery journey it had made: still at the service of the doctors in their great ministry of healing.

It is not dissimilar with truth. It passes through the fires of fierce distortion and seems at times to be utterly lost, but the flames cannot permanently harm it, and it returns to its remedial work again.

Albert Schweitzer, like most thoughtful men, dislikes to be asked whether he is an optimist or a pessimist, finding the question essentially shallow. He admits that only at quite rare moments has he felt really glad to be alive; that he is burdened with a sense of the world's suffering, and believes that, by the renunciation of thinking, mankind is delivering itself into spiritual and material misery.

One thing, however, keeps hope alive in him: belief in truth. He says: "One belief of my childhood I have preserved with the certainty that I can never lose it: belief in truth. I am confident that the spirit generated by truth is stronger than the force of circumstances.... Therefore, I do not believe that mankind will have to tread the road to ruin right to the end."

That, then, is the first ground of our hope—the indestructibility of truth. In all our anxiety in these days lest we become nationally self-righteous, none need hesitate to offer the prayer, "God defend the Truth."

The second ground of our confident hope is this:

God is on the Throne. Many people, most of whom live their normal lives in neglect of God, complain in times of national stress that He never seems to *do* anything. They set out the enormities of our enemies, touch with a light hand (or entirely ignore) our own national sins, and querulously enquire why God does not intervene.

The problem is a very old one. It puzzled the Psalmist. It perplexed the Prophets. It baffled poor Peter in the Garden of Gethsemane. When he stood, bloody and ineffectual, in the gleam of the lanterns, and watched them march his betrayed Master away, something came nigh to bursting in his mighty heart. He knew that it was devilry—every bit of it. But why did He suffer it? Surely, the same word that cured the leper, gave sight to the blind, and summoned the dead to life, could blast these evil men for their wickedness. Yet, He allowed them to lead Him away, and, of His own will, bowed His meek head to mortal pain. As Peter stumbled into the darkness, that was the question which hammered in his reeling brain: "Why?" "Why?" "Why?"

Let this be plainly said again, however elementary it must seem to those who deeply think on the things of God. He does not work our way. His might finds fitting expression, not in the power to wound, but in the power to woo. His power is not coercion, but constraint. Never does He violate the personality that He has made. With infinite patience, He seeks to win the wayward and the wicked by all the dear inducements of love, and our hard task is this: *to have patience with the patience of God.*

When we remember our own obdurateness to His pleadings, and for how long our prayers were compact of just personal petition, and how impervious we seemed to His call: when we remember His own long patience with us through all the years when we were proud and repulsive in sin . . . it should not be too hard for us to have patience with the patience of God. Let us accept this fact, however difficult, or even impossible, we may judge it to be for ourselves. God does not work our way. The Cross symbolises both His power and His wisdom. He meets all the massed hatred of wicked men with bleeding love, and, in the hour of their triumph, His only reply is a prayer.

But He is still on the throne! He is uncompromising about sin, and only blind ignorance can interpret His restraint as weakness, or indifference to moral worth. The Eternal God will vindicate the unalterable distinctions of right and wrong. The world can only work His way.

> Crowns and thrones may perish,
> Kingdoms rise and wane.

Already one nation has been entirely engulfed in the bloody tide of this new war. Others may share the fate: our own even. But justice and righteousness shall not vanish from the earth. Out of the chaos of these times, and by the bitter agony of this doubly afflicted generation, the will of God will ultimately be done "on earth, as it is in heaven."

He will never leave us nor forsake us. The Cross is the pledge of that. In those moments of unmeasurable horror, when we fear that even God's patience will be exhausted with our wicked race, and all the windows of heaven closed from within against the scenes of earth, let us repair again to Calvary. Here is the ground of unquenchable hope. He will never forsake the world of His incarnation and sacrificial death. God is on the throne. Truth is indestructible. When the shallow hopes of the world are all dead—hope on in God!

For additional information about W. E. Sangster:

Dorr, Luther Maxwell. "A Critique of the Preaching of William Edwin Sangster." Th.D. dissertation, New Orleans Baptist Theological Seminary, 1968.
Morris, A. Clifford, comp. *A Sangster Anthology*. London: Epworth Press, 1964.

Sangster, William Edwin. *The Approach to Preaching.* Philadelphia: Westminster Press, 1952.
———. *The Craft of the Sermon.* London: Epworth Press, 1954.
———. *Let Me Commend.* London: Hodder & Stoughton, 1949.
———. *Power in Preaching.* New York: Abingdon Press, 1958.
———. *Sangster of Westminster.* London: Marshall, Morgan & Scott, 1960.

FOR OTHER SERMONS BY W. E. SANGSTER:

Special-Day Sermons. New York: Abingdon Press, 1960.
Westminster Sermons. Vol. 1. London: Epworth Press, 1960–61.
Also: *Sangster of Westminster* (1960).